Manufacturing Enterprise in Asia

Issues relating to the size of firms in manufacturing are central to the discussion of development strategies. This book offers an interpretation of growth trajectories in selected Asian economies in terms of the size structure of enterprises in the manufacturing sector of these economies.

The book presents a comparative survey of the distribution of enterprises by size across Asia, including Japan, Taiwan, Korea, Thailand, Bangladesh, and Vietnam. It identifies three distinct patterns of manufacturing sector development and makes the connection between enterprise development and the overall impact on the economy. The book goes on to investigate the problem of the peculiar dual size structure of manufacturing in India, with its two modes at the low and high end of the size distribution and conspicuous "missing middle", and the effect that this has on the economy. It is an important contribution to studies on Asian Economics and Manufacturing Industries.

Dipak Mazumdar is Senior Research Associate at the Munk Centre for International Studies at the University of Toronto, Canada. He is the author of numerous publications on development economics. His co-authored book, with Ata Mazaheri, *The African Manufacturing Firm* was also published by Routledge in 2003.

Sandip Sarkar is currently working as a Senior Fellow with the Institute for Human Development (IHD), New Delhi, India. His main areas of research interest are industry, poverty, labour, and employment, on which he has over two decades of experience.

Routledge studies in the growth economies of Asia

Manufacturing Enterprise in Asia

Size structure and economic growth

Dipak Mazumdar and Sandip Sarkar

Routledge
Taylor & Francis Group
LONDON AND NEW YORK

Canada

IDRC | CRDI

First published 2013
by Routledge
2 Park Square, Milton Park, Abingdon, Oxon OX14 4RN

Simultaneously published in the USA and Canada
by Routledge
711 Third Avenue, New York, NY 10017

Routledge is an imprint of the Taylor & Francis Group, an informa business

Co-published with the
International Development Research Centre
PO Box 8500, Ottawa, ON K1G 3H9, Canada
info@idrc.ca / www.idrc.ca
(IDRC publishes an ebook edition of this book, ISBN 978-1-55250-549-6)

British Library Cataloguing in Publication Data
A catalogue record for this book is available from the British Library

Library of Congress Cataloging in Publication Data
Mazumdar, Dipak, 1932–
Manufacturing enterprise in Asia: size structure and economic growth/
Dipak Mazumdar and Sandip Sarkar.
    p. cm. – (Routledge studies in the growth economies of Asia; 113)
Includes bibliographical references and index.
    1. Manufacturing industries–Asia. 2. Small busines–Growth. 3.
Economic development–Asia. I. Sarkar, Sandip, 1961– II. Title.
HD9720.5.M398 2012
338.095–dc23
                                                            2011048402

ISBN: 978-0-415-62333-9 (pbk)

Typeset in Times New Roman
by Wearset Ltd, Boldon, Tyne and Wear

Contents

Figures

Tables

Part I

Introduction

1 Introduction

This book offers an interpretation of growth trajectories in selected Asian economies in terms of the size structure of enterprises in the manufacturing sector of these economies. The issues relating to the size of firms in manufacturing have been central to the discussion on development strategies, ever since the birth of development economics as a subject. The concerns in this area have, however, concentrated mainly on the optimal development of small enterprises (SEs) in developing economies. In particular, a large part of the literature in the 1960s and 1970s was concerned with the problem that market forces were not favouring the growth of SEs to the extent that might be desirable, given the factor endowments of these economies. Even more of the literature was devoted to the topic of the divergence of shadow prices of factors of production (principally labour and capital) from their market prices. A range of factors make the ratio of market prices of capital to labour significantly lower than the ratio of their opportunity costs in the economy and hence the technology of production is more capital-intensive than what is socially optimal. It is assumed that SEs are generally more labour-intensive. Hence the size of the SEs in manufacturing (in the absence of intervention) in a typical developing economy is less than desirable.

Older literature has examined the other end of the size distribution, exploring the large conglomerates in the process of development, particularly in East Asian industrialization, and the problems of political economy that the oligopolistic structure created.

I

A prescriptive model

It is difficult to find references in the literature that deal with the entire size distribution for the macro-economic trajectory of the economy. One exception might be the Mahalanobis model of Indian planned development. This was a prescriptive model of planning, concerned not with the current or historical development of the economy, but with a set of guidelines for the planned development of future growth. Based on the Marxist–Stalinist model of growth, it had, as we shall see, enormous impact on the size structure of the manufacturing sector in India and the source of its development. In fact, the Mahalanobis model seems to have its most obvious antecedent in the model described by Feldman, a Russian engineer in the late 1920s, at the beginning of the Stalinist program of industrialization. The model starts with the Marxist distinction between Department I of the industrial economy, catering to consumer goods, and Department II, producing capital goods. The growth model envisages that in a closed economy, the growth rate of Department II propels the growth of the economy through the expansion of the capital goods sector, supplying machinery to combine with labour that will enhance labour productivity over time. The object of planned growth is to allocate as much of the flow of capital goods produced at a point in time to Department II to maximize the production of further capital goods for a future increase in the capital labour ratio, and so maximize the growth rate of labour productivity. Obviously, this model assumes an unlimited supply of labour that can be employed in the developing sector. The only constraint on the allocation of labour to Department II is the necessity to produce consumer goods to satisfy the needs of the workers in the developing sector. The rate of growth of wages (and hence of consumption) is a problem of choice for planners and depends on their decision about the trade-off time paths of consumption in the short run and growth in the long run. At the extreme, the consumption growth in the immediate period might produce just enough growth of Department I goods (wage goods) sufficient to satisfy the demand of workers employed in the developing sector at the minimum level of consumption acceptable to them. This way, the largest proportion of investment could be devoted to the capital goods sector, thus maximizing the feasible growth rate of the economy.

In Mahalanobis's interpretation of the Marxist-Feldman model of the Indian economy was the particular view that the growth rate of the economy was exclusively dependent on the supply of capital goods produced at home. Some of the specific assumptions about this growth process include the following:

- The growth rate of the economy (and of manufacturing in particular) is constrained by the supply of capital goods, not by demand or other cooperant factors of production. Similarly, the importance of technological progress is underplayed.
- The problem of savings (or finance for investment) is assumed to be taken care of by the planner's ability to choose between consumption and savings, subject to the requirement of a minimum supply of wage goods.
- The economy is closed, so that there is no opportunity of augmenting resources needed to increase growth rates through international exchange.

When we move away from a perspective planning model to that of the effect of the size structure on the trajectory of the economy, other considerations come to the forefront of the discussion. These relationships can be studied by considering the impact of the manufacturer's size structure on the growth rate of the economy, and its possible impact on trends in inequality.

II

Three types of size structure in Asian industrialization

As we shall see in detail in the next chapter, a classification of size distributions of manufacturing in Asian countries shows three distinct types:

*   Equitable: a fairly even distribution in which small, medium, and large firms play more or less equally important roles and the productivity difference between the size classes is small (SME model).
*   Distinctly skewed to right: the distribution of employment by size groups is distinctly skewed to the large firms (LE model). Typically in this pattern, the productivity difference between large and small firms tends to be substantial.
*   Dualistic: there is a strong mode at both ends of the distribution; a relatively large proportion of employment is found in both the small and the large firms (BM model).

In what follows, we discuss the implications for these three types on growth and inequality trends. The empirical examples of each type are examined later in the book.

An important point should be made about the boundaries of employment in manufacturing covered in this book. In most developing economies, particularly those with a large agricultural sector, an important type of manufacturing is carried out by households. These enterprises, producing simple manufactured goods for local consumption, are called "household enterprises" because they are operated mostly by family labour, with perhaps some marginal help from wage labour. In the Indian economy, this sector constitutes some 55 per cent of all manufacturing employment, although the value added contributed by these enterprises is no more than 10 per cent. The employment in these enterprises, together with similar types of jobs in the service sector, constitutes the bulk of the so-called "informal" sector in these economies. Historically, household enterprises decline in importance with modernization and economic growth. Because of the large amount of employment in household enterprises, an analysis of the size structure of employment in manufacturing that includes this subsector would almost certainly give a pattern of a marked bi-modal distribution with a "missing middle". This would be true of many countries, in the developing countries of Asia (other than India) and also in Latin America and Africa. Our analysis in this book is, however, concerned with the development of modern manufacturing with more sophisticated technology. Thus the bulk of the analysis in the following chapters excludes this traditional household sector from consideration.

The problem arises as to where to draw the line in terms of size groups of manufacturing when we consider non-household enterprises. We accept the international standard of drawing the line at five workers. This has the advantage of comparing the size structure across countries. Further, it has the analytical basis of including only enterprises which depend mostly on hired labour.[1]

III

Size structure of manufacturing and the growth rate

Bi-modal structure

We can first consider the impact of the bi-modal size distribution in manufacturing (BM model) on the growth rate of the economy. The starting point of the analysis is a set of three observations:

- The growth rate of manufacturing is constrained by the rate of expansion of demand for manufactured goods. (This is contrary to the assumption of the prescriptive planning model discussed above, in which the growth rate is constrained by supply factors, and the production of producer goods in the capital goods sector.)
- There is surplus labour in agriculture (similar to the Lewis model) and the expansion of demand in manufacturing is directly related to the growth rate of employment in the manufacturing sector.
- But, unlike the classical Lewis model, labour is not homogeneous in the non-agricultural sector. There is a hierarchy of wage and productivity levels directly related to the size of the enterprise.[2] Thus the rate of expansion of wage incomes and the demand for manufactured goods, which the transfer of labour from agriculture ensures, depend very much on the point of the "ladder" where labour is employed.

A size distribution with two strong modes and a missing middle implies that a great deal of employment is created at the low end of the size distribution. Because of the low labour productivity in this size group, employment per unit output is, by definition, high. But because of the relatively low wage per worker, the income per consumer unit among such workers is also low. The demand for manufactured goods for this low level of consumption per capita also tends to be very low. Thus, although employment is large in the short run, the rate of expansion of demand for manufactured output is much less than would otherwise be the case. There is then clearly a trade-off between the volume of absorption of labour in manufacturing in the short run and its rate of growth over time.

Second, the low productivity of labour, working at low levels of technology, means that the economy is generally not very competitive in export markets. Thus the demand expansion of manufacturer output is constrained by the limitations of both the domestic and the export markets.

The low rate of growth of employment in manufacturing has a multiplier effect. In a surplus labour situation in agriculture, the increase in income per capita among farm households is determined partly by the increase in land productivity, but also significantly by the transfer of surplus labour to manufacturing. The low rate of growth of employment in manufacturing (which the predominance of low-wage labour in this sector entails) means that the rate of absorption of labour in manufacturing is also relatively low. Thus the increase in income per capita in agriculture, which would feed the growth in demand for manufactured goods, is also low, reinforcing the slow rate of increase in employment in manufacturing.

Two further arguments complete this line of reasoning:

- In a bi-modal distribution of employment in manufacturing, there would be a significant presence of labour at the high-productivity, high-wage end of the distribution. But the contribution of these large firms to employment growth in manufacturing is not enough to compensate for the low rate of expansion of demand in the low wage subsector. The large firms in the high-productivity sector typically have a low elasticity of employment and the rate of growth of the wage bill (which would support demand expansion at the relatively high level of wages) would be limited.[3] In fact, this type of economy with a bi-modal distribution of employment in manufacturing is likely to develop a distinctive pattern of product market segmentation in this sector. The low-wage, low-productivity sector is likely to dominate the market for relatively cheap manufactured goods for the mass consumer market, while the high-wage sector specializes in the production of intermediate goods and high-income goods for middle-class consumers and export markets. The combined size of the latter segment might be limited in terms of employment.
- Because of the limited growth of employment in manufacturing, the lead in employment growth outside agriculture could be taken by the tertiary sector. There are cumulative processes involved here too. With the limited transfer of surplus labour from agriculture, the low supply price of labour keeps the price of an array of services relatively low. This further constrains the demand growth for manufactured goods since often such services are substitutes for a range of manufactured goods. In other words, the price elasticity of demand for manufactured goods reinforces the effect of income elasticity in constraining demand expansion for manufactured goods.

Historically, the lead in the reallocation of labour from agriculture has been taken everywhere by manufacturing. While there is some discussion in the literature suggesting that advances in technology have shifted the emphasis from manufacturing to services in the development process, there is little evidence to suggest that a major shift has taken place in the early stages of development. Furthermore, the factors usually cited in the position of manufacturing rather than services as the spearhead of successful development remain true. The multiplier effect on growth of sectors related to manufacturing is generally much stronger—from the perspective of both inter-industry linkages and skill formation of the labour force.

Another problem with tertiary sector-led growth is the impact on inequality of this type of development, since tertiary sector earnings are generally more unequally distributed than those in manufacturing. This concern is explored in the next section.

Size structure skewed to the right

The logical question that follows is whether the alternative pattern with the size distribution skewed to the large firms takes care of some of the problems discussed above. No doubt the higher wage per worker would help in the process of demand expansion for manufactured goods in the domestic market, but the problem is that, because of the much higher capital intensity in large-scale production, the volume of employment created by the expansion of this subsector is low. Thus, unless output growth is very high, the rate of growth of the wage bill would be low, and the expansion of demand would also be low. At the typically low level of per capita income in developing economies, this implies that manufacturing growth would depend quite a bit on expansion in export markets. Too many developing economies, including some in Asia, have successfully got a foothold in export markets on a narrow range of goods (e.g. garments). The impact of such limited export growth has not been significant in expanding manufacturing employment and has not fostered a substantial transfer of surplus labour from agriculture. This pattern of development can hope to be successful only if the economy is able to develop a wide range of export markets to make a substantial impact on employment expansion in manufacturing—at least in the initial stages until increased incomes support a growing domestic market. In recent years, China has followed this path with considerable success.

A problem of some importance should be mentioned here which can hamper even widespread, large-scale, industry-based development. Export-oriented development is exposed to the cyclical problems of the world economy. Apart from the difficulty of maintaining sustained growth, such a development model might face the severe problems of Dutch disease and the attendant loss of competitiveness. The problem can be illustrated by the case of Thailand (dealt with in detail in Chapter 11).

Thailand had successfully developed a wide range of manufactured exports by the second half of the 1980s. However, industrial development was biased in favour of large firms, and there was heavy regional concentration in the province surrounding Bangkok, thus a good deal of the economy was distant from the centre of the development process. Permanent urbanization was slow, with the labour market in the region heavily dependent on migrant and seasonal migration from the impoverished North and North-East. The net result was that the transfer of labour from agriculture was slow and the difference in income per capita between agricultural workers and non-agricultural workers remained very high, one of the highest in Asian countries.

At the same time, low employment elasticity in large-scale manufacturing meant that labour absorption in manufacturing was low and the tertiary sector provided a larger part of employment creation in non-agricultural sectors.

All these developments contributed to the high income inequality in the Thai economy (one of the highest in Asia). The unequal income distribution supported a peculiar pattern of growth, as high-income consumers spent a large amount on tertiary sector goods and real estate—with high capital and import intensity. The process was aided in no small measure by the lax monetary and exchange policies favouring foreign capital inflow. There was no attempt to control short-run capital flows and distinguish them from long-term productive ones and foreign speculators fuelled the banking system's support of speculative investments, particularly in real estate.

The net result was a steep increase in the real exchange rate with the prices of non-traded goods increasing relative to those of traded goods, leading to an erosion of Thailand's international competitiveness. This eventually led to a flight of short-run foreign capital, ushering in the sharp Asian financial crisis of 1997.

The Thai economy has recovered somewhat in the first decade of this century. But the problem of non-participation of a major part of the labour force in the growth process and the corresponding inequality have contributed to continuing political instability which has created serious problems of governance to this day. The Thai case raises a red flag about the pattern of industrial development skewed to large firms, and could serve as a warning to other economies following similar strategies.

The SME model

The SME model, in which small and medium enterprises participate as much in employment growth in manufacturing as the large ones, would seem to avoid the pitfalls of the two other types of size distribution discussed above. Japan, Taiwan, and Korea no doubt had their manufacturing growth kicked off by large-scale industries geared to the export market. This was particularly important for Japan and Korea, where giant conglomerates dominated the industrial scene for much of their development history. But while the lead in industrial growth might have been taken by large export-oriented enterprises, the domestic market soon started to play a substantial part in the growth. The integration of small and medium enterprises with larger firms in a dynamic and cooperative relationship would seem to have been a crucial factor in the expansion of domestic markets. First, labour was absorbed at higher wage levels (unlike in the missing middle case). Second, the high rate of employment growth in manufacturing led the way to a rapid transfer of labour from agriculture. The consequent increase in income per worker in agriculture added significantly to the increase of consumer income per capita, which expanded the demand for manufactured goods. Our discussion would show that the export market accounted for no more than one-third of the market for all manufactured goods produced for much of the course of industrial development. Since employment growth was led by manufacturing rather than by the tertiary sector, the problems arising from growing inequality and growth linkages noticed in the BM and LE patterns were avoided.

Growth with equity has in fact long been singled out as a major characteristic of East Asian growth (World Bank 1993). The connection between the SME pattern of size distribution and equitable growth is discussed in the next section, within a more general analytical framework.

IV

Decomposition of inequality trends

Dynamic decomposition

The factors causing change in inequality in the different types of growth can be explored using the standard dynamic decomposition technique. This involves accounting for changes in the level of inequality by means of a partition of the distribution into subgroups. It then decomposes the change in inequality into two broad components: one due to changes in average income among the subgroups, and the other due to change in inequality within the groups. The former can be further broken down into two components: the change associated with changes in relative mean incomes between the subgroups, or "income effect"; and the change due to changes in the size of the subgroups, or "allocation effect".

Hence, as asserted by Mookherjee and Shorrocks (1982), the change in total inequality over time can be decomposed into three general components: an allocation effect due to changes in the number of people within different partitions, an income effect due to changes in relative incomes among partitions, and a pure inequality effect due to changes in inequality within partitions. This decomposition can be applied to the Theil index as follows:

$$\Delta I = \left\{ \sum_{k=1}^{K} \overline{p}_k \Delta I_k \right\}$$
$$+ \sum_{k=1}^{K} \overline{I}_k \Delta p_k + \sum_{k=1}^{K} \left[\overline{\frac{\mu_k}{\mu}} - \overline{\ln(\frac{\mu_k}{\mu})} \right] \Delta p_k \qquad (1)$$
$$+ \sum_{k=1}^{K} (\overline{\lambda}_k - \overline{p}_k) \Delta \ln(\mu_k)$$

where p is the population, μ stands for the mean wage, and λ is the relative wage share; the bar stands for the average over the two periods and the k stands for the subgroups.

In general, summarizing Equation 1, the change in inequality within groups, as measured by the first two terms, can be attributed to either the changes in intra-group inequality levels (pure inequality effect) or from the compositional changes in population. It is sometimes useful to combine these two elements and consider the sum to represent the pure inequality effect as distinct from the other two elements covering the part of the inequality change attributable to reallocation of labour during the growth process. The change in group inequality, measured by the last two terms, also consists of two components: the allocation effect and the pure between-group inequality effect (income effect), respectively. The pure between-group inequality effect (income effect) reflects divergence/convergence of income levels that corresponds to differential growth rates across subgroups. A faster rise in the income of higher-income groups leads to divergence of income levels and hence rising inequality, and vice versa. The allocation effect captures the effect of changing composition of the population.

The Kuznets process

The allocation effect in fact underlines the importance of the speed of transfer of surplus labour from agriculture in the growth process. A crucial variable in this process is the subgroups among which the redistribution of labour takes place.

In an economy divided into a low-productivity (agricultural or rural) sector and a high-productivity (industrial or urban) sector, the shift of labour from the former to the latter increases inequality even as the growth rate accelerates. This is because, as suggested by Kuznets, the proportion of labour in the high-productivity sector would remain small until development had gone some way, and the productivity gap between the two sectors would remain significantly large, creating a minority of workers who enjoy high incomes while the vast majority of them remain at a low level of productivity.

But in terms of Equation 1, the compositional change can lead to the so-called inverted-U shaped Kuznets curve (Jeong 2005). The relative strength of the movement from low- to high-productivity sectors declines as the percentage shift falls. At the same time, the inequality-augmenting effect of this shift is countered by the narrowing of the income differential between the sectors. Thus, eventually inequality declines.

The pattern of size distribution in manufacturing and trends in inequality

It is easy to see that the turning point in the U-shaped curve, with the allocation effect causing a reversal in the trend to increasing inequality, would be reached sooner with greater speed of transfer of low-productivity surplus from agriculture to other sectors. How does the expected speed of reallocation in the SME model compare with the other two?

Since the output ratio is smaller in larger enterprises, we could reasonably expect the SME model to have higher employment elasticity in manufacturing than the LE pattern. But this effect might be offset if the LE model in fact attains a higher rate of growth of manufacturing output. It is often believed that large enterprises are generally more effective in developing export markets. But as our review of the East Asian story will show, although some might have started their manufacturing growth with export expansion based on large conglomerates, they were quick to develop institutions which enabled SMEs to participate in the export markets actively. As far as the domestic market is concerned, the more widespread distribution of wages in the SME pattern also seems to have sustained a higher demand for manufacturing growth in these economies. In this sense, the SME model seems to be some sort of a "golden mean" between the LE and the BM patterns. While employment elasticity in manufacturing is higher than in the LE model, the wage level at which labour is absorbed outside agriculture is not so low as to constrain the expansion of markets for manufactured goods.

Apart from the quicker approach to the right arm of the Kuznets U-shaped curve, the SME model can be expected to produce a trend to greater equity than either the BM or LE models on both the other two fronts—the "within sector" and the "between sector" effects:

- The rapid transfer of surplus labour from agriculture, of course, reduces "within sector" inequality relative to the BM and LE patterns.
- As far as manufacturing is concerned, "within sector" inequality is clearly smaller and decreasing in the SME pattern. It is largest and probably increasing in the BM model. It is less important in the LE model, but the "between sector" inequality between agriculture and manufacturing is much larger.
- A further set of influences emanates from the role of the tertiary sector and moves in the same direction. We have discussed above that manufacturing takes the lead in employment growth in the SME model, while the tertiary sector plays the dominant role in the other two types, unless the export-oriented manufacturing growth from the large-scale sector is very strong (as in China). The higher level of "within sector" inequality in the tertiary sector compared to manufacturing is very much a universal phenomenon. The range of activities in the tertiary sector is wider, extending from petty trade and services to high-income business and financial services. The dispersion of skills and earnings in this sector is so much greater. This is true even in the Indian case, which has a particularly heterogeneous pool of labour in manufacturing, with its bi-modal distribution.
- Other important factors leading to growth with greater equity in the SME model stem from the geographic dispersion of industrial activity in this type of development and the more widespread formation of skills which it promotes. The decentralized industrialization which the SME-biased development promotes has a downward impact on the inter-sector productivity gap, since smaller urban areas have a smaller productivity gap with respect to the rural sector. The inflation of the rural–urban gap is dampened by the redistribution of labour to smaller urban labour markets. Further, the development of SMEs within the rural sector might provide huge opportunities for off-farm income and this might have a significant effect on decreasing "within group" inequality in the low-productivity farm sector, if indeed low-income farm households participate disproportionately in off-farm activities (as we shall see happened in Taiwan).
- Since much skill formation in industry takes place through on-the-job training, decentralized industrialization leads to a more widespread acquisition of skills. This effect extends to entrepreneurship. The East Asian SME model is well known for developing an extensive network of subcontracting, helping the integration of SMEs with large-scale production—even in exports—facilitated by the widespread development of small entrepreneurs.

- The process of growth with equity in East Asia was also heavily influenced by the strong growth of post-primary education, thanks to deliberate government efforts. The policy was successful in creating and maintaining adequate standards of schooling because the population recognized the economic value of education as the demand for more educated labour grew. It is apparent that the SME type of development increased the demand for skilled labour (including those with formal schooling) over a wide area.

- Finally, it should be emphasized that the increasing inequality and the relatively larger employment share of the tertiary sector, in the BM and LE patterns, produces a self-reinforcing effect. The low income per worker in agriculture keeps the supply price of labour in the tertiary sector low, thus boosting the demand for relatively cheap services in the households of high-skilled labour in non-agricultural sectors. At the same time, the large profit income created in manufacturing ramps up demand for some high-income tertiary products like high-end restaurants, hotels, shopping malls or expensive real estate. These two developments feed off each other in a cumulative process, boosting the incomes at the upper end of the distribution in non-agricultural sectors. This process is an especially likely outcome if the export demand for manufactured goods is supported by a large inflow of foreign investment.

2 An international comparison of the size structure of manufacturing firms

This chapter examines the size distribution of employment and productivity differentials by size groups in the manufacturing sector of selected Asian countries. For this analysis, we are confining ourselves to the size distribution within the modern manufacturing sector (i.e. excluding the household enterprises that generally employ own-account workers, perhaps with some help from one or two wage workers). In our earlier work (Mazumdar and Sarkar 2008), we presented a snapshot of the size distribution of the manufacturing sector in selected countries and compared them with India. The data that we managed to get for Asian countries were quite dated and referred to various years in the 1980s.

Here, we have tried to cover more countries and collect data for more recent years. We were fortunate in having a collaborative effort with Asian Development Bank staff, who obtained data on size distribution from government surveys and censuses of member countries.[1] As a result, most of the data belong to this millennium (for a few countries, we had to be satisfied with data for the late 1990s). In addition, for several Asian countries, we were able to collect data at two or more points in time; this has given us the opportunity to analyse the changes in size distribution for a few countries over the last two decades.

The trend observed in recent Asian industrializing countries—particularly among the most rapidly growing ones like China—seems to be quite different from that in the major industrialized countries in the last quarter of the preceding century. These contrasting trends suggest important changes are under way in the international spread of technology and in the international division of labour as reflected in trade patterns in manufacturing.

I

Comparison of size structure of manufacturing employment in South-East and East Asian countries

We will examine whether the size distribution of other Asian countries can be classified into the three categories distinguished in the earlier work (Mazumdar and Sarkar 2008):

Equitable: a fairly even-sized distribution in which small, medium-sized, and large firms play more or less equally important roles and the productivity difference between the size classes is small.

Distinctly skewed to right: the pattern in which the distribution of employment by size groups is distinctly skewed to the large firms. Typically in this pattern, the productivity difference between large and small firms tends to be substantial.

Dualistic: the dualistic pattern in which there is a strong mode at both ends of the distribution; a relatively large proportion of employment is found both in the small and in the large groups.

An inspection of our data sets enables us to classify the 11 Asian countries in our sample (nine in East and South-East Asia, and India and Bangladesh in South Asia) into the three types as presented in Table 2.1. The data sources are given in the Appendix. As already indicated, most of the data come from the submissions made by the National Statistical Offices to the Asian Development Bank. The Indian material was generated at the Institute of Human Development (IHD) in Delhi and the Bangladesh data in the Bangladesh Institute of Development Studies (BIDS) in Dhaka, as part of the research project. They were both generated from original unit-level data of the official enterprise surveys in these countries.

Equitable pattern

This group is best represented by the case of Hong Kong in the year 1982. We could gather size distribution of employment data for Hong Kong for later years but relative productivity data are available only for much smaller numbers of size classes of manufacturing employment. The Hong Kong data of the early 1980s illustrate one of the best examples of what equitable distribution could be. It can be seen from Table 2.1A that employment is quite evenly distributed among the various size groups, with the small enterprises playing as much a role in the island's manufacturing structure as medium and large enterprises. At the same time, the difference in labour productivity between the smallest and largest size group is one of the smallest in the sample.

The pattern of distribution in Hong Kong can be compared with the other countries in this category (Korea and Taiwan). They are characterized by a marginally stronger role of small establishments. It can be seen that, although the modal size group is the small size class of 10–49 workers, the proportion of employment in large enterprises of 500+ workers is significantly larger in Korea and Taiwan. Further, Table 2.1A shows that the productivity difference between the small and large enterprises is much less in Hong Kong particularly in relation to Korea. The wage differential between small and large units is accordingly much lower in Hong Kong. Average earnings in Hong Kong in 1982 were only 55 per cent higher in

Table 2.1 Percentage distribution of employment by size group and relative labour productivity of selected Asian countries

A. Equitable

Korea 1995

Size group	Employment distribution (%)	Relative labour productivity
5–9	9.4	25
10–49	30.3	31
50–99	12.4	41
100–199	10.7	51
200–499	11.4	65
500 and above	25.8	100

Hong Kong 1982

Size group	Employment distribution (%)	Relative labour productivity
1–9	12.2	54
10–49	27.4	61
50–99	15.6	66
100–199	14.5	71
200–499	13.8	82
500 and above	16.5	100

Taiwan 1996

Size group	Employment distribution (%)	Relative labour productivity
5–9	9.9	33
10–49	31.9	41
50–99	13.1	38
100–499	20.4	63
500 and above	24.7	100

B. Skewed to right

Malaysia 1995

Size group	Employment distribution (%)	Relative labour productivity
5–49	11.9	56
50–199	23.4	80
200–499	19.7	93
500 and above	45.0	100

Thailand 1996

Size group	Employment distribution (%)	Relative labour productivity
10–49	12.9	39
50–99	8.4	53
100–499	31.8	73
500 and above	46.9	100

Vietnam 2005

Size group	Employment distribution (%)	Relative labour productivity
5–9	1.1	34
10–49	7.0	69
50–99	5.9	92
100–199	8.6	107
200–499	17.5	112
500 and above	59.9	100

China 2004

Size group	Employment distribution (%)	Relative labour productivity
<9	1.8	59
9–19	4.8	50
20–49	13.4	41
50–199	24.8	48
200–499	16.7	64
500 and above	38.5	100

Bangladesh 2001–02

Size group	Employment distribution (%)	Relative labour productivity
6–9	5.3	29
10–49	10.7	38
50–99	6.7	72
100–199	8.5	64
200–499	26.0	65
500 and above	42.8	100

C. Dualistic

Indonesia 2006

Size group	Employment distribution (%)	Relative labour productivity
5–49	36.7	18
50–199	11.3	69
200–499	11.2	98
500 and above	40.8	100

Philippines 1988

Size group	Employment distribution (%)	Relative labour productivity
1–9	21.5	9
10–49	13.6	30
50–99	6.5	56
100–499	8.9	74
500 and above	49.5	100

India 2004–05

Size group	Employment distribution (%)	Relative labour productivity
DME (6–9)	46.6	8
10–49	10.4	24
50–99	5.7	34
100–199	7.1	43
200–499	9.9	57
500 and above	20.3	100

Note
The DME data are for 2005–06 and the rest for 2004–05.

establishments with more than 500 workers than in those with 1–9 workers. In Taiwan, workers in the largest firms earn on average double that of those in the smallest establishments and in Korea the difference is even greater.

As discussed in Mazumdar and Sarkar (2008), Hong Kong in 1982 comes closest to the free market model of development of Asia. The inference that can be drawn from it is that, left to itself, modern industry makes efficient use of small enterprises in a striking manner. In the absence of policy biases that protect both capital and labour in large firms, labour productivity and wage differential can be kept within fairly narrow bounds.[2]

Historically speaking, the Korean case presents an interesting scenario. In Korea, the size structure of employment in 1975 resembled the category of "skewed to the right" when proportion of employment in the largest size group peaked at 45 per cent. But from that time, Korea has been consciously trying to develop its small and medium enterprises and now it resembles much more closely the size distribution of traditionally equitable countries of Hong Kong and Taiwan. It is clear that the size distribution in 1995 has become even more equitable than it was in 1986, continuing the trend that was noticed in Mazumdar and Sarkar (2008).[3]

Skewed to the right pattern

The second pattern in our sample of countries represents the size distribution of employment which is skewed to the right with modal size groups employing 500+ workers. These countries constitute the largest number of countries in our sample, namely Bangladesh in South Asia; and Malaysia, Thailand, Vietnam, and China in East and South-East Asia. These countries exhibit one common trend. Malaysia and Thailand in the mid-1990s were hailed as success stories of export-oriented industrializing countries. In the present era, the most successful manufacturing exporting nation is China; Vietnam is also shaping up as a major labour-intensive manufacturing exporting country. Bangladesh also followed the policy of export development but with less success, being confined largely to garments.

The productivity differences among the various size groups of firms are not as substantial as in the dualistic pattern. One can discern two variants. Bangladesh, Thailand, and Vietnam show larger productivity differences between the smaller size classes employing fewer than 50 workers and the largest size classes employing 500+ workers. On the other hand, the productivity differential between the smallest and largest size classes in Malaysia and China is similar to that of Hong Kong in 1982, exhibiting the classical case of equitable size distribution. The wage differentials between small and large units in these countries are accordingly much smaller. Average earnings in Malaysia and China are only 50–55 per cent higher in establishments employing more than 500 workers than in those employing 5–49 workers.

One possible caveat to the account given in this subsection should be noted. We have grouped Malaysia along with the others in the "skewed to the right" group, but we see that, even though the share of the largest size group of employment in Malaysia is as high as in the other countries (close to 50 per cent), Malaysia is distinguished by having a substantial proportion of employment in the medium 50–199 size group. This presence of a successful group of medium-scale enterprises distinguishes it from the more clear cases of the "skewed to the right" group. The comparison of the size distribution of employment in Malaysia at the earlier date of 1981 (as given in Mazumdar and Sarkar 2008) is instructive, and is commented on below.

Dualistic pattern

India's size structure of manufacturing employment clearly reflects a dualistic pattern. It is characterized by, first, the strong presence of both small and large firms and, second, the substantial economic distance between small and large firms (see Table 2.1C).

A word of clarification is needed about this nomenclature. The dualistic pattern has been long discussed in the literature on Japanese manufacturing. Indeed the data presented in Chapter 8 show the two prominent modes at the low and the high employment size groups. This pattern of simultaneous growth of small and large firms had its root in the initial surplus-labour conditions prevailing in Japan during its initial industrialization (which contributed to labour market segmentation) and the simultaneous development of a complex system linking large industry, the state and financial conglomerates, which accentuated capital market dualism.

It is, however, important to note that, while the Indian case might sometimes be interpreted as an exaggerated case of this model, the quantitative difference with the elements of the Japanese model is so large as to constitute a qualitatively different type. First, the modes at the lowest and the highest size groups in India are much more prominent, with a conspicuous trough in the proportion of employment in the intermediate size groups, from 10–500 workers. In India, the proportion of employment in the middle-sized groups was around 30 per cent (1984–85), while in Japan it was double that at 60 per cent (1960). Second, the productivity difference between 5–9 and the 500+ groups was markedly larger in India relative to Japan. In Japan, it was of the order of 1:3 compared to India's 1:8.

It is indeed true that the characteristic of the Japanese model has been almost equally strong participation in manufacturing employment of firms of various size groups, including the small, medium, and large. But this is true of other East Asian economies as well, notably Taiwan and Korea. The Japanese case would thus logically belong to the model of equitable size distribution, while the Indian case is distinctly of a different dualistic type.

Unlike India, the modal size groups in both Indonesia and the Philippines are establishments employing 500+ workers. Still, these countries employ a large proportion of workers in establishments employing fewer than 50 workers. In both these countries, the productivity difference between small and large groups is much larger than in the economies studied other than India. Consequently, the average earnings of workers are three times higher in establishments with more than 500 workers than in those employing fewer than 50 workers. These two cases can then be classified as belonging to the dualistic pattern like India. The surplus labour situation in these countries has made the dualistic pattern emerge; these countries have not been able to establish themselves as successful manufacturing exporting countries compared to countries belonging to the category of "skewed to the right".

II

Changes in size structure of manufacturing industries over time

Data of size distribution of manufacturing industries for different years could be put together for some of the countries in our sample. The data for the two most recent years are from the set collected by the Asian Development Bank. We have added the figures for an earlier year from the material presented in Table 9.1 of Mazumdar and Sarkar (2008, p. 204), which also gives the original sources for the countries concerned (see Table 2.2).

Equitable

In the equitable group, we have three countries: Taiwan, Korea, and Hong Kong. Korea and Hong Kong show similar patterns of change. Both these countries depict an increase in the employment share in 5–49 size class of firms and a substantial decline in the employment share of large enterprises employing 500 and more workers. In contrast, in Taiwan, the large enterprises have increased their share in manufacturing employment at the expense of small firms employing fewer than 50 workers. This different pattern cannot be ascribed entirely to deindustrialization. Hong Kong does show strong deindustrialization, in the sense that total manufacturing employment in the study period has been reduced to half. Evidently, most of this fall in employment has come from the downsizing or demise of large firms. But Korea, which also shows a gravitation of employment to small firms, has in fact held its ground or even increased somewhat the absolute numbers of employment in manufacturing. Taiwan, which has also had only a small or negligible growth of manufacturing employment, has witnessed the opposite trend: increasing significantly the share of employment in the largest size group, mostly at the expense of middle-sized enterprises. Interestingly, in Taiwan, the relative labour productivity of large firms (employing more than 500 workers) has increased from three times to four times that of the lowest size class employing fewer than 30 workers. A plausible hypothesis is that the export expansion of manufactured goods based on the large-scale strategy (exploiting economies of scale of production and marketing), which has characterized the economic development of mainland China in recent years, has also spilled over into Taiwan. Hong Kong has not shared in this trend because its specialization has shifted from manufacturing to services and perhaps also to different types of manufactured goods.

Skewed to the right

In this category, two clear trends are observed. Malaysia exhibits a stable size structure over the decade 1995–2005. Evidently the trend towards larger firms, which was exhibited between 1981 and 1995 and increased the share of large as well as medium-scale firms at the expense of the small, had come to a halt. At the end of the period, Malaysia is left with a manufacturing sector which has a strong mode in the largest size group. But unlike the other countries in the group, Malaysia has a significant share of middle-sized firms. By contrast, Thailand, Vietnam, and Bangladesh show a clear trend towards further domination of the large-sized class of firms employing 500+ workers at the cost of small firms. All these countries have substantially increased total manufacturing employment, and much of it has been in the largest size class of firms.

The explanation of further strengthening of the largest firms in manufacturing employment can be found in the changes in the pattern of international trade. This category of countries has performed better in the export of manufactured products. In the last two decades, there has been a large-scale shift of manufacturing enterprises from developed countries to developing countries. This shift has been most pronounced in labour-intensive manufacturing industries. These products are purchased in bulk by large retail chains in developed countries at low prices. The major products in this group are garments, leather products, and electronic products. Production of garments and leather products and assembly of final electronic items are increasingly undertaken by large firms as they have the capacity to deliver large consignments of these products. This aspect is quite clear from our case studies of Bangladesh and India where there were persistent claims that small and medium-sized firms are unable to get large volume orders from the major retail chains of developed countries. Further discussion about the relationship between export patterns and size are to be found in the case studies of India, and also of the "balanced size structure" countries of East Asia, and our example of the "skewed to the right" type, Vietnam.

Dualistic

For the dualistic case of India, we have data over a 20-year period covering the era of important changes and the reforms that are considered to have started with the 1991 devaluation. We can see that in the two decades since the reforms, there is no trend towards a reduction of the characteristics of this dualistic structure. The only discernible fact is that the lowest size class (6–9) has gained in employment share in the manufacturing sector at the cost of large firms (500+) with hardly any increase in the employment share in the mid-segment. The missing middle phenomenon has been extremely persistent. Rather we can observe a strengthening of this dualistic pattern as the economic distance between smallest and largest size class has been widening in the last two decades. The relative productivity of labour in the smallest size class with respect to the largest has fallen from one-eighth to one-twelfth from the late 1980s to the present. This has

Table 2.2 Percentage distribution of manufacturing employment by size group

A. Equitable

Taiwan

Size group	Employment distribution (%)		
	1986	1996	2006
5–49	34.4	41.8	34.8
50–499	41.6	33.5	34.5
500 and above	24.1	24.7	30.7

Korea

Size group	Employment distribution (%)	
	1988	1995
5–9	3.9	9.4
10–49	22.6	30.3
50–99	12.5	12.4
100–199	12.3	10.7
200–499	13.9	11.4
500 and above	34.9	25.8

Hong Kong

Size group	Employment distribution (%)		
	1982	1997	2007
1–9	12.2	22.2	24.0
10–49	27.4	30.2	27.7
50–99	15.6	12.7	10.8
100–199	14.5	10.3	9.5
200–499	13.8	10.6	13.2
500 and above	16.5	14.0	14.7

B. Skewed to the right

Malaysia

Size group	Employment distribution (%)		
	1981	1995	2005
5–49	24.8	11.91	12.67
50–199	28.9	23.39	23.77
200–499	16.6	19.72	18.48
500 and above	29.7	44.99	45.09

Thailand

Size group	Employment distribution (%)	
	1989	1996
10–49	18.9	12.9
50–99	10.2	8.4
100–499	30.8	31.8
500 and above	40.1	46.9

Vietnam

Size group	Employment distribution (%)	
	2000	2006
5–9	2.1	1.4
10–49	7.4	6.5
50–199	16.1	14.5
200–499	19.2	16.5
500 and above	55.1	61.1

Bangladesh

Size group	Employment distribution (%)		Relative productivity	
	1995–96	2001–02	1995–96	2001–02
6–9	12.7	5.3	19	31
10–49	15.4	10.7	36	38
50–99	5.5	6.7	62	61
100–199	10.5	8.5	53	69
200–499	22.8	26.0	65	79
500 and above	33.1	42.8	100	100

C. Dualistic

India

Size group	Employment distribution (%)					Relative productivity				
	1984–85	1989–90	1994–95	2000–01	2004–05	1984–85	1989–90	1994–95	2000–01	2004–05
DME (6–9)	40.3	44.9	41.5	45.4	46.6	19	12	10	9	8
10–49	9.5	10.3	10.4	10.2	10.4	42	35	37	39	24
50–99	6.1	6.9	8.0	6.6	5.7	45	38	45	41	34
100–199	5.7	6.4	7.4	7.0	7.1	62	58	54	56	43
200–499	8.3	8.6	9.5	9.4	9.9	86	77	84	84	57
500 and above	30.2	22.9	23.2	21.5	20.3	100	100	100	100	100

occurred in spite of an increase in labour productivity of all size groups over the years. The major factor in this trend is the faster increase in labour productivity of the largest size class (500+) relative to all other size classes.

This is a very important point to emphasize about the trends in the Indian size structure. The dualistic structure seems to have originated during the old system of the controlled economy, one aspect of which was the protection of small-scale enterprises. But it seems to have not only persisted after the dismantling of the system but also probably prospered in the post-reform years. The implications of India's pattern of growth and inequality on this dualism in manufacturing are profound.

III

Factors determining the different types of size structure

In the country studies to follow, we shall be discussing the specific factors which might have had an impact on the particular pattern of size distribution observed. But it might be useful at this stage to give an outline of some of the more general factors that researchers have suggested in the literature as influencing the development of one type of size structure rather than another.

Factor market segmentation

Economists examine the hypothesis that segmentation in factor markets—principally in the markets for labour and capital—cause different factor-price ratios in different size groups. Thus the co-existence of small and large firms is assured even if they are facing the same production function. In this rather textbook view, a major element in the inter-country difference in the structure of enterprises by size would be the difference in factor-price ratios by firm size.

Labour market segmentation

The literature has noticed for a long time that size-related wage difference is significant in many economies and seems to be larger in developing economies (see the examples given in Mazumdar and Mazaheri 2003). Some discussions have emphasized labour market institutions, and particularly the role of labour legislation which covers only the larger enterprises. But the size-related wage differential has been known to exist in the absence of significant labour legislation (Mazumdar 1983 and the references cited).

The literature has discussed extensively the many factors connected with the non-homogeneous quality of labour—and why they seem to be more important in developing countries. A major factor to be considered in the Asian economies is the coming of modern industry to an economy where family farms have been dominant. The nature of labour use in peasant agriculture gives rise to major differences in the supply prices of labour for irregular and casual employment and for more sustained regular industrial work. While wage work in farm and off-farm activities and in small manufacturing enterprises can make use of casual or irregular labour with a high turnover, large plants in industry demand more sustained effort from a committed and regular workforce. Internal skill formation is also more important as firms grow. Thus large firms are induced to hire workers with a higher supply price.

It might appear that, although wages per worker are higher for labour in large firms, the wage per efficiency units of work (the efficiency wage) would not differ much. But an important point to note here is that, since the superior labour demanded by large firms has to acquire firm-specific skills for efficiency, the supply of such labour to the individual enterprise would be inelastic. Thus, even if the marginal efficiency wage for large and small firms is equated at the margin, the average value of the efficiency wage would be higher for larger firms.

Capital market segmentation

In most economies, capital (finance) is available much more readily and at much cheaper rates to large firms. A great deal of finance, in the start-up phase and subsequently, is supplied by the entrepreneur's own savings and retained profits of the business. The unequal distribution of wealth in the economy already ensures that self-finance is available in larger amounts to the larger firms. To offset this, financial institutions need to have the ability and incentive to provide a larger proportion of the required finance to smaller firms. The working of capital markets in most economies—developed as well as developing—ensures that the outcome is exactly the opposite. Small firms have fewer types of collateral that are readily acceptable to lenders. Insofar as lending is based on personal information about the prospective borrower, the fixed (overhead) cost of obtaining information is invariant to the loan size and will be higher per dollar for small loans.

In the developing countries, where modern industrialization has often been started by the formal sector, the role of the formal financial institutions favours the businesses in this subsector. The link of the industrial and financial structures through large conglomerates like the *zaibatsu* in Japan or the *chaebol* in Korea has worked powerfully to deepen the segmentation. Government policies are meant to offset the advantage of small firms by specially directed efforts to make finance cheaper for small firms. But they have often ended up doing the opposite. They have included financial policies depressing the cost of loans from the large-scale oriented banking sector, as well as industrial policies making it easier for large firms to avail themselves of cheap loans (sometimes even at negative real interest rates).

Product market segmentation

In sum, the combination of the two factors (i.e. the marginal price of capital would be, in all probability, significantly lower for large firms and the observed wage differential is likely to be smaller than the efficiency wage differential) makes it very likely that the large firm would be faced with a factor cost ratio which would encourage more capital intensity. There is a further point to consider about the overall profitability of firms in terms of total cost per unit of output. Since the lower cost per unit of capital for large firms is not wholly offset by higher wage costs, it is probable that, with the same production function, large firms are more efficient overall. The fact that small firms are able to survive can then be traced to small and large firms producing different products with widely different production functions. This is indeed so, as many capital and intermediate goods in modern economies have much more significant economies of scale than consumer goods. Second, there is product market segmentation in terms of quality of products even within the same line of consumer products. In a range of consumer goods of wide use (such as garments, washing materials, processed food), the attributes appealing to high-income consumers are widely different from attributes demanded by low-income consumers. The "poor man's" quality of such consumer goods could be more cheaply produced by labour-intensive small firms often using non-mechanized techniques (Little *et al.* 1987: Chapter 14). Such differentiation of product markets served by different-sized groups of enterprises must be an important explanation of the co-existence of small and large firms even in ostensibly the same product line. Countries differ in the degree of differentiation of products of different qualities serving the same basic consumer need, like clothing. They would primarily vary by income levels, but also by consumer tastes and marketing conditions.

Transaction costs

The cost of business transactions between different economic agents differs enormously from country to country and has a significant impact on the size structure in manufacturing. Levy (1991) emphasized this factor, as it related to inter-firm transactions in the production process, in trying to account for the difference in the size structure of manufacturing between Taiwan with its even size distribution and Korea with its dominance of large firms prior to the post-1975 reforms. The link between the state and the corporate business class in the first phase of Korea's "guided industrializing" encouraged vertical integration of the different stages of the production process. The system contrasted with the situation in Taiwan, where the industrialization was spearheaded by much more native entrepreneurs who were socially distinguished from the government (dominated by the Kuomintang immigrants from the mainland). The social homogeneity of the entrepreneurial class in Taiwan and its historical base in small-scale production enabled a vital system of subcontracting to develop. This enabled the integration of production stages through inter-firm relationships between production units of various sizes.

Inter-country differences in the levels of transaction costs would be found not only among producing units, but also between producers and traders of different size groups. The institution of subcontracting which has played such a large role in the development of small-scale enterprises in Japan had its origin in the *ton-ya* or wholesale house system of subcontracting. Large-scale merchant houses had extensive networks of cottage enterprises. This laid the basis for the reduction of transaction costs in the relationship between traders and small and mid-sized producers in modern manufacturing. A particularly good contemporary example of the difference in transaction costs in the trader–producer relationship comes from the globalization of the manufacturing industry and the contrast between developing and developed countries. In developing countries, traders serving mass markets of labour-intensive products in the Western markets have found it easier (and less costly) to deal in large batch orders. This has resulted in bias in the size structure of manufacturing in a number of Asian countries skewed to large enterprises. The traders of manufactured consumer goods originating in developed countries, on the other hand, have been able to deal with a multitude of SMEs, which has facilitated a dramatic change in the size structure of manufacturing in these countries.

Government policies

Industrial policies pursued by governments have almost always had a component that had an impact on the size structure—and sometimes a crucial one. Hong Kong is the one country in Asia which seems to have had an industrial policy that was reasonably neutral to the evolution of the size structure in manufacturing (Beng 1988). Thus the fact that the size structure of its manufacturing enterprises has been characterized by an even distribution over a long time period has been noticed by economists. It has been suggested that, left to itself, industrial development in Asia would give opportunities for small firms as well as large ones.

The country studies in subsequent chapters demonstrate the different ways in which government policies have been biased in their impact on the size of firms. Korea is a striking instance of a country in which state policies were able to deliberately change the size structure of firms in a short period of time, from one biased towards large firms to a more even distribution. India's post-independence policy of protection of the small-scale firms established the dual structure with two modes and a missing middle, which we see even today. The Indian policy contrasts starkly from the Chinese post-reform industrial policy, which seems to have encouraged the rapid growth of large export-oriented firms based on foreign direct investment.

IV

The special case of China

The Chinese case is an especially interesting one, not only because of the importance of China in recent Asian industrialization, but also because industrial policy and its changes over time have critically influenced the relative importance of different types of enterprises, which has resulted in the skewed distribution to the right, as shown in Table 2.1B. There are in fact six important categories that are distinguished by Chinese researchers: state-owned enterprises (SOEs); collective-owned enterprises (COEs); domestic private enterprises (PRVs); other domestic enterprises, mainly shareholding enterprises (SHRs); Hong Kong–Macau–Taiwan invested enterprises (HMTs); and other foreign-invested enterprises, mainly by investors from OECD countries (OECD). The relative importance of these types and the shares of each type in terms of critical economic magnitudes are given in Table 2.3 below. Table 2.4 gives the mean values of selected variables per establishment.

Before the reforms of the Chinese economic system, the manufacturing sector was dominated by SOEs. In the first stage of the reforms in the 1980s, SOEs lost their importance through privatization or acquisition by indigenous private enterprises and multinationals. Unlike the privatization process followed in the former Soviet Union and Eastern European countries, China did not pursue a policy of quick and massive privatization. At a later stage of the gradual privatization programme, China initiated the shareholding programme in 1993, which became a principal vehicle of privatization creating the SHR category in Table 2.3. The SOEs have lost their share of output gradually but quite substantially. Apart from the significant growth of SHR units, the growth of private firms has been quite remarkable, when we remember that legally such firms were not officially written into the constitution until March 2004. An unusual type of enterprise, nominally under the control of local governments but propelled largely by local entrepreneurship, made its appearance in the first decade of post-reform China. Also called town and village enterprises (TVEs), these establishments grew rapidly in the 1980s, increasing their share of industrial output from 22.4 per cent in 1978 to 39.4 per cent in 1996. A shift in industrial policy preferences in the post-Tiananmen decade saw an equally significant decline in the importance of this category as its share of output fell to 10.3 per cent in 2004 (Xu 2009, p. 12, quoting the figures from the China Statistical Yearbook; see below for a fuller discussion of the policy changes).

Table 2.3 Percentage distribution by ownership categories, 2004

Ownership type	Number of firms	Output	Fixed assets	Employment
PRV	65.6	21.8	11.7	34.6
COE	10.3	4.4	2.6	7.6
SOE	2.2	14.3	31.9	13.8
SHR	14.3	27.9	31.7	23.6
HMT	3.9	11.1	8.7	11.1
OECD	3.7	20.3	13.2	10.1
Total	100.0	100.0	100.0	100.0

Source: Xu (2009, Table 3). The original source is the First National Economic Census of China conducted in 2005. The reference time for the Census is 31 December 2004, and the flow data cover the whole of 2004.

Table 2.4 Mean values per establishment in different ownership categories, 2004

Type	Number of firms (000)	Output	Employment	Capital–labour ratio	Labour productivity	Wage per employee	College employee ratio (%)
PRV	898	4.4	35	51	124	9	6.9
COE	142	5.7	49	57	116	9	6.3
SOE	30	85.7	421	346	204	19	21.3
SHR	196	25.8	107	208	240	13	14.9
HMT	54	37.2	188	118	198	14	9.3
OECD	50	73.0	184	196	397	18	14.2
All	1370	13.2	87	150	197	13	11.7

Source: As in Table 2.3. Unit of values: thousand RMB. Unit of employment: persons.

Turning to the mean values of relevant variables in Table 2.4, it is clear that the SOEs remain the really large firms, even though their high capital–labour ratio and relatively low labour productivity point to their relative inefficiency. The SHRs are the next group of large firms, and are clearly more efficient than the SOEs, with a much lower use of capital per labour and higher labour productivity. We also see that the purely private firms, which as indicated grew under an uncertain legal environment, are generally on the small side. Although accounting for nearly two-thirds of all manufacturing firms, their mean output is very small, pointing to their low capitalization and labour productivity. Although the share of total output of such firms was much higher than that of the COEs in 2004, these two categories are on more or less the same level in terms of key economic ratios such as capital per worker, labour productivity, and wage levels. Nevertheless, in 2004, private firms accounted for no less than one-third of manufacturing employment, compared to only 7.4 per cent for COEs.

There are substantial differences between labour productivity and wages—which indeed partly relate to firm size. But there is a spectacular difference between SOEs and OECD firms. Although the wage per employee is as high in SOEs as in OECD firms, the labour productivity in the former is substantially lower, again pointing to their relative inefficiency.

The difference in wage level by ownership category otherwise follows labour productivity differentials. This is partly the consequence of differences in average size and partly in the use of educated labour.

Ownership category and size distribution

The fact that the mean employment size of SOE firms is so much larger than that of the others might suggest that the overall size distribution of Chinese manufacturing firms is the result of mixing up different categories of firms. This is only partially true. It can be seen from Table 2.1 that the proportion of employment in units of the largest size group (with more than 500 workers) was 38.5 per cent. But the share of SOEs, which would be in this group, was only 13.8 per cent. At the other end, although the mean employment size of PRVs was 35, the proportion of employment in all manufacturing with fewer than 50 workers was 20 per cent, with the PRV units accounting for 34.6 per cent of all employment. It is apparent that the size distribution of the different categories is overlapping. The proportion of employment in the largest size group is enhanced by the inclusion of SOEs, and the share of the smaller size groups is augmented by the inclusion of PRV and COE firms, while the foreign categories (HMT and OECD) augment the share of middle-sized groups between the two extreme groups.

The different pattern distinguishing China from the East Asian equitable distribution size structure should, however, be apparent. The large proportion of employment in the 5–9 size group found in the East Asian economies is absent in China. Indeed, even if we increase the upper limit of small firms to 50 workers, the share is much larger in East Asian (and indeed other Asian) economies. The middle size group of 50–199 workers in China employs about a quarter of the total workers in manufacturing. This is the modal group of private and TVE (COE) firms. But it is easily swamped by large units, which account for the bulk of employment in the state-owned, joint ventures (SHR), and foreign categories.

Impact of policy changes

Changing industrial policies in China have been critical in the evolution of the current size structure of manufacturing in the first decade of the century. When the first stage of the reforms was implemented in the 1980s, China saw the emergence of the COEs or TVEs. This wave of reforms was in the first place fuelled by the desire to decentralize the power of the central government to local branches of the state, including provincial and rural authorities. Some of the industrial enterprises owned and promoted by the local governments were collective enterprises. But the 1980s also saw the widespread development of individual enterprises, which are household enterprises typically having fewer than seven employees, and the so-called "alliance enterprises", which were in fact private enterprises with multiple investors. In 1985, out of a total of 69.8 million people employed by the TVE sector, 59 per cent were in collective TVEs, 33.7 per cent in household businesses, and only 6.8 per cent in the larger private businesses. But it was the last category that grew in importance over the years. By 1996, with a doubling of the total employment in the TVE sector, the proportions of the different categories had changed to 47.1 per cent, 37.8 per cent, and 18.2 per cent respectively (Huang 2008, Table 2.1). For much of this period, Chinese official policy did not recognize private ownership. Thus many of these private enterprises were counted in official documents as TVEs theoretically under the ownership and control of local governments, although the authorities knew very well that they were really private enterprises. The majority of these effectively private TVEs were medium-sized enterprises located in rural areas.

The second wave of reforms in the 1990s saw the official recognition of private enterprises as viable establishments for industrial development, and this was also the period which saw a substantial privatization of SOEs. The TVE sector declined in a significant way in this period but the "private" TVEs continued to increase in total employment, if not in number of units, along with the growth of non-TVE private enterprises. These private TVEs grew at the expense of the collective TVEs, although in the Chinese official statistics they are both covered under the umbrella of COEs (Table 2.3).

Privatization of the large SOE sector in the 1980s and beyond has followed a different route from the Soviet or other East European models. The rate of shrinkage of the state enterprise sector has been much slower and the ideological resistance to wholesale privatization has been strong. The resultant impact on the size structure of manufacturing has been threefold. First, the state sector has continued to play an important part in manufacturing. Second, the private sector, although showing a great deal of dynamic growth, has not produced a sizable number of large firms. They are significant in the 50–199 size group but there has been a very limited development of conglomerates which have been so important in the growth of East Asian economies and even of the Indian manufacturing sector. Third, the importance of foreign-invested enterprises (FIEs) from both neighbouring areas and from the OECD has been a significant development of Chinese manufacturing.

Huang (2003, 2008) has strongly argued that the second and third features of the size structure are related. It is the constrained development of domestic private sector firms that left a vacuum in the Chinese system for FIEs to fill. Foreign firms also participated significantly in joint ventures when a section of the SOEs were privatized. Huang attributes this superior performance of FIEs to elements of the Chinese industrial policies. The result was the product of political aspects of the policy, rather than economic aspects. The argument, in a nutshell, is that in the political pecking order, SOEs were the preferred type of enterprise, but that private domestic enterprise was further down than foreign investment. This ordering was the result of a profound and continued suspicion of private property even after the reforms.

Thus when an opportunity for export-led growth presented itself and SOEs were not efficient or flexible enough to seize the opportunity, it was FIEs rather than private domestic enterprises which were in the forefront of growth. Two of the important reasons for the dominance of political, rather than economic, advantage of FIEs cited by Huang are the following. To begin with, China was already building up a sizable pool of surpluses on the current and capital accounts when FDI liberalization took place in 1992. Thus, FDI dominance was not driven by the necessity of augmenting the savings ratio. In fact, China has been one of the world's largest recipients of foreign capital at the same time as it has been one of the largest capital exporters, with a rising savings rate. A further relevant point to consider is that foreign capital inflow took the form of foreign-invested enterprises rather than the alternative of contractual arrangements (by which foreign firms contract domestic suppliers to provide the necessary output for export markets). In fact, China is unique among other economies with large incidences of FDI in having FIEs in a whole range of industries; the more common experience is for FIEs to be concentrated in a few industries in which domestic production might be constrained for technological reasons.

The principal instruments through which the less-favoured position of domestic private firms became effective were the institutions for the supply of finance capital and land—both of which were subject to dominant forms of state control.

While the detailed process of FIE development and the factors affecting it remain a subject of discussion (and further research outside the scope of this book), the results given in Tables 2.3 and 2.4 are striking. FIEs accounted for 21 per cent of total manufacturing employment in 2004, and an even higher proportion (32 per cent) of output. The role of FDI would of course be significantly higher in both employment and output if we take account of its participation in joint ventures (SHRs).

Finally, we should make some reference to the virtual absence of small firms from the size structure of manufacturing in China—a striking contrast with the experience of other Asian economies. This is particularly remarkable since the development of TVEs showed the dynamic nature of Chinese entrepreneurs. It seems that the household enterprises (employing fewer than eight workers), which flourished under the TVE umbrella, were very much a rural phenomenon. Evidently the *houkou* system under which households were required to register their residence (which was rationed for migrants into the urban area) had an impact on the development of small-scale urban enterprises. Another relevant point to emphasize is that the constrained development of private manufacturing firms itself dampened the growth of small enterprises.

V

Size structure of manufacturing in developed countries

A contrasting picture

We have seen that the recent experience in the trend in size distribution in manufacturing in developing Asia has not particularly favoured the SME sector. In quite a few cases of the fast-growing economies—notably China—the growth process has been driven by a relatively rapid growth of larger enterprises in manufacturing. In the two cases in which the small enterprises have held their own (India and to a smaller extent Indonesia), the pattern of size distribution has shown a conspicuous feature of the missing middle, with its attendant problems. The classical East Asian pattern with the healthy development of the SMEs, which seems to have supported the striking period of growth with equity in the later decades of the last century, does not seem to have been repeated.

The recent experience of developed countries has been quite different. There has been a remarkable tilt towards small enterprise development in the size structure of manufacturing in a large batch of developed economies (starting in the 1960s, and persisting until at least the end of the 1980s).

The evidence

Figure 2.1, taken from Carlsson (2006), portrays the trend in the share of employment in small plants (fewer than 100 workers) in total manufacturing employment over the 1945–88 period.

The diagram shows that the developed countries after the Second World War had different levels of small enterprise (SE) presence in the developed world. Japan and Italy were exceptional in having more than half their manufacturing employment in SEs, with the UK, USA, and Germany occupying the bottom of the table at around 25 per cent of total employment, and France and Sweden in the middle. All these countries showed a similar pattern of development over the succeeding decades. After an initial spurt of larger enterprises, the share of SEs started to increase from the beginning of the 1970s (the only exception being Sweden, which lagged behind this trend for about a decade).

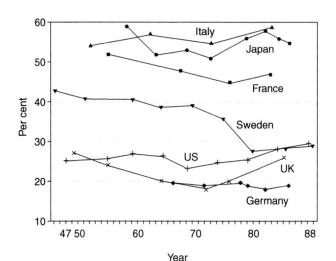

Figure 2.1   Employment shares of small plants in manufacturing in various countries, 1945–88 (source: Carlsson (1996, Figure 2.1, p. 65)).

Note
Small plants are defined as those with fewer than 100 employees. Original sources:
Loveman and Sengenberger (1991); US Bureau of the Census, *Census of Manufac-
turers*, various issues; Statistics Sweden, *Industrial Statistics*, various issues (in
Swedish).

The similar experience of these developed countries suggests that there were
common factors at play explaining the decline and then the increase in the share
of SEs in the industrial economies, with the turning point occurring in the 1970s.

Factors affecting trend towards SEs

There are broadly four groups of factors which have been discussed in the literature attempting to explain the remarkable tilt towards small units in the manufacturing sector of developed countries. These are:

•   change in the nature of world competitiveness
•   change in the structure of demand for manufactured goods
•   technological progress affecting the process of production
•   changing nature of entrepreneurship.

While the first group is particularly relevant for the size structure in developed
countries, the other three are relevant for understanding the trends in both developing and developed countries.

The intensification of global competition in the post-Second World War years is manifested in the significant increase in the world trade in manufactured goods, as exports outstripped production for the domestic markets in most developed countries. A second element pushing firms towards a more competitive environment was the integration of national economies achieved through much larger volumes of FDI flows and the growth of intra-firm trade within multinationals. These developments coincided with the breakdown of the Bretton Woods system of fixed exchange rates. All this added to the uncertainty facing individual firms, which were forced to adopt defensive measures to specialize in increasingly narrow markets and reduce the coverage of a wide spectrum of products.

One result of this response to uncertainty and competitiveness was the downsizing of corporations and the need to develop the strategy of "flexible specialization". Firms, on the one hand, needed to narrow their product specialization to specific areas in which they could achieve niche markets, and at the same time to prepare to switch to other product lines in response to developing pressures in the market.

THE CHANGE IN THE STRUCTURE OF DEMAND FOR MANUFACTURED GOODS

Rising incomes in developed countries led to much greater variety in the demand for consumer goods, forcing firms to develop more intense product differentiation. Carlsson, writing in the 1990s, remarked that a glance at supermarkets in the USA showed that these stores stocked roughly twice as many items on the shelf as they did 15 years previously. The implication for the size of firms is this: it is cheaper for a producer to build a new, more flexible line to accommodate the shifting demand than to change existing lines. It is then more advantageous for businesses to aim for smaller production units, which would involve much smaller fixed costs than specialized machinery, which would be profitable only with large and steady volumes of production over a long period.

This development in markets for manufactured goods in developed countries was accompanied by developments of specialization in international trade patterns. Firms in developed countries found it more profitable to farm out production of more standard consumer products to producers in developing countries with lower labour costs. Similar forces induced the shift of production of more standard intermediate goods to developing countries, to be used by producers of a variety of final goods in developed countries. This process of spatial redistribution of manufacturing was of course aided by a trading system which saw an enormous increase in FDIs and expansion of multinationals in the newly industrialized countries. This new form of division of labour is surely one of the major differences in the evolution of firm size in the two types of economies. The rapidly industrializing countries in Asia, notably China, have found it more profitable to exploit the economies of production and marketing in large units specializing in standard products with large world demand. The developed countries gravitate to smaller producing units, which can provide more easily differentiated final goods through their flexible specialization.

TECHNOLOGICAL PROGRESS AFFECTING THE PROCESS OF PRODUCTION

Carlsson (1984, 1993) has written extensively on the shift in production technology from one which favoured large-scale production for the mass market (which dominated modern manufacturing ever since the industrial revolution) to a system based on the discovery of micro-chips involving numerical control and favouring small and medium-sized production units. This major shift in basic technology affected particularly the metalworking industries (which account for half or more of total manufacturing in industrial economies) but the change is not limited to this subsector.

The two major prongs in the older technology were the interchangeability of parts and the moving assembly line. They required vastly improved speed and accuracy in the production of machine tools which supported high-volume production. It was subsequently helped along the same path by the introduction of transfer machines (which made it possible to transfer a workpiece automatically from one work station to the next) and the eventual Detroit automation (which permitted linking several work stations into a continuous production line). The technology (which got a major fillip during the Second World War) was extended to a variety of sectors of mass production and became the standard for high-volume production in most of the industrial world.

The development in recent decades of numerically controlled production methods involving a shift from mechanical to electronic control devices has, by contrast, favoured small and medium-scale units involved in batch production.

> When the Japanese introduced microcomputer based numerical controllers in the mid-1970s two important things happened. First, the programmability and therefore the flexibility of NCMTs [numerically controlled machine tools] increased dramatically. Second, cheaper and more flexible numerical controllers in combination with other changes led to mass production of NCMTs, resulting in drastically reduced prices.
>
> (Carlsson 2006, p. 90)

For the first time, automated technology came within both the technological and the financial spectrum of small producers. Taken in conjunction with the evolution of markets for finished goods to more differentiated products (discussed above), this change in technological possibilities gave a major push to the growth of SMEs in the economies of developed countries.

THE CHANGING NATURE OF ENTREPRENEURSHIP

The possibility of technological breakthrough is not the complete story of successful evolution. It needs a growing pool of entrepreneurs who can respond to the possibilities opening up in a substantial way. This is indeed what seemed to have happened in developed economies in the last quarter of the twentieth century.

Audretsch and his co-researchers (Ace and Audretsch 1993) found that entry by firms into an industry is not preferred at all in capital-intensive industries in which scale economies can be expected to play a significant role. Rather, new firm start-ups tend to be substantially more prevalent in industries characterized by the entre-preneurial regime, in which the bulk of the innovations are by small firms. This finding suggests a model of entry and survival of small firms which is rather differ-ent from the classical model of new firm entry, which stresses that the motivation is the prevalence of excessive rents in the existing industry. Rather, differences of beliefs about the expected values of new ideas play the dominant role. Small firms entering industries with the entrepreneurial regime have a greater likelihood of making a successful innovation, and thus would not exit even in the face of short-term negative profits. The expected gains from a successful innovation and a new regime of profitability motivate their survival and possible growth.

The question arises: how is this hypothesis to be reconciled with the older Schumpeterian model, which held innovations to be the dynamic factor propelling industrial growth, but implied that only large firms can bear the cost of innovations and have the advantage in the size structure of industry (rather like Audretsch's conical revolving door)? Research has explored the sources of new knowledge about technology and production processes and has pointed to a larger role of uni-versity and research institutions, rather than the firm's internal R&D investments. Such a shift in industrial economies like that of the USA has been instrumental in making the innovative ideas available more easily to small and new firms.

VI

Conclusions

While an extended discussion of the trend towards small firms in industrialized countries of the West is beyond the scope of this book, our brief review of the literature might be useful in providing interesting clues in the discussion of the three types of Asian countries which follow.

An example is the point about entrepreneurship. The importance of the small firm in the evolution of modern industry in developed countries depended heavily on the existence of a pool of emerging entrepreneurs who were ready to exploit the opportunities provided by innovation. This and the institutional support given to the production of new knowledge have been instrumental in the small-firm biased development in the USA and some other advanced economies. Equally, the absence of these conditions has led to large-firm development in the transitional economies and in Sweden (an exceptional case in developed Western countries).[4] In their lack of small entrepreneurs, the experience of China and Vietnam can best be considered an extension of the case of transitional economies of Eastern Europe. As discussed above, and in the case study of Vietnam, this is a major factor in the size distribution of manufacturing skewed to the right. However, different economic conditions, particularly with respect to the export market, ensured that the former Asian planned economies had a much more rapid growth experience. The nature of entrepreneurship, and in particular its non-homogeneous nature, would be central to our extended discussion of the Indian case of the missing middle. The contrasting picture of the East Asian countries (Japan, Taiwan, and Korea) provides the example of an alternative path in which a number of factors enabled small entrepreneurs to graduate to middle-sized ones, and led to the more even size structure of manufacturing in these countries.

Another important example of factors helping to produce different types of size structure is the changing pattern of specialization in manufacturing and in the export trade in manufactured goods; East Asian countries depended significantly on manufactured exports in their earlier periods of growth.

Appendix

Data sources

The statistics on the size structure of manufacturing (unless otherwise stated) have been collected by the Asian Development Bank (Manila) as background work to *Enterprises in Asia: Fostering Dynamism in SMEs*, published as a special chapter of their *Key Indicators for Asia and the Pacific, 2009*. The original sources are as follows.

Bangladesh

Data for 1–9 persons are constructed from the *Annual Establishment and Institutional Survey*, Manufacturing Sector. The data for 10+ establishments are from the *Census of Manufacturing Industries.*

China

First National Economic Census of China 2005. The reference time for the Census was 31 December 2004, and the flow data covered the whole of the year 2004. "The Economic Census covered all legal person units, establishments and individuals who were engaged in tertiary and secondary industries" (ADB 2009, p. 7).

Hong Kong

Data obtained from the Census and Statistics Department of Hong Kong.

India

Data tapes of the different rounds of the National Sample Surveys, Government of India. The tables are generated from the data tapes at the Institute of Human Development, New Delhi.

Indonesia

Economic Census 2006, BPS-Statistics Indonesia.

Korea

Statistical Yearbook of Korea.

Malaysia

Annual Survey of Manufacturing Industries, Department of Statistics.

Philippines

Annual Survey of Philippine Business, National Statistical Office.

Thailand

Own calculations from the *Establishment Surveys of Thailand*, Department of Statistics.

Vietnam

Own calculations from the data tapes of the *Enterprise Census* conducted annually by the General Statistical Office.

Part II

The case of India

Introduction

The post-reform growth experience in India has been characterized by three significant trends:

- While the growth rate has accelerated, there has been increasing inequality.
- Indian growth has been led not by the manufacturing sector as in most of the history of development, but by the tertiary sector. Further, labour productivity in the tertiary sector of India has been higher than in the manufacturing sector, in contrast to the experience of other Asian developing countries.
- The manufacturing sector has been characterized by a pronounced dualism, with strong modes at the low and high size groups, a conspicuous "missing middle", and an unusually large productivity gap between the two.

The hypothesis developed here is that these three phenomena are inter-connected. It is the problem in the manufacturing sector, with its dualistic size structure and missing middle, that has led to relatively low productivity in manufacturing. This in turn has slowed the growth rate of manufacturing in domestic and export markets and has produced the unusual pattern of growth led by the tertiary sector. The inequality in the growth process is also partly due to relatively faster development of the tertiary sector and to the dualism in manufacturing itself.

Chapter 3 describes the growth process in India over the last two decades, exploring the sectoral composition of the economy and the contribution of the tertiary sector through value added and employment. Chapter 4 examines the size structure of manufacturing and the characteristics of the small-scale (DME) sector, contrasted with the large-scale sector. Chapter 5 argues that dualism in manufacturing has been crucial to the slowdown in growth in this sector. Chapter 6 expands the analysis of the impact of dualism on income inequality in the economy, and brings in supply-side factors, like the development of education. Finally, Chapter 7 discusses the important issue of why dualism in manufacturing has persisted even after the initial factors helping to establish it in the pre-reform era were largely dismantled.

3 Salient features of the growth pattern in India

I

Trends in growth and inequality in recent decades

Acceleration of the growth rate

Indian economic growth has spurted in the post-reform years. This has led to an accelerated decline in the poverty rate, but (like many other countries in recent decades) the increase in the rate of poverty reduction has been accompanied by a growing inequality.

Growth in GDP

India's acceleration in terms of the GDP growth rate is generally thought to have started with the reforms undertaken following the balance of payments crisis of 1991, but many authors have suggested that the acceleration started earlier, in the 1980s. The difficulties of the early 1990s produced a dip in the growth rate, and the reforms seemed to have restored the higher rates at least of the second half of the decade (see Table 3.1).

The new century, particularly after 2003–04, seemed to have ushered in a phase of accelerated growth. Unfortunately the latest "thick round" of the National Sample Survey (NSS), on which much of the analysis of inequality has to be based, is at the moment only available for 2004–05. Thus the full effects of this most recent acceleration of the rate of growth of GDP cannot be assessed just yet. The NSS does not collect data on household income, but only on expenditure (consumption). We are therefore interested in concentrating on the rate of growth of consumption, rather than GDP.

Growth rate of consumption per capita

The basic data based on the National Accounts (NAS) and the NSS thick rounds are given in Table 3.2. It is well known that there is a major discrepancy in the growth rate of consumption given by the NSS and the National Accounts: the

Table 3.1 Growth rate of GDP, % (annual average for period)

1950–59	1960–69	1970–79	1980–82	1983–85	1986–88	1989–92	1993–95	1996–98	1999–2001	2001–03	2003–07
3.3	4.4	2.9	5.6	5.6	6.4	4.3	5.9	6.1	5.9	5.8	9.1

Source: Bhalla (2010, Table 1.6). Original sources are the Reserve Bank of India and the World Bank.

Table 3.2 India: economic growth in the 1980s and 1990s (%)

Period	Average annual growth of per capita[1]				
	GDP	Private consumption NAS	Private consumption NSS[2]	Private consumption rural NSS[2]	Private consumption urban NSS[2]
1983–93/94	3.11	1.84	0.91	0.76	1.23
1993/94–2004/05	4.43	3.30	1.31	1.12	1.74

Source: IMF WEO, NSSO 38th, 55th, and 61st rounds; and Fund staff estimates.

Notes
1 In constant prices.
2 Converted in real terms using the official deflators of the Planning Commission.

NSS reports a much lower level of consumption and the discrepancy has grown over time. The NSS consumption returns seem to have captured only 62 per cent of the private consumption estimated by the NAS in 1993–94 and the figure fell to 41 per cent in 2004–05 (Topalova 2008, footnote 8, p. 5). As a consequence, the growth rate of consumption estimated from the NSS data was only a half of what was reported by the NAS in the decade 1983–93, and it had shrunk to about 40 per cent of the NAS figures in the 1990s.

It is generally accepted that this discrepancy is, to a large extent, due to the NSS respondents not reporting high expenditures, particularly on durables or other assets.[1] The under-reporting of high expenditures is of course related to the under-reporting of high incomes, a large chunk of it undeclared for tax purposes. Banerjee and Piketty (2005) studied the time-series of income tax data over the entire period 1922–2000. They found that there was a turnaround in the share of the top 1 per cent of the taxpayers' income starting in the early 1980s. After a secular decline lasting throughout the period until the 1980s (interrupted only by some erratic movement in the years of the Second World War and immediately following), the income share of the top 1 per cent started to go up. It decreased from 12–13 per cent in the 1950s to 4–5 per cent at the beginning of the 1980s, but then increased gradually to 9–10 per cent in the late 1990s. There was a similar turnaround in the narrower group of the top 0.1 per cent, except that the share of this very rich group seems to have accelerated in the 1990s. The authors ascribe this turnaround to the impact of globalization, which enabled a small minority of the population to reap the benefits of the contacts established with the world economy.[2]

The implication of this finding for the NAS–NSS gap in the growth rate of consumption is this: if in fact the very rich taxpayers declared all their income to the tax office, but were wary of admitting their high income to the NSS (since there is no legal requirement for the response to NSS questions), then the omission of this share from the estimated consumption growth would underestimate the latter. Using the income share of the top 1 per cent from the tax returns of the late 1980s, Banerjee and Piketty conclude that such an omission would account for about 40 per cent of the observed gap between the NAS and NSS estimates of growth rate of consumption between the period covered, between the 38th (1983) and the 55th (1999–2000) NSS rounds.[3]

We conclude that the increase in measured inequality from the NSS rounds is likely to be an underestimate, useful for defining the lower bounds of the increase. It should also be emphasized that the analysis of the components of inequality and their changes over time would be more important than the absolute magnitude of the change.

Growth with poverty reduction and increase in inequality

The story of Indian growth, particularly in the post-reform decade, has been one of increasing inequality accompanied by a significant reduction in the incidence of poverty. This can be seen clearly in the changing pattern of distribution of the average per capita expenditure (APCE) for all households, as reported by the successive rounds of the NSS. The graphs of the kernel density functions for APCE for the different rounds (rural and urban areas) are presented in Figure 3.1. The vertical line shows the poverty line as defined by the Planning Commission, based on nutritional requirements at constant 1993–94 prices.[4] The distributions move to the right in both areas, signifying an improvement in household APCE. The modes of distribution were left of the poverty line in the pre-reform years, but in 2004–05 (after a decade of post-reform growth) they have shifted to the right of the poverty line. But it is apparent that the modes continue to be prominent and sizable percentages of households are in the vicinity of the mode (less so in the urban sector). This means that the incidence of poverty as measured, for example, by the headcount ratio (the percentage of population below the poverty line) would be very sensitive to growth (the elasticity of poverty with respect to income growth is high). At the same time, it is apparent that the APCE of wealthier households increased more in the urban sector, suggesting that the inequality in the distribution of income increased more in this sector.

Poverty incidence

An implication of the distribution of APCE portrayed in Figure 3.1, with the concentration of a significant proportion of the population around the mode, is that the trends in poverty incidence would be affected only in a small way, with reasonably small changes in the position of the poverty line. The exact definition of the poverty line is not that important. What is more relevant is the limitation of the income–expenditure definition of the poverty line used by the official Planning Commission standard, and which is used here. Non-income dimensions of poverty are important in a wider definition of poverty: a major example is the availability of health care and education for poor households. This wider view of household welfare is, however, a large topic and is not pursued in this chapter further.

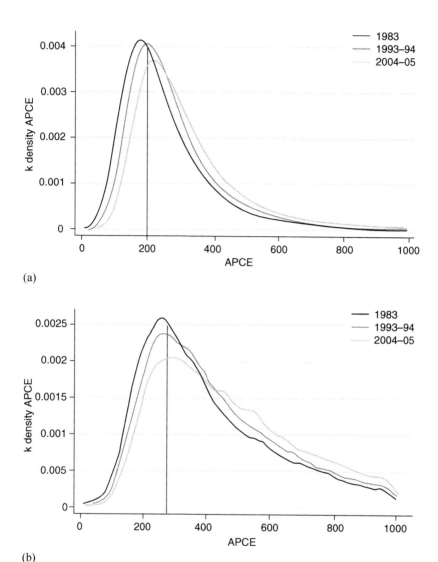

Figure 3.1 Kernel density functions, rural and urban (a) Distribution of APCE in rural areas (b) Distribution of APCE in urban areas (source: author's calculation from the data tapes of the NSS).

Notes
a Vertical line is the poverty line (Rs.205.64) at 1993–94 prices.
b Vertical line is the poverty line (Rs.281.31) at 1993–94 prices.
The kernel density function is a probability density function of a variable. It may be viewed as a histogram that has been smoothed to iron out minor irregularities in the observed data (Deaton 1997) and draw the eye to the essential feature of the distribution.

The actual measures of poverty incidence for the successive rounds of the NSS are given in Table 3.3. Topalova (2008) has presented a simple decomposition of the change in the poverty rate into two components: one due to growth and the other due to change in the distribution of consumption. This is done by calculating a counterfactual measurement of poverty change holding the initial distribution unchanged, and comparing the result with the actual change. Results clearly show that, while in the 1983–93 decade redistribution helped to reduce poverty (particularly in the rural areas), in the post-reform decade the distribution element shrank the extent of poverty reduction significantly in both the rural and the urban sectors. "Distribution neutral growth would have generated a poverty decline in rural India (in the latter period) that was 22 per cent higher; in urban areas the decline in poverty would have been 76 per cent higher" (ibid., p. 8).

Inequality

Table 3.4 gives the summary statistical measures of inequality of household welfare (as measured by the average per capita expenditure (APCE) of households) for the three periods 1983, 1993–94, and 2004–05. It is clear that inequality increased significantly in India only in the second period (generally regarded as the post-reform years) and was much more pronounced in the urban areas. In the 1983–93 decade, the NSS data show that there was a small decline in overall inequality—about two percentage points in the Gini in the rural areas and one percentage point in the urban areas.

For the more recent decade (1993–2004), all measures agree that inequality increased more in the urban areas. Although the extent of the increase was stronger in the measures that give greater weight to higher incomes, even the GE(0) index showed a significant increase. It is interesting to note that this increase in inequality across the board was substantial in the rural areas as well—although the urban indices show a somewhat larger increase.

Table 3.3 India: evolution of poverty[1] (%)

	Poverty rate[2]			Poverty depth[3]		
	All India	Rural	Urban	All India	Rural	Urban
1983	45.2	46.2	42.1	12.6	13.0	11.5
1987–88	39.3	39.3	39.2	9.6	9.4	10.4
1993–94	35.8	36.8	32.8	8.4	8.4	8.3
2004–05	27.5	28.0	25.8	5.7	5.5	6.2

Source: NSSO various rounds, and Fund staff estimates.

Notes
1 At 1993–94 prices in rural India.
2 Defined as the share of the population below the poverty line.
3 Defined as the poverty rate multiplied by the average value of the shortfall from the poverty line.

Table 3.4 Measures of inequality of APCE

	GE(-1)	GE(0)	GE(1)	GE(2)	Gini
Rural					
1983	0.1843	0.1690	0.1952	0.3244	0.3193
1993	0.1528	0.1480	0.1840	0.4537	0.2982
2004	0.1787	0.1724	0.2233	0.5312	0.3199
Urban					
1983	0.2627	0.2226	0.2487	0.4217	0.3670
1993	0.2354	0.2093	0.2387	0.4166	0.3568
2004	0.2871	0.2501	0.2902	0.5344	0.3891
Total					
1983	0.2070	0.1876	0.2170	0.3698	0.3370
1993	0.2081	0.1967	0.2397	0.5042	0.3465
2004	0.2489	0.2326	0.2920	0.6254	0.3758

Source: author's calculations from the NSS data tapes.

Sarkar (2009), following Topolova (2008), looked at the changes in the percentile distribution of APCE in detail, in rural and urban areas. Panels A and B in Figure 3.2 present the compound annual growth of percentile APCE for pre- and post-reform periods in the two sectors separately.

The conclusion from these graphs is striking and is consistent with the points made above. In the first period, the growth pattern in rural areas was decidedly pro-poor, producing a faster rate of growth for those at the lower end of the distribution. In urban areas, the growth was intriguingly distribution-neutral. There was a marked change in the post-reform decade. The richer groups in the rural areas were favoured, but the urban areas had a much stronger bias towards pro-rich growth and embraced a larger proportion of the richer consumption slabs.

While consumption per capita grew faster in the urban areas (the median growth rate of consumption is shown as being considerably higher than in the rural areas), the richest households grew the fastest (above the eightieth percentile). The rural households had a similar upturn in their growth incidence curve, but this seems to have occurred only for households above the ninetieth percentile of the distribution per capita consumption.

The positive rate of growth of APCE in both the rural and the urban areas in both the pre- and post-reform periods (refer to the straight lines in each panel) implied that the poverty rate fell in both periods and both areas. The reduction in poverty tracked the growth rates of median APCE. As the data presented in Table 3.4 show, although inequality increased faster in the urban areas, and more so in the post-reform decade, the difference in this experience with respect to the rural areas did not significantly alter the fact that poverty incidence was reduced at a somewhat faster rate in urban areas.

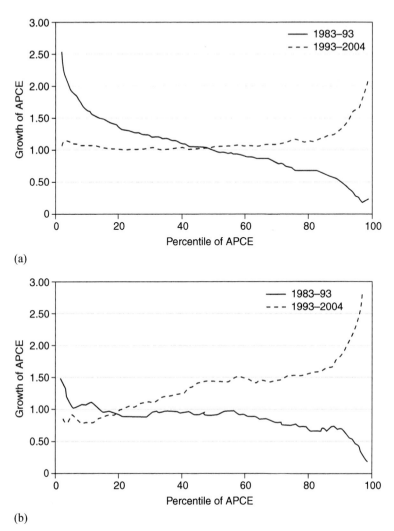

(a)

(b)

Figure 3.2 Growth rates of APCE by deciles, 1983–93 and 1993–2004 (a) rural (b) urban
(source: Sarkar (2009)).

II

The importance of the tertiary sector in Indian growth

A peculiar feature of Indian development is that it has been led by the tertiary
sector, rather than by manufacturing, in terms of both employment and value added.
Although historically, structural change in employment in India has been very slow,
it seems to have accelerated a little in the post-reform decade. The share of employment in agriculture in the post-reform decade of 1993–94 to 2004–05 had declined
by 6.5 percentage points, or nearly double the decline in the previous decade.

Table 3.5 Sectoral composition of growth, 1983/84–2004/05

	Average growth rate (in %)		Share in GDP (in %)		
	1983/84–1992/93	*1993/94–2004/05*	*1983–84*	*1993–94*	*2004–05*
Real GDP	5.22	6.23	100	100	100
Agriculture	3.56	2.71	37	30	20
Industry	5.6	6.59	24	25	26
Services	4.62	7.97	39	45	54

Source: Topolova (2008), RBI, National Account Statistics, and IMF estimates.

Barely 1.1 per cent of this decline was absorbed by manufacturing. The tertiary sector, along with construction, accounted for the bulk of the relative change in the employment structure. The sectoral composition of growth is shown in Table 3.5.

Is India an outlier in the sectoral shift of employment?

How does the Indian experience of reallocation compare with that of other Asian countries? Table 3.6 sets out some relevant data. We go earlier in time to take account of the historical experience of the rapidly growing economies of East Asia, and we end our comparison in 2000. (Note that, in this table, construction and a few other minor sectors like mining have been left out.)

It would appear from the data presented that India is indeed a clear outlier insofar as absorption in the tertiary sector is concerned. The newly industrializing countries of Asia—Korea and Taiwan—saw their share of employment in manufacturing increase much faster than that of the tertiary sector during their initial period of growth. Only in the later years, after they had developed into mature industrialized economies, did their tertiary sectors become the dominant provider of employment outside agriculture. By contrast, India's share of employment growth in the tertiary sector was already 60 per cent higher than in manufacturing. The decades of the 1980s and the 1990s saw a virtual stagnation in the share of employment in manufacturing, with the tertiary sector absorbing almost the entire loss of employment share by agriculture. The figures also show that other developing countries of Asia (Thailand, Malaysia, and Indonesia) have their larger shares of employment created in the tertiary sector. Unlike India, none of them had a stagnant share in manufacturing in any decade. On the contrary, one-third to one-half of the often large decline in the share of employment in agriculture was taken up by manufacturing. The only country in the sample with an experience close to that of India is the Philippines.

The role of the tertiary sector in absorption: alternative theories

The widespread view that the share of the force employed in the tertiary sector is directly related to income level has been advanced in the literature by a body of

Table 3.6 Changes in sectoral share of employment in elected Asian countries

Country	1971–80			1980–91			1990–2000		
	Agr.	Manuf.	Tertiary	Agr.	Manuf.	Tertiary	Agr.	Manuf.	Tertiary
Rep. of Korea	-14.4	8.3	6.0	-17.3	5.0	12.9	-7.6	-6.7	14.5
Taiwan, China[1]	-15.6	11.1	3.7	-6.6	1.7	8.9	-5.0	-4.1	9.2
Thailand	-1.4	0.3	1.7	-10.5	3.2	7.3	-15.3	4.3	10.2
Malaysia	-14.8	6.1	9.9	-10.4	4.6	6.6	-7.9	2.9	3.0
Philippines[1]	-1.4	-0.7	2.1	-6.2	-0.6	6.7	-7.8	0.3	7.6
Indonesia	–	–	–	-2.7	1.3	1.1	-10.9	2.8	7.1
India[2]	-5.5	1.8	3.0	-4.6	0.0	3.4	-3.6	0.3	2.4

Notes
Figures for first two periods are from Mazumdar and Basu (1997, Table 3.2, p. 38). Figures for the last period are calculated from *ILO Yearbook* data.
1 For all periods, calculated from ADB key indicators, 2001.
2 For all periods, calculated from NSS, adjusted by population from decadal census. The periods refer to 1973–83, 1983–93, and 1993–2000.

writing generally called the Clark–Fischer–Kuznets (C–F–K) hypothesis.[5] At low levels of income, agriculture is the dominant sector. As the economy develops, manufacturing (or, more generally, the secondary sector) increases its share of the force at the expense of agriculture and the tertiary sector follows, but at a slower rate of increase in its share. Once incomes have gone beyond a certain level, the share of the tertiary sector becomes dominant. The reason for this pattern—which is observed in the history of economic growth of developed countries—is twofold: the income elasticity of demand for services becomes higher than that of manufacturing only at relatively higher income levels; and the rate of productivity growth through technical progress is high and increasing for manufacturing relative to the service sector.

This prediction had been questioned even years ago when some writers had noticed that, contrary to the C–F–K hypothesis, a great deal of non-agricultural employment was to be found in tertiary activities in developing countries (Bauer and Yamey 1951). These economists ascribed the use of in service-type activities to the importance of such tasks as labour-intensive transport, the importance of bulk-breaking and retailing in small quantities in poor countries, and also to the lower supply-price of self-employed (dominating the service sector) compared to wage earners (more prevalent in manufacturing). Thus the relationship of the share of tertiary employment to GDP per capita is more likely to be negative than positive. Nevertheless, this set of factors would suggest that, with economic growth, the need for labour-intensive service sector goods will fall, leading to a slower rate of growth of employment in this sector.

In recent economic development, many branches of tertiary activity have emerged which might take the lead in income growth. The most spectacular example is of course the information technology (IT) sector. Furthermore, the rate of growth of this subsector depends as much on income growth of developed economies (which outsource these activities) as on the growth of the poorer economies themselves. Singh and Dasgupta (2005) and others suggested that the rapid development of the tertiary sector has changed the equation sufficiently to upset the substance of the C–F–K hypothesis. As such, the tertiary sector in this changed world economy could indeed be the engine of growth and the dominant source of employment reallocated from agriculture.

In sum, the tertiary sector in the modern economy embraces a more heterogeneous bundle of activities than years ago. What is the evidence on the growth in subsectors of tertiary activities in India?

Growth of tertiary subsectors in India

The changes in percentage share of the broad subsectors in tertiary activity in the post-reform decade are given in Table 3.7.

There has been a significant shift of employment from community services to other sectors, reversing the trend in the pre-reform decade. This loss, added to the overall increase in the share of the tertiary sector in total employment, allowed the other subsectors to gain a substantial share in the force. But it

Table 3.7 Changes in percentage shares of the work force 1993/94–2004/06

Category	Change in percentage share
All tertiary	+2.9
Community, social, and other services (9)	−1.5
Finance and business services (8)	+0.7
Transport and communication (7)	+1.2
Trade, hotels, and restaurants (6)	+3.2

Source: own calculations from the NSS data tapes. Note that the labour force counts are those of the Usual Principal Status (UPS) of the NSS.

appears that trade, hotels, and restaurants, the biggest subsectors at this level of aggregation, were also the sectors to post the highest gains in the share of employment. The IT sector, part of finance and business services, came a distant third in the incremental change in shares. Thus at this level of classification we find that the growth of new business services has *not* been a quantitatively dominant factor in the growth of tertiary employment.

In the last analysis, any diagnosis about the shift to the tertiary sector boils down to the question about the level of earnings being absorbed in this sector. In other words, one needs to examine whether labour is being pulled or pushed into this sector. This can only be answered by examining the trend in the relative earnings of labour in this sector.

Productivity differential between sectors

We start our examination of the relative level of earnings in the tertiary sector by looking at the sectoral values of labour productivity by combining the employment data obtained from the NSS with the National Account estimates of GDP by sectors. The results for the different rounds are reported in Table 3.8. They negate the hypothesis of labour being pushed out into the tertiary sector.

The average productivity of the tertiary sector is high largely because of the financial services segment. When examined at one-digit level, the trade sector absorbs a substantial part of incremental employment, and the productivity difference with manufacturing is less. But both these sectors have increased their mean earnings vis-à-vis agriculture over the 20-year period between 1983 and 2004–05. It is the construction sector which shows a decline in relative labour productivity, and indeed this is the sector that has started absorbing labour at a higher rate in the post-reform decade (50th to 61st round; Table 3.8). As far as the tertiary sector per se is concerned, even in the subsector with the lowest level (trade, hotels, and restaurants), mean earnings have been on a par with the manufacturing sector over the last ten years ending in 2004–05, although they have increased more slowly than in manufacturing since the earlier rounds (Figure 3.3).

The higher mean labour productivity in the tertiary sector is a second peculiar feature of Indian development, along with the larger proportion of employment

Table 3.8 Productivity by sector

Sector	Labour productivity (UPS) at constant prices (Rs)					Relative labour productivity (agri = 100)				
	38th 1983	43rd 1987–88	50th 1993–94	55th 1999–2000	61st 2004–05	38th	43rd	50th	55th	61st
1 Agriculture	11,818	11,312	13,507	15,288	16,842	100	100	100	100	100
2 Mining and quarrying	64,948	64,827	82,308	128,726	141,881	550	573	609	842	842
3 Manufacturing	26,139	30,091	38,949	55,307	59,902	221	266	288	362	356
4 Electricity, gas, and water supply	93,445	119,430	143,416	261,708	297,676	791	1056	1062	1712	1767
5 Construction	39,484	27,193	37,702	37,019	33,818	334	240	279	242	201
6 Trade, hotels, and restaurants	34,905	36,713	42,293	55,686	60,809	295	325	313	364	361
7 Transport, storage, and communication	39,219	46,970	52,200	63,907	70,115	332	415	386	418	416
8 Financial, insurance, real estate, and business services	211,516	256,215	277,806	350,016	306,209	1790	2265	2057	2290	1818
9 Community, social, and personal services	24,091	29,269	30,316	46,694	62,436	204	259	224	305	371
Tertiary sector (6–9)	36,511	42,833	49,573	79,568	96,080	309	379	367	450	472

Source: several years of Economic Survey and unit level data of quinquennial employment and unemployment rounds.

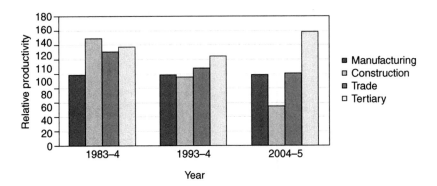

Figure 3.3 Relative productivity by economic sector (source: author's calculations from the NSS dataset).

growth in this sector. Papola (2005) compared the experience of changing shares of GDP and employment over the period 1960–2002 in five Asian countries (China, Indonesia, Thailand, Malaysia, and India) and brings out the striking point that only in India has the relative productivity in services increased over this long period. Further, productivity in services exceeds that in industry only in India, and by a substantial percentage. Service sector growth in India has been productivity-led and not employment-led, contradicting the views of some economists who state that employment grew in services because this sector has been a repository of low-income labour pushed out from agriculture.

Comparison of labour productivity or earnings at the mean is not sufficient. It is possible for mean earnings in a sector to be higher and at the same time the earnings in the bottom range of the distribution to be significantly lower. What is needed is a comparison of the distribution of earnings across sectors. The proportion of main earners in the tertiary sector in different quintiles of the distribution of household expenditure per capita for successive years is shown in Figure 3.4.

In rural areas, there are distinct changes: whereas in the pre-reform period (1983–93), the slopes of the curves increased, signifying a much faster increase in the upper quintile groups in the tertiary sector, during the post-reform period (1993–2004), there is a parallel movement outwards, except for the fourth quintile. It would appear that in the post-reform decade more jobs in the tertiary sector were being created in the lower as well as the highest quintile than in the decade before 1993. In the urban areas, the post-reform decade saw a relative increase in the lowest quintile, as in the previous decade, accompanied by a smaller increase in the middle quintiles than in the previous decade. At the same time, the highest quintile registered a larger expansion of tertiary sector households.

The next step in the analysis is to compare the earnings in the tertiary sector relative to those in manufacturing at different parts of the earnings distribution. For this purpose, the technique of quantile regressions is used, which enables us to compare the earnings differential by sector, after controlling for human capital factors, not at the mean as in the standard least squares regression, but at selected points of the distribution.

Quantile regressions for the 1999–2000 NSS unit-level data are run to estimate net differential at five quintiles of the distribution. Dummies for manufacturing and tertiary sectors (with primary as base) were used in the regressions along with a set of other explanatory variables. The latter included education, age, sex, and urban–rural location. The regressions were undertaken for the APCE of households, and the characteristics used as explanatory variables pertain to those of the heads of the households in the sample. The coefficients of the sector dummies (with primary as base) of the regression equations give the net differential in APCE with respect to the primary sector at the five quintiles of the distributions. These are plotted in Figure 3.5.

The results suggest that the income levels for tertiary sector households are above those in both the primary and the secondary sectors for all quintile groups, even after controlling for the higher levels of education of labour in the tertiary sector. There is no evidence whatsoever of labour being pushed into the sector, as the hypothesis of immiserization due to pressure of population would suggest. On the other hand, there is some evidence of dualism being higher in the tertiary sector, contributing to the higher inequality in the Indian economy.

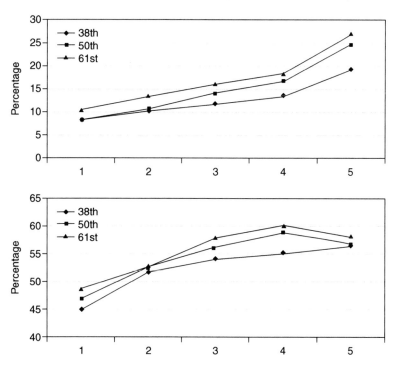

Figure 3.4 Employment share of tertiary sector by earnings quintile groups (different rounds) (source: author's calculations from the NSS data tapes).

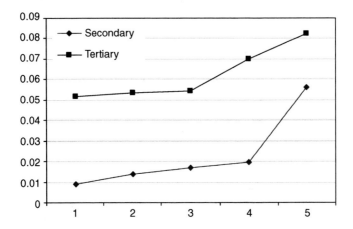

Figure 3.5 Coefficients of sector dummies in quantile regression model for APCE, 1999–2000 (source: own calculations from data tapes of the NSS 1999–2000).

III

Conclusion

We have identified a major difference in the structural feature of India's pattern of growth, not only with the historical pattern of growth of developed countries, but with that of other Asian comparator countries as well. This is the substantially higher rate of growth of employment and value added in the tertiary sector relative to manufacturing, and the higher mean productivity of the tertiary sector. The popular hypothesis which is advanced for this distinctive pattern is that the tertiary sector in India leads the growth process because of its unusual growth of high-income business and technical services. At the same time, a great deal of surplus labour finds its way into the low-income jobs of the tertiary sector, which are easy to enter. If this were truly the locus of relative income, quintiles of the distribution in the tertiary sector would cross that in the secondary sector. But our analysis, in terms of the time profiles of the distributions and the quantile regression at a point of time, refutes this hypothesis. It is clear that tertiary sector incomes are higher at all points of the distribution. Thus it is the peculiarity in the structure of the manufacturing sector in India that has to be looked at for an explanation of the relatively high earnings in the tertiary sector together with the excessive growth (by international standards) of the tertiary sector. This peculiarity might also be a large part of the story of the growth with increasing inequality, which seems to have gathered momentum in recent decades. This is the topic of the next chapter.

4 The non-household sector in Indian manufacturing

The low productivity in the Indian manufacturing sector is partly due to the large share of employment and value added in its "unregistered" subsector. A substantial amount of employment is in household enterprises which operate in the owner-worker's household with no help or just one or two hired workers. The productivity of labour is quite low in these units, with their non-mechanized technology. But modern industry has grown extensively outside the household subsector. Even in the non-household sector, however, labour productivity is low, as we will demonstrate below. This is due to the dualism in non-household manufacturing (which has been referred to as the "missing middle"). Indian manufacturing in the non-household subsector with extensive use of hired labour has a strong bi-polar distribution of employment: the lower mode of small units with fewer than ten workers and a higher mode of large-scale units employing 500 or more workers. The productivity (and wage) gap between these two strong modes is very large.

I

The DME sector

The Indian statistical authorities distinguish four types of establishments. There are three sub-categories within the unorganized sector:

- own-account manufacturing enterprises (OAMEs), which are household enterprises making use only of family labour;
- non-directory manufacturing establishments (NDMEs), which employ at least one wage (hired) worker and have between two and five workers in total; and
- directory manufacturing establishments (DMEs), employing between six and nine workers in total, at least one of whom would be a hired worker.

These three sub-categories co-exist with the formal or organized sector where establishments are statistically defined (by the *Factory Act*) to be employing ten or more workers. This sector is covered by the *Annual Survey of Industries* (ASI). Table 4.1 provides a statistical profile of the manufacturing sector in India distinguished by these four categories of establishments. The dominance of the household sector, as well as its low productivity, is apparent from this table.

While some writings on Indian manufacturing draw the line of the formal sector at the organized or ASI sector, it can be seen from Table 4.1 that this line does not distinguish the very large household sector in Indian manufacturing (where the operations are largely carried out by family labour) from the non-household sectors (the establishments making use of hired wage labour). The mean number of hired workers in the DME sector is large. More detailed analysis of the NSSO unit level data showed that the proportion of hired labour in the workforce of the DME units accounted for 80 per cent of the total, of which 6 per cent were part-time. In other words, the DME sector covers establishments in which the use of hired labour is not just marginal. A meaningful study of size distribution of manufacturing in the non-household sector should include these units, even if it excludes the NDME units which can be considered an extension of the household sector (with only marginal use of hired labour).

An added reason for including the DME units in our study of non-household manufacturing is that it would bring India in line with international comparison. For most countries, the lower cut-off point for non-household manufacturing is five workers.

Size distribution of employment in the DME sector

The legal definition of the DME sector is that it contains units with 6–9 workers, with at least one full-time hired worker. In practice, this legal definition has not been strictly enforced. A growing number of units employing more than nine workers have been allowed to be outside the purview of the registration needed for the ASI sector. This does not mean that the legal authorities have ignored the law indiscriminately. Rather, as we shall soon see, this relaxed enforcement has been confined to only a very small number of industries in which the use of mechanized methods of production is minimal.

Table 4.1 Employment and value added in manufacturing by type of establishment, 2000–01

	OAME	NDME	DME	Organized
Distribution of employment (% of all manufacturing)	55.9	12.4	14.4	17.3
Mean number of all workers in category	1.7	3.2	10.0	63.9
Mean number of hired workers in category	0	1.8	7.8	60.9
Distribution of value added (% of all manufacturing)	10.3	6.1	8.0	76.6
Mean value added/worker in category	Rs.6929	Rs.18,479	Rs.20,800	Rs.163,775
Labour productivity (organized=100)	4.2	11.3	12.7	100

Sources: unit level data of 56th round of NSSO and ASI unit level data of 2000–01.

Figure 4.1 gives the distribution of employment by size groups within the DME sector at different dates. The proportion of employment in the DME sector is substantial in the 10–19 size group. Also the proportion above the legal limit seems to be increasing over time.

A remarkable feature of this sector is that the employment in DME units above the legal size is largely confined to just three industries (defined at the two-digit level). Table 4.2 shows that these industries together account for 43 per cent of all DME employment in the 10–19 size group and 75 per cent in the 20 and above group.

A second notable feature of DME employment is that the increase in the employment size of DME units does not lead to any increase in the labour productivity in the sector. In fact, as the data brought together in Table 4.3 show, the productivity of the DME units remains at the same 10 per cent level of the large (500+) ASI units whatever their size category, and considerably below the small (10–49) ASI units.

We conclude that the DME establishments which are larger than the employment size of the legal maximum are not employing any significantly different

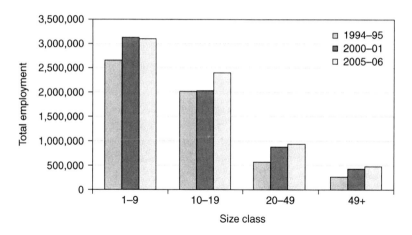

Figure 4.1 Size distribution of employment in DME units (source: own analysis of NSSO unit level data for the different rounds).

Table 4.2 Share of three industries in each size class of DME employment in 2005–06 (%)

Industry	6–9	10–19	20–49	50 and above	20 and above
Textiles	19.7	26.2	21.8	8.1	17.2
Non-metallic minerals	6.5	8.3	25.5	51.3	34.2
Furniture and fixtures	10.3	8.7	24.7	22.7	24.0
Combined	36.6	43.2	71.9	82.2	75.4

Source: own analysis of NSSO unit level data.

Table 4.3 Employment, value added, and productivity by size classes in ASI and DME
sectors

Size class	Workers	Value added	Productivity	Relative productivity, 500+ = 100
ASI 2004–05				
1–9	149,111	147,297	98,784	15
10–49	1,391,759	2,212,020	158,937	25
50–99	854,750	1,873,798	219,227	34
100–199	1,055,396	2,913,300	276,039	43
200–499	1,474,708	5,437,348	368,707	57
500 and above	3,018,600	19,533,187	647,094	100
Total	7,944,304	32,116,951	404,276	62
DME 2005–06				
1–9	3,123,613	1,545,205	49,469	8
10–19	2,397,130	1,235,811	51,554	8
20–49	933,392	435,113	46,616	7
10–49	3,330,522	1,670,923	50,170	8
50 and above	474,136	251,615	53,068	8
Total	6,928,271	3,467,744	50,363	8

Source: unit level NSS data of 62nd round and ASI unit level data of 2004–05.

Note
Value added in Rs. Lakh (at 2005–06 prices) and productivity Rs. per worker.

level of technology than the smaller units. In fact, they are mostly found in those
industries which compete successfully with a low level of technology. The
expansion of these units above the legal maximum is of the "horizontal" kind
(increasing the number of the same type of simple capital equipment as those
used by the smaller units). Thus they do not attract the attention of legal authorities enforcing the boundaries of the ASI sector.

In fact, further details for the three industries which account for the bulk of
employment in the 10+ DME establishments show that labour productivity in two
of the three industries actually falls in larger size classes (Table 4.4). This suggests
that the larger units possibly use a larger proportion of part-time workers or adopt
inefficient organization of production beyond the optimum scale size. This can also
reflect substantial seasonality of demand that these enterprises face.[1]

Review of the problem of the missing middle in non-household manufacturing

Given the size distribution of DME employment as discussed in the previous
section, the nature of the problem of the missing middle as presented in Chapter
9 of Mazumdar and Sarkar (2008) has to be revised somewhat. In the previous
analysis, we had assumed all DME employment was in the legally defined size
group of 6–9 workers. The new information presented in the last section leaves

us with two options about how to present the size structure of Indian industries in the non-household sector, comprising the DME and the ASI units. We could either merge the reported numbers in both the DME and the ASI sectors in the 6–9 and 10–49 size groups, or report the DME employment separately, irrespective of size. There is merit in both types of portrayals. But given the point established above that there is a qualitative gap between the technologies separating the DME from the ASI sector, it is probably more meaningful to go with the picture of the size structure presented in Figure 4.2, with the important caveat that the bottom bar in Figure 4.3 should be more correctly labelled as the "DME enterprises" rather than the 6–9 size class.

The picture of the size distribution with a missing middle is seen in both graphs, but the lower mode is higher when we consider the actual employment sizes of the DME units covered, rather than the legal definition of a maximum of nine workers for such units. The striking fact about Figure 4.3 however is that, with comparable definitions, the size structure in Indian manufacturing around 2005 is almost the same as was given in Mazumdar and Sarkar (2008) for 1989–90. If anything, the incidence of the missing middle has been accentuated over the 15-year period, with the DME sector now accounting for more than 45 per cent of total non-household manufacturing employment compared to a little over 40 per cent in 1989–90. The only other significant change is that, at the upper end of the size distribution, there has been some redistribution of employment from the very large 500+ units to the 200–499 size group.

In Chapter 2, the Indian size pattern in manufacturing was characterized not just by the bi-polar distribution of employment with a conspicuous missing middle, but also by the substantial productivity gap between the two extremes of the size distribution—much larger than in comparator Asian countries, or indeed in other countries like Japan which have had a long established dualistic pattern of development (see also Chapter 9 of Mazumdar and Sarkar (2008) for an extended discussion of this point). It is worth emphasizing the result already given in Chapter 2: that over the two decades extending from 1984–85 to 2004–05, there seems to have been an intensification of both these aspects of dualism with a missing middle. The proportion of all non-household manufacturing employment in the DME sector has increased from 40.3 to 46.6 per cent. The relative productivity in this subsector has fallen drastically from 19 to 8. There might have been a contrary tendency of the

Table 4.4 Labour productivity across size groups of DME in 2005–06 (at current prices)

Industry code	1–9	10–19	20–49	50 and above
Textiles	34,276	37,446	42,159	34,715
Non-metallic mineral	61,574	43,943	50,890	35,043
Furniture, jewellery, etc.	55,829	73,143	30,651	26,887

Source: own analysis of NSSO unit level data for the different rounds.

Note
In Rs. per worker.

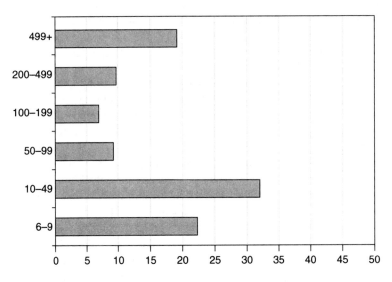

Figure 4.2 Size structure of Indian manufacturing employment, 2005–06 (with reported employment size of both DME and ASI units).

Note
The data are for DME 2005–06 and ASI 2003–04. The graph is based on actual employment in different size groups, including both DME and ASI counts.

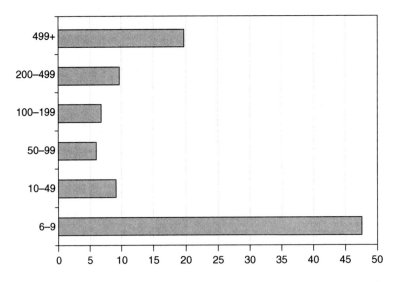

Figure 4.3 Size structure of Indian manufacturing employment, 2005–06 (with all DME employment included in 6–9 size group).

Note
The data are for DME 2005–06 and ASI 2003–04. All DMEs are considered to fall in the 6–9 employment group and all ASI establishments are considered to have at least ten workers.

distribution of employment within the ASI sector, as the proportion of employment in the top modal group (500+) has fallen (although a good deal of this reduction seems to have occurred between 1984–85 and 1989–90). In the 15 years since then, the proportion of employment in this largest size group has declined only marginally from 22.9 to 20.3 per cent. Furthermore, even this mild improvement within the ASI sector is overshadowed by an intensification of dualism in its other characteristic. The relative productivity in all the size groups smaller than the 500+ is reported to have declined significantly in 2004–05 compared to the previous years for which we have official data.

Difference in capital intensity in different size groups of firms

We have concentrated our discussion of the economic distance between different size groups in manufacturing on differences in labour productivity, both in the Indian scenario and in the comparisons with other Asian economies. Differences in labour productivity might be due to a combination of two factors: difference in the use of capital per unit of labour, and difference in the productivity of capital or the efficiency with which the capital is used as a cooperant factor of production. The contribution of each to the difference in labour productivity is an interesting question for many purposes—but not for the argument of this chapter. For most of our purposes in the analysis of this chapter, it is the ultimate result of these two influences (as embodied in the difference in technology) which matter, and not the relative contributions of the two to the outcome.[2]

II

Industrial composition of DME and ASI establishments: product market segmentation

It has already been noticed that the industries in which there are larger DME units (ten and above size groups) are few in number. It is now necessary to expand the enquiry to a more detailed level of analysis, to see how the DME units compare with the ASI sector in terms of their industrial composition. For this purpose, we undertook a detailed comparison of employment in the two sectors at the five-digit level of industrial classification. The questions of primary interest are: (i) How far are the DME industries overlapping with the ASI ones? How many of these five-digit industries are present both in the DME and in the ASI sectors? (ii) What are the proportions of employment in such overlapping industries, and how much is the overlap? (iii) Are there any significant trends in the direction of the overlap – that is, what can we say if the DME industries compete more or less with ASI industries in recent years?

In Table 4.5, we have picked up the industries in which both DME and ASI units have substantial representation. It should be noted that the data we have for ASI is for the year 2003–04, which is more or less at the mid-point of the two DME surveys of 2000–01 and 2005–06. It will be seen in several industries that

Table 4.5 Employment in overlapping industries

Industry five-digit code	ASI employment 2003–04	DME employment 2000–01	DME employment 2005–06	Description of industry
15312	210,701	67,376	91,016	Rice milling
15493	198,143	16,897	310,690	Processing of edible nuts
15002	418,420	60,565	18,471	Manufacture of *bidi*
17115	61,900	468,019	372,635	Weaving, manufacture of cotton and cotton mixture fabrics
17118	58,607	101,197	194,168	Weaving, manufacture of man-made fibre and man-made mixture fabrics
17121	88,539	38,728	66,354	Finishing of cotton and blended cotton textiles
17301	99,960	54,291	71,263	Manufacture of knitted and crocheted cotton textile products
18101	348,218	314,769	247,856	Manufacture of all types of textile garments and clothing accessories
19201	78,237	47,064	24,093	Manufacture of footwear, except of vulcanized or moulded rubber or plastic
22219	45,752	66,341	90,753	Printing and allied activities, n.e.c.
24231	27,992	75,588	5776	Manufacture of chemical substances used in the manufacture of pharmaceuticals
25209	79,003	60,849	36,472	Manufacture of other plastic products
26931	99,981	904,900	634,569	Manufacture of bricks
26960	78,910	106,025	62,799	Cutting, shaping, and finishing of stone
34300	212,021	41,977	55,106	Manufacture of parts and accessories for motor vehicles and their engines
36912	39,415	280,646	430,920	Diamond cutting and polishing and other gem cutting and polishing
Total	2,145,799	2,705,232	2,712,940	16 overlapping industry groups
All manufacturing employment	7,735,049	6,454,121	6,928,271	Includes all industries in sector
Percentage share of overlapping industries in all manufacturing	27.7	41.9	39.2	Ratios of the last two rows

Source: unit level data of different NSS rounds and ASI 2003–04.

there are substantial changes in DME employment over the span of the two surveys. But only in a few cases do we see a spectacular change in DME employment. The industries which have registered a sharp increase in DME employment are rice milling, processing of edible nuts, weaving of man-made fibres, knitted cotton textiles, printing, and diamond cutting. On the other hand, a sharp fall in DME employment is observed in the manufacturing of *bidi*, weaving of cotton fabrics, garments, and footwear. It is noteworthy that some of these declining industries for DME employment are in fact older ones in which the presence of DME units had been substantial. It remains to be seen if these reported trends continue in subsequent surveys. Overall, however, the growing industries in the DME sector have outweighed the decline in the shrinking ones, so that the share of the overlapping industries picked up in our analysis in all DME employment has virtually remained constant at around 40 per cent. The corresponding share of these industries in the ASI sector is 27 per cent of the total.

These proportions give an idea of the extent of product market segmentation in Indian manufacturing. The ASI sector has more than two-thirds of its employment in industries which (at our detailed five-digit level) have only a small presence in the DME sector. On the other hand, the DME units have a larger proportion of their employment in industries (around 40 per cent) which overlap with ASI products. Two points need to be emphasized. First, overlapping industries still amount to significantly less than half of employment in manufacturing, with the ASI units showing a much higher degree of specialization in products which only this sector can produce. Second, there is considerable churning of products within the DME sector, but overall the total share of employment in the overlapping industries has not changed much in the early years of this century. Note that our estimate of the overlapping industries provides only an outer limit. Although the five-digit level of classification is quite a detailed one, quality variations of the products cannot be captured in this classification. To the extent that the DME units can be expected to produce a larger share of their products for the lower end of the market, the overlapping industries of equivalent quality would be much less.

A detailed examination of DME employment for the two dates also enabled us to identify some new growth points for emerging industries which are becoming important in this sector. These industries (presented in Table 4.6) had, in the early years of this century, just about the same volume of employment in the DME sector as the ASI, but increased their volume of DME employment to three times ASI employment by 2005–06.

Comparison of the sectors in terms of value added

The analysis given above is in terms of employment. The low productivity in the DME sector relative to the ASI already noted implies that the share of the former in value added would be much lower than that of employment. As we have already seen, in 2000–01 the organized sector of Indian manufacturing produced 77 per cent of value added in all manufacturing, although it employed only 17 per cent of the labour force in the sector. We classified the 65 subsectors of

Table 4.6 Newly emerging DME industries[1]

Industry five-digit code	ASI employment 2003–04	DME employment 2000–01	DME employment 2005–06	Description of industry
19121	734	4894	50,266	Manufacture of travel goods like suitcases, bags, and holdalls, etc.
24291	47,692	32,367	61,802	Manufacture of matches
26954	1330	12,248	66,132	Manufacture of bricks and blocks
28996	4505	20,699	53,842	Manufacture of hollow-ware, dinnerware, or flatware
29299	26,512	15,354	71,295	Manufacture of other special purpose machinery, equipment, n.e.c.
35923	25,123	12,577	59,833	Manufacture of parts and accessories for bicycles, cycle-rickshaws, and invalid carriages
Total	105,895	98,139	363,170	

Source: unit level data of different NSS rounds and ASI 2003–04.

Note
1 Industries where DME employment was greater than 50,000 in 2005–06.

Indian manufacturing at the inter-sectoral transaction matrix level into four groups (taking the organized and the unorganized subsectors together): (i) those in which the organized sector accounted for nearly all of the value added (80 to 100 per cent), (ii) those in which the organized sector produced the major part of the value added (50–79 per cent), (iii) those in which the two subsectors are equally important, and iv) those which are dominated by the unorganized sector. The results are given in Table 4.7 in the next section.

Globalization and Indian manufacturing

The dominance of the organized sector in value added in Indian manufacturing begs the question: how far is it due to the exposure of the industry to world markets? It can be assumed that the organized sector would play the lion's share in the links to the world market in terms of both exports and imports, and it is this which propels the dominance of this subsector in terms of output. We do not have detailed data to quantify the export orientation of the unorganized sector, although it is well known that some lines of activity are export-oriented to well-developed marketing channels—which themselves might be parts of the national (and international) organized sector. But it is possible to quantify the external exposure of the manufacturing sector as a whole from official data sources.

The input–output (IP-OP) matrix used for this calculation is detailed in the input–output transaction table (commodity × industry) of the Indian economy available for 115 sectors in 1998–99 and 130 sectors in 2003–04. It is at factor cost and is prepared by the Central Statistical Organisation (CSO) of the Government of India every five years.

The sharp difference between the ASI-dominated group of industries and the others is revealed in these figures. In particular, the results show that industries in which the unorganized sector dominates cater almost entirely to the demands of the final domestic market. The export markets are almost exclusively served by industries dominated by the ASI sector.

There are, however, a limited number of industries in which both the ASI and the unorganized sectors are important, and which are important players in the export market. These are garments (53), and leather and leather products (60). Some traditional products produced mainly in the unorganized sector do indeed provide a significant proportion of their output to the export market, but their relative importance in the value of total exports is not high (less than 1 per cent in each case).

We will see in the next chapter that the role of consumer non-durables in India's export structure is limited, accounting for no more than one-third of the total of all manufactured exports. Since the unorganized sector—and the DME sector in particular—is concentrated in the manufacture of non-durables, it stands to reason that the role of this subsector in Indian exports would be limited. But it should be emphasized that the causal relationship goes in both directions. It is the low productivity and general orientation of the unorganized sector which partly account for its limited participation in the export market. After all, a small proportion of non-durable exports from India originate in this subsector.

Table 4.7 Classification of industries by degree of dominance in value added of the organized and unorganized sectors, 2003–04

Category	Number of industries	Industry code (IP-OP matrix)	Share of export in total final use	Share of intermediate use to total use
Fully/mostly ASI	47	38, 40–42, 47, 48, 50, 54, 57, 58, 61, 63–70, 72, 73, 75, 77, 78, 80, 82–92, 94–100, 102–105	38.1	67.9
Major share of ASI	9	45, 49, 51, 52, 56, 71, 76, 79, 101	2.0	6.0
Equal importance of two subsectors	6	43, 53, 59, 60, 62, 81	10.6	4.8
Major share of unorganized	6	39, 46, 55, 74, 93, 44	1.1	3.7
Total			11.7	21.4

Source: Inter-sectoral Transaction Matrix of the Indian Economy, 2003–04.

In the garment industry—one of the labour-intensive industries which has figured prominently in the recent expansion of exports from developing countries—India's participation in export markets has been positive but nowhere near the scale seen in the major exporters like China. The production technology in garments (particularly in knitted garments) is not of the kind that offers a great scope for economies of scale. But the marketing channels seem to favour large firms as foreign buyers show a distinct preference for batches of large orders. In fact, even within South Asia, the preference of buyers for garments for the mass market seems to be for the large units of Bangladesh, which can meet the demand for large batches, while their demand for garments of higher quality are directed to India with its dominance of small units of production (Tewari 2006).

III

Growth of output and employment in different size groups

In this section, we revert to the aggregative view of all industry and focus on the growth rates over the last two decades in employment and value added in the DME subsector and in different size groups of the ASI. The data are presented in Tables 4.8a and 4.8b.

It is remarkable that the DME sector has picked up the rate of growth of value added in the last two five-year periods, catching up with the growth rate of the ASI sector. Employment elasticity (ratio of growth of value added to growth of employment) for the two broad sectors was also quite close to the last period. This was a distinct change from the earlier years, when in two of the three five-year periods, employment growth and employment elasticity were both significantly higher in the DME sector. In fact, the adjustment came from both sides—the elasticity of employment increased in the ASI sector, and it fell in the DME sector.

Unfortunately, the NSS survey of the unorganized sector is not available after 2005–06. It is therefore not possible to give a reliable account of the change in the relative importance of the DME sector during the recent period of accelerated growth in India, which saw an increase in the growth rate of manufacturing. We have to rely on the estimates by the Central Statistical Office in their presentation of the National Accounts. This source distinguishes between output in the organized and unorganized sectors of manufacturing, presumably based on indicators available to the Central Statistical Office.[3] The data show that, even when manufacturing in the organized sector had an upward jump, the share of output (gross value) declined only marginally from 27.5 per cent in 2003–04 to 25.5 per cent in 2008–09. The unorganized sector was able to hold its own because some industries with substantial output saw an increase in the share of the unorganized sector. The chief contributor in this regard was the group of miscellaneous manufacturing (which constitutes a variety of consumer products), whose unorganized sector share increased from 27.3 per cent to as much as 55 per cent. Other important sectors which increased the share of the unorganized sector are

Table 4.8a Levels and growth of employment in DME and different segments of the organized sector

Type and size	1984–85 (number employed)	2005–06 (number employed)	1984–89 (% growth)	1989–94 (% growth)	1994–2000 (% growth)	2000–05 (% growth)
DME	4,535,870	6,928,271	4.52	–0.64	2.78	1.42
10–49	1,066,941	1,652,272	4.08	1.07	0.99	3.17
50–99	685,977	952,509	4.89	3.88	–1.92	0.38
100–199	646,159	1,118,200	4.52	3.80	0.34	3.07
200–499	931,494	1,528,308	2.96	3.06	1.08	3.42
500 and above	3,397,638	3,063,092	–3.25	1.24	–0.04	0.05
Organized	6,728,209	8,314,381	0.62	2.15	0.14	1.67

Source: unit level data of NSS and ASI for several years.

Note
For the year 2005–06, only DME is for 2005–06 and ASI is for 2004–05.

textiles (25.1 per cent to 31.2 per cent) and chemicals (10.8 to 14.3 per cent). Some other industries with smaller contributions to total output also saw significant increases in the share of the unorganized sector. These include wearing apparel, tobacco products, and transport equipment.

Trends in employment

Turning now to trends in employment in the recent period, the most striking point to note is the sharp increase of employment in the organized manufacturing sector, increasing from 7.9 million in 2003–04 to 11.3 million in 2008–09. The 37 per cent increase in ASI employment is only partly due to the acceleration of output growth. A more important part of the increase is due to the increase in the elasticity of employment, jumping to an unprecedented value of 0.53. This compares with the maximum value of employment elasticity of 0.33 reached in the 1986–96 years in the post-1980 period, and with the negative value in periods prior to and subsequent to this decade (Mazumdar and Sarkar 2008, p. 167).

A possible reason for this remarkable jump in employment elasticity in the ASI subsector might be the greater use of contract labour permitted in several states (World Bank 2010). But another reason could be a more vigorous attempt by the ASI to bring within its ambit the DME units which had exceeded the legal limit of ten workers but had not been registered (see above).[4]

IV

Productivity and wage differentials by desegregated industry

Labour productivity by size groups

The results reported above for relative labour productivity and wages by firm size categories refer to all manufacturing. But as we have seen, there is considerable separation of industries within manufacturing, particularly between the DME and

Table 4.8b Levels and growth of value added (in Rs. Lakh at 1993–94 constant prices)

Type and size	1984–85	2005–06	1984–89	1989–94	1994–2000	2000–05
DME	706,831	2,027,920	3.32	2.66	5.97	8.59
10–49	357,920	1,364,656	9.90	8.03	7.36	1.36
50–99	245,161	1,097,600	11.21	13.43	1.86	5.85
100–199	321,542	1,660,704	12.92	7.94	7.11	6.18
200–499	640,689	3,042,244	10.46	10.63	4.37	7.75
500 and above	2,726,616	10,784,208	5.99	6.84	5.53	11.37
Organized	4,291,928	17,949,412	7.92	8.20	5.36	8.94

Source: unit level data of NSS and ASI for several years.

Note
For the year 2005–06, only DME is for 2005–06 and ASI is for 2004–05.

the ASI sectors. How do these differentials by size groups look when we consider them separately for particular industries within manufacturing?

The relative labour productivity by size groups in selected industries in the privately owned manufacturing sector is given in Table 4.9. We confine our sample to the nine major industries and also classify them into two groups: labour-intensive and capital-intensive.

It is clear that the increase in productivity with firm size is much less steep in the labour-intensive industries, at least within the ASI sector. Nevertheless, even in this group of industries, the difference in labour productivity between DME and the smallest ASI firms is quite substantial (except in the small tobacco industry). Second, the big relative difference in labour productivity is between the DME and the small ASI group (10–49 workers): for higher size groups in the ASI sector, the increase in productivity is moderate for these industries and becomes even more so in the later year.

Wages by size group

Wage differences by firm size follow the trends in labour productivity. There are, however, some important points to note about both the size–wage profiles and the wage–productivity relationship by size:

- The wage in the ASI sector (relative to the DME) increases much more mildly for the labour-intensive industries than for the other group. In fact, in 1989–90, the acceleration did not happen before the size group of 100–199 workers.
- The divergence in the size–wage profile for the two subgroups of industry really takes place after the group of 100–199 workers (see Table 4.10).
- The rate of increase in average wage by size is smaller than that of labour productivity. It is already significantly smaller than for productivity in the

Table 4.9 Productivity by size and industry groups

	DME	10–49	50–99	100–199	200–499	500 and above
Labour-intensive						
1989–90	100	318	300	479	614	659
2004–05	100	293	380	393	487	463
Capital-intensive						
1989–90	100	377	478	718	1078	1481
2004–05	100	284	439	832	1279	2483

Source: own calculations from the NSS and ASI unit level data.

Notes
Labour-intensive industries are food and beverages; tobacco and products; textile products; and wearing apparel.
Capital-intensive industries are basic metals; chemicals; non-metallic minerals; fabricated metal products; and machinery and equipment.

two smaller ASI groups. This is true for both years and for both subgroups. The gap between wage and productivity increase became much more for higher size groups and was wider for the capital-intensive industries. While the *wage–size* relationship had moderated between the two years, the *productivity–size* relationship increased sharply in 2004–05.

An important point about the data analysed so far has to be emphasized. The wage earnings reported above are really the wage bill per worker as reported by the enterprises surveyed by the NSSO. The limitations of this measure are twofold:

- First, they refer to all workers of varying skills, and include blue-collar as well as white-collar workers. This consideration implies that we could expect some of the wage differential in favour of larger enterprises to increase because of the changing composition of the workforce, since we could expect the proportion of white-collar and higher skilled workers to increase with firm size. The data, however, give no indication of the quantitative importance of this effect.
- Second, the wage per worker is really the wage paid out by the employer; it does not represent average earnings of the worker. This is because of the varying incidence of under-employment among workers employed by different classes of enterprise. In particular, the enterprises in the unorganized sector employ a large proportion of labour with a high turnover, often with little regularity of employment. It contrasts with the organized sector, which is generally characterized by regular year-round employment for much of its labour force (including contract labour, who do not have security of employment). We would then expect the incidence of under-employment (measured by the number of work days not employed over a time period like a year) to be significantly higher in the DME sector.

Studies which analyse the size–wage relationship in Indian labour markets, after controlling for the measurable quality of labour, have been very rare, unfortunately. The study by Mazumdar in a World Bank-funded research project in Bombay City at the end of the 1970s is one of them (Mazumdar 1984; also

Table 4.10 Average wage per worker by size and industry group

	DME	*10–49*	*100–199*	*200–499*	*500 and above*
Labour-intensive					
1989–90	100	107	131	179	302
2004–05	100	127	139	187	198
Capital-intensive					
1989–90	100	146	166	325	586
2004–05	100	124	130	169	432

Source: own calculations from the NSS and ASI unit level data.

Little *et al.* 1987, Chapter 14). The study analysed the determinants of the earnings of male wage workers by the nature of the unit of employment, after controlling for education, age, knowledge of English, training, and occupation. The results revealed a wage ladder for net earnings, rising for casual workers in unregistered small factories (roughly coinciding with the DME sector discussed above) and registered ASI factories of different size groups. There were three major jumps in net earnings: the first, between casual workers and regular workers in small unregistered factories, the second between the latter and small ASI factories, and the last between these factories and the larger ones. Within the ASI subsector, the differential between size groups within the 100+ factories was relatively small. The log difference between the earnings of workers in small unorganized units and the casual workers was 0.18. The difference increased to 0.50 for small units and to 0.86 for large factories.

Detailed analysis of the NSS data on the earnings of the two categories of labour (casuals and regulars) has been undertaken by Vasudeva-Dutta (2005). In 1999–2000, confining the sample to prime-age males, regular wage workers earned 3.3 times more than the casuals when measured at the mean, and 2.87 times more measured at the median. The dispersion of wages among regular workers is much more than among casuals. This is because age and education variables play a much larger role in the determination of regular wages, as does industry and occupation. The single most important explanatory variable in the casual wage function for males was region, with age playing a minor role, and education none. For manual workers alone, and controlling for age and education, regulars earned nearly double that of casuals. For rural females, the differential was less (around 50 per cent).[5] Although no data were available, it should be clear that a major cause of the differential of average earnings between the casuals and the regulars is the number of days of employment secured by the casuals (relative to the regulars) over the time period of the survey.

Sharrad Chari (2004) refers to the issue of under-employment among the unorganized sector workers, whom he surveyed in the labour market of Tirupur. Chari collected data on days of employment secured by workers in the different industries in Tirupur. His striking finding was:

> Across the knitwear industry, it seems that some firms work all year, many continue to work for only about half the year, and as many work all year as for less than two months. Most workers are employed for less than half the year, demonstrating that knitwear work is profoundly seasonal.

The field data collected by him revealed that daily wages (including supplements and allowances) were comparable to those of cotton mill workers in the area (in the organized sector) and considerably higher than in unorganized-sector enterprises like food processing (in which the problem of seasonality and under-employment was less severe). But when he compared gross annual earnings, the level in knitwear units was nearly one-third that of the larger textile factories, though more or less on a par with that in enterprises like food processing (pp. 97–98).

Productivity and wage increase over time

Has the recent growth of manufacturing in India resulted in any significant change in the relationship of firm size to productivity and wage levels? Figure 4.5 portrays the ratios of r productivities at these two dates by size class of enterprise. While there has been an increase in labour productivity over the period in all size groups, an important point brought out by the graph is the substantially larger increase in productivity in larger enterprises as far as the capital-intensive industries are concerned. This contrasts sharply with the experience of the labour-intensive industries in which the trend, if anything, has been slightly in the opposite direction.

In both the subgroups of industries, the DME units have improved their relative productivity with respect at least to the small (10–49) ASI units.

In sharp contrast to the change in relative productivity of large enterprises, average wages have suffered a relative decline in the larger units employing more than 100 workers (see Figure 4.5). Indeed for the largest enterprises of 500+ workers, there has been an absolute decline in the average wage. Generally speaking, labour-intensive industries have suffered more in the downward trend of relative ages than capital-intensive industries. The decline in wages in the corporate sector (while the relative productivity of these enterprises has trended upward) is an important development of Indian manufacturing. It points to the increasing share of value added going into profits and investment in the largest enterprises.

V

Interstate differences

In this section, we select eight major states for a detailed analysis of size structures in manufacturing and their differences among states. These states are Andhra Pradesh (AP), Gujarat (GU), Karnataka (KA), Maharashtra (MA),

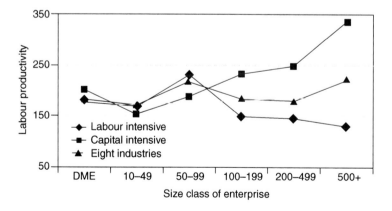

Figure 4.4 Change in labour productivity between 1989–90 and 2004–05.

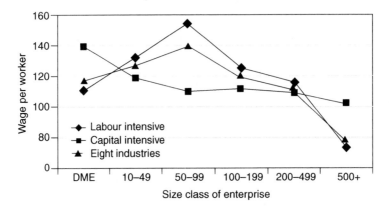

Figure 4.5 Change in wages per worker between 1989–90 and 2004–05 (1989–90 = 100).

Punjab (PU), Tamil Nadu (TN), Uttar Pradesh (UP), and West Bengal (WB). Together, these major states account for three-quarters of total manufacturing employment. Furthermore, we concentrate on eight major industries that together cover 70 per cent of all manufacturing employment (see Table 4.11).

Size distribution of employment by state and industry

This section describes the size distribution of the eight industries covered in the analysis for the eight states covered, as well as for all of India. It will be seen that the industries do have substantially different size structures but that within each industry there are significant differences by employment size group (see Figure 4.7).

The eight industries at the two-digit level can be classified into three groups:

- Group A: industries which are dominated by the DME units: food products, wearing apparel; non-metallic minerals, and machinery not elsewhere counted.
- Group B: industries in which large-scale units are dominant: tobacco and basic metals.

Table 4.11 Share in manufacturing employment

	DME	*ASI*	*All*
Selected eight industries	67.8	71.1	69.5
Selected eight states	78.5	73.6	75.9
Selected eight industries and eight states	53.5	52.3	52.9

Note
ASI data is for 2003–04 and DME data is for 2005–06.

• Group C: industries in which employment is more evenly spread among DME, smaller ASI, and large ASI groups: textiles and chemicals.

It has, however, to be noted that there are interesting interstate differences within each group.

For Group A, in food products, three states, Gujarat, Maharashtra, and Punjab, have substantial presence of the ASI sector (although not many very large units). The same is true of wearing apparel in Karnataka and Tamil Nadu, but in both these states, and particularly in Karnataka, large ASI units have a significant presence. Smaller ASI units are of importance in non-metallic minerals. The dominance of DME units in machinery seems to be due to the large presence of this type of unit in Gujarat and West Bengal, while the ASI has an equal or bigger role in the other states.

For Group B, the dominance of large ASI firms in tobacco products at the all-India level is due to the importance of such firms in two states, Andhra Pradesh and Maharashtra. In the other states, small and medium ASI units (but not DME) have a significant role. In basic metals, small ASI units in the 10–49 group have a much more important role in Gujarat and Punjab than in other states.

For Group C, in textiles, West Bengal and Punjab have a large role for large 500+ ASI units, while in most other states, small 10–49 units are more important, along with DME units. In chemicals, DME units are more important in Uttar Pradesh and Karnataka, while larger sized ASI units are important in Gujarat.

Interstate differences in size structure of manufacturing

Table 4.12 presents the size structure of manufacturing for all eight industries taken together in the eight states selected. The size distribution depends partly on the characteristics of the different industries and partly on state-specific

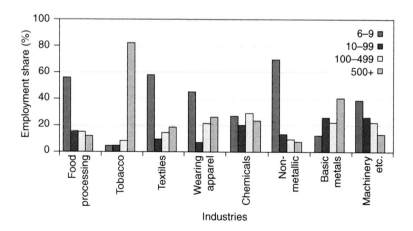

Figure 4.6 Distribution of employment by size groups in eight industries, 2004–05.

factors affecting the size distribution of all industries in that state. We control for the variations of industrial composition among the states by calculating the hypothetical size structure in a state by using the industry-specific size structure of the state but imposing on it the industrial composition of our reference state, West Bengal. This way we can see the quantitative importance of the difference in industrial composition in accounting for the interstate difference in size structure of manufacturing as a whole.

West Bengal was chosen as the reference state because the size structure of manufacturing in this state is the clearest example of the missing middle. Employment is concentrated in the small-scale DME sector and in the very large, with the medium and large sectors accounting for less than 10 per cent of the total. All the other states have a smaller proportion in the DME sector, which is compensated by a larger contribution to employment by small firms in the ASI sector.

A lesser proportion of employment than West Bengal in DME units is particularly conspicuous in three of the eight states: Andhra Pradesh, Punjab, and Tamil Nadu. It will be seen that only a very small part of the difference on this point with West Bengal could be accounted for by the difference in industrial composition. Evidently, there are important state-specific differences reducing the share of DME employment in these states.

Table 4.12 Size distributions in manufacturing across eight major states

State	DME	ASI small 10–99	ASI medium 100–199	ASI large 200–499	ASI very large 500 and over
AP actual	**40.3**	**14.3**	**4.3**	**8.0**	**33.0**
Hypothetical	43.5	16.1	5.5	11.4	23.5
GU actual	**52.8**	**15.3**	7.2	9.2	**15.6**
Hypothetical	43.0	19.8	9.2	12.2	15.8
KA actual	**54.2**	**12.4**	**5.1**	**10.5**	**17.0**
Hypothetical	52.3	15.8	6.8	10.9	14.3
MA actual	**50.2**	**14.5**	**5.9**	**9.8**	**19.5**
Hypothetical	57.0	12.5	4.8	8.7	17.1
PU actual	**23.2**	**30.1**	**6.7**	**12.9**	**27.0**
Hypothetical	26.8	29.3	6.7	10.1	27.1
TN actual	**44.3**	**19.3**	**10.2**	**12.7**	**13.4**
Hypothetical	46.1	21.2	9.6	10.1	13.1
UP actual	**58.1**	**12.0**	**7.1**	**9.5**	**13.3**
Hypothetical	56.2	13.5	6.9	10.0	13.5
WB	**58.4**	**8.3**	**3.9**	**5.2**	**24.3**

Note
The hypothetical figures are the percentages in this size group on the assumption that this state had the same industrial composition as West Bengal but the industry-specific size distribution was as found in the state concerned.

Gujarat, Maharashtra, and Uttar Pradesh come near to the size structure of West Bengal. But the difference between West Bengal and these three states is that in the latter the upper mode of the distribution in the very large (500+) group has a much lower value.

Another interesting point to observe is that in four of the eight states (Gujarat, Karnataka, Maharashtra, and Uttar Pradesh) the size distribution within the ASI subsector is much more even than in West Bengal. The upper mode of 500+ units is much less prominent. Two states (Andhra Pradesh and Punjab), however, show a marked U-shaped distribution within the ASI, with relatively large shares of employment at the two ends of its size distribution.

The following tentative hypotheses can be offered as explanations of these interstate differences. Further research is needed to substantiate the suggestions made here.

- It is hard to deny the hypothesis that the large percentage of DME employment in the base state (West Bengal) is related to the difficult labour relations in the state which eroded the viability of larger ASI establishments over a long period of time (Chakravarty 2010).

- In Maharashtra and Uttar Pradesh, the DME share is also very high, although smaller than in West Bengal. But the reasons for this high share are different in the two states. Uttar Pradesh is in large part a developing state, in which factory industry is not widespread and less mechanized units predominate. Maharashtra, however, is historically a leading industrial state which is home to the city and environs of India's commercial capital, Mumbai. But it has a history of industrial disputes, which had induced many larger factories to shut down and production shifted to smaller units to escape the power of industrial unions. The textile industry is the classic case of this kind of transformation (Mazumdar 1984). Although there has been a marked reduction of hostile union power and also significant slackening in the operation of labour laws affecting ASI units, particularly relating to the use of non-permanent workers (World Bank 2010), the bundle of factors included in hysteresis have maintained the importance of non-ASI units (Mazumdar and Sarkar 2008; Mazumdar 2010).

- Gujarat also has a large proportion of DME employment. Like Maharashtra, it has a history of militancy, but it has equally made efforts in recent years to amend labour laws in a pro-employer way and is generally thought to have a much better climate of labour-management relations (Streefkerk 2001). But more detailed examination (not presented here) shows that this high percentage of employment in DME is due to a markedly large proportion of employment in larger units of 10+ workers. Furthermore, the hypothetical distribution shows that, if Gujarat had the same industrial composition as West Bengal, its share of DME employment would have been much less. More than any other state, the relatively high share of DME employment in Gujarat is due to its peculiar industrial composition favouring the larger of the DME units (very likely due to the importance of gems and jewellery in Gujarat).

- In Andhra Pradesh and Punjab, a smaller percentage of employment in the DME sector has gone hand in hand with a substantially larger share of very large (500+) units. Labour regulations are known to be implemented much more liberally in these states and the union power has hardly been disruptive. Newly developing industries in these two states have been free to expand in size with fewer impediments in the ASI subsector.
- Punjab is unique: it has a large proportion of employment in the small 10–99 group of the ASI sector. Admittedly, there is a hint of the missing middle within the ASI but this is probably less of an issue for healthy manufacturing growth than in the cases in which the lower mode of distribution is in the DME sector. Tewari (1998) drew attention to the case of Ludhiana district of Punjab in which "unlike the more sophisticated states of Maharashtra and Gujarat, Ludhiana's industrial is dominated by small and medium-sized firms even in sectors which tend to be characterized by large and hierarchical firms in other regions" (p. 1387). She discussed at length the origins of Punjab's entrepreneurship and market for skilled labour which made this type of development possible. In fact, the data of Table 4.13 suggest that this growth of small entrepreneurs co-exists with that of very large enterprises.

VI

Two features of Indian industrialization not favouring even size distribution

We will see that the two factors that aided the relatively even distribution of manufacturing in the East Asian model were the decentralized nature of industrialization and the importance of subcontracting. In the following sections, we explore how these features have been conspicuously absent in Indian industrialization.

Table 4.13 Eight NSS regions where ASI and DME have substantial presence

State	NSS region	Share in employment	
		DME	ASI
UP	Western	6.0	4.9
WB	Central Plain	7.1	5.5
GU	Eastern	3.7	4.7
MA	Coastal	11.8	6.0
AP	Inland Northern	4.3	7.1
KA	Inland Southern	3.1	4.8
TN	Coastal Northern	4.2	5.1
TN	Inland	4.8	5.0
	Total	*45.1*	*43.1*

Note
ASI and DME values are for 2004–05 and 2005 06 respectively

Concentration of manufacturing in selected regions

While analysis at the state level has brought up some interesting points about regional differences in the size structure of manufacturing, more can be gained by looking at a detailed level of spatial dispersion. One alternative is to use NSS regions for our analysis. This approach reveals a striking picture of concentration of employment in manufacturing in a few selected regions—and the concentration is virtually the same in the DME and the ASI subsectors. Although the industries involved are different, eight common NSS regions (out of 72 NSS regions of India) have around 45 per cent of total manufacturing employment in each of the two subsectors. This is shown in Table 4.13, which specifies the regions.

There are a few exceptions to the broad generalization that the same NSS regions are home to the bulk of manufacturing in both the DME and the ASI sectors. Table 4.14 specifies the few regions which employ a significant part of manufacturing in each of the subsectors without a commensurate share of manufacturing employment in the other subsector. This type of employment together accounts for 11–14 per cent of total manufacturing employment in each subsector.

We conclude that location advantages for manufacturing as a whole (rather than for specific industries) are similar in strength for DME and ASI establishments. This is, however, not to say that these industrial NSS regions all have a high concentration of non-farm employment in manufacturing. Only one NSS region (Gujarat) has a high density (more than 70 per cent of all non-farm employment) in manufacturing. In all the other regions, the density ranges from 12 per cent to 20 per cent, even though all of them account for a significantly higher proportion than the all-India proportion (9.6) per cent taking DME and ASI subsectors together.

Subcontracting

In the manufacturing sector, two types of product outsourcing or contract manufacturing can be observed:

Table 4.14 Regions where DME has substantial presence not common with ASI

State	Name of NSS region	Share in employment within	
		DME	*ASI*
UP	Eastern	3.2	–
GU	Saurashtra	5.0	–
KA	Inland Eastern	3.1	–
GU	Plains Northern	–	3.0
MA	Inland Western	–	4.7
PU	Northern	–	3.1
TN	Coastal Northern	–	2.9
	Total	*11.3*	*13.7*

- Vertical inter-firm linkages: larger firms outsourcing specific tasks to smaller-sized firms in formal and informal sectors. It is difficult to measure the extent of this type of subcontracting from firm-level balance sheets.
- Horizontal subcontracting: Ramaswamy (2006) has expressed it as the ratio of goods sold in the same condition as purchased to the total value of products and by-products.

On the basis of the Annual Survey of Industries data of 2000–01, Ramaswamy (2006) observed that horizontal subcontracting has a substantial presence in export-oriented industries like wearing apparel and footwear across employment size class of industries. He found the highest outsourcing intensities in the size class of 10–99 employees and concluded that outsourcing by large firms to smaller firms in the formal sector would not form a significant proportion of the latter's output. However, this analysis was undertaken at the all-India level. The prevalence of outsourcing practices needs to be examined in a limited geographical area, say at NSS region level (within a state).

Nevertheless evidence for significant subcontracting practices has not been noted in detailed industry studies in India. Further, where subcontracting arrangements have been found to be important, it has not been of the type involving transfer of technology from large to smaller units (a model of much significance in East Asia). Thus in the garments industry of Tirupur, subcontracting of both types is widespread, but it is confined within the DME sector with its predominantly less mechanized technology (Satyaki Roy 2010). Similarly, the automotive industry reports extensive subcontracting, but the relationship is between large assembly units and SME units, which are separated by an apparently insurmountable barrier from smaller units of the DME type (Ushikawa 2011).

VII

Conclusions

A substantial part of the DME sector is not confined to the legal limit of units employing 6–9 workers. While this needs to be noted, it does not change the nature of the problem in a qualitative sense. The larger DME units (in excess of the legal limit) are largely confined to three labour-intensive industries, and do not differ significantly from smaller units of this subsector in terms of labour productivity (and hence technology).

The research demonstrates the importance of product market segmentation between the two subsectors: the overlap of industries at the detailed five-digit level amounts to rather less than one-half of total employment in manufacturing. Even this gives only a lower limit to the extent of segmentation because DME units can be expected to produce lower quality brands within the five-digit classification, which is not recorded in the statistics.

The sharp difference between the ASI-dominated group of industries and the others is revealed when we consider the markets for goods produced by industries dominated by the ASI and the DME subsectors separately. In particular, the results in Table 4.7 showed that the unorganized sector industries cater almost entirely to the demands of the domestic market. The export markets are almost exclusively served by industries dominated by the ASI sector.

It is remarkable that the DME sector has picked up the rate of growth of value added in the last two five-year periods, catching up with the growth rate of the ASI sector. Employment elasticity for the two broad sectors was also quite close in the last period. Accordingly, the differential in labour productivity between the DME and the ASI sectors—which had been widening in the earlier years—narrowed in the first five years of this century.

The chapter has also looked at interstate differences in size distribution. We selected eight major two-digit industries and considered their size distribution for eight major states.

Looking at all the eight industries together, West Bengal was identified as the state with the strongest incidence of the missing middle, with a very large presence of employment in the DME units and a substantial percentage in the largest ASI units. This striking bi-modal distribution can be traced to historical factors originating in militant trade unionism tolerated by left-leaning state administrations. It affected industrial relations in the traditional ASI sector, which induced a major disinvestment and migration of industry to other states. We compared the size distribution of manufacturing in other states with West Bengal as of the year 2004–05. Since the size distribution is affected by the specific industrial composition of a particular state, we provided the hypothetical size distribution in each state using the industry weights of the reference state, West Bengal.

The last section in this chapter addressed two special issues which have been critical in the development of mid-size manufacturing firms in the history of industrialization in East Asian countries. The East Asian pattern contrasts strongly with the Indian experience of the missing middle. First, India has suffered from marked spatial concentration of manufacturing employment, both in the ASI and in the DME sectors. Second, Indian manufacturing has experienced a much more limited role of subcontracting, a phenomenon which has helped the more dispersed industrialization across size groups in East Asia.

5   The impact of the missing middle on the growth rate

In this chapter and the next, we discuss the first two interrelated consequences of the dualistic structure of manufacturing in the Indian economy: the rate of growth and the trend to increasing inequality in the growth process. We start with the impact on growth in this chapter.

The two most important avenues through which dualism in manufacturing would have a negative effect on the growth rate of the sector would seem to be the slowing down of the markets for industrial goods and the dampening effect on the formation of industrial skills. (We first discuss only the growth of the domestic market for manufactured goods; the problem of exports is dealt with in a separate section below.)

The growth of markets

The starting point of the argument is that, unlike in the classical model of development (say, the Lewis model), labour is not available at a uniform supply-price to the whole of the non-subsistence sector. In particular, there is a hierarchy of wages closely related to the size of firms and it should be emphasized that these differentials are net of measurable worker quality, like education and experience.

Given this heterogeneity of wage and productivity levels in the non-subsistence sector, the segments in which jobs are created is a matter of critical importance. The growth of employment in the non-subsistence sector depends both on supply factors (the cost of labour) and the increase in the demand for the goods it helps to produce. If at the first round, most jobs are created in the low-wage, small-scale segment of the market, the cost of labour would be low, but the expansion of demand for industrial goods would also be low since the increase in per capita income is small. With more jobs being created in the middle-sized segment, income per capita could be expected to increase faster and hence the markets for non-agricultural goods could be expected to increase faster. The higher wage per worker does not lead to a proportionate increase in the cost of labour because part of the higher wage reflects higher efficiency. Finally, when we come to the large-scale segment of the market, many of the firms in this segment are geared to high-productivity technology. They are based on a high-wage, low-employment approach to labour deployment (partly because of the threat of union pressure and partly the desire of management to deal with a limited body of labour). Thus compared to middle-sized firms, even though wage per worker is higher, employment and the wage bill per unit of output could be significantly lower. In extreme cases, the employment elasticity of output in this large-scale sector could be very low (as has been the case in India). As a result, the contribution of this sector to the growth of domestic markets for industrial goods (particularly for the mass of low-income consumers) would be limited.

The impact on skill formation in the labour market

An adequate supply of skilled labour attuned to industrial work is partly a function of the development of the educational sector (including primary and lower secondary education) but is also dependent on widespread on-the-job training. Dispersed industrialization is important for such a pool of trained labour over a wide area. Many developing countries suffer from a concentration of skilled labour in specific metropolitan areas; researchers have identified this phenomenon as an important element in the limited dispersal of industrial employment. The concentration of industry and of skilled labour feed on each other, creating high infrastructural and social costs and adding significantly to the unequal distribution of capital and income.

I

The growth of domestic markets for manufactured goods

The growth of demand for manufactured goods in India has been slow due to the slow growth of income among the vast majority of India's population. Over the post-reform decade of 1993–2004, the growth rate of average per capita consumption for 80 per cent of the households rarely went above 1.25 per cent per annum in the rural areas, and in the urban areas it increased slightly from a low of under 1 per cent for the bottom 20 per cent to 1.5 per cent for the deciles up to 80 per cent. This is a far cry from the nearly 6 per cent growth rate in GDP, even if we allow for a growth rate of the population of nearly 2 per cent. The reasons for the relatively slow rate of growth of average per capita consumption for the bulk of the Indian population are:

- the dualistic development in the non-agricultural economy, which has meant that only a small proportion of the labour force is absorbed in the high-wage formal sector, while the larger part is in the low-wage informal sector; and
- the relatively slow reallocation of labour from agriculture, with its low productivity growth and high incidence of surplus labour it has to support.

Slow reallocation of labour from low-productivity agriculture

A large proportion of the population in Asian economies is supported by the agricultural sector. Thus a major factor in the rate of expansion of demand for manufactured goods would be the course of agricultural productivity (and income) per worker. The trend in agricultural labour productivity is determined partly by the course of land productivity and partly by the land-worker ratio. The latter magnitude in its turn is determined by the amount of surplus labour which is supported by the sector. The crucial variable in the increase in the demand for manufactured goods is the success of these economies in reallocating surplus labour to productive activities outside agriculture. A relatively slow expansion of employment in manufacturing implies that the reallocation of under-employed labour from agriculture to the more productive sectors of the economy is damp-ened. Table 5.1 provides some data on the reallocation of labour from agricul-ture in the Indian growth process and sets them in the perspective of the experience of selected economies of Asia which have recently experienced (or are currently experiencing) accelerated growth.

The major point which stands out from the comparative experience is that India had a particularly low rate of reallocation of labour away from agriculture. The slow rate of reallocation led to the low rate of growth of land productivity in agriculture. The net result was that, over the three decades, India showed a more striking rate of decline of relative labour productivity in agriculture.

Table 5.1 Share of employment in agriculture and relative productivity

A. Share of employment in total (%)

Year	India*	China[1]	Vietnam	Indonesia	Philippines[1]	Malaysia	Thailand
1980	65	69	73	56	52	37	71
Change *1980–90*	−4	−9	0	0	−7	−11	−8
1990–2000	−7	−10	−8	−11	−8	−8	−14
2000–07	n.a	n.a.	−8	−4	−1	−3	−7
Total since 1980	−11	−19	−16	−15	−16	−22	−29

B. Relative labour productivity in agriculture

Year	India*	China	Vietnam	Indonesia	Philippines	Malaysia	Thailand
1980	57	43	49	43	48	61	33
1990	49	45	45	35	48	59	20
2000	36	41	59	34	42	47	19
2007	n.a.	n.a.	67	34	39	68	26

Notes
Figures for first period are from Mazumdar and Basu (1997, Table 3.2, p. 38). For the second period, they are calculated from *ILO Yearbook* data. For the last period, they calculated from ADB Key Indi-cators 2010.
   Relative productivity is the ratio of labour productivity in the sector to GDP per worker, multi-plied by 100.
1 For all periods, calculated from ADB Key Indicators 2001.
* The Indian data are from the NSS (UPS count) 1983–84, 1983–84 to 1993–94, and 1993–94 to 2004–05.

The two socialist economies, reforming into relatively free market economies, performed much better in their agricultural sector. Vietnam actually increased the relative productivity of its agricultural sector significantly, while China held its own. The rate of reallocation of labour out of agriculture does not seem to have been unusually large, thus we can conclude that policies in these economies achieved an unusually high rate of growth of land productivity—significantly higher than in India.

The other countries in the sample suffered some decline in the relative productivity in agriculture, but much less severe than the experience of India. Thailand is a special case in many ways, characterized by a particularly low relative agricultural productivity—which seems to get worse over its period of industrialization after 1980. The Thai case is discussed in detail in Chapter 11. The pattern of industrialization, skewed to large enterprises and depending on capital-intensive methods for producing goods for export, led to particularly low employment elasticity in manufacturing. Further, the highly localized growth of non-agricultural activities surrounding the Bangkok region led to peculiar developments in the pattern of labour flows, which ensured that a significant proportion of farm families remained dependent on low-income farming activities in depressed regions. The result was that the proportion of the labour force dependent on agriculture—already unusually high at the beginning of the era of strong industrial growth—caused relative incomes in agriculture to remain particularly depressed.

Table 5.2 enables us to compare the Indian case with the historical record of the high-growth countries of East Asia. It is clear that the reallocation of labour from agriculture was substantially larger in the two East Asian economies during their period of industrialization. It is also revealed that this higher rate of reallocation of labour helped to maintain relative productivity in agriculture at higher levels than in India, in spite of the much higher growth rate of non-agricultural output. Particularly striking is the higher rate of reallocation of labour from agriculture in Korea during the second period, when Korean industrial policy successfully influenced the size structure of manufacturing to lean towards a higher proportion of small and medium-sized enterprises.

The evidence presented supports the hypothesis proposed in Chapter 1, that the reallocation of labour from agriculture is faster and the relative productivity in agriculture is maintained at a higher level in the East Asian type of model with an equitable size distribution of manufacturing enterprises than in the case of the missing-middle type typified by India.

II

Household income and the demand for manufactured goods

Figures 5.1 and 5.2 use data from the consumer expenditure survey of the NSS for the 2004–05 round to examine the demand for manufactured goods (separately for durables and non-durables) for the percentile groups of average per

Table 5.2 Employment share and relative productivity in agriculture, Taiwan and Korea

Country	Years	Employment share in agriculture (%, initial year)	Decline in employment share (%)		Relative productivity in agriculture (all sectors = 100)	
			Period	Per annum	Initial year	Terminal year
Taiwan	1952–60	60.5	1.8	—	55	47
	1960–66	58.7	15.2	—	—	49
	1966–70	43.5	6.7	—	—	45
	1970–75	36.8	7.8	—	—	43
	1960–75		29.7	2.0	55	43
Korea	1965–70	58.6	8.2	—	66	51
	1970–75	50.4	4.7	—	—	55
	1975–80	45.7	11.7	—	—	44
	1980–85	34.0	9.1	—	—	58
	1985–88	24.9	4.2	—	—	52
	1965–88		33.7	1.5	66	52
	1965–75		12.9	1.3	66	55
	1975–88		25.0	1.9	55	52
India	1983–2004		15.0	0.7	57	36

Source: Chapter 9, Table 9.2 and Chapter 10, Table 10.2 for Taiwan and Korea respectively.

capita consumption expenditure (APCE). It is seen that, in rural India, the share of non-durable manufactured goods increases rather smoothly up to the seventieth percentile group—doubling over the range from 4 per cent to 8 per cent. There is a kink at this point and a steeper increase of the share of non-durables for higher expenditure groups. By contrast, no such kink is found in urban India, and the plateau for manufactured non-durables is reached at the sixtieth percentile. The impact of relatively high income levels is found dramatically in the demand for durable manufactured goods. In both the rural and the urban sectors, a dramatic upsurge in the share of expenditure on such goods is found in the last 5 per cent of the APCE distribution.

We demonstrated in Chapter 4 that there is a significant degree of segmentation in the manufacturing sector in India, with the unorganized sector producing basic labour-intensive manufactured goods of mass consumption (e.g. textiles and footwear) and the organized sector producing high-value consumer goods (including durables), and intermediate and capital goods. The participation of the unorganized sector in exports of manufactures is also very limited.

Figures 5.1 and 5.2 show that the level of expenditure of the vast majority of consumers has not reached a high enough level for a substantial proportion to be spent on manufactured goods. The expenditure on high-value manufactured goods, including durables, is largely confined (in the analysis of 2004–05 data given above) to the top 5 per cent of the expenditure distribution. In spite of the high rate of GDP growth in recent years, the growth rate of consumer expenditure has not been sufficiently high to make a significant dent in this pattern.

Manufacturing production in the organized (ASI) sector has accordingly been dependent on the growth of the market for durables, intermediate goods, and exports. The nature and problems of Indian exports of manufactured goods will be dealt with below in a separate section. Here, we can give an idea of the

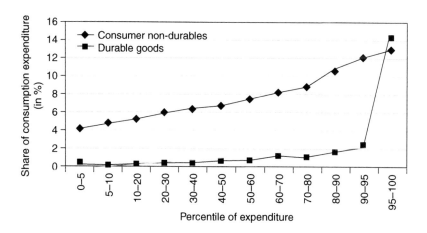

Figure 5.1 Share of consumer durables and non-durables in rural India, 2004–05 (source: our own estimates from the NSS Household Expenditure Survey 2004–05 round).

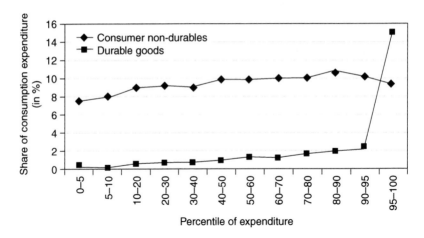

Figure 5.2 Share of consumer durables and non-durables in urban India, 2004–05 (source: our own estimates from the NSS Household Expenditure Survey 2004–05 round).

composition of the manufactured goods of the organized sector, classified by their usage. The weights of the different categories of manufactured goods in the Industrial Production Index by the Central Statistical Office (CSO) are given in Table 5.3.

It should be noted that, for the years prior to 1993–94, the Industrial Production Index included only the organized sector (ASI). The basis for the index was changed at this time to include the unorganized sector. We find that the production of consumer durables in the ASI sector had indeed gone up between 1980–81 and 1993–94, but in the latter year it still constituted a small proportion of total production. The ASI sector was dominated by the production of basic, intermediate, and capital goods. Table 5.4 gives the growth rate of production by usage categories for the years since 1998–99.

Remembering that part of the growth of consumer goods is produced in the non-ASI sector, we can see the growth of ASI has been much more due to the other categories (which are dominated by the ASI sector). The production of durables has been an important source of growth in this subsector, and has shared its leading role with the capital goods subsector—and the latter has indeed been important in the recent surge of manufacturing production since 2002–03.

The picture of the limited role of the growth of the subsector of durable consumer goods which emerges from the discussion of the last paragraphs is consistent with our analysis of the development of the middle-class markets in India. The growth of the middle class is undoubtedly significant in the development of Indian manufacturing in the organized sector, but the limits of its quantitative importance should be recognized. A relevant point to note here is that, while the reform process has unleashed economic forces which have created a growing

Table 5.3 Weights for the industrial production index (%)

Year	Basic goods	Capital goods	Intermediate goods	Consumer goods	Consumer durables	Consumer non-durables
1980–81	39.42	16.43	20.51	23.65	2.55	21.10
1993–94	35.57	9.26	26.51	28.66	5.37	23.30

Source: Central Statistical Organization, Government of India.

Table 5.4 Index of industrial production, 1993–94 to 2009–10 (base: 1993–94 = 100)

Years	Basic goods	Capital goods	Intermediate goods	Consumer goods	Consumer durables	Consumer non-durables
1998–99	121.4	115.0	125.7	126.5	146.2	122.1
2002–03	168.6	201.5	199.0	200.9	265.4	186.1
2006–07	209.3	314.2	242.4	276.8	382.0	252.6
2009–10	246.2	474.8	294.3	329.9	498.6	291.1

Source: Central Statistical Organization, Government of India.

middle class of consumers, it has liberalized the import structure, which now supplies an increased proportion of the consumer goods demanded by high-income consumers.

III

The middle-class bulge: how important is it in Indian growth?

The conclusion reached above seems at first to be inconsistent with the prevailing popular notion that Indian growth has created a large bulge in the middle-class population in India, which provides a large and growing market for modern manufactured goods. The first question is: what is the middle class?

Ravallion (2009) has tried to answer the question about the definition of the middle class from the point of view of the observed distribution of income and an acceptable definition of the poverty line. His empirical definition is that the middle class can be defined as the percentage of the population living on between US$2 a day of per capita income (or expenditure) and US$13 per day. The former is the median used by a selection of national governments in developing countries, and the latter the US poverty line (all at 2005 PPP prices). A very large percentage of India's population still lives below the US$2 line, even though we have seen that Indian growth has produced a significant decline in the headcount ratio of people under the poverty line. Table 5.5 gives the percentages of the population in different APCE blocks, as calculated by Ravallion. The contrasting picture of China is also presented in this table.

Table 5.5 Population in different ranges of per capita household income (expenditure) in India and China

Country/ range	Population (in millions)				% of population			
	Below US$2		Range US$2–US$13		Below US$2		Range US$2–US$13	
	1990	*2005*	*1990*	*2005*	*1990*	*2005*	*1990*	*2005*
India	701.6	**1091.5**	146.8	**263.3**	82.6	**75.6**	17.3	**24.1**
China	960.8	**473.6**	173.7	**806.0**	84.6	**36.3**	15.3	**61.8**

Source: Ravallion (2009).

The percentage above the US poverty line (US$13) is tiny for both countries. Table 5.5 shows that Indian growth pushed up the percentage of people in the US$2 to US$13 range quite a bit so that over 250 million people were out of poverty (even in terms of the higher international poverty line). This is probably the figure which is being used in popular discussions about the growing middle class in India.

But as we have seen above, the really substantial demand for manufactured goods, and in particular durables, occurs only at levels which are enjoyed by the top 5 per cent of consumers.

The analysis of the Asian Development Bank

The *2010 Annual Report* of the Asian Development Bank (ADB 2010a) includes a special chapter on "The Rise of Asia's Middle Class". This work included the Indian case in its detailed study of household survey data and other sources. The report considered the middle class of developing countries to include those with consumption expenditure of US$2–US$20 per person per day (in 2005 PPP dollars). It further divided the middle class into three groups: lower-middle class (US$2–US$4 per person per day) as vulnerable; middle-middle class (US$4–US$10) as above subsistence, and able to save and consume non-essential goods; and upper-middle class (US$10–US$20). In terms of our argument above, the lower limit of the earnings of households with a significant demand for manufactured goods could at most coincide with the lower boundary of ADB's middle-middle class.

The NSS data processed by the ADB shows that, in 2004–05, the population share of the middle class in India (above US$4 per person per day) was around 18 per cent, up from 12 per cent in 1993–94. The increase in the share of the middle class over the decade was much more pronounced in the urban areas, increasing by ten percentage points to 33 per cent. To put the Indian growth in perspective, the population share of the middle class in China, with the same definition, grew from 18 per cent in 1995 to an astonishing 70 per cent in 2007. The Chinese increase in the share of population in the middle class was also much more impressive in the rural economy (ADB 2010a, Tables 2.5 and 2.6),

There is a substantial difference in the population share belonging to the middle-middle section between these two countries. The differences in the absolute size of the middle class in the two economies are of course multiplied because of the larger population base of China. This underlines the point about the huge difference in the market size for manufactured goods in the two economies. The difference in the rate of growth as well as the difference in sectoral patterns of development is crucial to the understanding of the disparity. This is a large topic which is beyond the scope of this chapter.[1]

The ADB report also draws attention to the difference in demand patterns for selected consumer durables in three Asian economies, contrasting the experiences of India with those of China and the Philippines. Large differences in the consumption of the individual durable items are found between the countries for the same expenditure class. For example, Indian consumers (at middle-class income levels) consume electronics and appliance goods much less than the consumers in the Philippines. The ADB comments:

> It seems unlikely that difference in tastes is completely responsible. Much more likely is the possibility that India's consumer electronic and appliances industry has only recently taken off, while the Philippines has relied on fairly reliable trade policy for importing such products, and the PRC has manufactured domestically sufficient low-cost options.
>
> (ADB 2010a, p. 37)

The point illustrates the crucial importance of differences in industrial policies and the manufacturing structures between Asian countries. In particular, the product market segmentation, which the Indian industrial policy encouraged between the unorganized and organized manufacturing sectors, has played a dominant role in the relative under-development of some types of consumer goods industries in the modern sector, until recently.

IV

The growth of markets for manufactured goods: exports

We have been discussing the problems connected with the growth of home markets for manufactured goods, but a good deal of industrialization in Asian economies in recent decades has been propelled by exports.

The autarkic model of growth and export stagnation

It is well known that India's industry-cum-trade policy was responsible for India taking a back seat in the world expansion of exports in the latter half of the last century. While the developing countries claimed an increasing share of world exports, India slipped continuously. In fact, the decline in India's share in exports was much sharper for the subset of developing countries than for world exports as a whole. This declining trend was particularly noticed in manufacturing exports. India's ranking in the share of manufacturing exports from developing countries plummeted from second in 1960–61, at 10.2 per cent in the 1960s, to ninth, at 2.6 per cent, in the 1980s and has remained at this level since then (Athukorala 2008, p. 4, and Figure 1b).

This was the period when developing countries were playing a leading role in capturing the market for basic labour-intensive goods in the world arena. India's failure to take part in the export boom in these decades has been ascribed in the literature to the import-substitution strategy of industrialization based on the widespread "export pessimism" typical among development economists of the period (e.g. Bhagwati 1993). But India had already established, in the years before the war, factory industry in basic manufactured consumer goods like textiles and footwear. The significant reason for the export stagnation in these lines of manufacturing has to be traced to the other aspect of the strategy of industrialization embodied in the Mahalanobis model (see Chapter 1) of reservation of a wide variety of consumer goods for the small-scale sector. The licensing system, which excluded large-scale units from expanding their productive capacity in these lines, led to product market segmentation in which manufacturing goods for mass consumption were increasingly produced in the non-ASI (or unregistered) sector of the economy, while the ASI (or registered) sector produced largely capital and intermediate goods. The unorganized sector served the domestic market, and it lacked the technological and marketing capability of expanding sales in the world market. Our analysis from the 2003–04 input–output matrix in Chapter 4 showed that, at the two-digit level, the industries in which the ASI sector was wholly or mostly dominant in terms of value added had an export share of 38 per cent of the total output for final use, but those in which the DME sector was dominant had an export-to-final use ratio of only 1 per cent (see Table 4.7). We should re-emphasize the point already made in the last chapter that this estimate in terms of value added is an obvious underestimate of the role of the DME sector in total industrial production and exports because we know that the DME enterprises tend to specialize in the lower end of the quality spectrum of products in each industry.

As indicated in the discussion of Chapter 4, there has been some dynamism in this sector and some new industries have been emerging which, on the face of it, seem to be the non-basic kinds (see Table 4.6).

Recent development of Indian exports

India's exports fared much better in the post-reform years, In fact, the decline in the share of India's exports of the total for developing countries had levelled off in the second half of the 1980s and started to inch up in the 1990s. But the recovery has not been all that marked, relative to the other countries in the group. Its ranking has gone up a couple of notches from the bottom. But while China's share increased from 25 per cent to 38 per cent in the years 1990–91 to 2005–06, India's share remained virtually static at 2.7 per cent (Athukorala 2008, Figure 1a).

The Indian manufacturing industry has been progressively globalized. The share of manufactured goods in export composition of India increased from 57.8 per cent in 1979–80 to 72 per cent in 1989–90 and further to 78.1 per cent in 2005–6 (Athukorala 2008, p. 7). But the small base of the manufacturing sector has meant that its impact on the world market has been limited. The export of manufacturing did not play a significant role in expanding the importance of the sector in the domestic economy either.

The two areas in which India seems to have missed the boat in the export expansion from Asia are labour-intensive basic consumer goods and manufacturing and transport equipment (SITC 7), within which information technology and communications (ITC) products have played the dominant role. It was expected that, after the abolition of the Multi-Fibre Arrangement in 2004, India and China would be major gainers of market share. But China has outstripped India by a large margin in this area.

The more important gain in the shares of world trade by China and other East Asian economies, however, has been in the machinery and transport equipment group, and the ITC subsector in particular. The developing countries of Asia increased the share of SITC 7 in their total exports from 15 per cent in 1979–80 to 53 per cent in 2005–06, while China's went up staggeringly from 3 per cent to 48 per cent over the same period. By contrast, India's share of this subgroup in total merchandise exports was a mere 8 per cent at the beginning of this period and increased slowly to 11 per cent at the end (ibid., Tables 3 and 4).

The emerging trends in the first decade of this century can be discerned from the data given in Table 5.6. In spite of the acceleration in the growth of manufactured goods in the export market, the value of such exports as share of total has declined in the recent decade.

It can be seen from Table 5.6 that resource-based products continue to be the most important group for India's exports. There has, however, been a major shift in manufactured exports from textiles to engineering goods and (to a smaller extent) to chemicals.

The growth rate of all exports from India has had an upsurge in recent years. The rate of growth in export volume was double digit on an annual basis for a number of years of the first decade of the century, and was aided by an increase in unit price (Government of India: Economic Survey 2011). India also seems to have rebounded quickly from the depression of the recent financial crisis of 2009.

But a feature of the upsurge has been that this growth, as with the output growth in the non-agricultural sector, has been led by services rather than goods. The positive term on the "invisible" item in the balance of payments has, to a large extent, offset the negative element in the goods trade. In the last four years for which finalized data have been reported, the inflow of non-factor services contributed an average of US$38 billion per year to the balance of payments against an average trade deficit of US$81 billion (the average value of exports of goods was US$120 billion).[2] A great deal of this increase in exports (particularly in computer services) is intra-industry trade, showing the extent of India's

Table 5.6 Percentage shares in total exports: 2000–01, 2008–09, and change in marginal shares over the period (change in value of item over period/change in total value of exports)

Year	Agricultural	Minerals	All manuf.	Leather	Chemicals	Engr. goods	Textiles	Gems	Petroleum
2000–01	13.5	2.9	**76.1**	0.4	13.8	15.9	23.3	16.7	4.8
2008–09	9.5	4.2	**66.5**	1.9	12.3	25.5	10.8	15.1	12.2
2000/01–2008/09	12.8	4.6	**63.5**	1.2	11.8	28.5	5.9	14.6	18.0

Source: Director-General of Commercial Intelligence and Statistics.

Note

The percentages are calculated from the absolute values given in current US dollars.

integration with the global supply chain. The same cannot, however, be said about trade in goods. While China's export growth has been helped by its active participation in the nexus of intra-Asian trade involving the fast-growing economies of East and South-East Asia, India's dependence on the EU market has continued to be important (UNCTAD *Trade and Development Report*).

The limited participation of the unorganized sector in exports

The impact of enterprise size on export participation is very strong in the Indian economy. This can be seen from the data collected by the Census of Registered Small Industries for 2001–12. It is to be remembered that micro, small, and medium-sized enterprises covers units up to a plant value of Rs. 10 million in terms of a total value of plant and machinery investment. Larger and capital-intensive units (including those in the organized sector) are not covered under it.

Figure 5.3 shows the markedly non-linear relationship between export participation and enterprise size for this group of small and medium-sized enterprises. It is evident that the vast majority of the unorganized sector enterprises (that mostly employ fewer than 50 workers) are unable to participate significantly in the export market.

This picture contrasts starkly with the quantitative data on export participation for Taiwan, where we find that SMEs had a substantially higher rate of participation in the export market than large enterprises (see Chapter 9).

The major reason for this limited participation of small-scale enterprises (and particularly the unorganized sector) in manufacturing exports is the product market segmentation discussed in Chapter 4. The unorganized sector (and especially the DME sector within it) has largely catered to the markets of low-income domestic consumers. Technology and the attitude of entrepreneurs in this sub-sector, as well as the trade outlets, have been adapted to this strategy.

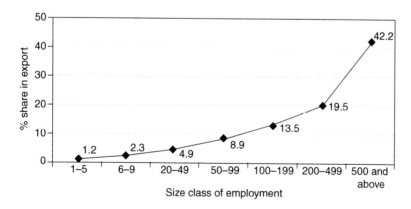

Figure 5.3 Share of exports in gross output of registered SSI units (source: unit level data of third MSME census, 2002–03).

A second important factor has been the limited participation of small establishments in the wider network of production through subcontracting relationships, such as existed in the East Asian economies (discussed in Part III of this volume).

We have seen that in certain areas—like in the textile town of Tirupur—an export market has become significant in recent years. The extraordinary homogeneity of the entrepreneurs in this industry (with the dominance of the Gounder community) has been singled out by observers as a critical feature in facilitating the development of the intricate patterns of vertical and horizontal subcontracting, which enabled the small units to develop the relationship with traders (many of them immigrating from outside the area) and made access to export markets feasible.

Appendix

The McKinsey report

Probably the most influential work to have publicized the spectacular middle-class growth in India, and the associated expansion of the market for consumer goods, is the *2007 Report* of the McKinsey Global Institute. The report adopted the classification of consumers by income slabs suggested by Shukla *et al.* (2004). The middle class was defined in this classification by two groups: the "seekers" (with annual household income between Rs.200,000 and Rs.500,000, in 2000 rupees) and the "strivers" (with household income between Rs.500,000 and Rs.1 million). They constituted (in 2005) 5.26 per cent and 1.16 per cent of the total number of households, respectively. They were flanked, on one side, by the "global" (very high income households, which accounted for 0.58 per cent of the total number of households) and, on the other side, by the "aspirers", with 44.12 per cent. The "deprived" with less than Rs.90,000 constituted the largest group of the pyramid, with 48.86 per cent of the total number of households. Using the figures by the McKinsey team, we give in Table 5.A1 the percentage of persons in each group expressed in 2000 US dollars per capita per day (and assuming the same exchange rate and number of people per household, an average of 3.85).

As mentioned in the discussion of Figure 5.1, the point of inflexion at which the demand for non-basic consumer manufactured goods turns upwards is at the top 5 per cent of the distribution of APCE—which would correspond roughly to the group of "seekers" and above in the McKinsey classification. It should moreover be noted that the NSS does not specify the quality of products. As we have seen in the previous chapter, a large proportion of the manufactured goods consumed by the APCE classes below the top 5 per cent are textiles and footwear, mostly of the quality produced by the non-formal DME sector. It is unlikely that the formal or ASI sector firms would be catering to the demand for manufactured consumer goods of 95 per cent of the households in 2005.

Table 5.A1 Percentage of households in different household income classes, 2005–25

Class type	Range in 2000 rupees per capita/per day (1000)	Range in US$2000 per capita/per day ($1 = 45.60 rupees)	Proportion of households (%) 2005	Projected proportion of households (%) 2015	Projected proportion of households (%) 2025
Deprived	<90	<1.40	48.86	30.36	17.54
Aspirers	90–200	1.40–3.12	44.12	43.44	33.28
Seekers	200–500	3.12–7.79	5.26	22.58	33.92
Strivers	500–1000	7.79–15.58	1.16	2.25	11.83
Global	1000+	>15.58	0.58	1.35	3.43

Source: derived from McKinsey Global Institute (2007), Exhibit 2.

The McKinsey report, of course, anticipates an explosion of the proportion in the middle-class income groups (the seekers and the strivers), going from an estimated 6.5 per cent in 2005 to 25 per cent in 2015 and an astonishing 45 per cent in 2025. The change is much more dramatic than the actual change seen from the ADB data (ADB 2010a, Table 2.5). Such an abrupt acceleration of the proportion of people above the poverty line of US$2 PPP seems rather misleading. In the absence of detailed information about the methodology of projection in the McKinsey report, and the data sets used by them, we are not able to examine critically the McKinsey projections as they might appear with alternative NSS data sets. But some general points about the assumptions of the McKinsey exercise might be made.

These projections assume a growth rate of GDP of 7.3 per cent (increasing by a full percentage point the growth rate of the 1995–2005 decade). It is forecast that the savings rates of households would gradually reach a plateau, so that aggregate consumption growth reaches 6.4 per cent in 2005–15 and 7.4 per cent in the following decade, 2015–25. This forecast means very substantial per capita consumption growth.

The first point of reservation we have about the McKinsey forecast is the likely over-estimation of the aggregate consumption growth. It is well known that the consumption growth rate of the recent past differs markedly between the NSS and the NAS (see Chapter 3). Some of the reasons for the massive disparity have been discussed in that chapter. Here, it is sufficient to note that the underestimate of the NSS of expenditure on durable and other luxury items would make the NSS figure an underestimate of consumption growth. On the other hand, the doubtful treatment of expenditure on asset creation by consumers would tend to overestimate the trend reported by the NAS (and McKinsey). In any event, even if the NSS growth rate of consumption is too low, it is clear that the basis of the McKinsey projection of consumption growth is much exaggerated, especially for non-durable consumer goods.

A second point of criticism of the over-optimistic McKinsey projection is the assumption that India's savings rate would increase only marginally and reach a plateau by 2015. The McKinsey report is useful in pointing out that India's consumption rate at 62 per cent of GDP is high, comparable to the rate in developed countries like Japan and the United States, and contrasts with the low consumption rate of 30 per cent in China (McKinsey Global Institute 2007, Exhibit 1.5). But some economists would doubt its prediction that this high consumption rate would be maintained with sustained high growth rate of GDP. There are indeed two different questions here: the investment rate needed to sustain the projected growth rate; and the contribution of household savings to the total national savings rate.

The McKinsey report expects the investment rate in the economy to grow in absolute terms but to grow at an equal pace with GDP. The report concedes that India's investment rate had climbed steadily in the few years before 2005, but expects it to stabilize at around 32 per cent of GDP as the Indian economy settles down to a sustainable steady growth of 7.3 per cent. The evidence from the latest

National Accounts is different. The growth rate has been climbing towards 9 per cent and, along with it, there is an increase in the share of investment to 37 per cent or more. It is clear that the optimistic scenario is due to the assumption that the pattern of growth will not change and, in particular, growth will be service sector-led.

India's household savings contribute a very large share of total national savings. At 69 per cent, it was among the highest of a sample of countries including the developed countries and China (Exhibit 2.9). The report rightly expects this contribution of households to diminish as the organized sector becomes a larger share of the growing economy and savings are financed more by the corporate and the public sectors (through the growth of the financial market and the widening tax base, respectively). But one of the more debatable conclusions of the report is that this shift in the composition of savings is unlikely to contribute substantially to a reduction in the projected increase in aggregate consumption.

The final point of criticism of the McKinsey projection is that it is based on a projection of the persistence of the present pattern of development—with growth being led by the service sector. The study makes no reference to the dominance of the non-organized sector in manufacturing in particular, or to any significant change in the role of the missing middle. But, as explained earlier in this chapter, the impact of a continuing existence of the size structure of manufacturing would be substantial on the growth of markets and hence on the overall growth rate of the economy. Furthermore, one result of the tertiary sector-led growth, apart from its sustainability, is its impact on the growing inequality in the distribution of income. Thus, with the persistence of the current pattern of growth, the hopeful scenario of the flattening distribution of income (with the severe weakening of the low income mode and a substantial growth of middle income groups shown in Exhibit 2.5) might be wide of the mark.

6   The impact of the missing middle on inequality

The phenomenon of the missing middle in manufacturing contributes to the process of growing inequality in India in several ways:

- Dualism slows down the rate of growth and the absorption of labour in manufacturing. Historically, manufacturing has taken the leading role in the growth of employment and the absorption of surplus labour from agriculture. The rate of reduction in the proportion of low-income labour in the traditional sectors of the Indian economy, suffering from under-employment, has been slower than it might have been. This has contributed to the maintenance of a large disparity in income levels between the agriculture and the non-agriculture sectors and increased inequality in the growth process (see the Kuznets decomposition of inequality discussed in Chapter 1). Admittedly, the growth of employment in small-scale manufacturing in India has been disproportionately high, and it has contributed significantly to poverty reduction. But the slow absorption of labour in the middle rung of the income distribution has increased inequality—with a large mass of low-income households co-existing with a small fraction of rich ones.
- The dualism in manufacturing, with its bi-polar distribution of employment, itself contributes to inequality within the sector. A more even size distribution of employment (as in East Asian economies) would contribute to greater equality of incomes and wage earnings in this sector.
- The slow growth of output and employment in the formal (non-household) manufacturing sector has meant that the lead in employment restructuring has, as we have seen, been taken by the tertiary sector. It is very much a universal experience that inequality is higher in the tertiary sector, partly because it has a sizable labour force of higher-than-middle education. The recent reversal of the trend to equality in East Asian growth has been ascribed to the change in the evolution of the employment structure, with the tertiary sector changing places with manufacturing as the leading growth sector (see the example of Taiwan in Lin and Orazem 2004). In the Indian case, the contribution of the tertiary sector to overall inequality has increased because of the low supply price of labour to the low-income services sector. This phenomenon is due to the slow reallocation of under-employed labour

from agriculture, and the dominance of the low-income subsector of manufacturing. The low supply price of labour in the poorer segment of the service sector keeps up the demand for these services in middle-income households and contributes to the bi-polar distribution of income, as is the case in the tertiary sector in India. The net result is a higher degree of inequality than would be seen with a more even distribution of employment.[1]

I

The shift of labour from agriculture

Agriculture does not directly contribute a great deal to inequality in the distribution of household expenditure because the distribution of income in this sector is relatively equal. This is consistent with the characteristics of peasant agriculture in Asian economies. This does not, however, mean that the sector's ability to shed labour and reduce the incidence of under-employment is not of major importance in the course of inequality in the economy over time.

We have seen in Chapter 3 that the transfer of labour out of agriculture in India has been on the low side relative to the experience of comparator countries in Asia. This is particularly true with respect to the period of growth of the East Asian countries in the 1960s and 1970s. This relatively slow transfer of labour keeps productivity low in agriculture, which is burdened with a significant degree of surplus labour in agriculture (see Table 5.1, Chapter 5). By itself, this probably does not fuel inequality. In fact, in agrarian economies dominated by self-employed farmers, the slow rate of growth of the modern sector has meant that, while income growth is low, the degree of inequality also stays at low levels. (This has most likely been the trajectory of Indian growth during the colonial era.) With accelerated growth of the modern sector, the between-sector inequality involving the agricultural and the non-agricultural sectors begins to open up. If at the same time the development in manufacturing and tertiary activities is dualistic, as discussed in this book, inequality in the economy increases further through the significant impact of intra-sectoral inequality. Two factors are of significance here: first, the gap in earnings at the base level in the non-agricultural sector, as determined by barriers to movement between sectors; and second, the degree to which dualism develops in manufacturing and services.

Table 6.1 shows the mean difference in average per capita household expenditure (APCE) between the industrial sectors, as well as the degree of inequality of per capita expenditure for the different dates of the NSS. The difference in APCE widened between agriculture and the two non-agricultural sectors between the two dates of the survey—the tertiary sector running ahead of the secondary. This was accompanied by an increase in the degree of inequality in the tertiary sector (which led, as we have seen, in terms of employment and income generated). But while this reallocation increased overall inequality, the between-sector inequality increased its share somewhat (but still accounted for only a small proportion of the total).

Table 6.1 Key statistics of households by broad industry groups, 2004–05 and 1993–94

Sector and inequality	Population share (%)	Income share (%)	Index of mean, APCE	Gini	Theil index	Atkinson A(1)
2004–05						
Primary	0.53	0.42	100.00	0.29	0.17	0.13
Secondary	0.19	0.20	135.17	0.36	0.28	0.20
Tertiary	0.28	0.38	172.42	0.38	0.29	0.21
Inequality (all sectors)	–	–	–	0.36	0.27	0.19
Within-sector inequality	–	–	–	–	0.24	0.17
Between-sector inequality	–	–	–	–	0.03	0.02
Inter-sector inequality as percentage of overall	–	–	–	–	10.98	10.08
1993–94						
Primary	0.60	0.51	100.00	0.29	0.18	0.13
Secondary	0.15	0.16	131.56	0.33	0.22	0.17
Tertiary	0.25	0.32	150.65	0.34	0.23	0.17
Inequality (all sectors)	–	–	–	0.33	0.22	0.16
Within-sector inequality	–	–	–	–	0.20	0.15
Between-sector inequality	–	–	–	–	0.02	0.01
Inter-sector inequality as a percentage of overall	–	–	–	–	7.83	8.07

Source: own calculations from NSS 1993–4 and 2004–05 rounds.

II

Inequality within the non-agricultural sectors

We turn now to the contribution to inequality of the dualistic development in Indian manufacturing. The phenomenon of the missing middle has an impact on inequality from two different routes. As far as the direct effect is concerned, the expectation is that the impact on inequality will be higher in the missing-middle type of size structure than in the East Asian type of even distribution, but that it would be less than in the case of a size structure skewed to the large size group. This is because with the bi-modal distribution we have a larger proportion of employment in the small size groups, whose earnings are quite close to the bulk of the labour force in agriculture and the tertiary sector concentrated at the lower end of the distribution. There is also an indirect impact of the missing middle on inequality—and this works through the relative growth of the tertiary sector. As we have seen, the missing-middle model slows down the demand for the manufactured goods. The consequent depression of the supply price of labour makes the price of services of various types available to consumers relatively low, inducing them to substitute the consumption of services for manufactured goods in their budgets. This would tend to increase the absorption of labour in low-income service activities and would (in conjunction with the growth of high-income services, which this type of development also encourages) increase inequality in the process of growth. In other words, the dualism with the missing-middle model originating in the manufacturing sector is translated into a similar type of dualism in the tertiary sector with an adverse effect on inequality. As we shall see, the impact on inequality through this route has been quantitatively more important in recent Indian development.

Inequality by industry (sector of activity)

The kernel density functions based on the APCE from the NSS for the three rounds are reproduced in Figure 6.1 for the three broad industrial sectors of the economy. While all three graphs show a movement to the right, signifying an increase in household welfare for all expenditure groups (particularly at the bottom of the expenditure distribution), it is apparent that the increase in the APCE of middle and higher expenditure groups is relatively more pronounced for the tertiary sector. This is particularly true of the latest post-reform decade. It suggests an increase in inequality in the tertiary sector relative to the others.

It is interesting to note the contribution of each type of household (distinguished by the principal industry of activity of the head) to the overall inequality of all household welfare (as measured by the APCE). For this, it is not enough to get the weighted average of the inequality measures of the APCE in the three types of households. We need to rank the household in any activity not in terms of the household welfare in that particular activity, but in terms of the household welfare of the total in all activities. This can be done by the computation of "pseudo-Ginis" for each household type (Table 6.2).[2]

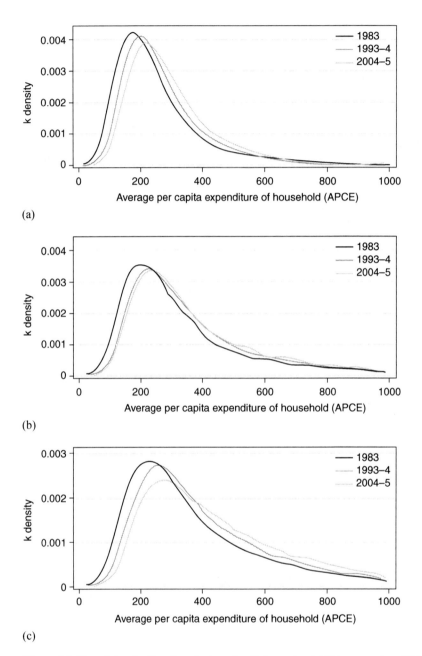

Figure 6.1 Kernel density functions by broad activity sector (a) Primary sector, (b) Secondary sector, (c) Tertiary sector (source: author's calculations from the NSS dataset).

Table 6.2 Contribution to inequality of households by sector of activity

Sector of activity	1983		1993–94		2004–05	
	Pseudo Gini	Gini	Pseudo Gini	Gini	Pseudo Gini	Gini
Primary	0.162	0.078	0.174	0.071	0.166	0.051
Secondary	0.461	0.081	0.446	0.076	0.330	0.065
Tertiary	0.552	0.191	0.555	0.235	0.525	0.262

Source: author's calculations from the NSS dataset for 1983, 1993–94, and 2004–05.

Note
The full results of the exercise are given in the Appendix to this chapter. The column Gini gives the contribution of each sector to the overall Gini. It calculates, for each sector, the share of the sector income in total household income, the pseudo Gini for the sector, and the Gini correlation of the sector with total income.

In all the years that the NSS studied, the contribution of the tertiary sector to overall inequality in the economy is the highest. What is important to note is that the contribution of this sector relative to manufacturing (whose contribution to inequality is large and comes second in importance) has increased dramatically in the post-reform decade.

Finally, we refer to the work of Topalova (2008) at the International Monetary Fund (IMF), which used state-level experience of varying growth patterns to study the causes of the "inclusiveness of growth". The degree of inclusiveness of growth depends on the evenness of growth rate of consumption over the period across household income classes. It is defined in one measure by the difference between the consumption growth rates of, for example, the poorest 30 per cent and the richest 30 per cent of the population. The higher the value of this ratio, the more pro-poor the growth rate would be.

The IMF study used variations across India's states and over time to examine an econometric model if the inclusiveness of growth depended in any way on the relative growth rates of different sectors. Growth rates of GDP per capita and of the three broad sectors were computed for each of the 15 large states of India for four time periods (defined by the dates of the thick rounds of the NSS: 1983–87/88, 1987/88–1993/94, 1993/94–2004/05).[3] The variable "inclusiveness of growth" was then regressed on the various per capita growth rates. State and time period fixed effects were used to control for time-invariant heterogeneity among states and for economy-wide changes. (See Table 6.3.)

Two important conclusions follows from the model estimated above. First, there is no evidence of the speed of growth as such being responsible for any of the different measures of inclusive growth. The coefficient of this variable is close to zero in all of the specifications. Second, of the three sector (industry) growth rates, the real per capita service sector growth is strongly significant and implies a negative impact on pro-poor growth. This result is consistent with the evidence presented above and in Chapter 3, from several cross-section exercises, that the trend in inequality observed in the growth of the Indian economy in recent decades is due to the contribution of the unusually fast growth of the tertiary sector.

Table 6.3 Determinants of growth inclusiveness

	Bottom 10–Top 10		Bottom 20–Top 20		Bottom 30–Top 30		Bottom 50–Top 50	
	(1)	(2)	(3)	(4)	(5)	(6)	(7)	(8)
Real per capita NSDP growth	−0.016 [0.202]	–	0.005 [0.159]	–	0.001 [0.134]	–	0.001 [0.095]	–
Real per capita agriculture growth	–	0.029 [0.072]	–	0.032 [0.051]	–	0.021 [0.040]	–	0.013 [0.026]
Real per capita industry growth	–	0.139 [0.109]	–	0.145 [0.087]	–	0.142* [0.071]	–	0.105** [0.049]
Real per capita services growth	–	−0.591*** [0.182]	–	−0.496*** [0.143]	–	−0.142*** [0.121]	–	−0.292*** [0.083]
Number of observations	45	45	45	45	45	45	45	45

Source: Topalova (2008, Table 5).

Note
All regressions include state and period fixed effects and are weighted by the square root of the number of observations within a state. Robust standard errors in parentheses. Data are from Schedule 1 of NSS 38th, 50th, and 61st rounds.

While the variations in per capita agricultural growth are not significant at all, those in the secondary sector have some significance in the later periods. These findings are consistent with the results presented in Table 6.1 above: that the contribution of the activity sector to inequality in the Indian economy is highest for the tertiary sector followed by the secondary sector, and that agriculture has by far the smallest contribution to it.

Why is inequality higher in the tertiary sector?

Formal and informal jobs within the tertiary sector

We have already discussed the heterogeneous nature of activities in the tertiary sector. An important aspect of this is the co-existence of formal and informal types of employment in this sector. It might be useful to know if the proportions of these two types of employment are as substantial in the tertiary as in the man-ufacturing sector of the Indian economy. Since it is well known that the gap in earnings between the two categories of employment is substantial, a significant proportion of employment in each is a good indication of the extent of dispersion of earnings and hence of inequality.

The 55th (1999–2000) and the 61st (2004–05) rounds of the NSS enable us to identify workers in the public sector. The questionnaire obtained information on the type of establishment in which a worker was employed. We grouped workers in all public and semi-public establishments as being in the formal sector. These rounds of the NSS also reported for the first time the employment size of the establishment in which a worker was employed. We take ten workers as the cut-off point, with those in establishments of larger size being in the formal sector. For the large group of self-employed workers, we adopt the usual definition in terms of the worker's education. Those with lower secondary education or less are in the informal sector, and the more highly educated (which would include the professionals) are in the formal sector. These criteria help us to give a rough picture of the composition of tertiary sector employment for the year 1999–2000 across formal and informal sectors, and the changes seen in the latest 2004–05 round. The data are given in Table 6.4.

Table 6.4 shows that the formal sector contributes one-third of total tertiary sector employment and its share over the last five years has gone up by three percentage points. In contrast, the formal sector contributes one-quarter of total manufacturing employment and its share has gone up only marginally. Clearly, most of the formal jobs are being created in the tertiary sector. This increasing share of employment in the tertiary sector, which was already higher than in manufacturing, clearly is related to the higher inequality in the former.

Aggregation of subsectors within tertiary activities

It might be suggested that we are getting the result about income inequality being higher in the tertiary sector because we are putting together the array of

Table 6.4 Share of formal sector in tertiary and manufacturing employment (%)

Sector	Share of formal in tertiary employment	
	1999–2000	*2004–05*
Rural tertiary	11.0	13.3
Urban tertiary	22.6	23.5
Total tertiary	33.6	36.8

Sector	Share of formal in total manufacturing employment	
	1999–2000	*2004–05*
Rural manufacturing	7.9	8.8
Urban manufacturing	18.2	18.1
Total manufacturing	26.1	26.9

Source: own calculations from NSS 1999–2000 and the 2004–05 rounds. Note that the formal and informal sector employment cannot be identified for the earlier rounds of the NSS. The definitions are as given in Mazumdar and Sarkar (2008, p. 226).

different activities in this sector—aggregating traditional tertiary activities with more modern ones. The dispersion of earnings obviously reflects the heterogeneous nature of activities in this sector, as we have already noted. But it is important to emphasize the point that, while this is undoubtedly a contributing factor, earnings dispersion is significant in all the four one-digit classifications of the tertiary sector. A perusal of the kernel density function distributions in Mazumdar and Sarkar (2008) shows that in the 1999–2000 round of the NSS (the 55th round) the dispersion of APCE (our measure of earnings proxied by the average per capita expenditure of households in the different subsectors) was, as expected, highest in business services, followed by community, social, and personal services, and the lowest in trade, hotels, and restaurants. But the magnitude of the dispersal was still substantial in the latter.

III

Determinants of inequality and its increase in the post-reform era

Wage inequality

Wage labour is less than half of the employed workforce in India, the majority being the self-employed. It is somewhat more important in the urban sector (Kundu and Mohanan 2009). Further, there are two different categories of wage earners: the regulars, who get contractual employment over a period of time, and the casuals, who are employed on a day-to-day basis as required. While casual labour is the most important category of employment in the rural sector, it also figures significantly in the urban economy. A major trend in the post-reform decade has been an increase in regular wage employment of females in regular wage jobs in the urban areas, which has come mostly at the expense of casual wage work.

The degree of inequality is much higher among regular wage earners, and has been increasing dramatically in the post-reform decade, while the trend in inequality for casual workers has been basically non-existent.

Vasudeva-Dutta (2005) analysed the determinants of inequality for wage earners only from the NSS rounds for 1983 and 1999–2000, focusing on the sample of male wage earners in the working age group (15–65). The study followed the standard Fields (2003) method of assessing the contribution of different explanatory variables for accounting for inequality among two samples: regular and casual workers.[4] The results from this work clearly show the difference between the markets for regular and casual wage earners. Human capital variables, education, and age in particular play a stronger role in the determination of the earnings of regular workers (age accounted for about one-quarter and education for one-third of the explained variance in 1999). The other important factor was industry affiliation (contributing another quarter). By contrast, human capital factors were of much less importance for casual workers (only age had any positive contribution, but at a much lower level of around 7 per cent). The single most important explanatory variable was geographical difference (the state of residence contributing no less than 62 per cent for casual workers against only 3.5 per cent for regular workers). In any event, the earnings function was much more effective in accounting for earnings differences among regular workers, explaining just over half the variance in their earnings (whereas it explained one-third of the variance for casual workers).

Although the wage gap between regular workers with graduate and primary school qualifications increased between 1983 and 1999 in Vasudeva-Dutta (2005), the share of education in the explanation of the variance declined from 23 per cent to 17 per cent. The importance of age increased as did that of industry affiliation. The study confirms that the increase in the "contribution of selection coupled with the fall in that of education suggest a rising importance of the unobservable for regular workers, possibly linked to the process of trade liberalization". Sarkar (2009) undertook a similar decomposition of factors that contribute to earnings disparity of all wage earners (regular and casual workers taken together) for the NSS round of 2004–05. Figure 6.2 shows the relative importance of the significant factors contributing to wage inequality. The regression equation for weekly wage earnings explained about 60 per cent of the variance in 2004–05.

The two major factors that contributed to differences in earnings were educational level and intensity of work (total days of work). Casual workers are paid only for the days they actually work, and thus the earnings of the casual workers are directly affected by the number of days of work. This factor had turned out to be the second most important factor contributing to earnings inequality. The level of education emerged as the most dominant factor contributing to the level of inequality in earnings of wage workers.

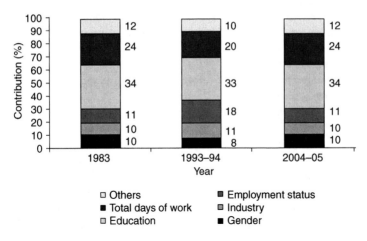

Figure 6.2 Contributions of significant variables to wage inequality (source: Sarkar (2009)).

The employment status (regular or casual) was the third most important factor. It showed that, even after controlling days of work, daily wage differential between regular and casual was substantial. Interestingly, the relative importance of these factors in explaining part of the contribution to earning inequality had not changed over the last two decades. The contribution of inter-industry disparity and gender differences in earning inequality were almost of equal importance. The education factor is the combined effect of all years of schooling. When Sarkar (2009) differentiated the education variable by levels, it was observed that the contribution to inequality of workers with education level "graduate and above" had gone up from 52 per cent in 1983 to 72 per cent in 1993–94 and further to 82 per cent in 2004–05. It shows that, even after controlling for several factors of location, gender, status of work, industry, and age, the relative earnings of workers of graduate level and above had registered huge increases in the last two decades of growth. It was also observed that the relative education premium of workers with only secondary education had declined substantially in the pre-reform period (1983 to 1993–94).

Inequality in household welfare (APCE)

This section extends the above analysis for the whole population. Since income measures are not available for the NSS, the dependent variable used was an index of household welfare, measured by the average expenditure per capita of the households. A problem with this measure is that it would be affected in a problematic way by the size of the household. A large household would show a low APCE but this effect is exaggerated because large household size is associated with a large number of dependent children. The impact of the number of children is exaggerated by the per capita measure of expenditure. A simple way of dealing with this problem is to allow for the influence of varying earner–dependant ratios in the household or the proportions of working-age members in the household. Unfortunately, the NSS records have an incomplete coverage of the ages of household members.

One option was to use household size as an explanatory variable in the model. Further, in the absence of detailed information on the main earner, all the characteristics used as explanatory variables referred to the head of the household. The dependent variable in this model was APCE, and the explanatory variables included age and age squared, household size and size squared, social categories or castes, religion, regions of the country, education, major industry groups, and labour market status (self-employed, wage labour, etc.) Only age and household size were used as continuous variables, the rest were used as dummy variables. The model explained 36 per cent of the variation in APCE in the rural areas and as much as 43 per cent in the urban areas.[5]

It appears that household size and education account for the major part of the explained variation in the model. Evidently these two variables are picking up some of the explanatory powers of other significant variables in the regression. Omitting "household size" only decreases the variance explained by the regression. It is gratifying to see that the relative importance of the various factors contributing to the inequality of APCE is unchanged. There are, however, some important differences in the factor inequality weights (the share of the variance explained by the explanatory variables) in the results reported above for the two different samples (the one confined to wage earners and the other embracing all households). It is, of course, expected that force status (self-employed, wage, etc.) would play a more significant part in the explanation of the variance in the equation for all households than in the one confined to wage earners. But some of the other explanatory factors which attain significance in the household welfare equation (APCE) need to be specially noticed. Both social category and region play a significant role in the explanation of APCE, although much smaller than education in the wage equation.

Another notable difference between the APCE and the wage models which should be emphasized is that while industry, apart from education, plays a major role in the explanation of the variance in the wage equation, this is not so in the APCE equation. This is partly because the correlation between industry and the other significant variables is stronger in the sample of all household heads than for the regular wage earners. Agriculture, for example, is likely to have a relatively more substantial presence for the lower social classes than for regular wage earners. Regional differences are similarly more significantly correlated with industry for all households than for the regular wage workers.

Conclusions from the regression-based models

The overwhelming point emerging from the regression-based models analysed above is the determining importance of education in the explanation of inequality both for all households and for regular wage workers. It is clear that the different contributions to inequality by the three major sectors of employment which have been discussed earlier in the chapter work through the education variable. This is indeed the conclusion of a detailed study by the Asian Development Bank (2010b) with similar regression models, but with slightly different variables.[6]

Thus we can say that if inequality is higher in the manufacturing and the tertiary sectors compared to agriculture, as we have seen, this is to a large extent because the variance in educational attainments among those working in the former is greater. It should be noted that both informal and formal sector workers are included in the classification of wage earners or household heads by industry of occupation. Casual wage workers are, however, mostly found in the informal activities. The degree of inequality among them is much less than for regular wage earners and, as already mentioned, this is due to the low variance among them of their educational attainments.

IV

The role of educated labour

The conclusion that the impact of sectoral changes in employment on the trend in inequality is permeated through the education variable implies that our analysis must turn to the role of education in the determination of earnings.

Occupation–education matrix

Table 6.5 gives the distribution of the principal earners in each sector by their reported educational levels. The table dramatically brings out the importance of educated labour in the tertiary sector. It employs disproportionately labour with more than middle-school education. The difference with even the secondary sector in the use of such labour is enormous. The comparison with the proportions given in parentheses for the 1983–84 round shows that this role of the tertiary sector in the preferential employment of educated labour existed even more strongly at this earlier date. In 1983–84, 76 per cent of the workers who were graduates were in the tertiary sector—and 20 years later this proportion has come down only slightly to 73 per cent (the corresponding percentages for the secondary industries were 21.4 and 20.8).

The same story of heavily disproportionate use of workers with secondary education in the tertiary sector is found in both years.

We conclude that the pattern of development in India with its relatively higher employment growth in the tertiary sector is a major element in the accelerating demand for educated labour. This can be expected to lead directly to increasing inequality if at the same time the rate of return to education is high, and even more so if it is increasing.

Table 6.5 Percentage of principal earners in each sector distributed by education levels, 2004–05 (1983–84)

Sector/education	Up to primary	Middle	Secondary	Graduate and above	Total
Primary	76.3 (90.7)	13.3 (6.3)	8.8 (2.6)	1.5 (0.4)	100.0
Secondary	59.8 (75.6)	19.5 (12.6)	15.8 (9.0)	4.9 (2.8)	100.0
Tertiary	38.5 (54.9)	17.5 (15.5)	26.8 (19.5)	17.2 (10.1)	100.0
Total	63.8 (81.8)	15.5 (9.0)	14.6 (6.7)	6.1 (2.5)	100.0

Source: own calculations from the data tapes of the NSS.

Return to education

An important part of the diagnosis of the growing inequality is clearly the rising return to education. The Asian Development Bank (2008) has presented results of an extended analysis of the NSS data on the trends in APCE in which the households are classified by the characteristics of household heads, including their education (see Table 6.6).

Table 6.6 Average monthly per capita expenditure (APCE) at 2004 prices and rates of change

A. Rural

Groups	1983	1993	2004	Annual change (%)	
				1983–93	1993–2004
Overall	774.98	837.33	955.74	0.74	1.21
Level of education					
Below primary	713.82	759.55	828.66	0.59	0.79
Primary	887.18	924.98	1013.01	0.40	0.83
Secondary	1133.68	1145.46	1244.41	0.10	0.76
Tertiary and above	1258.53	1415.91	1746.64	1.13	1.93

B. Urban

Groups	1983	1993	2004	Annual change (%)	
				1983–93	1993–2004
Overall	864.01	981.02	1184.14	1.22	1.73
Level of education					
Below primary	658.77	689.85	742.62	0.44	0.67
Primary	794.55	867.96	960.00	0.85	0.92
Secondary	1117.06	1182.06	1362.71	0.54	1.30
Tertiary and above	1529.51	1697.02	2147.62	0.99	2.16

Source: ADB (2008, Tables 4 and 5).

Note
The absolute numbers are in 2004 rupees (the deflator used in all cases is for urban Delhi).

It is clear that, while the APCE of households with tertiary levels of education was already growing at a higher rate in the decade of 1983–93, their differential rate of growth in the subsequent decade of 1993–2004 has increased significantly. This growth is more marked in the urban areas, where the households with secondary education have also experienced a significantly higher growth rate.

The volume of employment and the price of labour in any subsector are of course affected by both the demand and the supply sides of the market. On the supply side, a major element is the structure of education and its development over time. These are to some extent determined by non-market forces, especially government policies and patterns of investment. This is a topic we need not pursue at this point. For our purposes, it is sufficient to note that the rate of return to both secondary and post-secondary education has increased in the second decade, that a significant cause of this acceleration has been the relatively higher growth of the tertiary sector in India's growth experience, and that this has been one of the major causes of the trend to increased inequality.

Appendix

Gini coefficient for total income inequality, G, can be represented as $G = \text{sigma}(Sk*Gk*Rk)$, where Sk represents the share of source k in total income, Gk (the pseudo-Gini) is the source Gini corresponding to the distribution of income from source k, and Rk is the Gini correlation of income from source k with the distribution of total income. Note that the pseudo-Gini for any income component is similar to the Gini coefficient for that component, except that individual units are ranked in terms of their total income rather than component income.

The influence of any income-earning activity upon total income inequality depends on:

- how important the income source is with respect to total income (Sk)
- how equally or unequally distributed the income source is (Gk)
- how the income source and the distribution of total income are correlated (Rk).

The Gini coefficient of the individual sectors is given in the last column of Table 6.A1, and the overall Gini (for the economy) is given in the last row of this column. The column "Share" is the proportion of the sector Gini to the overall Gini. The column called "% Change" gives the change in sectoral Gini for a marginal change in the share of this sector to total GDP. This last magnitude can be shown to be equal to the sector's share of the Gini minus the sector's share of GDP. (The algebra is spelled out in Chapter 13 in the discussion of inequality by sectors in Vietnam.)

Table 6.A1 Contribution to inequality of households in different industry groups

A. 1983

Sector	Sk	Gk	Rk	Share	% change	Pseudo Gini Gk*Rk	Gini sk*Gk*Rk
Primary	0.4784	0.5972	0.2713	0.2219	−0.2565	0.1620	0.0775
Secondary	0.1756	0.9030	0.5106	0.2317	0.0561	0.4611	0.0810
Tertiary	0.3461	0.8283	0.6661	0.5465	0.2004	0.5517	0.1910
All						0.3494	

B. 1993–94

Sector	Sk	Gk	Rk	Share	% change	Pseudo Gini Gk*Rk	Gini Sk*Gk*Rk
Primary	0.4070	0.6623	0.2620	0.1853	−0.2217	0.1735	0.0706
Secondary	0.1701	0.9027	0.4939	0.1989	0.0288	0.4458	0.0758
Tertiary	0.4229	0.7950	0.6981	0.6158	0.1929	0.5550	0.2347
All							0.3812

C. 2004–05

Sector	Sk	Gk	Rk	Share	% change	Pseudo Gini Gk*Rk	Gini Sk*Gk*Rk
Primary	0.305	0.7406	0.2235	0.1339	−0.1711	0.1655	0.0505
Secondary	0.196	0.8699	0.3798	0.1717	−0.0243	0.3304	0.0648
Tertiary	0.499	0.7491	0.7005	0.6944	0.1954	0.5247	0.2618
All							0.3771

7 Causes of dualism in Indian manufacturing

What are the major factors causing the emergence of dualism: the phenomenon of the missing middle and the unusual productivity gap between the small and the large units? What are the reasons for its persistence over time, even when the reform process reducing some of the strength of the causes of dualism has been eroded?

I

Protection of small-scale units

The protection of small-scale units has been an important aspect of Indian industrial policy since independence. It has taken the form of reservation of a large number of items for production in small units and the provision of incentives (fiscal, financial, and legislative) as long as the units stay below a certain size. The threshold size was first defined in terms of the enterprise employment size. In later years, it was changed to a definition based on capital size. On the one hand, the package of measures provided an umbrella for the establishment of a large small-scale sector (and, in particular, non-household units employing fewer than 20 workers using less mechanized technology), and on the other, it discouraged such units from expanding beyond a threshold size. The policies provided an incentive over a long period of time for entrepreneurs to expand horizontally with more small units, rather than vertically with larger middle-sized units (see Little *et al.* 1987 and Mazumdar 1991 for details).

The reservation policy targeted consumer goods industries as the Mahalanobis model suggested (see the discussion in Chapter 1). The policy was implemented in the Second Five-Year Plan in the 1960s and governed Indian industrial policy until the reforms of the 1990s. The policy developed as more and more lines of production were added to the reserved list. At its peak, no fewer than 850 lines of production were reserved for exclusive production in the small-scale sector, and the capacity of large units in the organized or formal sector was frozen at existing levels.

The consequence of this policy was far-reaching. It led directly to product market segmentation of a fairly rigid kind. Consumer goods (particularly those of mass consumption) were produced exclusively for the small-scale units. The policy of dual protection also prohibited the importing of such items from foreign countries. The organized sector of manufacturing produced intermediate and capital goods. Export licenses and some preferential systems did exist for the manufacturers irrespective of size, but examples of the formal sector being enthusiastic about entering the market for basic consumer goods like South East Asia (or China or Bangladesh today) are very rare. The evidence given in detail in Chapter 4 shows the extraordinary persistence of this basic pattern of product market segmentation in Indian manufacturing to this day.

The policy of reservation was effectively dismantled in the reform process initiated in the late 1980s and after the liberalization of 1991. What explains the continued dual size structure in Indian manufacturing?

II

Labour laws in the formal sector

Labour legislation has been traditionally at the top of the list of proximate causes of the phenomenon, and its importance persists since the reforms have not touched this body of regulations. The present legal framework consists of major acts and a number of minor state-level laws. Most of these laws apply to all units under the umbrella of the *Factory Act*, which covers all workers in enterprises in the registered sector employing ten or more workers using power, or 20 or more not using power. Additionally, the *Industrial Development Act* with its job security legislation section applies to units with 100 or more workers. Both types of legislation would impose costs on units increasing beyond the threshold sizes.

Laws affecting wages and benefits

The basic wage scales in the formal sector have been set by industry-wide wage boards, which provide a tripartite framework for the setting of occupation-specific wage scales in major industries. Actual earnings include supplementary benefits (some of which are negotiated by employers and labour unions), but others are legislated by a number of acts which are revised from time to time. These include the 1923 *Workmen's Compensation Act*, the 1948 *Employees State Insurance Act*, and the 1952 *Employees Provident Fund Act*. The courts backing up this legislative framework of wage-setting have been reasonably strong and pro-worker. The net result has been that average earnings (including benefits) in the formal sector have been substantially in excess of those in the informal sector.

The evidence on wage differentials shows that, while wages increase along with productivity, the extent of the size-related wage difference is not nearly as much as that of the productivity differential. There are two reasons for this: first, the industrial composition of the DME of the ASI sectors is substantially differ-ent. The DME establishments concentrate on light consumer goods industries and the productivity differentials by size for this group are much smaller than for other heavier industries. Second, DME (and the smaller ASI units) employ a smaller proportion of skilled and/or experienced workers.

Further, not all of the wage differential can be traced to institutional impact. Workers in the formal manufacturing sector obviously have higher skills and human capital. In fact, the wage differential in favour of modern large-scale factories had been established well before the coming of institutions or state intervention in Indian markets (Mazumdar 1973). The difference in efficiency wages between the informal and the formal sectors would be much smaller than the observed gross differential. Further, the chicken-and-egg problem diminishes the causal effect of institutions and of efficiency wage considerations on earnings. The desire to select higher quality workers might partly precede the institutional intervention, but on the other hand might be prompted as a response to the elevation of wages by institutional factors.

In fact, individual firms decide where to locate themselves in the efficiency–wage space and the point of their location would vary by the characteristic of the firm and the industry in question. We would expect larger and older firms to opt in favour of a core labour force of high productivity, and they would have the resources and the experience to invest in the creation of a carefully selected high-efficiency labour force. Smaller firms, and those in less skill-intensive industries, would have a labour force of lower wage and efficiency. Wage differentials between the formal (DME) and the formal (ASI) sectors in India, and within the formal by size groups, would then vary by type of industry. This is what we find from the data on wages available in the official surveys. This is illustrated in Table 7.1.

It can, however, be legitimately argued that, while larger firms can neutralize at least part of the higher cost of institutionally determined wages by selecting a higher quality of workers, this is likely to be possible only over a period of time by established units. Smaller units, wanting to increase the size, could indeed be deterred from expansion by the prospect of higher gross wages in the short to medium term.

Laws affecting security of employment

It has been suggested that the laws relating to job security in the formal sector have been more important in raising the effective cost of labour in the formal sector, slowing down employment growth in this sector and discouraging small firms from graduating from the informal sector.

The 1948 *Industrial Disputes Act* states that units employing more than 100 workers require authorization from the government for retrenchment, layoff, and closure. The legislation adds to the fixed cost of employment of regular workers in formal manufacturing units. Many firms have to maintain an administrative wing to deal with the problem of retrenchment with inspectors, labour boards, and ultimately the judiciary. Clearly the burden of such costs would vary inversely with firm size. The possibility of such dealings with labour courts

Table 7.1 Wages of directly employed workers in private firms 2004–05 (DME = 100)

Industry	DME <10	10–49	50–99	100–199	200–499	500–999	1000+	Total ASI
Food and beverages (15)	100	112	130	136	214	281	183	**170**
Tobacco and related (16)	100	144	160	163	246	221	184	**185**
Textile products (17)	100	121	128	138	160	182	210	**169**
Wearing apparel (18)	100	100	99	89	91	88	95	–
Chemicals and products (24)	100	123	160	154	237	415	543	**247**
Basic metals (27)	100	115	112	166	330	458	390	**213**
Metal products (28)	100	110	143	157	240	359	457	**246**
Machinery n.e.s. (29)	100	134	156	211	277	366	489	**243**
All industries	**100**	**124**	**142**	**153**	**206**	**260**	**294**	**198**

Source: NSS (Unorganized Sector Survey) and ASI.

would be a significant deterrent for small firms to expand beyond the point at which they would come under the coverage of the job security legislation. Thus it has been a well-known practice among small-scale entrepreneurs to expand horizontally by setting up more units rather than expanding the employment size of their enterprise.

The administration of the act is the joint responsibility of the central government and the states. In fact, individual states have introduced their own modifications about the provision of job security, and implementation has varied from state to state. Apart from the varying effectiveness of inspection, the most important means of easing the grip of the job security legislation has been the treatment of contract workers. Contract workers, temporaries (with fewer than 240 days of work in any 365-day period), and *badlis* (substitutes) are exempt from the provisions of the legislation. The *Contract Regulation and Abolition Act* was enacted to control the use of non-permanent workers but, under section 10 of the act, individual states were given the opportunity to introduce their own regulations about the industries in which the job security law was to be applied strictly. The result has been a substantial increase in the use of contract workers in recent years—from 12 per cent in 1985 to 23 per cent in 2002 (World Bank 2010, Figure 5.1), and the proportion of contract workers used in formal manufacturing has varied significantly from state to state.

Interstate variations: the Beasley–Burgess studies

Besley and Burgess (2004) (B–B) exploited the interstate variations in amendments to the laws to use the degree of strictness of the laws to study their impact on economic outcomes in formal manufacturing. This work, however, considered only *de jure* variations. Ahsan and Pages (2007) have sought to extend this work to include interstate variations in de facto differences in the implementation of regulations as revealed by the varying proportions of contract workers. Both sets of studies find a significant negative effect of the net bias of regulation on state-level employment and value added growth in formal manufacturing. They also find that a lower level of labour protection is associated with higher elasticity of demand.

Topalova (2008) used the amended B–B classification of states as pro-worker, pro-employer, or neutral, to explain the ratio of tertiary to manufacturing output over the period 1980–2004. State and year fixed effects were used in the regression. The strong result was that the (lagged) regulation dummy was significantly negative. The service sector was seen to expand more quickly than the industrial sector in states that amended regulations in favour of workers. "This is logical, as the Industrial Disputes Act applies to manufacturing workers, but not to service workers" (ibid., Table 7, p. 17). The slower growth of the manufacturing sector is partly due to the discouragement of the graduation of small-scale establishments (particularly DME units) to expand into the formal sector.

While the recent extensions of the original B–B analysis are impressive and tend to support the general conclusion about the negative role of legislation, extensive doubts about the methodology remain in the discussions of this type of exercise. Quite apart from technical problems of econometric estimation, substantive points have been raised in the literature about the method of construction of the indices of state-level amendments to the legislation. It should be noted that all the studies referred to above share the methodology used in the construction of the indices. Some of the major points about the deficiencies of the analysis are discussed below.

The specification of the dependent variable

Most of the studies consider the growth of manufacturing employment as being identical as the growth rate of workers employed by ASI (organized sector) enterprises. Thus the growth rate of manufacturing employment in the large unorganized sector is not considered at all. Admittedly, regulations will affect organized sector employment more intensely. But it should be apparent from the arguments developed in Chapter 4 and elsewhere in Part II that employment in the organized sector will be affected by other factors, notably the growth of those product categories in which the ASI sector specializes. The growth rate of both value added and employment in this subsector of manufacturing in individual states might indeed be affected by state-specific variables, including the varying incentives given to location in some states rather than others. A relevant point to emphasize is that an awareness of the structure of manufacturing should suggest that the dependent variable to specify is the proportion of total manufacturing employment (in the ASI and DME sectors together), which in fact is found in the DME sector. If regulations are biting, we would expect them to affect this variable positively, after controlling for state-specific factors which influence location of ASI industries.

Weakness in the treatment of the state-level intensity of regulations

The following is a summary of the critique which has been discussed in the literature:[1]

1   Non-commensurability of different pieces of reforms. Even when limited to one class of legislation (such as the *Industrial Disputes Act* dealing with security of tenure), major reforms are rated at the same level as minor ones in this methodology.
2   Since state legislation is meant to supplement central legislation, it is often difficult to determine if a particular reform is more in the nature of clarification/reiteration rather than a genuine substantial extension.
3   The methodology attaches a score of just +1 or −1 to state amendments to the act in a particular year, and then cumulates them over time to calculate the regulatory index in the state. The methodology, which results in a state just scoring +1 or −1, creates problems when states make more than one amendment in a year.

With this procedure, 113 amendments collapse to 19 episodes of legislative changes within the period of the B–B econometric study (1958–97), four of them in West Bengal alone, with the remaining 15 spread over nine other states over 40 years. Changes in the B–B index are thus infrequent, and of equal magnitude (either +1 or –1) in the ten states in which amendments occurred, regardless of their relative importance or the extent to which they were implemented.

(Bhattacharjea 2006, p. 9)

4   The cumulative scores up to year t-1 are used as dummies in the regression model, with the observed state and year-specific employment or output growth as the independent variable. Does it mean that the impact of the amendments is felt with a one-year lag and is exhausted after that year? It seems that the impact would be less over a period of years if the amendments were bunched in one particular year rather than spread out over several years.

5   More generally, it is probably quite misleading to concentrate on one, albeit important, piece of legislation (the *Industrial Disputes Act*). Bhattacharjea (2006) points out several serious errors in misspecification of states as being "pro" or otherwise because the methodology has chosen to ignore other pieces of legislation and their implementation.

Lack of attention to interstate differences in the implementation of laws

The assumption behind the B–B analysis is that the significant player in labour regulation is the state government and that its success in enforcing the regulation is strongly correlated with its administrative decisions to enact amendments to the *Industrial Disputes Act* (IDA) as discussed above. This, however, is a highly simplistic view of the political process governing the treatment of labour in the state concerned. This process involves a complex relationship between the political parties, the organizations, and the administration at various levels of the state.

The issues can be illustrated by considering briefly the case of West Bengal. We found in Chapter 4 that this state had the largest share of employment in manufacturing in the DME sector, such that we can reasonably conclude that there have been powerful forces which have led to the lack of incentive to employ in the ASI (organized) sector. This is particularly significant when we remember that this state was very important in developing large-scale manufacturing in the past.

While West Bengal has not been at the forefront of amending the IDA regulations, it is rather naïve to suggest that the decline in employment in organized manufacturing is mostly due to the support of job security of labour in this subsector. The state has been only one (and perhaps not even the leading) player in the political process affecting labour. The other two players have been the ruling political party (the CPM) and the unions which it supported. The CPM has had an unbroken rule in the state over nearly three decades and has developed close relationships with several state institutions including the unions. Its cadre penetrated the leadership of the unions and became deeply involved in the process of selection and deployment of labour. In fact, the party domination of labour institutions was not confined to the organized sector but permeated the DME enterprises as well. But while the all-India and multinational enterprises exited the state altogether in response to the constant interference of the party–union nexus in all aspects of deployment, the DME units with their more local base had to adapt themselves to the conditions. The dominance of the DME subsector is then more the result of the impact of the party–union nexus than of any legislation and its implementation by the state.[2]

Ignoring regulations other than IDA

The original B–B analysis concentrated on the regulations on job security. This ignored two types of regulations which clearly would affect the enterprises: other regulations relating to labour and regulations affecting factors other than labour.

Other regulations

Several writers on Indian labour issues have pointed out that IDA is only one of many labour laws enacted by the central government and many more promulgated by individual states. Given this plethora of labour laws, to concentrate on just the job security aspect of the IDA might indeed be a distraction (Popola and Debroy, among others, in Debroy and Kaushik 2005). Dougherty (2008) reports on an OECD attempt to take a more comprehensive look at reforms of the entire spectrum of laws thorough a customized survey instrument to "identify the areas in which Indian states have made specific discrete changes to the implementation and administration of laws". The survey sought information from each state about changes made in eight major labour law areas, identifying 50 specific objects of possible reform (see Dougherty 2008, Annex 1 for details).

The overall score for all states was just 21. Looking at the relative importance of the main areas of reform, the study found those dealing with IDA accounted for just 20 per cent of the total. Reforms of laws governing the use of contract workers were just as important (ibid., Figure 4, p. 17). The interstate variations in the total score extended from a low of 14 for West Bengal and Chhattisgarh to a high of 28 for Uttar Pradesh. There was a bunching of 11 of the 20 states covered in the narrow range of 20–24. The study found that there was a significant correlation between an index of flows in the organized ASI sector and the state scores, in spite of this bunching (ibid., Figure 5, p. 19).[3] But the analysis did not address the question of whether the regulations had a statistical relationship to the proportion of manufacturing employment in the DME relative to the ASI sector, the variable which we have identified as the appropriate one to consider.

Another important point to note is that the average score of 21 against the maximum of 50 suggests that there were many areas of regulation which were not subject to any significant amendments in any state. In particular, it is likely that the provision in the *Factory Act*, which specifies that all registered factories in the covered sector are liable for payment of social security benefits, could be a significant deterrent to "graduation" and does not seem to have been touched by the reforms.

III

Non-labour regulations

The preoccupation with labour regulations distracts attention from other fields in which regulations exist and are enforced at state levels. These range from laws covering land use to licensing procedures for starting a firm and to control over numerous business practices. Surveys of sample businesses carried out by the World Bank, reported below, find these non-regulations to be of much greater concern for formal sector firms.

The World Bank surveys

A more reliable (if less sophisticated) body of evidence about the importance of legislation in India comes from the regular World Bank surveys: the *Investment Climate Assessment* (ICA) surveys, which seek the opinions of business owners/managers through structured questionnaires, and the *Doing Business* surveys, which record the assessment of lawyers and other professionals with long experience with the laws and procedures affecting business operations.

The ICA surveys found that India's overall ranking in terms of business climate was fairly low—134 out of a total list of 175 countries (compare this to the ranking of 29 for South Africa, 121 for Brazil, and 93 for China) (World Bank ICA survey 2006). Corruption tops the list of the five most important business constraints reported (37 per cent), followed by power shortage (29 per cent), tax rate (28 per cent), tax administration (27 per cent), and policy uncertainty (21 per cent). Labour regulations are not on the list for India.

The report remarks that India's reforms have been initiated by the central government but the implementation of the regulations are still the responsibility of state governments, and the administration of the regulatory framework leaves room for elaborate opportunities for corruption. (This way, the "License Raj" of India's old controlled economy has been succeeded by the "Inspector Raj" at the state level.) It might be suggested that the prime difficulty pointed out by Indian businesses (corruption) partly refers to the bribes needed to be paid to inspectors to evade laws. But the important point to note is that labour regulations are only a part of the total regulatory framework and businesses seem to think that difficulties related to these are not the most important.

Doing Business agrees with this assessment. Its 2010 report ranks India highest at 169 in terms of the difficulty of starting a business and at 175 for dealing with construction permits, against a rank of 104 in terms of the problem of employing workers (World Bank *Doing Business* survey 2010, p. 5). While the conclusions from these World Bank surveys and indicators would seem to show that this is not at the top of the list of the difficulties faced by private businesses in India, two important caveats should be mentioned:

1   Ahsan and Pages (2007) were able to break up firms' perceptions of regulations by their employment size groups. This analysis of the 2002 ICA survey revealed that the score attached to regulation as a constraint to growth increased progressively with firm size group, from around 60 for the 1–9 size group to 100 for the 100+ group. For the latter, regulation was as important as electricity problems, although corruption, tax rates, administration, and policy uncertainty scored higher.
2   The ICA report of 2006 emphasizes the point that managers of firms in the formal sector represent a biased sample, insofar as they have already succeeded in establishing their existence in the subsector. They do not provide an evaluation of the constraints faced by firms which seek to grow in size from the informal to the formal sector.

IV

Conclusion on the impact of regulations

Our best judgment from the available evidence is then twofold:

• Both small and large firms have been able to adjust to the incidence of legislation. The problems of adjustment seem to increase with firm size, as with other types of regulation.
• The fact that firms are able to adjust to the regulations does not mean that laws are not a factor in the upward mobility of firms from small to large. But factors other than regulations might be equally, if not more, important in discouraging such mobility.

Before coming to these other factors, it might be useful to elaborate on how large and small firms have adjusted to the laws with some success.

Adjustment to regulations

The way firms adjust to the labour laws is not really due to loopholes in the laws, but in the governance, or the way the laws have been administered.

Large firms

Indian manufacturing firms in the formal sector have long used the distinction between the permanent core of their labour force and a sizable complement of temporaries. The distinction is similar to the distinction made in universities between tenured and non-tenured staff. The permanent core typically enjoys social security benefits as laid down by the law and has a seniority-driven wage scale, such that its earnings are significantly above those of the temporaries. In addition, the permanent staff enjoy greater job security and have a low rate of turnover. Mazumdar (1973) described this system as it had traditionally prevailed in the Bombay textile industry in the first half of the twentieth century—long before the coming of post-independence regulations. The temporaries constituted perhaps a quarter or more of the workforce employed in the factories at any point in time. In addition to the reduction in the average wage, the system helped in at least two other important ways: the adjustment of the input to fluctuations in demand not just over the cycle, but also over day-to-day variations; and recruitment of requisite quality to the permanent core.

In recent years, Indian industry in the ASI sector seems to have ramped up its use of various types of non-regular workers, including temporaries, casuals, and contract workers. The incentive for the greater of use of non-regular workers has been a spate of amendments to the IDA permitting the use of non-regular workers under certain conditions in a number of states (see Ahsan and Pages 2007 for a listing of the major amendments). A survey by the Institute of Human Development of about 900 firms spread across ten states found that non-permanent workers comprised 36 per cent of total employees (Karan and Sarkar 2000).

Small firms

Turning to the adjustment in small firms, we note that the legal limit of employment in DME units is 6–9 workers, but in fact the size distribution of employment as reported by the official survey of the NSS shows that only just over a half of total employment is in the group with fewer than ten workers. Over one-third of all DME employment is in the size group of 10–19 workers and a significant proportion is in larger units. Further, the proportion in the 10+ size groups seems to have increased over the decade 1994–95 to 2004–05. Evidently, the formal requirement that firms employing ten or more workers are required to register in the ASI sector is not strictly enforced. Respondents to a review were of the opinion that so long as DME units did not become very large (say, in excess of 75 workers) inspectors were not very careful about registration of the firms with the ASI. From the employers' point of view, the bribes one might need to pay off the inspectors were more than compensated for by the savings on social welfare dues. From the inspectors' view, it is always very difficult to identify the size of the firm belonging to an owner; small firms are often related to one another through production, trade, and kinship relationships.

The lack of a rigid and legally enforced limit to firm size in the DME sector offers a significant degree of flexibility to the production organization in this sector. Field studies in Tirupur have suggested that the flexible upper limit to firm size is not so much the scope for substantial economies of scale[4] as the opportunity it offers for different forms of horizontal and vertical integration among production units in this industrial area (Cawthorne 1995; Chari 2004; Roy 2010).

Limitations of the adjustments

The limitations of the adjustments to labour regulations discussed above for large and small firms alike should be emphasized. While the use of non-permanent labour does mitigate the constraints on the use of labour, considerable ambiguity remains about the interpretation of the numerous provisions of the *Contract Act*, variations in the individual states, and the way they are implemented by a combination of executive action and judicial decisions. The uncertainty increases transaction costs and is in effect a tax on the use of labour. Similarly, the flexibility of the upper limit of employment size in the DME sector has its limits. It confines the concentration of DME production to those industries in which this particular form of productive industry is most competitive—largely, light consumer industries with an emphasis on domestic consumption. We have seen in Chapter 4 that there is definite product market segmentation between DME-dominated and ASI-dominated industries within Indian manufacturing. DME units were concentrated in just six of 65 sectors distinguished in the intersectoral transaction matrix of the Indian economy in 2003–04 and overlapping industries in which DME and ASI employment was equally important added up to just six more. The concentration of DME employment in a limited range of product lines could be even more severe, since the data do not distinguish product quality in detail and DME products are concentrated at the lower end of the quality spectrum. Second, an important point to note is that the level of labour productivity within DME units does not increase with employment size groups, and the gap in productivity with the ASI sector is as substantial for the larger DME units as for the smaller ones. This result shows that technological progress within the DME sector is limited and larger units within the sector use as low a level of technology as small ones.

We conclude that, as the entrepreneurs' responses show, firms in both the ASI and the DME sectors do adjust to labour regulations, but that does not mean that the regulations do not have an impact on their trajectory of development. In particular, they are likely to constitute a significant impediment to the vertical mobility of firms from the DME to the ASI sectors.

It is, however, wrong to conclude from this evidence that labour laws are the only, or even the primary, cause of the discouragement of the informal sector to expand into the formal, giving rise to the phenomenon of the missing middle. This brings us to a review of other constraints which limit the upward mobility of small firms and their graduation into the formal sector.

V

Other constraints to upward mobility of firms

Infrastructure

LAND AND SPACE

During the field survey of unorganized sector enterprises, the persistent answer to questions about obstacles to growth was that the binding constraint was the availability of space. As we found in Chapter 4, the spatial concentration of DME units was very high. Their location was strikingly in the same geographical areas as the ASI units (see Chapter 4). The enterprises in the two subsectors (the organized and the unorganized) had to compete for the same commercial space.

INADEQUACY OF TRANSPORT

The spatial concentration is a consequence of the inadequate development of infrastructure and adds to the problem of urban services. In spite of the recent boom in construction, India suffers from inadequate road and transport systems to support a dispersed industrialization. In the post-war growth of East Asian economies, spatial decentralization in the manufacturing sector has fostered growth of small and medium enterprises and contributed to the impressive record of growth with equity (see the review of the classic case of Taiwan). By contrast, much of the employment in important industries which have dominated the DME sector in India is located in a few cities or towns where they often have to compete for infrastructural facilities with large units (such is the case with garments in Tirupur, and leather and footwear in Kolkata and Agra).

SHORTAGE OF POWER

Inadequate supply of power not only produces low productivity of small dispersed units, but also accentuates the need for heavy lump-sum capital investment for firms needing to provide their own generators for electricity, and biases the economies of scale favouring very large units. While the development of wireless systems of communication has helped ease the heavy costs of information flows in marketing, the inadequate supply of electric power has hampered the transfer of computer-based technology that is critically important to the enhanced productivity and growth of SMEs in more developed economies, including parts of East and South-East Asia.

Entrepreneurship

The types of entrepreneurs found in the DME and the ASI subsectors of manufacturing are quite different. An obvious difference is in formal manufacturing:

while the owners and managers in the ASI units are highly educated profession-als, the proprietor-managers have typically less than college education with often imperfect knowledge of English.

Entrepreneurs in the informal sector are characterized by qualitatively differ-ent approaches to business:

1 Owner-managers in informal enterprises, who are often themselves involved in the actual operation of the firm, work in a much less structured environ-ment, involving less formalized contracts and bookkeeping. They would be uncomfortable dealing with inspectors and officers of various kinds found in enterprises registered in the formal sector. Thus we find that, even when the DME enterprises have significantly exceeded the legal upper limit of employment size, they are in no hurry to register in the ASI sector. As long as they are not too large in employment size (typically not more than 50 workers), the ASI registration system is not very stringent in enforcing the law.

    Our interviews revealed that the cost of registration in terms of laws was only a small part of the DME entrepreneurs' concern; what was uppermost in their minds was entering a world in which bureaucratic relationships with official institutions would be the norm of the day.

2 Informal sector entrepreneurs generally pursue business relationships which are rather different than the structured, contractual modes of the formal sector. Labour-intensive industries catering to basic consumer demand in the Indian scenario developed in clusters, which were typically served by one or more distinct community groups. The networking relationships within the community involving different stages of production and market-ing have been vital to the success of these clusters. The different tasks in the production process in garments or footwear, for example, are not necessar-ily vertically integrated into a single large firm. Rather, there is an intricate relationship of horizontal subcontracting with a number of small firms sup-plying different parts of the product to the coordinating firm. The efficiency is enhanced by the social network of these multiple firm operators belonging to the same community.

    The knitted garment industry of Tirupur has been the classic and much-studied case of this type and has been described in Chapter 4. The fact that the major role in the growth of this industry was played by one community (the Gounders, with an agricultural base) was instrumental in providing the extensive social network needed in all stages of development of the indus-try. Other communities from outside the region participated in later stages of the development of the cluster, particularly in the growth of export markets. In spite of the strong growth of exports, however, vertically inte-grated, large units have not been major players. As discussed, the size distri-bution of enterprises has been "normalized" to some extent with a strong mode in the 20–50 employment size group. Since much of this development took place after 2000 (export growth was particularly strong after 2004–05), the limited emergence of large-scale units cannot be ascribed to the direct impact of small-scale reservation policy (which had been largely dismantled by then). Rather, a significant factor most likely has been the continuation of the industrial organization based on community-based network relationships. There was indeed technological progress in the exporting firms but the innovations stopped short of generating growth of large integrated units in the model of big exporters like China or even Bangladesh. The other side of this development has been the exclusion of India's garment sector from the export boom of garments based on large batches of orders for the mass markets in developed countries.

3   The industrial organization based on social networks rather than structured contracts carries over into the processes typically found in the DME sector in most industries. In the footwear and garments clusters studied by us, the labour used was distinguished by its close relationship to the region of origin of the entrepreneurs—often coming from the same villages. A large body of the labour force had a high turnover, and in the footwear industry in particular had a high degree of seasonality with one foot in the agricultural activities of the region of origin. This does not mean that this type of labour was unskilled: rather, the clusters develop a pool of labour that acquires skills needed in the operations of the industry concerned and is continuously renewed by the same migrants returning after a sojourn in their native areas. We have seen that there has been a sharp increase in the last decade in the use of contract labour, even in the organized sector of manufacturing, working alongside a core of regular workers. To that extent, labour use in the unorganized sector would seem to differ from the system in the formal sector enterprises only to a degree. But a qualitative difference might be that the role of the patron–client relationship embracing the owner-entrepreneur and his workers in the small enterprises is different from the much more impersonal relationship found in large, formal sector units.

We conclude that the difference in the socio-cultural worlds of entrepreneurs found in the two subsectors of Indian manufacturing is very large. If unorganized sector entrepreneurs are wary even of registering in the ASI sector after they have passed the legal size of ten workers, their transition to a full-scale, medium-sized entrepreneur in the latter could be expected to pose insurmountable difficulties.

Education policies

Education policies have been biased towards the promotion of tertiary education and have neglected basic primary and low secondary education. It has been maintained in the literature (e.g. in the work of Adrian Wood among others) that modern manufacturing requires a minimum of basic education for a workforce to be able to perform up to minimum standards in modern manufacturing. Small and medium-sized units in East Asia (adopting comparatively intensive but modern technology) benefited from an ample supply of such workers. They are contrasted with smaller units with less sophisticated technology units (as in the Indian DME sector), which could use nearly unskilled workers with less than primary education for low-grade production, but would find it difficult to grow beyond a certain scale with such a workforce. The relatively plentiful supply of skilled workers with higher education, which the Indian education system has produced, biases production towards skill-intensive industry and modes of production. Large units have a comparative advantage in using such workers which smaller units cannot afford.

A related point, more in the purview of sociologists, might be suggested here. The relative neglect of the lower rungs of the educational system in post-colonial India has created an educational divide which in fact has cemented the class divide within the society. The entrepreneurs and administrative employers in the formal sector tend to come from the upper branch of this divide and are culturally separated from the bottom rung. It is often difficult for entrepreneurs from the latter to cross the cultural barrier and graduate into formal sector units. At the same time, it would be unusual for entrepreneurs from the upper rung of the divide to look for profitable opportunities in the informal (including the non-household small-scale) sector when the natural ambition is to emulate the successful members of their class in the formal sector of manufacturing.

This cultural–educational divide could also be one of the elements in the explanation of the limited development of subcontracting in Indian manufacturing. We could again refer to the widespread development of subcontracting by manufacturing and trading establishments as a key element of East Asian industrial development. Not only did this development promote the small and medium enterprises in manufacturing, but it led to significant transfer of technology from large to small and medium enterprises, leading to growth of productivity in the SME sector. Economists investigating the problem have been struck by the lack of dynamism and technological backwardness of the subcontractors in Indian industry.

Hysteresis

Finally, the limited impact of the reforms on the size structure of establishments might be due to widely recognized processes in which a socio-economic system established over a long period of time tends to persist even after the original causes have disappeared. This persistence is not just due to inertia; economic agents and institutions acquire characteristics which sustain the system. For example, entrepreneurs develop with ambitions to think in terms of horizontal rather than vertical growth. Marketing channels, financial institutions, and infrastructure are geared more towards supporting small units serving limited markets rather than dynamic units growing into larger sizes and different markets. Of particular significance in this connection is the organization of retail trade. If the retail sellers are organized in a system of small outlets serving local markets, production also thrives in small units. The transition to production with larger firms exploiting economies of scale would need simultaneous growth of large-scale retailing. Recent developments in India have seen the development of large-scale retailing and Western-style malls, but these are so far confined to metropolitan cities and lines of products catering to the upper-middle class market. There might indeed be a chicken-or-egg problem here as to which takes the lead in larger-scale economic activity—producers or retailers—when both are intimately connected in the consumer goods industries. The traditional system of small-scale production and retailing might hold its own for a long time.

We have argued above that the segmentation of the markets for manufactured goods into low quality "poor man's goods" and higher quality "rich man's goods" is one of the major reasons shoring up the dualistic structure, with small firms producing the former and larger firms playing a bigger role in the latter. This type of segmentation had been encouraged strongly by the Indian industrial policies of protection for the small-scale firms. Market segmentation impacts the nature of growth in a peculiar way which tends to strengthen the degree of segmentation. The process sees a disproportionate growth of employment at low wages, while the absorption of labour at higher wages in the large-scale sector is constrained. Thus we get a relatively higher rate of expansion of demand at the lower end of the quality spectrum of manufactured goods. There is then a cumulative process involving the protection of small units producing "poor man's goods" and a pattern of expansion of markets for manufactured goods, which favours the growth of demand for such goods.

V

Policy conclusions on dualism

The conclusions for policy makers tackling the problem of the limited upward mobility of small firms in the Indian manufacturing sector—and its attendant problem of the "missing middle"—are rather pessimistic. There is no single big recommendation, like tackling labour regulation, which is likely to result in a quick and significant solution to the system. Rather, progress has to be made using a wide spectrum of policies, including reform of non-labour regulations, improvement of infrastructure, development of primary and secondary education, and decentralized industrialization, among others. The impact of these measures is likely to be slow and long term. A major factor perpetuating dualism is product market segmentation (as we recall from Chapter 4 in particular). The best way to whittle away this type of segmentation is to increase income levels at the lower end of the distribution. If non-agricultural growth of the type India has been urgently witnessing is of limited scope in this respect, attention of policy makers has to shift decisively to increase land productivity in agriculture.

Part III

The East Asian model

8 The role of small-medium enterprises in manufacturing and economic development

The case of Japan

This chapter examines in some detail the size distribution of enterprises in manufacturing during different phases of Japan's growth. For the most part, the period covered is the first three decades of the twentieth century. Studies of Japanese development have often pointed to the importance of small firms. This chapter goes beyond this issue to examine the entire spectrum of the size distribution of manufacturing industries, depending on published English-language sources.[1] We show that the problem of the missing middle did not emerge in Japan in any of the different phases of growth considered. To set this discussion in context, we discuss the pattern of reallocation of labour from agriculture and, in particular, the relative importance of the manufacturing and tertiary sectors in the process of development. The contrasting pattern of size distribution in Japan relative to India is also associated with a different experience of growth, in which manufacturing led the tertiary sector in terms of both employment and value added.

We explore different factors which enable the co-existence of firms of different size classes during Japan's economic development, as well as export capability and firm size. Did the Japanese pattern of growth, with its apparent export dependence, hinder the healthy growth of small firms, and if not, why not?

I

Manufacturing as the leading sector in economic growth

The average growth rates by decades are given in Table 8.1, which also shows the relative importance of the broad sectors in each period.

Manufacturing contributed most to the increment in GDP throughout the growth process (except in the first period in the late nineteenth century). The pre-Second World War average of the relative contribution was 38.4 per cent for manufacturing by itself, and 61.5 per cent for the M sector (including construction, transportation, and communication), way above the S sector (including service activities and all sectors outside M and P sectors; 28.9 per cent), not to mention the primary sector (9.6 per cent).

What was the contribution of manufacturing to labour absorption? Employment in the primary sector had been declining since the beginning of the period being studied. It is estimated that the growth rate of the labour force in this sector was –0.03 in the 1899–1900 period and –0.33 in the 1901–10 period, compared to 1.84 and 1.77 in the non-primary sector respectively. But reliable data separating the growth rate of employment in the M and S sectors are apparently available only after 1910.

It is clear that for the period for which the data are available, the M sector contributed more to employment of the labour displaced from the primary sector. Over the entire 1910–38 period, the relative contribution of the M sector to the absorption of the increase in the labour force was 69 per cent, far exceeding the contribution of the S sector at 48.4 per cent (see Table 8.2). The only exception was the downswing of 1921–30.

What explains the much more substantial role of the M sector in labour absorption in the historical process of Japanese economic growth—compared to India, for example?

The rate of growth of the M sector does not seem to have been significantly higher. The mean growth rate in the pre-Second World War period was 6.34—slightly below that of the formal manufacturing sector in India in the post-reform years.

The elasticity of employment was, however, higher. Over the entire period it was 0.39, probably larger than India, certainly compared to the formal manufacturing sector, but perhaps also taking all manufacturing into account.

Per worker growth rate of the economy was significantly higher because of the much slower rate of growth of the total force in Japan—0.68 for the period. A higher growth rate of productivity means higher per capita income growth, and this supports the growth in the domestic market for the M sector goods as well as the S sector services.

Table 8.1 GDP growth rates and relative contribution of industry groups

Period	Real GDP growth rates (average for period)	Percentage contribution to GDP growth		
		Primary	M sector	S sector
1888–1900	2.92	17.8	31.6	50.6
1901–10	2.62	20.8	52.6	26.8
1911–20	4.13	11.0	45.0	44.0
1921–30	2.41	7.1	85.9	7.0
1931–38	4.86	4.9	69.7	25.4
Pre-war average	3.31	9.6	61.5	28.9
1955–60	9.23	5.7	49.2	45.1
1961–70	10.24	1.9	53.8	44.3
1971–80	5.42	–0.1	54.6	45.4

Source: Minami (1986, Table 5.1, p. 102; Table 5.5, p. 116).

Notes
The GDP figures are simple averages of the annual growth rates based on seven-year moving averages (five years for 1938, 1955, and 1980). The percentage contributions were calculated by dividing the increase in real GDP accounted for by the respective industry groups by the increase in total real GDP. The original source is Klein and Ohkawa (1968, p. 227).

Table 8.2 Relative contribution of major sectors to growth of labour force (percentage)

Years	Primary	M sector	S sector	Non-primary	Total
1889–1900	−3	n.a.	n.a.	103	100
1901–10	−47	n.a.	n.a.	147	100
1911–20	−49.5	104.2	45.3	149.7	100
1921–30	2.3	30.7	67	97.7	100
1931–38	−13.3	80	33.3	113.3	100
(1910–38)	−17.4	69	48.4	117.4	100
1956–60	−44.8	80.6	64.2	144.8	100
1961–70	−69.3	94.5	74.8	169.3	100
1971–80	−64.6	36.2	128.4	164.6	100
Post-war average	−61.7	73.3	88.4	161.7	100

Source: Minami (1986, Table 9.1, p. 272, Panel B).

Note
The figures for employment are seven-year moving averages (five-year averages for 1938 and 1980).

The relative contribution to absorption compared to the relative contribution to GDP growth defines the relative productivity in the individual sectors. A relatively low productivity in manufacturing means that there is a greater potential for absorption. On the other hand, it would also imply that the impact of the sector on growth rate—on manufacturing output and hence total GDP—would be negative. Low productivity makes manufacturing products non-competitive in export markets, and the low wage associated with low productivity slows down the expansion of the domestic market.

The hypothesis is that, in the early stages of industrialization, manufacturing would be dominated by household enterprises and by small firms without much use of mechanical power. Thus, in spite of the low productivity (and disguised unemployment) in the agricultural sector, the productivity differential between manufacturing and agriculture could be low. Higher productivity (and education) would be found more in the tertiary sector, which includes government and the rudimentary framework of a modern economic structure. Although the dispersion of earnings (and productivity) in the tertiary sector would be high, we could expect to see the mean labour productivity in this sector to be higher than in manufacturing. When industrialization gets going at a reasonable rate, the relative mean productivity of the manufacturing sector would increase, perhaps above that of the mean of the tertiary sector and also of agriculture. A more advanced stage of development would see the current developed country scenario, in which average productivity in the tertiary activities again exceeds that of manufacturing. Thus the prediction is one of an inverted U-shaped manufacturing sector differential with respect to the tertiary sector, with the differential with respect to the primary sector depending very much on the trend in disguised unemployment in the latter.

The time-series of growth rates of GDP and employment in Japanese development given in Tables 8.1 and 8.2 support the above hypothesis. In the early stages of industrialization (1910–20), productivity in the tertiary sector was more than 30 per cent higher than in manufacturing. Although large-scale factories had developed strongly in this period, manufacturing was dominated by textiles, and the labour-intensive nature of this sector was characterized not only by unskilled workers but also by the large-scale use of young females (a special feature of Japanese growth). In the more mature stage of industrialization in the following years, the relative productivity of manufacturing went the other way— increasing with respect to the tertiary as well as the agricultural sector.

This experience contrasts strikingly with that of India's recent intersectoral changes in the structure of employment and of relative productivities by broad sectors. We have seen that, first, the Indian growth process seems to have been led by the tertiary sector, both in terms of value added and employment, rather than manufacturing. Second, while the expectation in a labour-abundant economy might be that the tertiary sector had disproportionately absorbed labour displaced from agriculture at low levels of earnings, the data seem to suggest that this has not been so. Earning levels in the tertiary sector have been significantly above those in manufacturing, suggesting that growth in the tertiary sector has been productivity-led rather than employment-led. We have advanced the hypothesis that both these trends in tertiary sector development relative to manufacturing are related to a third peculiarity of Indian manufacturing, the persistence of dualism, with a missing middle. We turn therefore to a detailed examination of the size distribution of enterprises in Japanese manufacturing, as developed over time, and contrast it with the Indian pattern.

II

Size distribution of firms in Japanese industrialization

It is well known that a distinguishing feature of Japanese industrial development has been the role of SMEs, the co-existence of a large sector of small and medium-sized firms along with very large firms, corporations under the control of the famous *Zaibatsu*. The phenomenon, often called dualism within manufacturing, can be illustrated by the comparative data presented by Broadbridge for the 1950–60 period (Broadbridge 1966, Table 12, p. 90).

The second feature of this dualistic structure, a wide differential in productivity and wage levels between small and large firms, was noticed in the Japanese case, but the differential, although much larger than in the Western industrial countries, was significantly smaller than in the Indian case. (In fact, for much of the history of Japanese industrialization, it was similar to the East Asian pattern.[2]) The size-related wage differential follows the pattern of productivity differentials.

Contrasting scenarios of India and Japan

Writing in the period of our discussion (the first decade after the Second World War), Ishikawa (1962) noticed the remarkable difference between the size structure of manufacturing between Japan and India. Ishikawa had to confine himself to the organized sector of manufacturing (with ten or more workers) because of the data constraints in India. His work revealed that in India:

> the size class covering 1000 or more employees occupies an outstandingly high position while other size classes have a shape of a gentle hill ... this feature is also common to 1948, 1954, and 1955 when viewed in terms of the total of 28 industries.... (Moreover) the study (VKRV Rao 1940, p. 139) although not strictly comparable to the present data, tends to indicate that the weight placed on the size of 1000 or more employees is even higher in 1931 as compared with 1956. In contrast the Japanese structure is character-ized by the almost parallel growth of respective size classes since the era of Meiji.
>
> (Ishikawa 1962, pp. 51–52)

The composition of industry in India was indeed not quite different from Japan's at this date, dominated as it was by light (and particularly the textile) industries. Ishikawa, however, calculated the "concentration ratio" in individual industries defined as the total number of workers in establishments of over 1000 employees to the number in those with 20 or more workers. His data showed that:

> in many industries the degree of concentration in India is considerably or remarkably higher than in Japan.... The industries for which the grade of concentration in India is lower than in Japan are small in number, covering only the automobile industry, chemical industry, power generating and transmitting industry, glass making industry, etc.

There were no data available at the time in India of the size structure of estab-lishments employing fewer than ten workers. But looking at some data on the small-scale sector and combining them with his results for the large-scale sector, Ishikawa concluded that "the pattern for India is the one characterized by an extreme division into two poles in respect of the size of establishment" (cf. Figure 1, p. 55), and within this pattern the smallest size class (the household industry) is decreasing and the largest growing over time, while the medium size classes have been extremely retarded in their maturity. This constitutes a con-trast to the pattern for Japan "where the smallest size class has been decreasing but all other size classes have been growing almost in parallel" (ibid., p. 55).

The availability of recent survey data has enabled us to refine the description of the phenomenon of the missing middle in India for the years after the mid-1980s. Dualism in India is dramatically apparent within the non-household sector and con-trasts with that of Japan.[3] The latter in fact does not so much reveal a dualistic dis-tribution of employment by size but the co-existence of enterprise of all size groups. A second striking difference between the two economies is the extent of the difference in productivity between enterprises of different size groups. The ratio of the productivities of the largest (500+) and the smallest (5–9) size groups is 3:1 in the case of Japan but 8:1 in the case of India.

It is, however, interesting to note that the extent of the size-related differential is so significant only if we include the smallest size group, 5–9 (or the DME units in the case of India). For the universe of firms in higher size groups (ten and above), the size-related productivity differential is very similar in the two countries. This is indeed what was found by Ishikawa for an earlier date (in 1955; op. cit., Table 6, p. 67). The point underlines the very significant role of the DME sector in Indian manufacturing development.

Size distribution in Japanese manufacturing in earlier periods

Japan in the decade after the Second World War was a fairly advanced industrial country (Table 8.3). It had already gone through a period of rapid industrialization beginning soon after the Meiji restoration. Indeed the preparation of the war economy itself helped to diversify its industry strongly away from light consumer goods to heavy industries. Could it be that the fairly uniform growth of different size classes (so different from the Indian scenario) is an outcome of its more advanced state of industrialization?

At first glance, a broad classification of manufacturing employment by small (5–49 workers), middle (50–499), and large (500+) enterprises suggests that it was not so.

There was indeed an increase in the share of employment in large establishments, first at the expense of small establishments in the 1909–19 period, then at the expense of middle-sized establishments in the 1930–40 period (Table 8.4). But all three classes continued to be substantial throughout. In fact it is interesting to see that, in the period of rapid diversification of the industrial structure in the period 1919–30, both the small and middle-sized establishments grew at the expense of the large.

Table 8.3 International comparison of employment distribution in manufacturing by scale of plant

Scale of plant (number of workers)	Employment (%)		
	Japan (1960)	USA (1958)	Britain (1951)
1–9	15	4	4
10–49	28	14	11
50–99	11	10	10
100–499	21	30	32
500–999	7	12	13
1000+	17	31	29

Source: Broadbridge for the 1950–60 periods (Broadbridge 1966, Table 12, p. 90). Original sources: Japan in 1960: *Japan Statistical Yearbook*, 1963, Table 90, p. 158. USA in 1958: *Chusho Kigyo-cho, Chusho kigyo kindaika (Modernization of Smaller Enterprises)*, p. 11; Britain in 1951: P. Sasrant Florence, *The Logic of British and American Industry*, 1961, p. 37.

Detailed industry-wise analysis of size distribution is available in the work of Yosuba (2006). The author classifies industries at two dates (1932–33 and 1951) into two groups: (a) the dualistic ones in which:

(i) wage differentials within industries are so wide as to include it in the upper half of industries ranked by the co-efficient of variation in wages; and (ii) such a significant tendency for the larger establishments to pay higher wages that the industry is in the highest quintile of industries ranked by size elasticity

and (b) homogeneous industries "in which wages were so uniform that the industry is in the lowest quintile in terms of the coefficient of variation" (ibid., p. 263). It should be noted that the pattern of size distribution need not necessarily be determined by the wage characteristic of the industry as defined. For example, an industry with a concentration of employment and the large size group might indeed be a homogenous one simply because wage earners in smaller establishments are a small proportion of the total. An industry with a widespread distribution among the size classes, on the other hand, might be either a dualistic or a homogeneous one depending on the wage differential prevailing between establishments of different size groups.

The data suggest the following conclusions about the industry-specific size distribution of employment:

- None of the 16-odd industries in the three years of the data presented show the peculiar Indian pattern in a number of industries (strong bi-polar distribution with modes at the very small and very large). Two industries (bricks and tiles, and bakery products) had a strong mode at the lowest size group, 4–9, before the Second World War, but in both cases middle-sized units were quite important.
- The larger number of industries had a very wide distribution of employment by size groups in all three years of the study. In particular, the phenomenon

Table 8.4 Percentage distribution of employment in manufacturing by size of establishment in Japan

Year	Size (number of workers)		
	5–49	*50–499*	*500 or more*
1909	45.7	33.6	20.7
1914	40.0	34.9	25.1
1919	33.9	34.6	31.5
1930	37.0	37.4	25.6
1940	36.5	27.4	36.2

Source: Minami (1986, Table 9.16, p. 318). Original source: *Kojo Tokeihyo* and *Kogyo Tokeihyo* *(Census of Manufacturing)*; pre-war: *Tsusho Sangyo Daijin Kanbo Chosa*, 1961, pp. 180–181.

of the missing middle is not observed in any of the years, before or after the First World War.

There were just three industries of the 16—spinning, silk reeling, and primary metals—that had a skewed distribution favouring the large size. This group might have been joined by matches after the war, though not spectacularly so. At the other end, there are just two (grain milling and tea) in which large units are conspicuous for their lack of importance.

III

Factor market segmentation

We turn now to a discussion of the factors stressed in the voluminous literature on the evolution of the Japanese economy relating to the factors supporting the "dualistic pattern" in manufacturing. We first turn to the issue of segmentation in factor markets, starting with the labour market and going onto the capital market later in the section.

The dualistic wage structure

The Japanese wage structure has been judged to be abnormal in the literature on this subject principally because it has been found to be large relative to other developed countries. Thus, Broadbridge (1966) produced a study after the war, quoted in Section II above, showing that the scale-related differentials for France, West Germany, and Britain were all much less than for Japan.

However, we have already seen that the quantitative dimensions of the size-related differential in wages in Japan are not at all unusual for other developing countries in Asia (Chapter 2 above). Furthermore, we might reemphasize the point that the absence of the phenomenon of the missing middle in the Japanese economy would itself lead us to expect that the differential between the establishments at the two poles of the distribution—the very small and the very large—would be moderate, even if it was large by the standards of developed countries.

Historical evolution

Japanese researchers have long maintained that the dualistic wage structure evolved after the First World War when Japan started to diversify into industries other than light industries, like textiles (see Shinohara 1970, p. 312, also Table 6). However, more detailed research has suggested that the absence of a large scale-related differential might be partly the result of the dominance of young female workers in the large spinning mills in Japan before the First World War. Yosuba has made a detailed study of wage differentials by scale for individual industries and has sought to standardize wages by adjusting for sex composition, operating days, skill, and age composition. He calculated two measures of wage differentials: first the coefficient variation, and second the size elasticity of wages (derived from a log linear regression). The two measures were plotted the first on the Y-axis and the second on the X-axis for the years for which good data were available: 1909, 1814, 1932–33, and 1951 (Yosuba 2006, Figures 3–7, pp. 260–262). The conclusion is that wage dualism already existed in 1909 in a significant way—with more than half the industries showing statistically significant size-related wage elasticity.

> By 1914 (Figures 4 and 5) the cluster moves somewhat upward (larger co-efficient of variation) and considerably to the right (higher wage elasticity with respect to size), but in general rather close to the origin. By 1932/3 the cluster moves from the origin to the north-east. A similar pattern can be observed for 1951.
>
> (ibid., p. 261)

Evidently, the dualistic wage structure was already established before the First World War, but increased strongly during the inter-war period, when it reached the level noticed after the Second World War.

It appears that the differential, while positive, was quite small in 1909, the smallest size group (5–9 workers) having a level about 20 per cent below the largest. The difference widened in 1914 and continued to increase during the inter-war years. In 1932–33, the relevant percentage was 61.2, but it declined in the post-Second World War years.

It should be noted that the size-related wage differential (which is related to differential in labour productivity), although of long standing in Japanese development, is considerably below that of some other Asian countries, notably India.

Industry-specific analysis provides additional conclusions. As indicated, homogeneous industries were distinguished from the dualistic ones on the basis of the two criteria of coefficient of variation and significant size-related wage elasticity. Yosuba is of the view that the import of foreign technology in the earlier years played a critical role in determining the demarcation between the two types of industry. Six of the ten dualistic industries were textile related. Tea (in 1909) and bakery products, medicines, and printing (in 1914) joined this list.

> Most of these industries became established at an early stage using imported technologies modified and acclimatized in different degrees. It is easy to imagine a productivity gap would appear when the larger and more modern branches of these industries happened to be very advanced in technology from the outset ... or when indigenous entrepreneurs and engineers had developed superior acclimatized technologies suitable for medium and large scale industries, while smaller establishments continued to use more traditional technologies.
>
> (ibid., p. 265)

The inter-war period saw a rapid diversification of industries and at the same time a rapid growth of small-scale enterprises as entrepreneurs developed acclimatized technology dependent on cheap labour. This trend was fostered by two important developments in the Japanese economy: first, the widespread availability of electric motors; and second, the growth of the subcontracting system, which enables larger firms to enlist the help of smaller establishments in reducing the cost of the finished product.

Dualistic industries in the years 1931–32 and 1951 are then found in many industries, moving away from the previous concentration to the textile-related ones. Dualism still occurred more commonly in industries which were experiencing rapid technological progress. These included iron and steel, fire bricks, printing, and flour milling after the First World War. They were subsequently joined by cement, Western paper, Western medicines, and parts of the ceramics industries (ibid., p. 271).

Homogeneous industries, on the other hand, consisted of spinning, silk reeling, paper, cloth, and bakery products in Yosuba's 1931–32 classification and were joined by matches, tea, hosiery, and wearing apparel in the 1951 classification. The demarcation between the dualistic and homogeneous depended on how far the process of polarization in particular size groups had gone. Industries which favoured the concentration of employment in large units—spinning and silk reeling being the most important examples—and those whose technology favoured concentration in small-scale units (e.g. tea) were clearly homogeneous since the size distribution of employment was not very wide. But the industries which had a large presence of middle-sized units with a widely dispersed size distribution (and the majority of industries developed in this way) were found as much in the homogeneous as in the dualistic category.

Turning to the size-related (standardized) wage differential, Yosuba noted an important change from the period before the First World War. The wage difference between small and large units was not now due to small units paying less than average wages. It was the other way round, with large units paying higher than the average in their size group. Homogeneous industries, however, seemed to pay roughly the average wage specific to their size group in all sizes of establishments (ibid., Table 9).

This finding has some bearing on the causes of the origin and persistence of the dualistic wage structure.

Segmented labour markets

Surplus labour

The Japanese economy, like many other Asian economies today, has been characterized by the existence of surplus labour in the farm sector. It was dominated by family farms and any working member of the family shared in the family pot and contributed to the farm activity, even if the marginal product of some units of labour time was very low. A plentiful supply of labour was available to the non-farm sector at low wages, corresponding to the low supply price of such labour.[4]

The significance of the surplus labour in agriculture (and to some extent in household enterprises in non-agriculture) is seen in the pressure on wages in small firms throughout the pre-Second World War period. We have already referred to Yosuba's finding that small firms in the early years of industrialization actually suffered a decline in real wages as the new competition from imported technologies put pressure on domestic industries. Subsequently, as the new technologies spread rapidly, larger firms raised wages while small firms recruited their labour at roughly constant real wages.

The surplus labour situation was instrumental in supporting the evolving labour system. It provided a continued cushion of flexibility for labour use in the high-wage, larger firms by allowing a flexible supply of temporary workers (to work alongside the stable core of high-wage labour) and a source of labour for smaller firms (which acted as subcontractors for some parts of the finished products produced by large firms).

Labour in large enterprises

To explain higher wages paid in large firms in the face of surplus of labour beating down wages in the small firm sector, we have to postulate a separation of the markets of labour for large and small firms. Such segmentation of the labour market could be achieved by institutional factors like government legislation or trade unions. But no such influence is detectable in Japanese labour history. "Enterprise unionism" did not come into any significance in Japan until well after the Second World War. While the percentage of workers unionized in manufacturing was 38 per cent in 1955, it was only 7.9 per cent in 1930, and actually fell to 4.6 per cent in 1938 as heavy industry expanded (Odaka 1967, p. 60). Furthermore, while in the more recent periods unionism varied directly with establishment size, in the pre-Second World War period it was found mostly in small and medium firms (ibid., p. 60, footnote 56).

Japanese economists have embraced the thesis that segmentation was an integral part of the Japanese labour system, in which the market for labour in large enterprises is separated from that for SMEs. Shinohara (quoting the results of a special survey conducted in the industrial district of Tokyo-Yokohama in 1951–52) reports that those workers who had experience only in large factories amounted to as much as 78 per cent. Those with working experience only in small factories amounted to 47.7 per cent but if we added to these percentages workers who moved from small to large factories and came back again to the former, the percentage rises to almost 80 per cent (Shinohara 1970, p. 314).

> In the field of the large enterprises, the recruitment of new personnel is dependent much more upon the new graduates than it is in the field of small enterprises, because workers who seek employment in small enterprises get it through the personal help of relatives and friends.... Once the large firm employs new graduates ... the practice of so-called life time employment is

enforced on them, and their wages increase like a sliding scale, in accordance with increase in the length of their services.

(ibid., p. 315)

The committed labour force in large enterprises ensured that the rate of turnover was extremely low—contrasting with the experience of SMEs, which showed much more instability of the labour force. The labour flexibility in large enterprises was largely provided by the "Reinjiko" (temporarily employed) who had different contracts and could be laid off at any time. The use of the temporaries made the wage levels appear to be lower than what they might have been because they were paid at a much lower rate (perhaps half of the regular wages, according to Shinohara), and the firm could expand and contract the relative size of the temporaries as demand conditions fluctuated.

The discussion leads to two important conclusions relating to labour market segmentation as a factor explaining the dualistic pattern. First, the scale-related wage differential will be of significance in the choice of techniques only if they do not reflect differences in the quality of labour. That is to say, the observed wage gap per man truly reflects differences in the cost of a labour unit in terms of efficiency. We have seen, however, that there are many reasons to suggest that a god deal of the differential reflects differences in labour quality, which are partly created by different methods of labour recruitment and deployment. Second, the welfare loss associated with size-related wage differentials would be significant only if there was evidence of an "abnormally" high differential, but we have seen that, in the Japanese case, the extent of the differential has not been high by the standards of many agrarian economies in Asia.

Capital market segmentation

As the wage per worker (W) increases with firm size, so does capital intensity or the capital–labour ratio (K/L) and the productivity of labour (Y/L). But it has been argued in the literature (e.g. Shinohara 1970, Chapter 8) that the causation might indeed run the other way, from right to left in the sequence: $[K/L \rightarrow Y/L \rightarrow W]$. The use of more capital-intensive techniques leads to higher labour productivity and to a higher share of capital. The surplus produced by this technology might conceivably result in sharing with labour and in higher wages per worker.

In the Japanese context, we discussed in the last section that the size-related wage differential widened significantly in the period after the First World War, when there was a large increase in industry with modern technology. This went hand in hand with an increase in overall labour productivity in manufacturing, which now pulled ahead of labour productivity in the tertiary sector. It would be hard to argue that these developments did not imply an enhanced productivity in the large-scale industrial enterprises based on higher capital intensity and increasing returns to scale. Thus, it would seem very likely that the line of causation led from higher surplus to higher wages in the larger firms

Yosuba makes an ingenious attempt to show the existence of profit sharing by using firm-level data for lifetime earnings of workers in the same firms at two dates in the post-Second World War period, 1958 and 1968. He first finds that the rank correlation between firm-specific lifetime earnings of workers between the two dates is very low—even when we consider groups of workers classified by sex, cohorts, and blue/white collar groups. "The drastic changes in short time span indicated by these low correlation coefficients suggest factors other than the quality of labour have to be introduced to account for these changes" (2006, p. 284). The telling result from his statistical analysis was that the "lifetime wage income in 1968 is most satisfactorily explained by income in 1958 and the increase between 1958 and 1968 in profit as a proportion of paid-up capital in 1958" (ibid., p. 285). In spite of the small sample (100 firms), the high R-square of the regressions suggests that "a part of the wage differentials should be accounted for by some form of profit sharing".

IV

Product market segmentation

If indeed segmentation in the capital markets makes large firms more profitable (and this advantage is not offset by higher labour costs because of the wage-efficiency mechanism), why are the larger firms not able to compete the higher-cost smaller firms out of existence? It is clear that we have to postulate some degree of non-competitiveness between the small and large firms, and this is most likely based on their specializing in different classes of products.

The Japanese case

Turning to the Japanese case, we need to emphasize a special feature of the consumer culture in Japan which has figured much in the literature. This is the persistence of traditional habits of consumption of goods, commonly used for daily consumption as well as rituals, even after post-Meiji Japan had opened up to the import of Western methods of production. These traditional consumer goods needed labour-intensive methods of production which could not be easily produced by Western mechanical technology—and were more generally produced in small-scale units.

Writing in 1937, G.C. Allen drew the distinction between the transformation during the industrial revolution of the West and the trends in Japanese industrialization.

> In those Western countries where the industrial revolution began ... the cultural traditions and habits of the people afforded little resistance to the application of mechanical methods to the production of articles in daily use as long as techniques had developed to produce them cheaply; and during the latter half of the nineteenth century machine-made furniture, ornaments, doors and window

frames. Clothes and domestic utensils of all kinds came into general use among the populations of England and America.... The degradation of the articles of daily use was a price which more men paid willingly for the abundance that machinery made possible.... The instinctive popular culture had no prestige, being divorced from the cosmopolitan (or European) culture of the ruling classes and so could not survive the onslaught; while the latter, having no roots in the masses, were easily degraded.

(Allen 1940, pp. 407–408)

By contrast, Japanese civilization had developed a tradition of consumption tastes which embraced people of all classes and were distinguished by:

a strong aesthetic habit.... This habit has a particularly close connection with the various ceremonies and accomplishments that are conducted or demonstrated in the home, such as the tea ceremony and flower arrangement. These require the use of utensils simple and commonplace in function, but beautifully made according to traditional designs, although the performance of these ceremonies and accomplishments was until lately limited to the upper classes. The coming of Western ideas and institutions has not yet destroyed them but has even made possible their development.

(ibid., pp. 408–409)

The ruling elites in fact encouraged them as an answer to the perceived superiority of the West, to encourage self-respect and patriotism among the Japanese.

The continued importance of traditional commodities, depending heavily on labour-intensive methods of production (at the everyday and ceremonial levels), gave the Japanese industrialization a unique flavour—different from many developing countries undergoing economic growth in recent years. If time-series data for traditional and Western items of consumption could be constructed, one would expect to find that the income elasticity of the former group has been much higher than that of today's developing countries.

The Japanese case contrasted with India today

Finally, a point might be made about the contrast between the Japanese case and that of India. Product market segmentation is an important part of the Indian economy and a crucial element in the dualism in the manufacturing sector. The small-scale sector produces a good deal of the "poor man's" consumer goods with labour-intensive, largely non-mechanized techniques. These are typically traditional goods with very low income elasticity of demand. They exist side by side with larger units in the same narrowly defined industries producing commodities with similar basic attributes, but having supplementary attributes which satisfy the "rich man's" tastes. While the small-scale sector in India undoubtedly does produce some luxury goods, their proportion is small relative to what has been the case in the period of Japanese modernization. The relatively limited size in India of a small-scale sector producing traditional goods with a high income elasticity of demand has meant that the sector has lacked the dynamism and growth which characterized Japanese manufacturing. This is indeed one reason why in India we have a predominance of the traditional sector in very small units—without the graduation to middle-sized units observed in Japan.

V

Other factors explaining the Japanese size structure: subcontracting

Another important reason why the productivity gap between small and large enterprises has been much smaller in Japanese industrialization is the success of the subcontracting system linking the two size groups. The importance of subcontracting in the Japanese industrial scene has been recognized for a long time. Two stages of the process have been identified: the early developments which depended much on the organization of merchant capital, and the subsequent graduation to systems in which large industrial firms took the lead, promoting what has been called "vertical inter-firm hierarchy" (Shinohara 1970).

Of the many advantages following from the subcontracting system, the most important are as follows:

- The relatively lower cost of labour because of the wage–size relationship discussed at length elsewhere.
- The savings in the amount of fixed capital which smaller firms are able to achieve not only because of the more labour-intensive techniques of production, but also because of their greater ability to use second-hand equipment, often from their patron firms. Shinohara (1970) estimated that in 1954 the ratio of second-hand to total fixed capital was 48 per cent in the employment size group of 4–9 workers, and the relative value would be considerably higher if the under-valuation of second-hand equipment in the books of the firms could be corrected. This economy in the use of fixed capital was particularly important for small firms because this enabled them to compensate to some extent for their decidedly significant disadvantage in the availability and cost of finance from lending agencies.
- The economy in the use of capital extended to working capital as well. Subcontracting units generally received raw materials from their parent firms. Subcontractors had greater flexibility in adjusting their production to demand fluctuations, thus saving in the cost of inventories as well as the fixed costs of the firms (including the permanent core of firm-specific labour).
- The economy in the costs of marketing, which the subcontracting system helped to achieve, would seem to be near the top of the list of advantages. Basically it enabled firms to take advantage of the considerable economies of scale in marketing and benefit from the reduction in the costs of production. The small subcontractors could concentrate on production rather than

marketing activities. Further, they could (and did) receive continuous help in the supply of technological information and training in the use of new technologies and production management.

Two distinct types of subcontracting systems could be distinguished. The first is the subordinate relationship, in which large firms use the small subcontractors mainly to reduce costs, and the transfer of technology to the latter is not very significant. The other is the dynamic relationship of active cooperation between large firms and their subcontractors involving real exchange of technical knowledge and facilities, with the latter producing a large variety of components which would be of high enough quality to be used in the manufacture of the final product.

The historians of Japanese business agree that, while some form of subcontracting was prevalent before the First World War, the system expanded during the period of economic fluctuations in the 1920s and developed further during the rapid growth of manufacturing in the 1930s. Hayashi (2005) maintains that the sharp increase in demand for the products of the machinery industry in the 1930s induced large firms to contract out parts of their requirements to small firms as they hit constraints on their existing capacity. The memory of economic fluctuations of the previous decade was a factor in their search for an alternative to the more permanent commitment to capacity expansion and vertical integration of the parent companies. At the same time, the lower wage levels in small firms were an added advantage to the expansion of subcontracting. Clearly this development required a graduation of the subcontracting relationship into a more developed one of mutual cooperation and creative exchange.

Nevertheless some writers have maintained that in this period developments in different markets for finished goods were probably more important for small firms than production of components (Friedman 1988). It is only the war economy that began with the Manchurian incident of 1931 which led to the large expansion of the subcontracting system as Japanese manufacturers tried to meet the upsurge in demand. The state played an important role in promoting a programme of organizing subcontractors serving large munitions manufacturers (Nishiguchi 1994).

With the disappearance of the demand for munitions after the Second World War, the subcontracting system took a new lease of life and evolved into a mature system within the new industrial structure. It was helped by a series of measures enacted by the post-war governments to protect subcontractors against unfair practices by larger firms (Nishiguchi 1994; Hayashi 2005). Nishiguchi, however, maintains that the conditions of small firms as subcontractors improved dramatically only in the 1960s and 1970s when the expansion of industrial goods of mass consumption led to increased competition among large firms. The need for flexible production helped the growth of small firms in expanded subcontracting relationships, and it is likely that this development has gone further in supporting the growth of small firms more than in other developed countries.

VI

Other factors explaining firm structure: the importance of electrification

Historically, the introduction of electric power increased productivity in power-driven factories which had previously been supplied by steam power. Electrification allows motive power to be available in small units. This divisibility helped large units as well as smaller factories. Large factories could reduce production costs by replacing group drive arrangements by unit drive ones, while many small firms could improve their competitive position in the market by installing small capacity electric motors.

The substitution of steam engines for water wheels took place in 1890–1905, and that of electric motors for steam engines was nearly complete by 1930. Minami comments: "It appears that these two substitutions occurred in a much shorter time than was the case in other industrialized countries" (1976, p. 303). Minami's data on the sources of power by size groups of factories show that, while factories of all scale participated in electrification, it was, if anything, somewhat faster in the smaller factories.

The point to note here is that small factories could not be equipped with steam engines with a large capacity. Electric power, on the other hand, could be used by the smallest units, in many cases by extending an electric wire to a small house and installing a small motor within the house. Thus for small firms steam as a source of power was not an option. But for larger firms the choice between electric power and steam engines was a question of choice involving relative costs and efficiencies.

The introduction of electric power increased the productivity of small firms and allowed them to compete with larger firms. This development could have been as important as the other factors (differentiated factor and product markets or the culture of subcontracting) in the flourishing of SMEs in Japanese economic growth. Minami comments:

> Without the use of introduction of motive power, many of the smaller plants would have disappeared during the 1920s, which were depression years in Japan. Large factories made some attempts to prevent declining profits by introducing new technologies, discharging unskilled workers, and so forth. On the other hand, smaller plants could introduce motive power and raise profitability because of the diffusion of cheap electric motors and the big decline in the cost of electric power.
>
> (ibid., p. 323)

VII

Exports and the firm size issue

An important set of issues concerned with the role of SMEs in Japanese growth is that of the impact of export orientation on the size structure of firms. It is generally thought that penetration of export markets is easier for large firms. Since Japanese growth has been traditionally assumed to have been heavily dependent on exports, and even export-led, we need to discuss the question: how is it that SMEs played such an important role in Japanese development, as the evidence presented above would seem to suggest? The question in fact has to be explored in two parts: did large firms dominate the export sector in Japanese manufacturing? How important were exports in the growth of Japanese manufacturing?

Export structure and firm size

Around the turn of the century, processed raw materials, including raw silk in the textile group, accounted for the bulk of exports. These industries were generally dominated by small firms. While early data on the silk reeling industry is scant, post-war data (1964) show that plants of fewer than 50 employees accounted for 13.7 per cent of total production, and plants with between 100 and 300 employees produced another 68 per cent of the total (ibid., p. 207, footnote 10). Given the obvious upgrading of technology and the optimal plant size over the post-war years, it is legitimate to expect that silk reeling in the first decade of the century was similar to the category of other processed raw materials industry—in which 60 per cent of output is produced in small units. We can conclude that "exports of these industries were produced by small- and medium-sized firms with little or no export concentration" (ibid.).

The second generation of export industries (textiles, ceramics, and miscellaneous manufactured goods, or the "light" industries), although generally labour-intensive, had a higher proportion of large firms than the raw material processors. The inter-war period saw a diversification of Japanese manufacturing to more capital-intensive industries, including machinery. Some of this trend spilled over into exports. But the dominance of textiles lasted and it was only in the later inter-war period that the share of textiles in total exports declined from its peak in 1925. There were, however, changes in the composition of exports within the textile and apparel group, which have significant implications for the firm size in the export sector.

Rapp (1976) reports that the mean employment size in Japanese manufacturing went up from 25.6 per cent in 1909 to a plateau of 41 per cent in 1925 but declined significantly after that, reaching a value of 30.9 per cent in 1937. Evidently the diversification of industry reduced the average firm size. It is interesting to note that this trend happened within the textile and apparel group itself, reflecting the diversification of textiles to subgroups in which economies of scale were less important.

Textile industries

COTTON

The textile group of industries dominated Japanese exports throughout the pre-Second World War period, although its share reached a peak in 1925, and its share in exports declined quite significantly in the next decade, from 78 per cent to 54 per cent. There were, however, important changes in the composition of exports and production within the group—principally from spun yarn to woven cloth in cotton, but also in the later years to rayon and wool. Did this changing composition have an impact on the role of large firms in exports?

Economies of scale are very important in spinning and, while this section of the industry was dominant, very large firms played the central role both in production and exports. The weaving of textiles, however, technically is not characterized by large economies of scale in production. Uyeda's data for the end of 1935 showed that employment in the non-household weaving industry was fairly evenly distributed among the small-medium sized groups (Uyeda 1938). Only 21 per cent of employment was in large units with more than 200 workers—in sharp contrast to spinning, in which most workers were seen to be employed in very large units of 500 or more workers. Furthermore, many of the weaving workers in the 200+ units were employed in composite spinning–weaving mills.

The important point made by Uyeda was that:

> these small textile mills are mostly engaged in weaving pattern goods for the home market, whereas the larger ones, even among the specialized textile mills, are producing goods for exports.... Most of export goods of wide measurement came from mills with 50 looms and over.
>
> (ibid., pp. 56–57)

> Large firms maintained their export orientation and volume by producing and exporting cotton fabrics using continuous production techniques. They specialized in exports to the extent of 80 to 90 per cent of their total fabric production, compared to 20 to 30 per cent for specialty goods producers.
>
> (Rapp 1976, p. 222, citing Uyeda 1938 as the source)

NON-COTTON

The textile industry diversified to fibres other than cotton (such as rayon) in the inter-war period. There seems to have been little difference in the output per worker between small and large firms in this industry (Uyeda 1938, p. 122). The non-existence of significant economies of scale meant that small and medium firms dominated the industry. Most of the output came from units employing fewer than 200 workers, evenly distributed among the size groups within the 15–99 employment range (ibid., Table 54, p. 122). But it was reported that, as in cotton, the wide-width textiles for export purposes were produced by relatively larger-scale units. Uyeda noted that the dynamic part of the industry in specialized regions of Japan (which produced the bulk of the output for export) had a significantly larger size of establishment. Another point to note is that, even if the production for exports took place in small-medium units, the organization for marketing was on a much larger scale—as was the case of the many other labour-intensive manufactures which grew rapidly in the inter-war period in Japan (see below).

Another fibre which developed in the inter-war period was wool. "Although larger firms (over two hundred employees) dominated early production and exports of *mousselines de laines* and wool fabrics, as this industry developed demand for mousselaines fell" (Rapp 1976, p. 220). There was a large increase in the demand for the use of wool for kimono—which stimulated the output of wool fabric of narrow width for the domestic market. A disproportionate amount of output of wide width for exports continued to be supplied by larger firms.

Non-textile exports

Japan diversified its export structure significantly in the inter-war period. The share of textiles in all manufactured exports, which had reached its peak at 78 per cent in 1925, came down significantly to 54 per cent in 1937. Some of the increasing share was claimed by industries of a capital-intensive nature: chemicals, metals, and machinery. We could expect that economies of scale were most likely significant, and the available data showed that the share of large firms (over 499 workers) was substantial in terms of both employment and shipments (ibid., Table 3, pp. 210–212). We could then reasonably expect the role of large firms to be even larger in the exports from these industry groups. But there was also a significant increase in the share of some labour-intensive products, aided partly by the devaluation of the yen. Although production on a small scale dominated industries like ceramics, wood, and the miscellaneous group, the organization of exports in terms of marketing was on a large scale. The trend can be illustrated in terms of one of these dynamic products: bicycles. Uyeda reports that in the 1930s "only a small number of larger factories manufacture more than two kinds of parts or accessories, the other factories limiting themselves to the production of just one or two parts" (Uyeda 1938, p. 234). Standardization of the various parts of the bicycle was a critical factor which made a small factory system possible. The distribution of workers in the industry by employment size groups in 1930 is shown in Table 8.5.

The organizational pattern for exports of bicycles (which accounted for 40 per cent of production in value in 1936) was rather different from that of the organization for the domestic market. While assembly plants played the role of putting the bicycle together for domestic production and then sold them to dealers and retail agents, in the export trade wholesale dealers played a pivotal role. In particular, they acted as banker to the numerous manufacturers of parts as well as the owner of the assembling factory. Typically the owner-wholesaler would be a large firm. Rapp concludes:

Table 8.5 Distribution of employment by size groups in bicycle industry (%), 1930

5–9	10–14	15–29	30–49	100–199	200–499	Total
15.05	10.13	18.45	17.43	10.53	28.27	100.00

Source: Uyeda (1938, Table 101, p. 236).

It would seem that 30 to 35 percent of exports may have been an appropriate figure for large firms' export share. By 1937 or even 1929, this was more nearly 45 to 50 percent, for we know from Uyeda's data that large firms' export share in many key industries exceeded their share of shipments during this period.

(Rapp 1976, p. 228)

Post-war years

Precise data on exports by firm size are available only for the period a couple of decades after the Second World War. By 1960, the post-war recovery of Japan had led to an increase in both the production and exports of several new industries—mostly of a capital-intensive character. At the end of the decade, the leading export-intensive industries were measuring equipment, transportation equipment, electrical machinery, iron and steel, and rubber. The net effect of the shift from the older export industries was towards sectors where larger firms dominated. There was also, of less quantitative significance, an increase in the share of large firms in exports within industries. The net result was that firms employing more than 300 workers accounted for three-quarters of manufactured exports. The export intensity of these large firms was also well above unity overall—and in most individual industries (ibid., Table 9, pp. 234–235).

The importance of exports in Japanese growth

It should be clear from the above discussion that exports came from large firms disproportionately—and it seems very probable that the importance of large firms increased with the growth of Japanese exports through its various stages of growth. This conclusion begs the question: how important were exports in the Japanese growth process? If SMEs were as important in Japanese economic development as the material presented earlier suggests, was it really the expansion of the domestic market for manufactured goods which acted as the major driver in the growth process?

A common perception among economists has been that Japanese economic development was export-led (Minami 1986, p. 223 cites Blumenthal and Shinohara supporting this hypothesis, among others). Manufacturing contributed to the bulk of the growing export ratio in Japanese development, as in British development. In Japan, the proportion of manufactured goods to commodity exports increased from 52.9 per cent in 1874–80 to 94 per cent in 1931–39 (ibid., Table 7.6, p. 227). There was also increasing diversification within manufactured exports as products other than textiles came into the picture. But although exports at first sight would appear to be the leading sector in Japanese growth in the pre-war period, a growing number of scholars have disputed the thesis of export-led growth.

Minami reports that the increase in exports accounted for a much smaller proportion of the increase in gross national expenditure (GNE) than private and government consumption expenditure and of fixed capital formation both during the pre-war and the post-war periods. The Minami averages for the increase in the share of the individual components to the increase in GNE in the entire 1888–1938 period was 57.6 per cent for personal consumption, 14.6 per cent for government consumption, and 30.7 per cent for gross fixed capital formation, as against 25.0 per cent for exports (ibid., Table 6.7, p. 177).

More important from the point of view of the point being discussed in this section is the contribution of different components of the demand for the manufactured products. The share of exports in manufactured finished goods rose through the end of the First World War but then levelled off in the inter-war period. But even during the period of expansion of manufactured exports, foreign demand did not reach 30 per cent of total production. Shinoya (1968) makes the point that exports did not imply impoverishment of the domestic market. On the contrary, exports made the importation of machinery and intermediate goods possible, and this helped build up the capacity of industry to sustain the increased supply of manufactured goods to the home market. The production of manufactured goods for the domestic market was constrained not by demand but by supply. The supply constraint was not labour—since the economy enjoyed conditions of surplus labour throughout the pre-war period (as evidenced by the limited increase in wages). Rather, the constraint was the necessary intermediate and capital goods which could only be imported. Exports eased this constraint and allowed production for the home market to grow along with exports. It is significant to note that, even during the rapid growth of heavy industries in the 1930s and the attendant increase in investment and military durables, domestic consumption provided the lion's share of the final demand for finished manufactured goods.

The analysis of the composition of the final demand for finished manufactured goods is not sufficient to quantify the relative importance of different factors in the causes of industrialization. This is because the exercise does not take account of the changing role of intermediate manufactured goods and of imports. Shinoya addresses this question as well, extending earlier work by Chenery *et al.* (1962). He attempts to classify industries into four categories according to the economic use made of their output in terms of the demand for which they are destined. The four categories are: consumer goods, investment goods, unfinished goods, and export goods. The classification of the output of each industry into these four categories require either input–output or commodity flow statistics. The latter method pioneered by Kuznets (1938) and Shaw (1947) is followed by Shinoya for the pre-war period in Japan and the input–output tables are used for the analysis after the Second World War (Table 8.6).

Shinoya's calculations suggest a trend decline in domestic consumption as a factor in industrialization—which was interrupted temporarily in the immediate aftermath of the First World War. But the major factors in the shift away from domestic consumption do not seem to have been exports; they were the increase in intermediate demand and in import substitution. The latter was severely interrupted in the period of trade disruption caused by the First World War, allowing

Table 8.6 Contribution of different components to increase in manufactured output

Years	Increase in output	Consumption	Investment	Intermediate demand	Exports	Import substitution
1892–1901 to 1902–11	100.00	35.5	15.8	26.0	27.6	–4.9
1902–11 to 1912–21	100.00	19.8	19.7	29.9	20.3	10.3
1912–21 to 1922–31	100.00	46.0	6.8	39.0	16.2	–8.0
1922–31 to 1930–39	100.00	16.0	12.6	36.5	20.9	14.0

Source: Shinoya (1968, Table 3–13, p. 95).

domestic consumption to increase its share of the increment of manufactured output. But the trend was resumed in the late 1920s. A rise in investment added to the declining share of domestic consumption.

The relatively constant role of exports during the pre-Second World War Japanese industrialization is an important finding. Here we have one explanation for the continued importance of SMEs in the industrial economy of Japan, although, as we have seen, larger firms had a bigger role in direct exports. SMEs played a prominent role not only in the market for consumer goods but also in that for intermediate goods because of the importance of subcontracting.

VIII

Income distribution

We have suggested that the relatively even size distribution of employment in manufacturing, with a limited productivity differential between small and large firms, would be helpful for a high growth rate with equity. Unfortunately, data on income distribution are unavailable for the pre-war period of Japanese industrialization. When firmer data are available, it is seen that the Japanese level of inequality in income distribution is indeed on the low side in an international perspective. Japan in 1962 was reported to have had a Gini coefficient of 0.39— well below the average for the group of middle-income countries (in the $500–$1000 range) to which it belonged. In fact, its Gini value was slightly higher than just a few low-income countries and a small group of egalitarian developed countries like those in Scandinavia (see Fields 1980, Table 4.3, pp. 65–66, quoting Palukert 1973). The World Bank study *The East Asian Miracle* confirmed that Japan in 1965–70 was, along with Taiwan and Korea, part of an outlier group with a low Gini coefficient and high growth rate (World Bank 1993, Figure A1.7, pp. 74–75).

While we do not have direct evidence on the trend of inequality or indeed of its level in terms of standard measures in the pre-Second World War period, key indicators might be looked at to see what they suggest about the trend. The first variable of interest is the role of agriculture—the rate of transfer of surplus labour from this sector and the magnitude of the productivity differential with respect to non-agriculture (see the discussion in Chapter 1 and the Indian case in Chapter 6).

Agriculture relative to non-agriculture

The situation of surplus labour which characterizes Asian peasant agriculture, and which seems to have been present in Japan as well in the earlier stages of industrialization, suggests that the faster the transfer of labour to the developing non-agriculture sector, the less likely an increase in inequality because of the faster rate of growth of the high-productivity non-agricultural sector (see discussion of the Kuznets process in Chapter 2). During the first four decades of the last century in Japan, the labour force in the primary sector declined as the rate of outflow exceeded the rate of natural increase. The rate of outflow was particularly high in the first two decades, declined somewhat in the 1920–30 decade, but picked up again in the next decade (Table 8.7).

It is seen that the massive transfer of labour out of agriculture in the first two decades of the century led to a maintenance of the relative productivity in the primary sector at its level at the turn of the century, in spite of the growth of the higher productivity non-agricultural economy. It contrasts with the experience of India where the relative productivity in agriculture was reduced by a third over the 1980–2000 period. The two decades in Japan following 1920 saw a slow-down in the rate of outflow of labour out of agriculture and this was partly responsible for a small decline (about 10 per cent) in the relative productivity.

Table 8.7 Share of the primary sector in the labour force and its relative productivity (%), 1888–1938

Years	Initial share (%)	Relative contribution* (%)	Relative productivity**	
			A/M	A/A+M+S
1888–1900	69.9	−3.0	n.a.	0.59
1900–10	65.0	−47.0	n.a.	0.53
1910–20	60.2	−49.5	0.38	0.52
1920–30	53.4	2.3	0.34	0.46
1930–38	49.5	−13.3	0.24	0.42
1938	–	–	0.20	0.36

Source: Derived from Minami (1986, Table 9.1, pp. 272–273 and Table 9.3, p. 279).

Notes
* Increase in sectoral employment divided by increase in total labour force.
** Initial year, at 1930–34 prices.

This downward trend was also helped by the rising importance of heavy industry, particularly in the later part of the period with the militarization of the economy, and also by the effect of the world depression turning the terms of trade against agriculture.

We conclude that this role of the primary sector in Japanese growth was a positive contribution to growth with equity, though this particular mechanism might have weakened after 1920.

Trends in wages and wage share

Another partial index to look at to judge the likely trend in inequality is the behaviour of wages in relation to GDP or sectoral growth (Table 8.8).

It is seen that the wages in agriculture had a substantial growth rate in the decade of 1911–20 when Japan took advantage of the First World War to embark on a major industrialization process, moving away from exports to domestic markets. This wage growth, of course, partly compensated for the declining trend in the preceding decade. But agricultural wages fell thereafter. Taking the entire pre-Second World War period as a whole, agricultural real wages remained almost constant.

Manufacturing did not share the experience of decline in the post-1921 decades, although it slowed down and had a slightly downward trend in the 1930s. The wage trends, however, contrast sharply with the post-Second World War situation when, for two or three decades, wage growth had a substantial upward trend in both sectors.

Real wage growth in both sectors took off after the Second World War and reached a level of around 4.5 per cent in both sectors over the 1954–80 periods. While the growth rate of GNP per capita was more than double in the post-Second World War decades, the fact that in the pre-Second World War period GNP per capita averaged just over 2 per cent (and wages were more or less stagnant) has prompted Minami to suggest that the labour market in Japan reached its Lewis turning point after the Second World War. Before the war, Japan was a labour-surplus economy and all of the increase in GNP per capita went to non-labour income.

Table 8.8 Growth rate of real wages (%)

Industry	1896–1902	1903–10	1911–20	1921–30	1931–38
Agriculture*	−0.65	−1.19	3.51	−0.87	−3.06
Manufacturing**	n.a.	0.46	4.64	2.73	−0.49
All non-primary**	n.a.	1.23***	4.15	2.54	0.38

Source: Minami (1986, Table 9.10, p. 301 and Table 9.11, p. 306).

Notes
* Deflated by the rural cost-of-living index.
** All (male plus female) workers: deflated by the urban consumer price index
*** 1900–09.

This view, however, ignores the significant cycles in the pre-war economy. It should be clear from the data presented that, in the second decade in particular, wage growth was very high in both sectors, exceeding the growth rate of GNP. The wage growth slowed down in the next decade, but so did the growth rate of GNP. It was only in the 1930s that a major discrepancy occurred between the trend rates of real wages and of GDP per capita. While the latter increased sharply, real wages were on a declining trend.

Table 8.9 gives the estimates of labour shares calculated by Minami (1986) and the data bear out the point just made.

The figures bring out the critical change in the decade of the 1930s. In the previous decade, when the wage growth rate accelerated along with the growth rate of GDP, the share of wages was maintained in both the corporate and the non-corporate sectors. The next decade saw a severe decline in the share in the non-corporate sector, although the share in the corporate sector also fell by 6 percentage points. We can reasonably conclude from these changes in labour's share that the trend in inequality in Japan was more or less unchanged until 1930, but that it suffered a significant decline in the last decade before the Second World War.

Different aspects of Japanese industrialization are responsible for these differing trends before and after 1930. The Japanese pattern of industrial development before the threshold year of 1930 most likely kept the degree of inequality unchanged. This pattern involved, as we have seen, a size structure of manufacturing in which small and large firms played an equal role with no missing middle, and only a limited differential in labour productivity (and wages) between the two groups. In the decade of the 1930s, inequality increased, particularly in the unincorporated sector. This is more likely to have been the consequence of Japan's increasingly militarized economy with a heavy emphasis on heavy industry and possible labour repression.

It might be tempting to conclude from the evidence of the increased share of wages that the degree of inequality fell significantly after the Second World War.[5] This is consistent with the restructuring of the Japanese economy under Allied occupation. It will be recalled from the discussion earlier in the chapter that the two critical elements in the size structure of manufacturing—the distribution of employment by size groups and the inter-group differentials in labour productivity—had remained more or less unchanged in the post-Second World War period. The decline in the degree of inequality is then a one-time shift of the

Table 8.9 Income share of labour (%)

Sector	1900	1910	1920	1930	1938	1955	1968
Incorporated	n.a.	52.7	55.4	58.1	52.2	69.3	63.5
Unincorporated	n.a.	66.7	57.9	56.6	44.7	72.6	77.7
All	67.8	62.9	56.9	57.2	48.1	70.3	66.7

Source: Minami (1986, Table 9.18, p. 321).

trajectory of the economy to a lower Gini value due to exogenous political economy factors, that is, the reform of the economy imposed by the post-war occupation.

IX

Conclusions

This chapter has explored the Japanese case of economic growth, particularly in the pre-Second World War years with a view to shedding light on the contrasts between the Japanese growth experience and that of India in recent decades.

We saw that Japanese development in much of the pre-Second World War period was led by manufacturing, not the tertiary sector, and that the relative productivity difference has been in favour of manufacturing. We saw that the use of the dualistic pattern is quite different from what we found in the Indian case. There is no evidence of the phenomenon of the missing middle emerging in any period of Japan's growth. Rather, small enterprise played as important a role in manufacturing[6] as middle-sized and large units. The upward mobility of small firms into medium-sized ones, reflected in this picture of stable size distribution, leads to the expectation that the productivity differential between small and large firms would not be very large. In fact, the difference in labour productivity between the largest and the smallest size groups was seen in Japan to be of the order of 3 : 1 throughout the period—a far cry from the 8 : 1 differential found in India.

The co-existence of small, medium, and large firms in Japanese manufacturing was helped by some important features of Japanese economic development. These included: the persistence of demand for traditional as well as modern consumer goods; the successful development of subcontracting; and electrification, which permitted the spread of technology. It has been maintained in the literature that large firms have an advantage in exports. While the evidence does suggest that export intensity was higher for larger firms, there are two major reasons why this factor did not hamper the relative profitability of smaller firms: first, taking intermediate goods into account, Japan had never been an export-dominated economy; second, subcontracting allowed smaller firms to participate actively not only in the export economy but even more so in the market for intermediate goods.

9 The role of small-medium enterprises in manufacturing and economic development

The case of Taiwan

Taiwan's spectacular economic growth starting in the mid-1950s was accompanied by large population movements. The expulsion of the Japanese in the aftermath of the Second World War was followed by a substantial migration of people from mainland China. Kuznets' estimates of the growth of the population, particularly in the last few years of the 1940s, put the growth rate well above that of natural increase—which itself was bumped up by sharply falling death rates (Kuznets 1979, Table 1.5). But apart from the impact on the growth rate of the population, the immigration of mainlanders was critical to the shaping of the course of Taiwan's economic development. The group had a disproportionate effect on government policy as a subset of it took charge of decision making. Moreover, with no connection to interest groups among the native population, they were able to push through growth-oriented reform measures. To quote Kuznets:

> The importance of the government's role is indicated by major decisions made during the 1950s—on land reform, on the public and private choices in industrial development, on curbing inflation through the control of money supply and government budgets, on regulating foreign exchange and controlling foreign trade, and most recently, on major public projects that seemed advisable to cushion the shock of recent world recessions.
>
> (ibid., p. 28)

I

Manufacturing as the leading sector

Taiwan's industrialization can be divided into four phases: from the initial primary import substitution phase to primary export orientation phase, stretching over the period from the early 1960s to the mid-1970s (that relied on unskilled labour-intensive manufacturing); to the higher skill content and capital-intensive secondary import substitution leading to exports of such manufactured goods; and finally to the so-called de-industrialization phase.[1]

Taiwan consistently experienced a high rate of growth of GDP from the early years of the 1950s. The relevant data on growth rates as well as the changing composition by industry of origin are given in Table 9.1. It should be remembered that the rate of population growth fell over time so that the growth rate of GDP per capita showed some significant acceleration. Kuznets reported that GDP per capita in 1971 prices accelerated from 3.76 per cent between 1951–53 and 1961–63 to nearly double its value in the next decade between 1961–63 and 1971–73 (ibid., Table 1.8, p. 45).

The data on GDP by industry of origin show the rapid decline of agriculture and related activities over the two decades. It is remarkable to see that—unlike the experience of many developing countries in later years—the tertiary sector did not play any role in compensating for this loss in agriculture's share of GDP. The secondary sector accounted for the entire rising share of non-agriculture in GDP. Furthermore, while in the first decade a small percentage of this increase (about 2.5 of the 7.5 increase in percentage points) was accounted for by subsectors like construction and transportation, in the subsequent decade manufacturing took care of the entire increase of the non-agricultural share from 36.1 per cent to 51.3 per cent of GDP.

Labour absorption

Galenson (1979) has put together the data on the changing sectoral composition of employment in Taiwan over the period 1952 to 1975. The series are from two different sources. The second of this series for the period after 1966 is from the more reliable labour force surveys. The series for the previous years are estimates based on census and household survey data. But we can see from the figures given in Table 9.2 for the overlapping year (1966) that the discrepancy between the two series is not very serious.

It should be remembered that the period covered in Table 9.2 experienced an accelerating increase in the labour force. "During the thirteen years 1953 to 1966, the labor force grew by 27 per cent; in the following nine years the increase was 48 per cent" (ibid., p. 384). Galenson notes that the spurt in the growth rate was in spite of a fall in the working-age population. It was clearly due to the rising participation rates for females, which more than compensated for the smaller fall in male participation, primarily due to schooling.[2] Despite this growing labour force, the substantial fall in the proportion absorbed by agriculture was only to a small extent accommodated in the tertiary sector. A much more important source of employment was industry (and the dominant manufacturing).

II

Size structure of establishments in Taiwan

Abe and Kawakami (1997) have put together the data for the distribution of employment and value added by size groups in Taiwan for the period 1966–91. These data are from the Industrial and Commercial Censuses of Taiwan

Table 9.1 Growth rates and shares of GDP by industrial origin (%)

	1951–53	1954–57	1958–60	1961–63	1964–67	1968–70	1971–73
Growth rates of GDP	–	7.49	6.24	6.83	9.76	9.20	6.24
Shares of GDP							
Agriculture	33.2	27.8	27.2	24.9	22.4	16.5	13.1
Secondary	26.2	31.8	33.8	36.1	39.9	46.0	51.3
Of which:							
Manufacturing	15.5	19.6	21.4	23.0	26.7	32.3	37.9
Other	10.7	12.2	12.4	13.1	13.2	13.7	13.4
Tertiary	40.8	40.4	39.0	39.0	37.7	37.5	35.6
Of which:							
Public	9.1	9.9	10.1	10.6	10.2	10.7	10.1
Social and business	5.2	4.8	4.7	4.9	5.2	5.1	5.5
Commerce	17.8	17.4	16.2	15.4	14.3	13.1	11.1
Finance	8.5	8.3	8.0	8.1	8.0	8.6	8.9

Source: Kuznets (1979, Tables 1.8 and 1.10).

(Republic of China). They contain data based on individual establishments (factories, etc.) and on the whole enterprises. The difference in the distribution for the two types of classification is not great—except for the largest size class (employing more than 500 workers). Since the data based on individual establishments are more comparable internationally, Table 9.3 presents the distribution for this classification.

The trend in employment towards establishments in smaller size groups started at the beginning of the 1970s and accelerated in the second half of the 1980s. The shift before this acceleration was more from large (500+) to medium-sized firms (100–499), with the share of the small (under 100) remaining roughly at around 40 per cent. But in the more recent period after 1986, there was a sharp increase in the share of the small at the expense of both the large and the medium. It is also important to note that this shift was accompanied by little significant decline in the relative labour productivity of the small units (except perhaps in the initial five-year period of 1966–71). This can be seen by comparing the value added relatives in Panel B of Table 9.3 with the employment relatives of Panel A.

Taiwan belongs to the group of Asian economies where employment is distributed fairly evenly between the different size groups—small, medium, and large—and the productivity difference between the size groups is also relatively small. While the productivity difference in Taiwan would seem to be larger than Hong Kong if we compare the lowest and the highest size groups, closer examination shows that this appearance is largely due to the high relative productivity of the largest (500+) size group in Taiwan. Value added per worker rises very gently up to the level of the large firms of 500+ workers and then seems to take a big jump.

Table 9.2 Sectoral composition of employment (%)

Year	Agriculture*	Industry**	Services***
1952	60.5	18.4	21.1
1955	58.8	20.0	21.2
1960	52.7	25.2	22.1
1965	46.9	28.9	24.2
1966	45.6	29.7	24.7
(1966)	*(43.5)*	*(28.2)*	*(28.3)*
1970	36.8	33.7	29.5
1973	30.5	39.5	30.0
1975	29.9	41.2	28.9

Source: Galenson (1979, Tables 6.2 and 6.3). The data for 1966 onwards are based on the more reliable labour force surveys.

Notes
* Includes agriculture, forestry, and fishing.
** Includes mining; manufacturing; construction; electricity, gas, and water; and transport and communication.
*** Includes all other industries.

Industrial composition and firm size

The specific features of Taiwanese industrialization which produced the rather even distribution of employment in different size groups can best be analysed by contrasting it with the case of Korea—the other case of export-oriented industrialization in East Asia after the Second World War. As we pointed out in Chapter 2 (and will elaborate in the next chapter), Korea favoured a skewed distribution to the larger size of firms until the late 1970s, but then reversed its course towards a greater presence of SMEs through deliberate government policies to promote the latter.[3]

The first point we need to investigate is whether the difference in industrial composition—related to the different patterns of industrialization in the two countries—was responsible for the difference in size distribution. The situation around 1971 is portrayed in Table 9.4.

The picture emerging even at the broad two-digit level is clear. Around 1971, the industrial composition of the two countries was not significantly different. However, it is seen that, while Taiwan had a larger share of employment in the largest 500+ employment size group in the more traditional industries like food and textiles, it was more than overshadowed by the much smaller share of this size group in the other subsectors. This is indeed the basic reason for the differing trends in the size distribution (Ho 1980, Table 4, p. 730). Taiwan favoured smaller establishments in these newer industries more than Korea.

It is well known that Korea emphasized heavy industry development, particularly during the years immediately following the first oil crisis in the 1970s. It is,

Table 9.3 Distribution of employment in manufacturing by size groups and relative labour productivity: Taiwan, various years

A. Percentage distribution of employment

Size groups	1966	1971	1976	1986	1991
1–9	12.8	9.4	10.2	10.4	14.1
10–49	21.2	17.0	17.7	24.0	29.6
50–99	8.7	9.2	11.1	13.5	12.8
100–499	22.5	28.2	30.4	28.1	21.3
500 and above	34.1	36.1	30.6	24.1	22.2

B. Relative labour productivity (value added per worker)

Size groups	1966	1971	1976	1986	1991
1–9	n.a.	40	33	34	30
10–49	n.a.	36	34	35	31
50–99	n.a.	47	36	38	35
100–499	n.a.	45	48	49	47
500 and above	n.a.	100	100	100	100

Source: Abe and Kawakami (1997, Table 1).

Table 9.4 Industrial composition and distribution of employment by size groups and industry: Korea 1973 and Taiwan 1971 (percentages)

Industry group	Share of employment (%)			% of industry total		
	Korea 1973	Taiwan 1971		1–99	100–499	500+
Food, beverages and tobacco	15.7	11.7	K	62.7	16.1	21.2
			T	39.6	18.7	41.7
Textiles, apparel and leather	33.5	25.8	K	37.4	29.1	33.5
			T	21.9	34.1	44.0
Wood and furniture	4.8	6.6	K	48.3	7.1	44.6
			T	43.1	21.1	35.8
Paper, printing and publishing	4.6	4.2	K	48.1	35.5	16.4
			T	52.8	26.8	20.4
Chemical, petroleum and plastic	10.9	15.4	K	22.5	22.1	55.4
			T	34.0	33.3	32.7
Non-metallic mineral	4.6	5.0	K	51.3	22.1	26.6
			T	63.5	20.6	15.9
Basic metals	2.8	2.4	K	23.1	29.5	47.4
			T	28.7	28.4	42.9
Metal production, machinery, etc.	17.8	24.7	K	31.3	23.1	45.6
			T	49.1	20.8	30.1
Other	5.3	4.2	K	34.3	29.8	35.9
			T	28.6	31.0	40.4
Total	100	100	K	37.3	24.2	38.5
(Thousands)	(1315)	(1250)	T	36.2	41.0	22.8

Source: Ho (1980, Tables D3 and D4).

however, not so widely recognized that Taiwan also went through a period of state-supported development of heavy industry in these years. Taiwan lost its diplomatic status around the time of the first oil crisis, which threatened the inflow of foreign investment. To counter this, the country moved towards a policy of self-sufficiency, particularly hoping to develop heavy industry. We conclude that, to pinpoint the reasons for the greater prominence of SMEs in Taiwan's manufacturing, we should look not to its composition of industry, but to the ownership pattern of firms, as influenced by differing government policies.

Government policies, ownership patterns, and firm size

In the early years of Taiwan's development, the state took over the Japanese private enterprises, and the direct involvement of the state in manufacturing was sustained in the import substitution phase. The importance of large firms in

Taiwan manufacturing during this phase was largely due to the central role of these state-owned establishments in a narrow range of industries. The direct involvement of the state in manufacturing enterprises was reduced in the next export-oriented phase, but there was a U-turn in the next phase of secondary import substitution, when the government felt the necessity to provide intermediate manufactured goods as inputs for the newer industries.

The government's attitude to foreign investment also changed after the initial import substitution (IS) period. Foreign investment was welcomed in the period since the early 1960s, first, as Taiwan sought replacement for US foreign aid, and second, after the diplomatic change following the US–China rapprochement of 1973, when the government felt that the presence of US and Japanese investment in the island would prevent a more drastic swing towards the political goals of the mainland regime. Nevertheless, the direct investment of foreign firms in Taiwan's economy was not all that large. Chou reports that the contribution of foreign direct investment to domestic capital formation was 1.9 per cent in the first phase, increasing to 5.5 per cent in the second period, but declining to 3 per cent in the secondary import substitution phase (Chou 1995, Table 4.1, p. 123). The proportion of value of production was much higher, but still not more than 20 per cent at its peak (ibid.).

Private domestic firms became important as Taiwan's industrialization proceeded. The role of business groups is of critical interest in the evolution of the size structure of Taiwan's manufacturing. The participants are "people linked by relations of interpersonal trust". In Taiwan, the groups were formed largely on the basis of family ties. The average scale of the individual participants of the group was larger than that of foreign firms and of manufacturing as a whole, but less than that of public enterprises (see Table 9.5).

There was, of course, considerable variation in scale among members of the group. There were eight groups whose individual turnover exceeded 1 per cent of GNP (headed by the Formosa Plastic Corporation, which contributed 4.1 per cent of GNP in 1980). The total turnover of these eight groups reached a little more than 15 per cent of GNP and one-half of the entire turnover of all groups put together. More than 90 other groups shared the other half (Chou 1995, p. 125).

It has, however, been emphasized by most researchers of Taiwan's industrialization that the Government of Taiwan had a preference for state enterprises and multilaterals rather than very large domestic private businesses. The ethnic difference between the ruling Kuomintang and the native Taiwanese bourgeoisie was probably a decisive factor in this suspicion of large native conglomerates. In this way, Taiwan differed markedly from Korea, where the link between political leaders and big business provides a distinct bias to giant business groups.

This discouragement of the growth of giant conglomerates was evidently one factor which provided space for SMEs to flourish in Taiwan manufacturing. But the other important reason was the strong growth of the subcontracting system, which was special to this economy. This system depended, on the one hand, on incentives for trading companies as well as larger manufacturers to seek out

Table 9.5 Number of firms and their characteristics on manufacturing industries, 1976

	Total manufacturing	Public enterprises	Foreign enterprises	Group's enterprises[1]
Number of firms	69,517	89	988	673
Average size in terms of assets in operation (NT$ million)	15.1	3474	119.3[2]	375.5
Employees (persons)	27	1493	266	446
Turnover (NT$ million)	11.3	1445.1	137.9	289.6
K/L ratios[3] (NT$ thousand to persons)	599	2327	449	842

Sources: DGBAS, Executive Yuan, National Income of the Republic of China, 1981, Tables 6, 7 and 12, pp. 137, 140–145 and 182–189; China Credit Information Services, Studies on Group Enterprises on Taiwan, 1982, pp. 24–35; The Committee on Industrial and Commercial Censuses of Taiwan Fukien District of the Republic of China (ICCT), Executive Yuan, The Report of 1976 Industrial and Commercial Census, 1976, vol. 3, Bool 1, Table 1, pp. 1–2.

Notes
1 Business groups include the non-manufacturing sector.
2 This is estimated from the ratio of foreign firms to total manufacturing firms in terms of fixed assets.
3 The ratio of assets of operation to employee.

SMEs which could supply a variety of components for the final products they wanted to market and, on the other hand, on the existence of a large number of small producers which could respond to this demand and provide the necessary components at the required pace and quality.

The literature provides a number of industry-specific studies which document and discuss the mechanics of SME development in Taiwan. We select two examples from this to illustrate the Taiwan case.

The footwear industry

Levy has studied the remarkable difference in the trajectories of development in the footwear industries of Taiwan and Korea. The industry in both countries was highly export oriented. The rate of growth of exports was phenomenal, increasing from only US$10 million in 1969 to over $2 billion in 1986 in each country (Levy 1991, Table 3, p. 134).

> But already in 1971 Taiwan had twenty times the number of firms as did Korea; but the value of exports per Korean firms was an average of fourteen times that of Taiwan. These early disparities widened over the course of the 1970s; by 1979 the average Korean firm (in terms of export value) was twenty-two times the size of its Korean counterpart.

In both countries, the initial surge in demand came from the decision of Mitsubishi, the leading Japanese trading company dealing in footwear, to relocate the manufacture of shoes for US markets from Japan to Taiwan and Korea. But the way this initial surge played out differed in fundamental ways in the two countries. Levy points out that:

- Taiwanese entrepreneurs established new firms much more readily than the Koreans. While in Korea the new orders were mostly channelled through an expansion of existing firms, Taiwan seems to have provided a breeding ground for numerous new producers. The Japanese started the process by identifying and encouraging suitable entrepreneurs to establish new productive units, and there is evidence to suggest that this effort continued into the 1980s.
- The process of diversification of production sources was strengthened by the ability of the Taiwanese industry to accept subcontracting much more easily than their Korean counterparts. The Korean manufacturers throughout the 1970s were organized on a vertically integrated basis, combining in the same firm the several stages of production (cutting, stitching of uppers, and lasting). By contrast, "it is rare for a Taiwanese footwear firm to perform in-house more than at most two of the various sub-processes" (ibid., p. 156). Unlike the historical model in Japan, and in any other Asian countries, the Taiwanese subcontractor did not typically cluster one or two big firms; Taiwanese subcontractors maintain supply relationships with multiple independent affiliates.

- The entry of small firms was rendered easy because of the proliferation of independent traders. Levy's data showed that between 1973 and 1984, while the number of export traders in Korea increased nearly fivefold from 1200 to 5300, in Taiwan (where the number was already double that of Korea) it increased nearly nine fold from 2700 to 20,600. The average value of industrial exports per trader (initially double the value of Taiwan in Korea) more than doubled over the ten years, while that of Taiwan remained constant (ibid., Table 4, p. 157). This growing number of traders was not all foreigners. In 1985, 70 per cent of the Taiwanese respondents in a survey reported that domestic traders handled 50 per cent or more of their exports.
- Finally, Levy underlines the point that the Taiwanese footwear industry was much more diversified than the Korean. Even after the Korean industry had seen a reduction in the average firm size during the period of SME promotion starting with the late 1970s, non-rubber athletic shoes continued to be the single most important element in Korean footwear exports, accounting for as much as 71.3 per cent of the total value. By contrast, in Taiwan this item was also the leading footwear export good in 1985 but accounted for no more than 27.5 per cent of the total export value. The next five items in order of importance in the export list provided an additional 42.4 per cent, while the remaining 30 per cent was composed of an array of different items (ibid., p. 158). The divergent export structure of the Taiwan footwear industry was both a cause and consequence of the decentralized industrial structure.

Amsden has made the point that "big firms in Taiwan's subcontracting system are not absent, but simply invisible". She maintains: "Except for tiniest establishments, many small firms are members of a business group. They are only independent for tax purposes. Moreover, global businesses operate in Taiwan's subcontracting systems offshore multinationals that contract for Taiwan-made goods and services" (Amsden 1991, p. 1129). Big businesses are important in providing the benefits of scale economies in marketing, but also help in the transfer of technology and the supply of inputs to the small manufacturers.

Taiwanese economists have commented on the "dichotomous market structure" in the economy. Large-scale producers, including state enterprises and top participants in business groups, are significantly inward looking, focusing on the domestic market. They enjoy monopolistic market relationships because of the limited competition. On the other hand, the numerous small-scale producers and trading companies are often dependent on foreign buyers with significant market power and operate in consequence in highly competitive environments.

The bicycle industry

Wan-wen Chu (1997) has documented the case of the bicycle industry, which started in Taiwan during the IS regime in the early 1950s. In the period 1952–54, four major assemblers and manufacturers of various parts emerged in Taiwan.

They also tried to cater to the domestic market by maintaining a country-wide repair network. But in spite of the protection afforded from imports, the income level in the economy was just not high enough to sustain these establishments, and they went into liquidation by 1965.

The growth of the industry started again with the export drive around 1969. But it was only with the upsurge in demand for bicycles in the United States after the first oil shock that the Taiwan industry took off. The sudden upsurge in US demand was channelled to Taiwan by a body of foreign traders. The role of the foreign buyers exceeded that of just transfer of technology:

> The role of the foreign buyer here resembled very much that of multinational corporations (MNC) making direct investment in the LDCs, except that the foreign buyers did not commit their capital directly. For they both initiated the process, helped the local producers to set up production, monitored progress, checked the product, offered financing via issuing letters of credit, and marketed the product in developed countries.
>
> (ibid., p. 60)

The response of Taiwan entrepreneurs to respond to this opportunity was spectacular. The data show an acceleration in the growth rate of the industry between 1971 and 1976, with the number of establishments increasing by over 60 per cent (see Table 9.6). Most of the units were of small scale—the average employment per enterprise was fewer than 20, even in 1981 after a massive period of growth. There was a slight upward trend in the average number of employees in the next decade, but the rate of growth was not as high as value added per employee and assets per employee. Evidently in the 1980s, the industry upgraded itself in terms of technology and labour productivity, while the employment size of enterprises remained small.

There were two types of SMEs involved in the production of bicycles: the producers of parts and the assemblers. Bicycle manufacture requires a great deal of assembly work and involves work with nearly 100 different parts. The Taiwan industry had little vertical integration from the beginning. A survey at the end of the 1980s showed that 90 per cent of the bicycle assemblers produced no parts at all. At the same time, the parts producers were highly specialized, with over 90 per cent producing only one type of bicycle part (quoted by Wan-wen Chu 1997, p. 61). The same survey found that "on average, each bicycle producer has about 60 parts suppliers and each parts producer supplies up to 20 bicycle assemblers. Thus, the degree of dependence on particular supplier or buyer is not very high" (ibid., p. 64).

In other words, the Taiwan bicycle industry depended on a network of suppliers and assemblers, most of whom were SMEs dealing happily with each other. At the same time, their contact with foreign sources and markets was well developed. Many small Taiwan suppliers exported a portion of their output of parts, and assemblers also imported foreign parts. It is this openness which sustained the process of continuous technological upgrading and gave the industry the

Table 9.6 Market structure of bicycle and parts industry

Item/year	1966	1971	1976	1981	1986	1991
(1)	255	279	447	541	867	1,307
(2)	3534	4463	9233	9726	22,948	30,647
(2)/(1)	15.71	16.00	20.66	17.98	26.47	23.45
(7)/(2)	25.86	29.58	62.93	193.39	254.96	464.28
(9)/(2)	53.85	9417	300.06	520.42	667.66	1315.21

Sources: The Report on Industrial and Commercial Census, Taiwan-Fuben Area, the Republic of China, 1966, 1971, 1976, 1981, 1986, 1991; Wan-wen Chu (1997, Table 4, p. 62).

Note
(1) refers to number of enterprise units, (2) number of persons employed, (7) annual gross value added, and (9) net value of assets in operation. Thus the third row lists the average number of persons employed per enterprise, the fourth row the average annual gross value added per employee, and the fifth row the average net value of assets used per employee.

flexibility to respond to opportunities, as in the demand surge in North America following the first oil crisis.

What was the role of the state in the development of the industry? It can be maintained with confidence that the leading role of the state in the early import substitution phase created the initial pool of know-how, even if the early producers under the IS regime did not last. The subsequent flourishing of the industry clearly depended on the availability of numerous small-scale entrepreneurs with necessary skills. The state played no more than a supporting role in this development. For instance, in the early years of the industry in the 1970s, the state:

> assisted the industry in solving production problems, and establishing national standards for the bicycle. Bicycles from different firms were examined, and those firms whose products failed to meet the standards were not allowed to export.... The coordinating role played by the government helped to remedy an obvious market failure at a crucial moment in the development of the industry.
>
> (ibid., p. 66)

III

Factors in decentralized industrialization

There is a large body of literature on the pattern of development in Taiwan. It has stressed two important aspects of the development process which favoured a growth path giving major importance to a dynamic SME sector: the bundle of historical and socio-political factors which lowered inter-firm transaction costs; and dispersed industrial development, which saw the widespread growth of firms in rural and small urban areas.

Reducing inter-firm transaction costs

Levy (1991) in particular has sought to interpret the difference in the size structure of manufacturing between Taiwan and Korea in terms of a theoretical
framework of transaction costs. "Economic agents select those contractual mechanisms that minimize the sum of production costs and the costs of contracting."
In economies in which transaction costs are higher, buyers and manufacturers
would tend to economize on these transactions by dealing in large orders, and
also by organizing production hierarchically within firms. We would then see a
high incidence of large business groups and vertically integrated firms. Con-
versely, in economies with low transaction costs, there will be a larger presence
of inter-firm exchanges in the process of production and marketing—involving a
large number of small-scale traders and producers.

The level of transaction costs would be heavily dependent on the specific
socio-economic structure prevalent at the beginning of the process of recent
development—as indeed Taiwan differed significantly from Korea in the post-
war scenario. But the difference could be magnified if state policies veered in a
direction which responded to these initial disparities but then this bias in policies
accentuated the differences.

Difference in initial conditions

Both Korea and Taiwan were Japanese colonies and their development (including some industrialization) took place under the colonial regime. Korea seems to
have industrialized ahead of Taiwan, but the civil war and partition had a profound impact on the relative economic position of the two countries at the beginning of their post-colonial development. Most of the Korean industry was
located in the North, so after the partition South Korea was less industrialized
than Taiwan. Agriculture also seemed to have been more developed in Taiwan.
In 1961, GNP per capita in Korea was only 55 per cent of the figure for Taiwan.

There was also higher stock of commercial enterprise in Taiwan. Most of the
industry in Korea, both large scale and SMEs, were owned by the Japanese. But
in Taiwan, while many of the large corporations were owned and managed by
the Japanese, SMEs seem to have been much more in the control of Taiwanese
entrepreneurs. Along with the higher level of GDP, the education level of the
population was higher in Taiwan. The proportion of the population aged six and
over and with 12 or more years of education in 1960 was 14.2 per cent in Taiwan—nearly three times that of Korea (Levy 1991, Table 8, p. 165).

Difference in the evolution of policies

As a result of the lower level of development of the Korean economy at the
beginning of its post-war development process, resources (particularly capital
funds) were seriously deficient. This prompted the state to be interested in a
more centralized way to guide the development path. The Park Cheng-hee

administration nationalized the financial institutions and took direct control of the inflow of foreign savings, which were managed by current account deficits and continued devaluation of the currency. By contrast, the approach to Taiwanese development was much less centralized. Taiwan also presented a contrasting picture of external accounts, which were in surplus much of the time, showing a lesser need for foreign capital inflow.

We should mention a sociological element in the difference between the two economies, which induced them to move in different directions in the size structure of manufacturing. This has to do with the relationship between state and society and the network relationships in the civil society. Taiwan after the war saw the arrival of the Kuomintang from the mainland, which created a deep rift between the state (dominated by the immigrants) and the native Taiwanese. The latter were not inclined to join the administrative elite. Their focus on economic rather than political advancement fostered a growth of industry without centralized support from the state institutions—including the financial. This produced a suspicion of the emergence of conglomerate giants, which dominated Korean economic growth in the early years, and which depended so much on the ties of mutual interdependence among the military, government, and political elites.

The less centralized Taiwanese development might also have been aided by the difference in the pattern of social networks in the two countries. The social networks among the traditional Taiwanese are reported to have been "horizontal, open, and flexible". By horizontal, we mean each network member is highly independent and cannot be controlled from above or subordinated. By open, we mean that network boundaries are not well defined and that they can be expanded when deemed necessary. By flexible, we mean that human relationships in these networks are very functional (active when needed and inactive when not needed).

Infrastructure development and rural industrialization

There are two major factors which have encouraged dispersed industrialization in Taiwan. The first is the strong historical development of agriculture and some agro-based industries. Second is the relatively early and substantial development of infrastructure.

While both Taiwan and Korea started modern agricultural development as Japanese colonies, Taiwan's colonial development started earlier and, in the 1930s, its agriculture was more developed and prosperous than Korea's. While the higher level of agricultural income would by itself support rural-based industry through higher levels of local demand, the process was helped by the promotion of agro-industries. One well-known example is the development of the colony as Japan's main provider of sugar.

The literature has noted that "throughout its modern period of economic transition rural Taiwan has had access to an adequate transportation system" (Ho 1982, p. 983). The railway ran through Western Taiwan, where most of its farming population is located, from as early as 1908. In 1962, the density of paved highway and feeder roads was 76.4 km per thousand sq.km. of area, contrasting with a figure of below 10.0 for Korea in 1960. Rural electrification also began early; by 1960, 70 per cent of farm households had electricity (ibid.).

The sequence of industrialization in Taiwan was then markedly different from Korea's. Taiwan progressed from agricultural growth, through infrastructure development to manufacturing, while Korea seems to have gone down the path of industrialization first with foreign finance and subsequent rural development.

It should be emphasized that the connection of infrastructure development to decentralized industrialization does not run necessarily through lower transport costs. It can indeed be argued that the reduction in hauling costs might be more beneficial to large firms with economies of scale in a centralized location. In the Taiwan case, a significant impact on decentralization might have been an element of government policy which set lower rates on short-haul movements and also restricted trucking companies to operations within one of seven geographic zones (Sylia 1974, p. 34). There are other avenues through which infrastructure development, together with agricultural growth, could facilitate decentralization of industry.

The literature on "growth poles" has stressed the economies of agglomeration which are spread out over a number of urban clusters away from the metropolitan cities. These economies include the supply of trading, financial, and other business services, and the creation of a pool of skilled labour. The labour market aspects of decentralized development are particularly pertinent in the Taiwanese context. Some of Taiwan's fastest growing industries (e.g. textiles, apparel, and electronics) employed a disproportionate number of female workers. Industrial units were located near rural areas, which enabled easy access to female wage workers from farm families who could easily commute to their industrial jobs. It should be noted that, by and large, these day workers were neither part-time nor secondary workers whose main job was farming. In fact, even as early as 1970 only about 13 per cent of the employed rural population in Taiwan reported a secondary occupation in the Census, and this proportion must have been reduced drastically by the 1960s. Ho quotes official Agricultural Census reporting that in 1970, of the 1.2 million Taiwanese farm household members who had off-farm employment, a half worked full-time off their farms and most in wage employment (Ho, op. cit., Tables 1 and 2 and footnote 13). The Taiwan model of labour supply to industry contrasts dramatically with that of Korea, which also used a growing proportion of female labour in its manufacturing sector. Unlike Taiwan, Korea depended much more on the traditional Lewis model of migration of labour from the rural to large urban areas. Because of the limited development of infrastructure, Korean industry was concentrated in the urban conglomerates. Ho gives figures to show that in Korea factory employment in the two major conurbations (Seoul and Busan areas) increased from 58 per cent in 1958 to 74 per cent in 1975. In Taiwan, the trend was just the opposite. The percentage of factory employment in Taiwan's five major cities was 70 per cent in 1966 and 52 per cent in 1971.

In fact, it can be argued that the relocation of medium and large units to these areas is a necessary pre-condition of the dynamic growth of small enterprises.

Agricultural development per se can have a dynamic impact on the growth of small industry through demand linkages—either the consumption demand of farmers as their income increases, or the increased demand for farm machinery and other inputs as farming methods become more sophisticated. But the supply-side effects on the growth of small enterprises emanating from the development of growth poles would come not just from agricultural growth, but from the development of small and large enterprises in urban locations away from the big cities.

Amsden (1991, Table 6) produces data to show that over the period of 1966–86 the growth rate of industrial employment was highest in the four suburban areas, followed by the rural region. The redistribution of employment from the five big cities did take place but the other urban areas played a more important role in the redistribution than the rural areas. A second important point to notice is that, although the average firm size was declining over time in both the big cities and the other urban areas, the mean size stayed consistently higher in the latter. Evidently, the redistribution involved not just a rising importance of small firms in all urban areas, but also a perceptible shift of larger firms to the newer urban locations. Industrial employment in the rural areas also increased, and indeed faster than in the big cities, although not as fast as in the suburban towns. The mean size of firms was the lowest in the rural sector.

IV

Exports and the role of SMEs

Exports versus domestic market in Taiwanese development

There was a major shift in the 1960s (particularly in the latter half of the decade) to exports as Taiwan increased its competitiveness in world markets. This was particularly important for non-durable consumer goods—labour-intensive light industries. Nevertheless, a decomposition analysis of sources of demand for growth for manufacturing, which takes account of inter-industry linkages produced by Ranis (1979, Table 3.10, p. 227), shows that growing demand in the domestic market continued to provide the bulk of the market growth for Taiwan's manufacturing industries. This demand continued to be fed by rapidly increasing income in the agricultural sector at the same time as the shift of labour to non-agriculture contributed to the rising GDP per capita. According to Ranis's calculations, the home market for all manufactured goods accounted for 74.7 per cent of the output in 1965–70, down from 82.5 per cent in 1960–65.

Export ratios of SMEs

While Taiwan was not an export-oriented industry in the extreme sense of supporting its industrial development through the dominant role of exports, the export ratio of its manufacturing sector was quite high. A more spectacular part of the story is that the export ratio of SMEs was substantially higher than that of the large enterprises for a long period of its growth. Heather Smith reproduces official data to show that in 1976 (the earliest year for which her series is reported) the export ratio of SMEs was 56.8 per cent as against 39.1 per cent for large enterprises. The export ratio of SMEs continued to increase at least until the early 1980s, reaching a maximum of an astonishing 75 per cent in 1982 (Heather Smith 2000, Table 2.15, p. 85). Looking at the export shares of SMEs by industry in 1984, it is easier to pinpoint the industries in which export ratio was low rather than high. Paper and printing, chemical production, metallic minerals, and machinery were the only ones in which the ratio was less than 50 per cent. Industries in which the ratio was more than 75 per cent included textiles, lumber and furniture, leather, rubber products, plastic products, electrical machinery and appliances, transportation, and precision instruments (ibid., Table 2.16, p. 86). It would almost appear that the SME sector in Taiwan was indeed geared to, and took advantage of, the available export markets, while the large-scale sector increasingly concentrated on intermediate goods.

It is of interest to note here that the Taiwan case of the participation of SMEs in the export of manufactured goods contrasts with that of Korea discussed in the next chapter. Abe and Kawakami report export ratios for Korea and Taiwan for SMEs and others for the years of the 1970s until the early 1990s (1997, Table VI, p. 396). In Korea, the export-sales ratios through the 1970s were at half the level of Taiwan's (in the 40–45 per cent range in the latter). Furthermore, in Korea there was a marked positive relationship between size and export ratio among SMEs in Korea.

V

Income distribution

The development of Taiwan has been long cited as a classic case of growth with equity. The trends in income distribution in the first decades of its post-war growth have been documented by Kuo (1983). It was not until the early 1980s that the downward trend in income inequality was reversed—when in fact Taiwan was beginning to attain the mature stage of deindustrialization (see Table 9.7).

At first glance, the drastic reduction in inequality seems to have been in the early post-war decade, during the phase of import substitution. A certain amount of scepticism must be attached to the drastic reduction in inequality as shown in Table 9.7 because these data emerge from only a pilot survey of this period. But it is plausible to some extent, since this period followed the Allied Land Reform Policy of extensive farmer-friendly policies to raise land productivity. As indicated in Table 9.1, Taiwanese agriculture in the early 1960s still accounted for a quarter of GDP.

The decreasing inequality during the early growth process, as Taiwan launched into the export expansion phase, was less drastic but continuous. It really gathered momentum after 1968 when Taiwan, according to some scholars,

Table 9.7 Income inequality measures in Taiwan

Item	1961	1964	1966	1968	1970	1972	1974	1976	1978	1980
Share of top 20%	52.0	41.1	41.5	41.4	38.7	38.6	38.6	37.3	37.2	36.8
Ratio of shares of top 20% and bottom 20%	11.6	5.35	5.25	5.31	4.61	4.49	4.39	4.19	4.18	4.18
Gini	0.461	0.360	0.358	0.362	0.321	0.318	0.319	0.307	0.306	0.303
Per capita GNP (1976 thousand NT dollars)	14.2	18.1	20.8	23.8	27.7	34.1	37.5	42.6	51.3	56.9

Source: Kuo (1983, Table 6.1). The original sources are official surveys: 1961, *Report on Pilot Study of Personal Income and Consumption*; 1966–80, *Report on the Survey of Family Income and Expenditure*.

reached the Lewis turning point. The importance of SME development in the Taiwanese growth process has been an important element in this evolution.

SME development and the trend in inequality

The course of income inequality would depend on three factors: the extent of the gap in productivity between the low and high productivity sectors, the trend in inequality within the low productivity sector, and the trend in productivity within the high productivity sectors. Kuznets (1955) concentrated only on the first item in his prediction that a transfer of labour from the low to the high productive sector would initially increase inequality. But this impact might be overshadowed if either (or both) of the other two elements has trends in declining inequality. Clearly the actual outcome will depend on the relative magnitudes of the three factors, both on the initial levels and the trends in inequality concerned.

The size structure of manufacturing, and in particular SME development, would have an impact on each of these three factors. A large SME sector with relatively high productivity—as in the Taiwan case—would make the level of the productivity gap between the two sectors as well as the inequality level within each sector relatively low, and even if there is no declining trend in any of these magnitudes, the impact of the labour transfer on overall inequality would be low. At the same time, SME-dominated growth could be expected to have a significant effect in reducing inequality for two separate reasons:

- The development of SMEs within the rural sector might provide huge opportunities for off-farm income and this might have a significant effect on decreasing within-group inequality in the low-productivity farm sector, if indeed low-income farm households participate disproportionately in off-farm activities (as we shall see happened in Taiwan).
- The decentralized industrialization which the SME-biased development should promote had a downward impact on the intersector productivity gap, since smaller urban areas have a smaller productivity gap with respect to the rural sector, and also the inflation of the rural–urban gap is dampened with the redistribution of labour to smaller urban labour markets.

We document below both these developments in the Taiwan case. But we need to emphasize that developments other than the size structure of manufacturing might have a substantial impact on the downward trend in inequality. The two most important in the Taiwan case are the impact of land reform on farm inequality and the expansion of the education system, which kept the return to human capital low and even reduced it over time.

Off-farm income of farm households

The Land Reform programme initiated by the allied authorities starting in 1949 increased the proportion of owner-cultivators among farm households significantly (from 36 per cent in 1949 to 60 per cent in 1957), according to Kuo (1983, p. 21). It also tilted distribution of landholdings to the small size groups:

> The impact of reform and technological progress in agriculture were felt to increase multiple cropping and an upward trend in land productivity. This increase in productivity, however, was not sufficient to prevent a continuous increase in the income gap between farm and non-farm households. In spite of this increasing intersectoral gap, the index of income inequality in the economy decreased significantly over the 1960s and 1970s. The reason for this was that the intrasectoral inequality decreased sufficiently to more than compensate for the widening of the intersectoral inequality. A major factor in the reduction in household inequality in the farm sector was the participation of small farmers disproportionately in off-farm activities.

It is clear from Table 9.8 that poor farm families took the lead in participating in off-farm activity at the early stages of the process, but as the cumulative development went on, most families started deriving a substantial proportion of their income from off-farm sources, and the inverse relationship between the size of farm and the proportion of income derived from farm sources disappeared. But even late in the 1970s, the poorest farm households had an astonishingly high (two-thirds) of their income from off-farm activities. It can truly be said, as mentioned by several researchers, that Taiwan became the land of part-time farmers.

Two points should be emphasized about this process:

- The activities in the off-farm sector were not generally a case of farmers devoting themselves to part-time work away from the farm. Rather, it was more the case of some members of the farmer's household working full-time in the off-farm sector, either as wage workers or family labour in an off-farm enterprise.
- The inverse relationship between the size of farm and off-farm income observed during the early years of Taiwan's development was not by any means the general scenario in Asian agriculture. It has indeed been observed in studies of the Indian farm sector, for example, that it is the richer families who more often than not get the higher-income jobs in the non-farm wage sector (e.g. Lunjow and Stern 1998, Chapter 5 on the economy of Palalnpur in North India). Another point to note is that in Palanpur, India the wage jobs in non-agriculture were typically in urban areas located at a distance from the farms, so that commuting jobs for farm families were rare.

We conclude, along with other authors, that "by 1966 the majority of farm families listed themselves as only part-time farmers, and after 1968 rural by-employment had become the dominant form of rural labor reallocation and sources of rural family income" (Fei *et al.* 1978, p. 34). This development increased labour-intensive growth rate and played a critical role in the reduction of inequality, particularly in the rural sector.

Table 9.8 Sources of farm and non-farm income

Ten equal divisions of family numbers	1966		1979	
	% of agri. income in total farm family income	% of non-agri. income in total farm family income	% of agri. income in total farm family income	% of non-agri. income in total farm family income
The richest 10% of families	67.6	32.4	24.4	75.6
The second richest 10% of families	70.2	29.8	27.9	72.1
The third richest 10% of families	70.1	29.9	26.8	73.2
The fourth richest 10% of families	68.5	31.5	25.5	74.5
The fifth richest 10% of families	65.5	34.5	27.5	72.5
The sixth richest 10% of families	64.3	3S.7	25.8	74.2
The seventh richest 10% of families	61.0	39.0	28.9	71.1
The eighth richest 10% of families	57.3	42.7	32.9	67.1
The ninth richest 10% of families	55.3	44.7	31.4	68.6
The poorest 10% of families	54.7	45.3	33.7	66.3
Total	65.9	34.1	27.3	72.7

Source: Kuo (1983, Table 6.4, pp.104–105). The original source is: Department of Budget, Accounting, and Statistics, Taiwan Provincial Government.

Decentralized industrialization

Widely dispersed industrialization enabled farm families to participate in rural, off-farm activities. In addition, this pattern of industrialization had an important effect on growth with equity from another angle—the dampening of the growth of income disparity between the urban and rural areas. Developing countries, which have concentrated growth of the non-agricultural sector in a few metropolitan areas, are often faced with the rapid increase in wage and rental costs in the growth poles, and employers are forced to respond to this development by promoting capital-intensive technical change which increases labour productivity—and adds to the widening of the income gap between rural and urban families. In addition, the income distribution within the large conurbations also tends to deteriorate. Then experience of the growth process in Taiwan seems to have been quite different.

Kuo (1983) divided the economy into four areas based on degree of urbanization and arranged the four groups in descending order. The characteristics of the four groups and the income disparities both between and within them were studied. The results for the years 1966 and 1980 are shown in Table 9.9.

It is seen that growth over the period 1966–80 saw the proportion of families at the two extremes of the spectrum decline, while the middle-sized urban groups gained in importance. An important feature of this growth process was that the income parity with respect to the most urbanized families improved for the third urban group, while the ratio for the second urban group declined only marginally. Even the relative decline of the least urbanized was small. In any event, the values of all the ratios were generally modest.

Kuo's analysis of trends of inequality for these spatial groups further shows that over the whole period 1966–80 the dominant effect on inequality was the reduction in within-group inequality. The mild increase in the inter-group income disparity effect was largely nullified by the negative (inequality decreasing) effect of the family weight effect (due to the decentralized process of development, which saw a redistribution of the population to smaller urban areas with relatively lower income levels) and rather stronger income disparity effects within each community group.

Table 9.9 Economic indicators for four groups characterized by degree of urbanization

	Most urban	*Second urban*	*Third urban*	*Fourth urban*
Share of families				
1966	0.2122	0.0952	0.1283	0.5643
1980	0.1505	0.1629	0.2500	0.4363
Sectoral income parity				
1966	1.00	0.96	0.79	0.81
1980	1.00	0.84	0.88	0.67
Coefficient of variation				
1966	0.6405	0.6380	0.5695	0.6760
1980	0.5228	0.4796	0.5155	0.5197

Source: Kuo (1983, Table 6.6, p. 114).

The continuous downward trend in within-group inequality is due to the substantial absorption of labour in the growth process at the lower end of income distribution. Clearly the dynamic role of SMEs was a key element in this pattern of growth.

Analysis of inequality changes, 1966–72

Fei, Ranis, and Kuo (1978), FRK hereafter, tried to put together the components of the trends in inequality over the period of 1966–72. While admittedly a short period under study, the intensity of changes in the Taiwan economy is revealed in this analysis that pulls together quantitatively the elements in the dynamics of inequality in this growth process.

The FRK analysis breaks down the change in inequality into three main components: family farm income, wage income, and profit income. Income in the first element is of a joint type functionally and hence is kept separate. Total change in inequality is the sum of the reallocation effect (R) due to the shift of labour from agriculture to non-agriculture; a functional distribution effect (D), reflecting the shift in the shares of wage and profit in the non-agricultural sector and their respective inequality measures; and a Factor Gini effect (B), which comprises the changes in the inequality measure of the three types of income measured: agricultural (G_A), non-agricultural wage (G_w), and non-agricultural non-wage or profit (G_π) (the three inequality measures weighted by their respective shares in their total income).[4]

The reallocation effect (R) could be either positive or negative depending on the nature of the economy. FRK maintained that it depended on the course of the Taiwanese economy with respect to the Lewis turning point. Before this point, the surplus labour situation prevailing in agriculture prevented labour income from rising too much, so that any increase in land productivity would be likely to favour the owners of non-labour factors of production and could be expected to increase inequality in the farm sector. The situation would be reversed after the turning point when pressure on labour income would begin to be felt with the exhaustion of surplus labour. The turning point in Taiwan has been dated by researchers as being some time in the latter part of the 1960s.[5] FRK fixes the date at 1968. This is the year the inequality of distribution of household income reversed direction and started to decline. Along with this reversal in the trend in inequality, the relative inequalities in the farm and the non-farm sectors also changed. Before 1968, G_A was higher than incomes in non-agricultural households (G_x) but the situation reversed after 1968. Thus in the years 1964–68, the reallocation effect on overall inequality was negative, and positive thereafter.

The other two effects refer to the relative distribution of income among the three types: farm income (a composite income), wage income, and profit income. The FRK empirical material reveals that there was a significant difference in the course of inequality before the turning point (BTP) and after it. In the BTP period (1964–68), the trend in overall Gini was more or less stable (in fact, increased marginally by 1.6 per cent). After the turning point (1966–73), it fell by 11.1 per cent. The difference between the two periods is even more dramatic if we distinguish between rural and urban households. For the urban households in the earlier BTP period, the Gini index actually increased by 1.91 per cent, but fell drastically after the turning point by 14.4 per cent.

In the BTP period, the contribution of agricultural income to the decrease in inequality was considerable—and affected the rural households more significantly. After the turning point, the wage share increased and the decreasing inequality in this component tended to have a disproportionate effect on the fall in inequality among urban households. Another significant conclusion from the FRK figures is that the profit (or property) component, which had been a positive magnitude increasing inequality in the earlier period, started to support in a strong way the negative impact on inequality emanating from the wage component after 1968. We can interpret this as at least partly due to the growing importance of small enterprises in the urban economy with a more dispersed ownership pattern.

It is important to emphasize the role of scale-related wage differential in manufacturing. We have already noticed that the differential in labour productivity between small and large firms in Taiwan manufacturing was quite low throughout its period of growth; it seems that the difference in average wages was even lower.

It appears that the period 1976–81 saw a narrowing of the wage difference between all classes of firm size less than the largest on the one hand and the 500+ on the other. This trend was reversed after this date. As Taiwan entered the later phase of a middle-income economy, the relative wage of the smaller size groups increased. In fact at the end of 1991, the average wage of the smallest size group with fewer than 30 workers was only around half of that of the largest size group (see Figure 9.1).

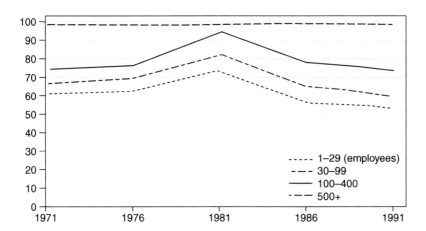

Figure 9.1 Relative emoluments per worker by size group, Taiwan (source: Tzannatos and De Silva 1998) (original data from *Industrial and Commercial Census of Taiwan-Fukien district of Republic of China*, various years).

Factors other than firm size distribution affecting inequality

We should discuss before concluding this section that important factors other than the size distribution in manufacturing had important effects on the trend in inequality in the different phases of Taiwan's development. Two such factors were the increased participation of women in the labour force and the increase in investment in education, which impacted on the supply side of the labour market.

Increase in female participation

There was a massive increase in the participation rate of females in the labour force in the post-1960 period of growth. The rate went from 25 per cent in 1960 to 41 per cent in 1975 (Galenson 1979, Table 6.1, p. 386). This large change in the labour market clearly affected the distribution of income, at the levels of individual earnings and of household income.

At the individual level, the increased participation rate of women could be expected to increase the relative supply of less skilled workers, and hence increase the skill differential. But at the household level, insofar as less-skilled female workers tend to come from relatively low-income families, it would tend to reduce the inequality of income.

Supply of educated labour

While wages of unskilled labour were being pushed upwards as Taiwan's labour market passed the Lewis turning point, large increases in the supply of educated labour were being planned by the state's education policies. Like Thailand, Taiwan had a fairly developed primary school system. However, high rates of primary enrolment and insufficient lower secondary systems meant rationing; entrance exams were set up to filter the huge demand. The immediate goal of the government in the mid-1950s was to furnish enough schools so that the entrance requirement for the lower secondary could be removed. The goal of universal lower secondary education was not immediately achieved, but the far-sighted policy dramatically increased the proportion of those who advanced to the lower secondary level from only 30–50 per cent in the 1950s to more than 80 per cent by the early 1970s. By the end of the 1970s, almost all students (more than 96 per cent) advanced to the lower secondary level.

Tertiary education expanded most rapidly in the 1960s because of the explosive increase in the number of junior colleges (from 12 in 1960 to 76 in 1972). In order to speed up the pace of industrialization, the education policy encouraged the expansion of institutions that were industry-oriented, while restricting the number of schools specializing in such fields as agriculture and nursing.[6]

The development of non-agricultural industries in Taiwan increased the demand for skilled labour substantially, but the increase in supply, resulting from the active government policy, was instrumental in reducing the premium on skilled labour. It thus reinforced the impact of the size structure in manufacturing with its importance of the SME sector (since they could be expected to use a smaller proportion of skilled or educated labour). A study of the returns to education in Taiwan has been made by Bourguignon *et al.* (2001) for the period 1979–94. Their results from regression analysis, corrected for selectivity, indicate that for male wage earners the rate of return to years of schooling in 1979 (the earliest year in their study) was just 0.0325, and for females it was 0.571. These are very low numbers, especially for males, and a far cry from Thailand, for example, which gives the rate at 0.081 for the private sector in 1996 at the end of its first period of strong growth (admittedly from a different wage model). Another strong result from this wage equation for Taiwan suggests that, unlike in many other developing countries, the rates of return to education for males are not increasing for successive levels. The marginal rates are 0.16 for primary over illiterates, 0.07 for lower secondary, 0.12 for graduated secondary (general), and 0.09 for higher education (ibid., Table 9.2).

The change in inequality in the later mature stage

The work by Bourguignon *et al.* extends over the period 1979–94 when Taiwan graduated to a middle-income country and was firmly established as one of Asia's newly industrialized nations. The rate of return to education had an upward trend over much of this period. The return to years of schooling for males increased from 0.0325 in 1979 to 0.0502 in 1983 and to 0.0620 in 1991.

The size structure in manufacturing over this period, if anything, increased the importance of small firms with an employment size under 50 workers. Thus the increasing return to education was not due to a growing importance of larger firms. It appears, on the other hand, that structural changes in the economy in this mature stage of growth have reduced the importance of manufacturing employment in the labour market scenario. Lin and Orazem (2004) divided the economy into three broad sectors:

- traded goods: agriculture, mining, and manufacturing
- traded services: finance, insurance, and commerce
- non-traded services: construction, transportation, utilities, and social and personal services.

The employment share of traded services increased significantly over this period of mature growth, largely at the expense of traded goods. The share of non-traded services also increased, but to a much smaller extent than the traded services sector. The authors produced education–occupation matrices to show that the use of highly educated labour was of greater and growing importance in the traded services sector. Evidently, the increase in demand for educated workers grew faster than the supply so that the returns to education increased over the period.

The rising rate of return to education eventually changed the direction of movement of the inequality index in Taiwan. Vere (2005) reports that the Theil index of wage inequality over the 1980s and the 1990s moved from an absolute change of –0.032 to +0.032 respectively (Table 5, p. 731):

Bourguignon *et al.* point that if we look at household inequality and (further control for its composition), inequality unambiguously increased over the 1979–94 period. This outcome was the result of an increase in the rate of return to education and of changes in participation and occupational choice.[7]

VI

Conclusions

Taiwan represents a remarkable case of industrialization based on growth of SMEs in manufacturing. It seems to have developed with a strong presence of SMEs after a very short period of state-sponsored large-scale industrial units. In this it differs from Japan, which started its period of industrialization with large textile factors breaking out into the export markets. Taiwan also differs from Korea, which switched gear after its industrialization had been under way for some time, and where the state took the lead in promoting a deliberate policy of SME development.

We have discussed in some detail the political economy background which enabled the highly successful SME model to develop. The major issues to stress are as follows: first, the historical stock of entrepreneurship, which the Japanese exporting firms in particular were able to exploit in the 1950s and 1960s; second, the political tension between the state dominated by the immigrants from the mainland and the native entrepreneurial class prompted the latter to take the lead in SME growth; third, the growth of a business network which enabled a multitude of small producers to work under the umbrella for large-scale trading organizations; and fourth, the process of decentralization helped by judicious state investment in infrastructure, as well as the successful land reform and agricultural policies which ushered in an era of dynamic rural development. A number of these and related points can be made clearer by comparison with the experience of Korea.

In spite of the export orientation of Taiwan's development model, the growth of agriculture and small-scale, off-farm activities ensured that the domestic market was growing at a substantial rate to provide the markets of industrial goods. Another striking feature of Taiwan's development is that the SMEs in manufacturing had a high export ratio, in fact higher than the large-scale sector, and that this ratio increased significantly over time until the transformation of the economy as Taiwan attained the middle-income stage in the 1980s.

Industrialization with strong growth of SMEs is probably the major reason for Taiwan achieving growth with equity, although the early development of education must run a close second factor.

10   The case of Korea

I

Phases of growth in the economy

Economic growth in Korea did not get under way in a sustained way until the early 1960s. Some development did take place after the Korean War under an import-substituting regime: the new military government of 1961 changed the previous set of policies drastically. The government normalized its relationship with Japan with a view to encouraging foreign investment to replace the flow of foreign aid. The currency was devalued 50 per cent and a floating rate regime was put in place. Interest rates were also increased drastically, but they served as one of the instruments in the drive to promote exports since an untimed low rate was allowed for export loans. The export-led growth ushered in a period of accelerated growth over the period 1965–73.

Problems in the growth process were already beginning to emerge. They included the continued deficit in the external account, which had to be sustained by continuous capital inflow and the macro-economic imbalance as investment rate exceeded savings, leading to a high rate of inflation and concern over spiralling wage costs, which threatened to undermine Korea's external competitiveness.

The response was, first, the policy which drew industries away from export promotion per se and towards the heavy and chemical industries (called the HCI policy of President Park, enunciated in 1973). As we shall see, this turnaround in industrial policy was followed quite soon, and at first sight rather incongruously, by an equally sharp and effective policy of encouraging the growth of SMEs to counter the weight of large enterprises in the growth process.

The shadows created by the HCI policy lingered until the second oil price hike ushered in a full-scale depression. Korea was hard hit because of its dependence on imported oil, the demand for which had mushroomed during the HCI initiative. It was clear that the Korean economic strategy was unsustainable and required drastic measures of restructuring.

The post-oil crisis developments strengthened the emerging initiatives in the direction of a comprehensive adjustment programme under the post-Park government.[1]

The package of reform policies was spectacularly successful. Korea resumed its fast growth rate of GDP in 1981, and the upswing continued to the end of the decade—the cut-off point of this chapter. The rate of inflation was kept in check and, for the first time in its development history, Korea actually registered a surplus in its balance of payments in the latter half of the 1980s. The hallmark of Korean development of this period was the upgrading of manufacturing from labour and capital-intensive to technology-intensive industries. The private sector took the leading role in this transition, with government playing a supportive but essential role. Unlike Taiwan, Korea's development in the 1960s and 1970s did not make significant use of technology transfer, hence the relatively small role of FDI. Rather, Korea's reliance on foreign capital took the form of vigorous external borrowing. The liberalization of the inflow of FDI in 1980 ushered in the phase of targeting more advanced technologies.

II

Structure of output and employment

Korea was very much an agrarian economy in the 1950s, with around 70 per cent of the labour force employed in the farm sector, even at the end of the decade. The transformation of the economy over the next three decades can be seen from Tables 10.1 and 10.2.

Table 10.3 summarizes the change in the employment structure and the relative productivity in the major sectors for the phases of the Korean growth process distinguished above.

All three periods of growth showed a substantial outflow of labour from agriculture. Manufacturing productivity over the first period of growth was more than two-and-a-half times that of agriculture. The absorption of labour in manufacturing was double that of the tertiary sector in relative terms and the labour productivity was higher in manufacturing than in the tertiary. This is the normal pattern of growth experienced in an agrarian economy led by the manufacturing sector. The period of heavy, directed industrialization saw a massive growth in

Table 10.1 Industrial structure of GDP (percentage)

Year	Agriculture, forestry, and fisheries	Mining and manufacturing	Others
1960	36.9	15.7	47.4
1965	38.7	19.5	41.8
1970	25.8	22.3	51.9
1975	24.9	28.0	47.1
1980	15.1	32.0	52.9
1985	13.9	30.7	55.3
1988	10.8	32.3	56.9

Source: Yoo, Jung-ho (1990, Table 1, p. 7). The original sources are *Major Statistics of Korea (Economic Planning Board)* and *Economic Statistics Year book (Bank of Korea)*

Table 10.2 Structure of the employed labour force (percentage)

Year	Agriculture, forestry, and fisheries	Mining and manufacturing	Others
1963	63.1	8.7	29.2
1965	58.6	10.3	31.1
1970	50.4	14.2	35.4
1975	45.7	19.1	35.2
1980	34.0	22.5	43.5
1985	24.9	24.4	50.7
1988	20.7	28.5	50.8

Source: As in Table 10.1. Because of the unreliability of the figures on the labour force for earlier years, we have substituted the figures from the *Korean Statistical Yearbook* for 1963.

Table 10.3 Change in structure of labour force and relative productivity

Change in sector share of labour force (%)				Index of relative productivity			
Years	Agriculture	Mfg	Tertiary	Year	Agriculture	Mfg	Tertiary
				1965	100	262	203
1963–75	−17.4	12.3	6.0	1975	100	267	244
1975–80	−11.7	3.4	8.3	1980	100	323	293
1980–88	−13.3	6.0	7.3	1988	100	217	215

Source: Yoo (1990, Tables 9.1 and 9.2).

labour productivity in manufacturing relative to agriculture, exceeding that in the tertiary sector. This was the period which also saw, as is to be expected, a substantially larger absorption of labour in the tertiary sector, as industry became more capital intensive. Growth in the 1980s after the post-crisis adjustment saw a return to more labour-intensive manufacturing development, prompted in part by the impetus given to SMEs. Absorption of labour in manufacturing improved in relative terms, while relative productivity with respect to agriculture fell sharply and attained a level similar to that of the tertiary sector.

The role of exports

It is well known that Korea's growth was based on a rapid growth of labour-intensive manufacturing exports. But the resource base was small in the Korean economy so much of the raw materials and intermediate products, as well as machines and equipment, had to be imported. The import content of exports was accordingly very high. Export growth accelerated in the early 1970s, and in the last years of the HCI regime, and again after the post-adjustment years of the 1980s. In each case, this acceleration was accompanied by sharp increases in the growth rates of imports, and in fact in the HCI period, by more than the export acceleration. Thus the net contribution of the external sector to the growth rate was quite small, or even negative, compared to either consumption or investment (Corbo and Suh 1992, Table 3–2, p. 39,).

While the above gives the components of the growth from the angle of macroeconomic aggregates, another issue is to see how the supply of goods and services by different industrial sectors of the economy are absorbed by different categories of demand. For this we must take into account not only the final vector of demand but also the inter-industry generated by it for the industrial categories. Chenery *et al.* (1986) have presented calculations based on input–output tables of the contribution of different components of demand for the absorption of the flow of goods and services. Their results are given in Table 10.4.

It is seen that Korea in the first phase of its growth was a significantly less export-oriented economy than Taiwan, although considerably more so than Japan in the second and more intense period of growth extending from the beginning of the First World War until the mid-1930s. This is true even if we consider the individual industry sectors separately.

But even in this phase of export-oriented growth, it appears that domestic demand absorbed as much of the flow of manufactured goods produced as the export markets. In the post-1975 period, the share of exports was most likely reduced with the increase in income levels and the development of small-scale industries.

Table 10.4 Sources of growth in East Asian economies during their periods of growth (%)

Country and sector	Growth rate	DD	EE	IS	IO	Total
Korea (1955–73):						
Primary	5.7	12.0	3.0	−1.7	−2.5	10.8
Light industry	13.6	19.7	15.1	0.0	−1.9	32.9
Heavy industry	22.3	11.1	10.7	1.4	1.9	25.1
Services	10.3	25.6	6.2	0.2	−0.8	31.2
Total	11.2	68.4	35.0	−0.1	−3.3	100.0
Taiwan (1956–71):						
Primary	7.1	8.8	5.3	−2.0	−1.8	10.3
Light industry	13.6	12.7	17.5	0.6	2.0	32.8
Heavy industry	22.5	10.2	13.5	2.4	1.0	27.1
Services	9.7	7.1	7.1	0.1	−1.0	29.8
Total	12.0	55.3	43.4	1.1	0.2	100.0
Japan (1914–35):						
Primary	1.9	7.6	2.8	−2.3	2.3	10.4
Light industry	4.6	15.1	10.5	0.2	−0.4	26.1
Heavy industry	8.1	15.2	4.4	1.9	−3.3	18.2
Services	4.2	35.2	9.0	−0.2	1.3	45.3
Total	4.1	73.8	26.7	−0.4	−0.1	100.0

Source: Chenery *et al.* (1986, Table 6.4, pp. 158–159).

Notes
DD = domestic demand; EE = export expansion; IS = import substitution; IO = change in inter-industry coefficients.

III

Korean labour markets, wage inflation, and the SME promotion policy

Korea was generally characterized as a labour-surplus economy at the inception of its economic growth. In the early 1950s, Korea had a very large amount of underused labour, largely in the rural sector. For nearly a decade after the end of the Korean War, the labour market situation did not improve. There was an influx of job seekers with demobilization, and the rate of increase of employment in the modern sector was close to zero. Official statistics measured the civilian rate at 13 per cent in 1959 and 18 per cent in 1960. Real wages in manufacturing fell at a significant rate in the first half of the 1960s (Richardson and Kim 1986, Table 6).

The upward thrust in the labour market occurred around the middle of the 1960s. Employment growth in the non-agricultural sector rose by about 2.5 million over the period 1967–75 (the total labour force in 1967 being about nine million). This growth was enough to absorb the surplus labour in the farm sector (Richardson and Kim 1986, p. 18 and Table 3). Although the date of the turning point is not clear, real wages started on an upward march in 1964–65.[2]

The upward trend in real wages in Korea has continued through its period of growth. Figure 10.1 gives the picture of real earnings per worker in key sectors of the economy for the period 1966–85. It seems that, starting around 1975, something happened to the real earnings in the urban sector and in manufacturing

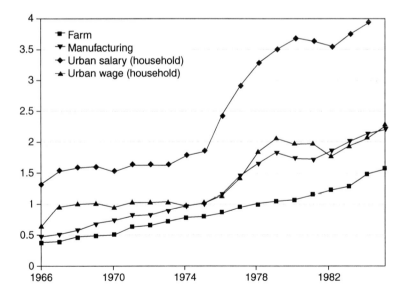

Figure 10.1 Real annual income per earner, by earner type, 1966–85 (source: Mazumdar (1990, Figure 6, p. 25)).

which took it relentlessly away from the real earnings in the farm sector. Before this date, earnings in the non-farm sector were growing only slightly more than in the farm sector. After this date, the growth rate diverged dramatically in the second half of the 1970s, the acceleration being most marked in urban salaries. The acceleration seems to have been controlled by the end of the decade.

It is quite striking that the acceleration in non-agricultural earnings coincided with the inception of the policy of heavy industrialization (called the HCL surge) shortly after the first oil shock. It also coincides with the beginning of the altered trend of the size structure of manufacturing enterprises now favouring small and medium-sized enterprises—a change which, as we have seen in the last section, could be ascribed strongly to the new departure in government policies favouring SMEs.

As an economy whose growth rate depended heavily on exports of manufactured goods, Korea was constantly struggling to keep a lid on the labour cost per unit of output in the sector against the continuing pressure on real wages. It should be made clear that the upward pressure on wages was not due to institutions like trade unions or other agencies of collective bargaining. In fact throughout the 1960s and 1970s, there was a succession of labour laws enacted to regulate the labour movement. Emergency provisions in 1971 prohibited collective bargaining by broad labour organizations. This effectively reduced the power of centralized or industry-wide unions. Wage settlements were negotiated at the level of individual enterprises.

But Korean economists at the same time have been quick to point out that "labour repression" did not imply an attempt to impose employer domination in the wage-setting process. In fact, the object of the Korean state, starting with the military government of 1961, was to preserve industrial peace under which expansion of output and investment could take place. The Korean state was interested as much in directing the owners of industry as directing their workers to achieve this end. Further, the economic philosophy of the state was not to keep wages low to help accumulation but to let workers benefit from a high productivity growth to create a "virtuous circle" of rising wages and rising productivity.[3] The Korean government did set wage guidelines to limit wage growth in key sectors (and which were enforced with the help of threats of withdrawing subsidies and support to offending enterprises).

In fact, with or without government encouragement, Korean manufacturing (at least the larger firms) had developed a strong predilection towards a profit-sharing system of remuneration in which bonuses constituted 70–75 per cent of total wage earnings; and an internal seniority-based labour market in which firm-specific skills were rewarded (see the discussion in Mazumdar 1993, pp. 365–367). Thus, as revealed in Figure 10.2 below, real wages increased pretty much in line with, and somewhat below the rate of, increases of labour productivity through the first half of the 1970s. This relationship seems to have been seriously disrupted in the second half of the 1970s. Starting with the aftermath of the first oil crisis and for the rest of the decade, the rate of real wage increase was higher than that of productivity, putting strains on unit labour costs. Korean

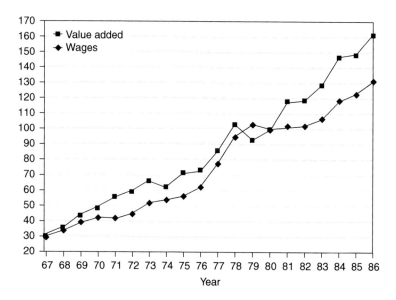

Figure 10.2 Indices of real value added and wages per worker, 1967–86 (1980=100)
(source: Mazumdar (1990, Figure 5, p. 17) (original sources: *UN Yearbook of Industrial Statistics*, "Principal Economic Indicators", Bank of Korea).

labour markets seem to have tightened considerably after a decade of rapid employment growth and fuelled by the HCL policy and the out-migration of Korean labour to the Middle East.

A second problem of labour market trends for the Korean export economy was the accelerating rate of inflation. It is well known that Korean growth policy depended crucially on foreign capital outflow, which enabled it to invest more than it saved. The attendant inflation produced an upward trend in the real exchange rate with the domestic consumer price index (in which the non-traded sector had disproportionate weight), increasing at a faster rate than the price index for manufactured goods (which was influenced by export prices). Korean policies tried to compensate for this increasing trend in the real exchange rate by continuous devaluation, in order to prevent a disastrous increase in unit labour cost at world prices (see Mazumdar 1993 for details). This was, however, a policy riding on a knife-edge. Inflationary expectations were an important determinant of wage increases. Since devaluation was threatening to fuel further inflation, a vicious circle of the rate of devaluation and acceleration in the rate of increase of the real wage was always on the books. This threatened to put upward pressure on the unit labour cost of Korean exports of manufactures in world markets and undermine the basis of the export-led growth strategy. One index of nominal wage in manufacturing shows an increase in the rate of increase from around 14–16 per cent in 1971–72 to a rate in the 30–35 per cent range in the second half of the 1960s (Corbo and Suh 1992, Chapter 10, Table 10–13).

The policy of promotion of SMEs

Korea has been known in the literature for the importance of giant conglomerates in the promotion of export-oriented economic growth. The equally impressive development of the SME sector from the mid-1970s onwards has attracted much less attention. The effective government policy to promote SMEs in Korean manufacturing, which gathered steam in the second half of the 1980s, can at least in part be traced to this instability in the labour market threatening to push the trend in the unit cost of labour above dangerous levels. The SME promotion policy could be expected to curb wage inflation because there was a substantial difference in average earnings between small and large firms.

The available figures clearly show that the earnings differential for medium-sized firms (50–199) had widened over the decade of the 1960s. Although the differential in favour of large firms relative to the medium had decreased somewhat, it was not sufficient to compensate for the widening of the small–medium differential (Mazumdar 1990, Table IV.2, quoting the figures from the Statistical Yearbooks of Korea). The reallocation of labour away from the large firms to SMEs would be one way to reduce the pressure of wage inflation, which was gathering momentum in the second half of the 1970s.

In this perspective, the pro-SME policy was another (and earlier) prong in the government effort to control the inflation of wages, which was clearly a danger that was seriously threatening damage Korea's competitiveness in world markets. After the second oil crisis, the new government introduced a comprehensive incomes policy, which included guidelines for wage increases, freezing of government salaries, and introduction of social welfare measures (Suh 1985, pp. 80–81).

Wage growth fell from a peak annual rate of increase of 34.3 per cent in 1978 to 8.1 per cent in 1984. As can be seen from Figure 10.2 above, the rate of growth of real wages after 1980 was significantly below the rate of growth of real value added per worker. The reduction of the unit labour cost (in dollars) over the first half of the 1980s restored Korean competitiveness in world markets.[4]

IV

Size structure in manufacturing and its evolution

It has been well documented in the literature that the size distribution of employment in Korean manufacturing reveals a marked V-shaped pattern over time, with the turning point coming some time in the first half of the 1970s. Nugent has produced a series of papers documenting this trend reversal and its proximate determinants (Nugent 1996; Kim and Nugent 1994; Nugent and Yhee 2002).

The share of SMEs (between five and 300 workers) in total manufacturing employment fell from 61.5 per cent in 1960 to 45.7 per cent in 1975, and then rose to 69.3 per cent in 1997 (or in terms of our time period to 61.7 per cent in 1990).

Two points about the reversal of the trend in the role of SMEs in Korean manufacturing should be underlined. First, in the upswing phase of this V-shaped pattern, the two largest SME size groups distinguished in the statistics, the 100–199 and 200–300 groups, also fell along with the share of large enterprises. It is the smaller of the size classes (in fact, the three groups below 50 workers) that showed the spectacular V-shaped trend. Second, as is to be expected from the point just made, there is evidence of an upsurge in the entry of many new firms in the SME sector.

The distribution of manufacturing employment and value added by selected employment size groups are given in Table 10.5. It is clear that all size groups below 300 employees participated in the redistribution of employment to SMEs. In fact, there is evidence that the redistribution to the smaller size groups (5–9 and 10–19) gathered momentum in the latter half of the period 1976–93.

Relative labour productivity by size groups

It can also be seen from the second half of Table 10.5 on relative labour productivity that this redistribution was achieved by not letting labour productivity fall relatively more in the smaller establishments. On the contrary, the productivity differential between the very small and the large remained roughly unchanged over the entire period. The relative productivity of medium-sized units employing 100–199 workers, however, improved over the period.

Composition of manufacturing and size distribution

The composition of manufacturing changed dramatically over the 20-year period we are considering. As indicated, Korea concentrated on an export-oriented strategy of employment in the first phase of growth. The policy changed into a directed development of heavy industry in the immediate aftermath of the first oil crisis.

Table 10.5 Distribution of employment in manufacturing by size groups and relative labour productivity

% distribution of employment				Relative labour productivity		
Size group	1976	1986	1993	1976	1986	1993
5–9	3.8	3.8	8.3	31	27	29
10–19	4.2	6.6	11.8	37	31	32
20–49	8.1	14.0	14.2	42	37	38
50–99	8.6	12.9	12.9	59	45	53
100–199	12.9	12.7	10.7	56	55	68
200–299	6.5	7.4	6.0	75	67	75
300–499	10.8	7.4	5.6	85	77	82
500 and above	45.1	35.0	25.5	100	100	100

Source: Korea Statistical Yearbook, various years. The original source is the Mining and Manufacturing Census and Surveys.

Table 10.6 Changes in composition of manufacturing value added

Year	Heavy and chemical (%)	Light (%)	Total manufacturing (%)	Total manufacturing value added (in billions of 1980 won)
1966	15.3 (15.4)	70.8	100.0	1193
1973	21.9 (20.1)	62.1	100.0	4432
1978	34.5 (24.0)	53.4	100.0	9925
1985	41.4 (31.9)	49.0	100.0	16,401

Source: Yoo, Jung-ho (1990, Table 10, p. 48).

Notes
The HCI group in this classification included "those favored by the HCI policy and the light the rest". However, the former excluded oil refining, and the latter tobacco since both were monopolies dominated by a few firms (see ibid., p. 46 for details).
The percentage of manufacturing employment in the heavy industry group is given in parentheses.

President Park Chung-hee announced the policy of promoting the heavy and chemical industry (the HCI policy) in a press conference on 12 January 1973. The tools of targeted industrialization were now used for promoting heavy industries rather than exports of light industry. The resultant transformation of the manufacturing sector can be seen from Table 10.6 below. The figures in parentheses make the further point that the proportion of employment in the heavy industry group also increased, but relatively more slowly than value added. That is to say the relative labour productivity increased faster in the favoured subsector.

It appears that the trend to a size distribution in manufacturing which tilted towards smaller establishments in manufacturing occurred at the same time as the push towards the development of heavy industry.

V

Trend reversal: elements of the SME promotion policy

The widespread nature of the trend towards SMEs suggests that there was something pervasive happening in the Korean economy. It is likely that this influence was supplied by government policies towards the manufacturing sector. The policies of targeted industrialization have been much discussed in the literature on Korean economic development (for example, by Amsden 1989). Generally, the literature has stressed the intimate connection between the political leadership and the financial-business elite. It has noticed the development and growth of the conglomerates like the *chaebol* that were instrumental in pushing the export-oriented industrialization of the 1960s and the early 1970s based on large industrial establishments. But the concern with the role of the conglomerates and their large firms has detracted attention from the equally important policies which sought to promote SMEs (Nugent and Yhee 2002, p. 85).

In fact, the concerns with SME development and government measures to help them have been in place for a long time in Korean policies but gathered momentum after the HCL policy of encouraging heavy industries was in effect. Somol Seong of the Korean Development Institute has compiled a list of government measures to encourage SMEs. It shows that a series of policies for the promotion and support of SMEs was pursued in the 1960s, although they were mostly on a trial-and-error method (1993, Table 13, p. 21). Evidently, the concerns with SME promotion were not strong enough to prevent a sharp downward trend in their share of employment and value added in manufacturing.

During the HCI polices of the first half of the 1970s, the "vulnerability of the SME sector emerged as a major structural problem" (ibid., p. 22). In 1975, the *Small Business Sub-Contracting System Promotions Act* was passed. It was meant to protect SMEs in vertical relationships with large firms. The purpose was to draw more SMEs into the growing industries in a complementary relationship with large firms. The act also made provision for more intensive support of products suitable for SMEs. In 1979, the Small and Medium Industry Promotion Corporation was established to implement various SME support programmes. A long-term plan for the promotion of SMEs was drawn up in April 1982 and the next few years saw a series of improvements of laws already on the books to help SMEs in different areas—ranging from technical, financial, and market support, to a limited protection in designated lines of production.

Several international agencies have already commended Korea as a leader in developing effective SME support programmes (e.g. UNIDO 1986). Four major points about the foundations of Korea's support policies deserve special emphasis:

- First, the Korean policies were not directed at merely protecting the existence of small enterprises; they were much more concerned with the development of SMEs.
- Second, in keeping with the concern with the dynamic growth of SMEs, attention is not focused exclusively on very small units. Along with neighbouring Japan, Korea defines the SME sector as enterprises employing fewer than 300 workers. This does not imply that only the larger units in the sector benefit from the programme. According to the sample survey carried out by Kim and Nugent (1994), most SMEs began with fewer than 50 workers, but many had grown to more than 200 workers, an indication of the generally high level of success of the support policies.
- Third, Korean policies discriminated among SMEs in directing the support schemes. The government used a system of "special designations", and in principle SMEs given special designation received priority in the allocation of various forms of support. Korea had even established "SME sanctuaries" to reserve certain product lines for SMEs like India had, but unlike India these were limited in number, carefully chosen, and limited to last no more than three years.
- Fourth, some important features of governance of Korea's support system have been noted by Kim and Nugent. The agencies were controlled and audited, and the authors emphasize that "Korea is unusual in that

competence is about equal in importance to political connections" in the appointment of principals and their subordinate executives. Most of the support agencies sampled in the enquiry emphasized educational qualifications, experience, and competence in their hiring practices. The average salary level was 50 per cent higher than the industry average. Finally, although the state support agencies had some advantage over private ones, such as the ability to offer services at below-market prices, there were very few restrictions on private sector participation in the supply of financial, technical, and marketing support, and the state agencies often felt significant competition from other private institutions and firms.

Turning now to the contents of the support schemes, financial assistance seems to be the most critical. State support comes in three major ways:

*   specialized financial institutions and funds catering to the SMEs
*   government-supported venture capital companies that finance technologically based SMEs
*   credit guarantee facilities.

In addition, commercial banks (which were heavily controlled by the government until the liberalization of 1993) were required to allocate a substantial percentage of their loans to SMEs. Another important source of financial support has been Central Bank discounting of commercial bills of SMEs and export finance. In the second half of the 1980s, government-led funds for SMEs increased the percentage of the net lending increase by commercial banks from 1–2 per cent in the early 1980s to an average of over 10 per cent (Nugent 1996, Table V.1, p. 68).

The next important area of public SME assistance is technological support. Korea has an extensive network of agencies providing support in the form of training programmes, information services, and joint research opportunities, headed by the Industrial Advances Administration under the Ministry of Trade and Industry.

The third general area of the support system is marketing. The largest public sector marketing agency is the Korea Trade Promotion Corporation (KOTRA), which originally was founded to help the export activities of large firms. But as these firms became more self-sufficient, KOTRA focused its activities more on SMEs. More than half of the firms in Nugent's survey used some form of collective marketing services (more so in the early stages of their export growth) but these agencies received lower approval and usefulness ratings than the large number of private channels of support available to Korean SMEs.

Nugent (1996) has attempted an econometric analysis of the relative importance of different factors which caused this V-shaped pattern, an increase in the share of employment in large enterprises until 1976 and decline in the next two decades.

The major conclusion of this exercise was that the financial variables, individually and collectively, were the most important in accounting for the divergent trends in the two periods. In particular, the share of minimum credit allocation to SMEs by commercial banks mandated by the government and the suppression of the curb market for informal finance were quantitatively important factors in the changing share of SMEs between the two periods. The technical-organizational factors, which have been much stressed in the literature, contributed little to the observed trends. But the trade-related variables, particularly the declining share of exports and the reduced importance of trading firms catering primarily to the large establishments, were also of importance. The last observation does not imply that SMEs were unimportant in exports. In fact, their share in commodity exports has increased strongly in recent years, from 22.1 per cent in 1982 to 42.1 per cent in 1990 (Nugent 1996, p. 1). However, to the extent that the export share of large firms has generally been at a higher level in the past, the fall in the degree of export orientation has been a factor working in favour of SMEs.

VI

Characteristics and economic performance of SMEs

Nevertheless, the Kim–Nugent Survey of 1994 provides a very healthy picture of the sector at this date:

- About 70 per cent of the sample was owned by individual entrepreneurs. They were largely in the age group of the 40s and 50s. Most of the units were established in the 1970s and 1980s, with half of them being less than ten years old, signifying their debt to the pro-SME policies pursued with vigour after 1975. The entrepreneurs seemed to be highly educated, the mean years of schooling being 15–16 years in the sectors selected. Almost 75 per cent of the sample had a college education, and more than 10 per cent had a graduate education. About half of them earned a science or engineering degree, often directly related to their line of business.
- Upward mobility seems to have been high. Most of the units were established as small enterprises with fewer than 50 workers, but 80 per cent in three of the industries had grown to a higher size group, and 50 per cent in factory automation (the latter probably replicating the technical conditions of small employment size in this sector). Considering the size group of relatively large SMEs (100+) in 1990, fewer than 20 per cent had been in this size group at the start-up (Kim and Nugent 1994, Table II.5).
- Subcontracting relationships have been in Korea, as elsewhere in East Asia, an important means by which SMEs have received support from larger enterprises. Korea seems to have been well aware of the Japanese subcontracting experience and government policies have tried to imitate the Japanese model. The Korean version, however, differs from the Japanese one in involving two levels instead of the complex pyramid found in Japanese industry.

Technical progress in SMEs

Korea was able to increase the share of SMEs in manufacturing employment in the post-1975 period without any adverse effect in relative labour productivity. Nugent has presented data on the growth rate of the relevant economic variables for SMEs and LEs together for the 1979–97 period (Nugent and Yhee 2002, Table VI, p. 90). These data were collected by the Bank of Korea. An important point suggested by this series is that, in spite of the fact that capital per worker (capital intensity) was three times higher in LEs at the beginning of the period, LEs tended to accumulate capital at three times the rate of SMEs in most years, so that it is very likely that, in spite of the higher rate of increase of employment in SMEs over the 1980s and 1990s, the capital intensity of LE firms increased even further. This can be reconciled with our earlier data on unchanged relative labour productivity of the two groups of firms (a finding confirmed by Nugent's Bank of Korea data taking one year with another) only on the assumption that SMEs experienced a significant rate of increase of capital productivity over time. In other words, there is evidence of a substantial rate of technical progress. In fact, Nugent's data report that capital productivity (the ratio of gross value added to total assets) in SMEs was consistently and substantially above that of LEs in most of the 18 years of observation—in fact higher by around 50 per cent—and did not show any trend in either direction. Along with the more or less unchanged ratio of relative labour productivity, employment cost per capita (a proxy for wage rates) increased at about the same rate for both groups over the years.

The study of sample firms in Kim and Nugent (1994) revealed that most of the firms had begun with primitive technologies and later upgraded both products and productive processes in a piecemeal manner through a long process of imitative learning. The authors refer to the specific industry studies of Kim and his associates, which find a consistent pattern of organic evolution in a wide spectrum of industries, including weaving textiles, electronics, automotive parts, and machinery (see the references cited in footnote 6, p. 4).

Export performance

Korea remained an export-oriented economy even after the restructuring of the late 1970s. At the beginning of the 1970s, the light industries (textiles, wood, and footwear) dominated Korea's exports and accounted for 80 per cent of manufactured exports. But in the course of the decade, the scope for further exports of light industries had largely disappeared. The HCL policy of encouraging heavy industry started off as an import substitution strategy to diversify the economy, but its ultimate objective was to prepare Korea to participate more strongly in the changing world market. This subsector did start to participate in exports quite quickly, although it never attained the level of export-orientation of the earlier light industry. The overall export/output ratio of manufacturing increased from 15 per cent in 1971 to 24 per cent in 1976, where it remained for the next decade, and increased to 28 per cent in 1993 (Corbo and Suh 1992, Table 8–14, p. 188).

It would thus appear that the restructuring of the size distribution of Korean manufacturing went side by side with the restructuring of industrial composition and with the changing nature of Korea's exports. The fact that this simultaneous change in the industrial economy in its several aspects was achieved so smoothly is a tribute to the dynamism of the newly emerging SMEs in venturing into the uncertainties of the world market and achieving the requisite level of competitiveness in a short period.

Woven textiles continued to appear on the list of exports until 1985 (dropping to second place at the end of the 1980s), though its share of total export value was reduced from 41 per cent in 1970 to 23 per cent (Kim and Leipziger 1993, Chapter 3, Table 1). In the 1970s, Korea displaced Japan as the leading exporter of woven textiles.

The woven textile industry was joined by electronics products by 1980 and footwear in 1985 as one of the five leading exports. Exports from the electronics industry were in the first stages after the HCL policy was dominated by capital-intensive products like semi-conductors produced by large joint ventures. But in the 1980s, exports of electronic parts from SMEs increased strongly (ibid.).

Abe and Kawakami give details of the export ratios[5] by size groups of SMEs for various years. In the aggregate, the export ratio was substantial and might have increased somewhat in the decade after 1975 from around 20 per cent to nearer to 25 per cent (1997, Table VI, p. 396). Their figures, however, make clear that the export sales ratio was positively related to the employment size of SMEs. In the late 1970s, the highest sales ratio was found in the largest 200–299 group of SMEs, but in the late 1980s the next size group of 100–199 had as high a sales ratio (30 per cent) as the largest size group (as against an overall average of 26 per cent), and even the 20–49 size group had a significant sales ratio of 20 per cent.

In sum, the policy-led change in the size structure of manufacturing achieved an extended participation of SMEs in Korea's export expansion. This objective was in fact built into the system of incentives for SMEs, which the government pursued after 1975. The demarcation of the borderline of SMEs at the fairly high level of 300 workers was in itself an opportunity of forward-looking enterprises. As we have seen, it is the size group of 200–300 workers which took the lead in export participation.

The role of SMEs in Korea, although substantial, was less than that in Taiwan, which we considered in the last chapter. Taiwan's industrialization had started earlier than Korea's and it was also more export-intensive. The SMEs in Taiwan attained their peak level participation in the early 1980s when their export-sales ratio was nearly three times that of Korean SMEs.[6] It appears that, while the Taiwan SMEs reduced their export ratio after their peak in the early 1980s, the export ratio for Korean SMEs went on increasing through the 1990s. At the latest date given by Abe and Kawakami, 1994, the Korean SME ratio was 42 per cent compared to the Taiwan SME ratio of 52 per cent.

VII

Trends in inequality

Korea has been used as an example of the East Asian model of growth which has enjoyed the benign experience of growth with equity. In the World Bank study of the East Asian Miracle, Korea was in the list of countries whose growth rate over the period 1965–89 was plotted against a measure of inequality in the 1980s (the ratio of the income share of the top 20 per cent and that of the bottom 20 per cent). The position of Korea is at the most benign top north-west corner of the scatter (the Y-axis measuring growth rate of GDP and the X-axis measuring the inequality index) (World Bank 1993, Figure 1.3, p. 31). The only other country in this sample with a better record could possibly have been Taiwan—which indeed had a somewhat lower index of inequality but also a slightly lower growth rate. The World Bank work, however, failed to notice the major changes in income inequality over the longer period of Korean growth.

Nugent and Yhee have put together a time-series of the "best available" measure of inequality, which shows that inequality as measured by the Gini coefficient increased over the period 1953 to 1975, and it declined thereafter to a value in the mid-1960s that was more or less the same as in 1953 (Nugent and Yhee 2002, Table XXIII, p. 113). It is quite revealing to note from Nugent's table that these divergent trends in the Gini over time coincide almost exactly with the divergent trends in the share of SMEs over the same time period.

The evidence on wage inequality—the inequality in earnings accruing to wage labour—is even stronger for the period after 1976. The calculations by Fields and Yoo (1998) from the data tapes of the Korean Occupational Wage Survey for the period 1976–93 showed that the value of the Gini was around 0.40 at the beginning of the period but declined continuously after that, reaching a value of 0.34 in 1986 and 0.29 in 1993 (ibid., Table 2.2). The Lorenz curves for labour income from this study are reproduced in Figure 10.3.

Factors in the reversal of trend in income inequality

It is no doubt true that, while the coincidence of the turning points in the size structure of manufacturing and in the trend in income inequality is remarkable and suggestive, it cannot be a conclusive factor without further detailed research, as Nugent himself maintains (Nugent and Yhee 2002, p. 113).

We will discuss the ways in which the reversal of the trend in the size distribution in manufacturing might have contributed to the remarkable decrease in inequality. This is best done in terms of our framework relating size distribution to inequality given in Chapter 1.

Taking the economy closer to the turning point

We hypothesized that a distribution of employment leaning towards the smaller size groups might Increase the rate of absorption of labour in manufacturing

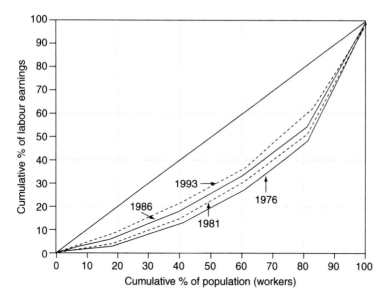

Figure 10.3 Lorenz curves of labour earnings (source: Fields and Yoo (1998, Figure 2.1)).

faster than a distribution skewed to large firms, thus getting the economy nearer to the point at which the era of elastic supply of labour from the agricultural sector at a low wage ends and wages begin to rise, with its favourable impact on distribution of earnings in the non-agricultural sector. This is not the case of the relevant period in Korean development.

The trends in the Korean labour market strongly suggest that Korea had ceased to be a labour-surplus economy by the end of the 1960s. Although after 1960 the Korean labour force grew at 3 per cent per annum, the unemployment rate was halved by the end of the 1960s from its level of over 8 per cent at the beginning of the decade (Richardson and Kim 1986, Table 3). The transition to the turning point was short and intense in Korea. Between 1962 and 1968, the wage per farm employee (in 1970 US$) grew at 0.74 per cent per year, but exploded to a rate of 8.8 per cent between 1968 and 1973 (Hong 2000, Table 5.2). In accordance with this development, the available series on average earnings in manufacturing, after registering negative rates in the first half of the 1960s, started to increase at a rapid rate, registering several double-digit growth rates in the late 1960s (Richardson and Kim 1986, Table 6). In fact, inequality in Korea was increasing even as manufacturing wages increased at a historically unprecedented rate. It is only after the change in the reversal of the trend in size distribution away from large-scale firms that inequality started to decline and, paradoxically, the rate of increase of real wages moderated. The conclusion from this story is that it is not the trend in average real wage in manufacturing (related to the rate of absorption of labour) which is the significant part of the trends in inequality, but in fact the behaviour of the distribution of wage earnings. This point is discussed below.

A size distribution skewed to large firms increases inequality among the self-employed

Income inequality data for Korea before the 1980s are not as comprehensive as one would like them to be. The household surveys on which empirical studies of inequality are generally based excluded self-employed households from the urban surveys and non-farm households from the rural surveys. Thus estimates of income distribution for these earlier years are based on a patchwork of various types of data—for example, estimates based on consumption expenditures and indirect inference from the trends for the known categories (Suh 1985, pp. 7–8). The evidence for the self-employed groups is best discussed separately for the rural and the urban sectors.

Rural

A feature of the increase in Korean inequality in the period 1965 to the late 1970s is that, although inequality was consistently higher for urban households, the trend of increasing inequality was more pronounced for the rural sector. Suh reports that the estimates prepared by the Korean Development Institute show that the Gini for rural households increased from 0.285 in 1965 to 0.356 in 1980, while the Gini for urban households fell slightly from 0.417 to 0.405. (ibid., Table 3, p. 9). This is rather unexpected since we have seen that the turning point in terms of farm wages was reached in the late 1960s, with wages increasing in the farm sector. The paradox is resolved if we remember that the market for wage labour is rather limited in Korean agriculture. The land reforms undertaken after the war had effectively made the cultivating farm family the dominant economic unit in agriculture. Thus the trend in inequality would be dominated by what had been happening to the distribution among the self-employed cultivators. The Korean government had taken a number of measures to bolster the income of farm families. Notably, a vigorous price support programme was initiated in 1968 for farm products, which improved the terms of trade for agriculture. But it is very likely that the relatively high price for rice and other farm products benefited the richer farmers disproportionately, as indeed did other measures to improve farm productivity.

The development strategy which encouraged the size distribution to large manufacturing firms tended to reinforce the trend to higher rural inequality in another way. It has been pointed out that in the early development of Taiwan the participation of smaller farmers in off-farm activities was a major factor in the decline in inequality in the early experience of Taiwanese growth. There was an inverse relationship between total household income in the rural sector and the proportion of household income originating from off-farm activities. This was possible because the Taiwanese development strategy led to widespread growth of small enterprises in manufacturing and related activities, which percolated to the rural economy. Decentralization of such activities also helped in a significant way in the participation of poorer rural families in these sources of growth.

Korea stands in marked contrast to this pattern of development. While in Taiwan the development of rural off-farm employment preceded the burgeoning SMEs in manufacturing in other urban areas, in Korea the farm sector had to wait for the post-1975 development of directed SME growth for it to participate in small-scale, non-farm activities.

Urban

It is very likely that an economy with a manufacturing sector development skewed to the large firms would offer less in incentives for small entrepreneurs to set out on their own in manufacturing than a scenario with a strong presence of SMEs. The prospects of successful risk-taking in planning an ambitious business venture would be so much less likely. It is more likely that the self-employed businesses would try to fill a role at the lower end of the income pyramid in repair and services geared to poorer consumers. Thus we would expect to see a significant presence of the self-employed working either with family workers or with the help of only a few hired help, co-existing with highly educated self-employed professionals and employers in medium-large businesses. The expectation then is that the income distribution for this group would be more unequal than for wage earners.

Choo's (1978) estimates are particularly relevant because they provide the course of inequality by sources of income. Table 10.7 gives the inequality measures separately for the two groups—employee households, and self-employed plus employer households.

It is clear that the degree of inequality of income for self-employed/employer households followed the movements of that of employee households. It does appear, however, that the increased inequality in the wake of the HCL policy was much stronger for the self-employed households and, further, the subsequent recovery towards greater equity was less sharp for this group.[7]

The inverted U-shaped change in wage inequality

In the wage economy of Korea, it is the widening of the wage structure, and its subsequent narrowing, that is critical to a proper diagnosis of the change in the

Table 10.7 Inequality measures for different groups

Gini	1965	1970	1976	1982
Employees	0.339	0.304	0.355	0.309
Self-employed and employers	0.384	0.353	0.440	0.445
*Decile ratio**				
Employees	0.331	0.536	0.347	0.537
Self-employed and employers	0.360	0.419	0.235	0.292

Source: Leipziger *et al.* (1992, Table 1–8 and 1–9). Original source is Choo (1978).

Note
*Share of bottom 40 per cent relative to share of top 20 per cent.

trend in overall inequality. Can the observed trends in the size structure of manufacturing be singled out as the most important single factor in the changing structure of wage differentials? Fields and Yoo (1998) have looked in detail at the determinants of wage inequality. Their work covers the period 1976–93, thus we cannot draw on this work to study the causes of increasing wage inequality before 1976. But some insights might be gained by looking at the determinants of wage earnings in 1976—the beginning of the period when the inequality started to decline.

The earnings function for 1976 estimated by Fields and Yoo shows that size of enterprise did have a positive and significant influence on earnings but its direct role in the explanation of the variance in earnings is not nearly as important as other factors like education.

While the estimated earnings functions were quite efficient, explaining 66–70 per cent of the variance, the role of firm size seems to be rather small and reduced drastically at the later date. Of course, the contribution of any factor to the change in inequality over a period of time is not the same as its contribution to the level of inequality at a particular date. If we take the results for Gini, we see that education and occupation are the single most important factors in accounting for the decline in the inequality measure. Experience and gender pulled strongly in the other direction, presumably because the variance in these variables became more important with the larger number of less experienced and female workers entering the wage sector. The direct effect of firm size was in the direction of aiding the decrease in inequality, but its quantitative contribution to the decline was small.

The direct effect of firm size, however, is far from giving the total effect of this variable on inequality. It is very likely that there would be significant interaction between this variable and at least two others—education and occupation—which have figured prominently in the estimation of the Fields and Yoo regression model. Smaller firms would have a smaller number or even a smaller proportion of workers with relatively higher levels of education or in the non-manual occupations. Both these interactions would tend to increase the net effect of firm size in the decline in inequality. But other interactions might be pulling in the opposite direction. We have already seen that the experience variable has tended to increase inequality. This is partly because there had been an influx of less experienced workers due to the birth of new smaller firms and partly because the smaller firms are likely to have been less entrenched in the seniority-based internal labour markets of large Korean enterprises.

Finally, we should draw attention to an additional important effect of the rising proportion of smaller firms in Korean manufacturing—an effect which is not captured in the estimated earnings functions. It is the impact of the larger role of smaller firms on the shifting demand for educated labour. The Fields and Yoo analysis of the change in wage inequality clearly shows that the most important driving force in the decline in wage inequality was the role of education.

Supply and demand in the market for educated labour

Supply

The rate of return to education would be the result of supply of and demand for educated labour. There were undoubtedly important changes on the supply side. Korea had near universal primary education at an early stage of its development history. One of the characteristics of the Korean education system in the first phase of development was the fact that the government gave priority to expanding the quantity and improving the quality of primary education, leaving demand for higher education to the private sector.

Universal primary education meant great competition for entrance into secondary schools. This coincided with an increasing need for skilled workers caused by a rapid economic growth and high wages associated with a college degree. The government responded by removing barriers of student flow and by increasing capacity at secondary schools through public financing and privatization.

The government introduced the High School Equalization Policy, which aimed to equalize school inputs—such as operating expenditures, student intake, class size, and education facilities—across schools. A new student admission policy, which is still in effect in most metropolitan areas, was adopted. The new system replaced the individual institution's own entrance examination with the locally standardized achievement test. The change in admission policy, under the presence of excess demand for secondary education, resulted in a boost in secondary education enrolments through a mechanism almost identical to that of middle schools. Private providers of education also responded quickly by increasing their capacity to accommodate an increasing flow of students.

The educational expansion policies significantly improved the quantitative measures of educational outcomes. The average years of schooling almost doubled between 1970 and 1995 from 5.74 years to 10.25 years. The illiteracy rate decreased dramatically from 13 per cent in 1970 to 2 per cent in 1999. The expansion process has been equitable as evidenced by school equalization policies. In particular, the rate of progression to tertiary education has more than doubled for high school graduates during the last three decades.

In general, the educational policies which have been adopted by the Korean government can be characterized as an expansion strategy, noted by Hout and Dohan (1996) as the typical path that the United States has followed. Educational policy in Korea has been strongly oriented towards increasing the quantity of education available, rather than improving equality of opportunity across social groups. Over the past few decades, no explicit effort to reduce social differentials in educational opportunity has been implemented. Indeed, it is demand by individuals and a willingness to pay for higher education, without a substantial government effort reducing barriers to higher education, that has shaped the dramatic expansion of higher education in Korea. The high demand for education among Koreans, the aspirations and efforts of parents to provide support for their children's educational success, and competition for college entrance in an effort to avoid disadvantage and stigma suffered by non-college graduates have been important driving forces for educational expansion in Korea.

Demand

We have seen in our discussion in earlier sections that Korean development had put an upward pressure on wages at an early stage, and presumably the pressure had translated to the higher levels of the a wage structure. It has been argued that the concern with wage inflation was one of the motives for the turnaround in government policy towards supporting the growth of SMEs. The heavy industrialization policies of the 1970s could be expected to add fuel to the increase in demand for more skilled and educated labour, but the faster development of SMEs from around the same period must have acted as a counter to this tendency. The proportion of educated labour in the workforce was considerably lower for SMEs than for larger firms.

In any event, the increase in demand for educated labour fell behind the enhanced supply of such labour from around the early-to-mid 1970s. The result was a relative fall in the relative wages of educated labour (Moon 2001).

We conclude that squeezing of the wage structure in Korean manufacturing must have been an element in the falling trend in wage inequality, even as Korea had swung towards a policy of promotion of heavy industry under the new import substitution strategy. While the large expansion in the supply of educated labour was clearly a relevant actor in this process, it was significantly aided by the dampening of demand for educated labour by the turnaround in the trend in the size structure of manufacturing (favouring smaller firms).

Other factors in SME development affecting wage inequality

We should draw attention to several other key channels through which the tilt towards SME growth helped to reduce inequality in this phase of Korean economic growth:

- First is the important point about the inverse relationship between firm size and the share of wages. We have seen above that the ratio of wages costs to gross value added at the end of the 1970s was around 60 per cent for SMEs as against about 45 per cent for LEs. The higher growth rate of SMEs increased the share of wages in value added in manufacturing and helped reduce inequality.
- Second, we have seen that the productivity differential between SMEs and the larger firms narrowed even while the share of employment and value added of the former increased. Accompanying this fall in productivity differentials, the wage differential between firms of different sizes also narrowed significantly—even within the same educational groups.[8]

• Third, the narrowing of productivity and wage differentials by size of firm is an aspect of the critical change in the Korean redistribution of manufacturing employment and output by firm size. This redistribution did not lead to the phenomenon of the bi-polar distribution with a missing middle as in India. The more even distribution in which SMEs played a larger role helped the distribution of income in two separate ways. First, it decreased inequality within manufacturing as just indicated. But second, it helped support the growth of employment in the manufacturing sector relative to the tertiary. The elasticity of employment (with respect to value added) was maintained at a high level even as the industrial composition changed in favour of heavy industry. Further, it has been argued in Chapter 1 that a relatively faster absorption of labour in the tertiary rather than manufacturing sector leads to greater overall inequality, for, as in the Indian case, the dispersion of earnings in the tertiary sector tends to be greater. The absence of the missing middle in the Korean restructuring meant that there was stronger growth of wages and hence domestic demand for manufactured goods, which was as important in sustaining the rate of growth of manufacturing as exports.

VII

Conclusions

Korea started off its successful growth process after the dislocations of the Korean War with the development of large-scale manufacturing. Since the export expansion was in labour-intensive industries, the rate of absorption of surplus labour from agriculture was very high. In the first stage of export-oriented growth in 1963–75, the share of labour in agriculture fell by 12 percentage points, and two thirds of it was absorbed by manufacturing, with the tertiary sector absorbing the residual. A new policy of diversification in manufacturing was pursued in the latter half of the 1970s as Korea took the bold step of promoting heavier industries. This phase slowed down labour absorption in manufacturing as employment elasticity in the sector fell, but it might have laid the groundwork for a different type of industrialization.

This new phase of industrialization was based much more on SMEs. The government made a conscious and fairly detailed effort to promote SMEs, even as it started pressing on with the HCI policies. The earlier pattern of industrial growth, based on dependence on a few light industries, but exploiting the economics of scale in large firms, was producing problems in the growth process. The large investment ratio involved in the rapid growth of large firms was only partly financed from domestic sources. Korea had to depend on a large flow of borrowings from foreign sources to sustain the growth. The inflation rate was high and the strong demand growth, accentuated by the internal labour market problems in the large enterprises, pushed up real wages at a high rate, and this wage inflation was accentuated by the high inflation rate induced by the net capital inflow. The rate of increase in money wages threatened to outrun the rate of increase in productivity, undermining the competitiveness of the Korean economy, which was the mainstay of the growth process.

The desire to control the labour market problem was one of the main motivations behind the shift in government policy in favour of promoting SMEs—moving away from the bias in policies and institutions which helped the emergence of giant firms in the earlier phase of industrialization. The survey of the data in the chapter shows a spectacular V-shaped picture of the proportion of employment and value added in SMEs with the turnaround occurring around 1975. The striking feature of the two arms of the graph of SME is that it seemed to cover all major industries across the spectrum—both light and heavy industries. The pro-SME policy seemed to have been developed simultaneously with the HCI policies. The effectiveness of the policies has been widely noted and appreciated not only by researchers but also by international institutions like the United Nations Industrial Development Organization. This trend reversal in the share of SMEs continued through the 1980s, such that, at the beginning of the 1990s, 20 per cent of manufacturing employment was in enterprises of 5–20 workers and a further 27 per cent was in units of 20–100 workers.

The objectives of the SME promotion policy seem to have been achieved as the rate of growth of wages in manufacturing slowed down in the early 1980s and was brought within the limits permitted by the growth of productivity. The adjustment of Korea to the sharp recession of 1979–80 was quick and successful (Mazumdar 1993). The turning point in the role of SMEs also coincided with a reversal in the trend towards inequality. The relatively faster growth of SMEs contributed significantly to the Korean example of growth with equality—which was beginning to be threatened by the rising role of large enterprises prior to 1975.

Part IV

Economies with the size distribution in manufacturing skewed to large enterprises

11   The case of Thailand

Thailand presents the case of an unexpected growth experience in the last quarter of the twentieth century, led by manufacturing growth centred on large-scale firms and geared to an export market. It was fuelled by substantial foreign capital inflow. This pattern of growth with its three key, interlinked elements—industrialization with the size distribution skewed to the large enterprises, export orientation, and foreign capital inflow—produced an adverse effect on the economy, which disrupted the virtuous circle in the form of a sudden and sharp financial crisis, and in fact spread beyond the bounds of the Thai economy to the Asian crisis of 1997–98.

I

The theory

This pattern of growth is in evidence in several Asian economies. There are two developments of this process: first, the trend towards increasing inequality; and second, the increase in unit labour costs, which threatens to erode international competitiveness and thereby undercut the foundations on which this type of growth has rested.

Increasing inequality comes from three different sources:

- The distribution of output and employment in manufacturing skewed to the large size group implies that the productivity and earnings differential in favour of manufacturing relative to the traditional (or agricultural) sector is larger than in the case of a more even size distribution. The contribution of the income difference between sectors (or occupations) to the change in overall inequality is accordingly larger.
- The absorption of labour in manufacturing is smaller. At the same time, we would expect much greater labour absorption in the tertiary sector. The demand for tertiary services is large because, first, the supply price of labour is low due to the low absorption of labour in manufacturing, and second, the demand for services from the incomes created in manufacturing is large. The dispersion of income in the tertiary sector is much more than in

manufacturing. Thus the relatively larger employment in the former increases overall inequality through the "within sector" factor in the inequality equation of Chapter 1.

- The third mechanism in the increase in inequality works through the change in factor shares within manufacturing. The pattern of industrialization skewed to large-scale firms involves both a smaller share of wages and a larger use of skilled labour. We then have a distribution of incomes created within the sector to higher income groups.

Determinants of competitiveness

The type of industrialization biased to large firms depends heavily on export markets, and thus maintaining international competitiveness is crucial to the continued growth of this type of economy. But this type of economy is also vulnerable to shocks, which have periodically created waves in global trade and growth. This is especially so because such export-oriented economies are typically dependent on foreign capital, which is very sensitive to changing climates of opinion, particularly related to the country's foreign exchange account.

The risks involved in export-oriented economies, dependent on continuing foreign capital inflow, are easy to understand as far as the short-run fluctuations in world markets are concerned. But there is a longer-run problem with such economies which is less obvious and not debated widely in popular economic writing. This is the aspect of the problem which we will be more concerned with in this case.

In our study of the trends in competitiveness of an open economy, we concentrate on the measure of unit labour costs in dollars (U_c), as analysed in Mazumdar (1993). Unit labour cost analysis can provide significant insights on the interplay between labour market functioning, the developments in the external account, and export performance. The index of unit labour cost, expressed in terms of a unit of foreign currency as defined below, is the measure of competitiveness. Its movement over time is influenced by three elements: the wage-productivity gap, movements in relative prices, and changes in the exchange rate.

The precise formulation of the measure is reproduced here from Mazumdar (1993).

Define the unit cost of labour in dollars, U_c, as:

$$U_c = W/V^\circ \, 1/e \tag{1}$$

where W denotes wages per worker, V denotes value added per worker, and e denotes the exchange rate (local currency per dollar).

The following relation can be derived from equation 1:

$$\dot{U}_c = \dot{W} - \dot{V} - \dot{e} = (\dot{w} + \dot{P}_c) - (\dot{v} + \dot{P}_p) - \dot{e} = (\dot{w} - \dot{v}) + (\dot{P}_c - \dot{P}_p) - \dot{e} \tag{2}$$

where the dots represent proportionate rates of change. The additional variables are defined as follows: w is the real wage (in terms of consumer goods), v is an index of the physical productivity of labour, P_c is an index of the cost of living, and P_p is an index of prices of manufactured goods. Equation 2 decomposes the percentage change in the unit labour cost into three elements: the wage-productivity gap, the shift in the ratio of consumer to producer prices, and the change in the nominal exchange rate.

The first term depends on the behaviour of the labour market. The second is what is sometimes called the domestic real exchange rate (DRER), on the assumption that P_c is the price of non-traded goods and P_p is the price of traded goods. This is by and large true in the open Asian economies under consideration.[1]

The relation between the domestic real exchange rate and foreign capital inflow

A simple story of foreign capital inflow is that it creates export capacity in the tradable (say, manufacturing) sector which should not create macro-economic imbalance. Its impact is benign as it increases the availability of resources for investment and also increases productivity through transfer of technology. But problems of imbalance might arise if the increase in domestic demand created by the capital inflow and its multiplier effect leads to an excessive increase in the demand for non-tradables. Demand inflation in the economy, particularly if it is concentrated on the non-tradable sector (services and construction), could lead to a sharp increase in the price of non-tradables, while the price of tradables geared to the world market remains more or less stable or at least increases much more slowly. Thus there is a sharp increase of DRER, leading to an increase in the unit cost of labour, unless it is offset by movements in the wage-productivity gap in the labour market or a decline in e, the exchange rate. However, the required offsetting movements are the exact opposite of what would be expected in the sequence of events. A rise in DRER accompanying the relative inflationary increase of non-tradable prices would tend to increase the demand for wage increase. The foreign capital inflow, together with the export boom, would tend to create a surplus in the balance of payments, which would put an upward pressure on e if the currency is free to float. The same process resulting in an increase in unit labour cost might be created by a surge in the price of commodity exports (other than manufactured tradables), leading to what has been called Dutch disease in the literature.

Two important points should be emphasized in this connection:

* First, the upward pressure on the demand and hence the relative price of non-tradables is likely to be larger: the more unequal the distribution of income, the larger the demand will be for non-tradable services and real estate. In fact, the demand for non-tradable services and inequality feed on each other in a cumulative process of cause and effect.
* Second, the upward pressure on the DRER can be controlled, at least to some extent, by suitable monetary and capital account policies which seek to "sterilize" the impact of capital inflow. It might seek to control demand

inflation through restrictive monetary measures and might control the free flow of capital seeking to extend its territory to sectors of the economy which need finance for less long-term productive investments.

We will see below that, in the Thai case, monetary policies needed to mitigate the Dutch disease impact of capital inflow were inadequate, leading to the rise in DRER, which threatened to undermine international competitiveness in a big way.

II

The pattern of economic growth in Thailand

From the beginning of the 1970s, Thailand announced the move to an export-led growth strategy. However, despite the official adoption of the export-led strategy, the mild form of import substitution of the 1960s was only replaced by a higher tariff rate (30–55 per cent), while the tariffs on machinery and intermediates remained at a lower level, as an attempt to encourage the domestic consumer industry. In the process, industries such as textile, pharmaceuticals, and auto assembly were particularly targeted, with high trade barriers as well as domestic content requirements. In the early 1970s, a range of incentives was extended to exporters as well. It has been argued that the duty drawback schemes were biased towards the upstream producers insomuch as the intermediates and raw materials were allowed to be imported almost without any protection. This may have hampered the development of the industrial base (Warr and Nidhiprabha 1996, pp. 35–37).

A combination of a relatively successful import substitution policy and a booming agriculture sector meant the Thai economy registered a healthy growth over the 1960s as well as the 1970s. But the second oil shock as well as a severe decline in the terms of trade (the result of a dramatic decline in the price of the agriculture products, in particular the price of rice) revealed some of the weaknesses of the Thai hybrid of import substitution/export promotion strategy and caused serious balance-of-payments difficulties. In 1981, Thailand's trade policy was further reinforced towards export orientation and, as a result, Thailand devalued its currency, simplified and reduced import restrictions, and shifted its objective from promoting import-substituting industries to promoting labour-intensive exports and inflows of FDI. The incentives adopted to implement such a policy were largely in line with other countries in the region.

Thailand faced serious economic difficulties after the second oil shock, and structural adjustment policies were implemented with the help of the International Monetary Fund. It abandoned the import-substitution policy altogether, devalued the baht one more time, abolished several export taxes, and reduced import taxes on materials destined for export. By 1986, Thailand was a full member of the export-promotion strategy group of countries encouraging labour-intensive manufacturing and implementing tax codes advocating FDI projects geared for export (Warr and Nidhiprabhu 1996). The impact of these policies was far reaching. By the mid-1980s, the imbalances were to a good extent rectified, the budget deficit was eliminated, and the current account deficit was dramatically reduced. Coupled with the end of the Cold War, and a depreciation of the US dollar (to which the baht was pegged) following the Plaza Accord, Thailand was in a prime position to take advantage of the flood of FDI that poured into the East Asian countries.

The impressive phase of export-led growth, which gathered momentum in the second half of the 1980s, contained seeds of economic difficulties, which could be traced to the structural features of the economy shaped by the specifics of the export-led growth model: the nature of capital inflow as well as the type of industrialization biased to large firms.

Table 11.1 presents the basic macro-economic data for the different sub-periods of the seven five-year plans ending in 1996. The data underline the quantitative importance of the acceleration of economic growth led by export expansion in the late 1980s.

As indicated in the post-1970s era, and more so in the 1980s, Thailand's growth was primarily on the back of the export-oriented growth of manufacturing. This is reflected in the Thai composition of export, which shows a dramatic shift from agriculture to manufacturing, with the majority of the shift happening in the pre-1990 era (see Table 11.2).

The change in the structure of production can be seen in Table 11.3.

While the shift in production to manufacturing is apparent, the change in the distribution of employment did not favour the manufacturing sector to quite the same extent (Table 11.4). First, the transfer of labour out of agriculture in the growth process was somewhat sluggish. In the more recent period of growth between 1980 and 1996, for example, while the share of value added in agriculture was halved, the employment share of the sector was reduced by only 23 per cent. Second, over the same period, manufacturing absorbed only a third of the share of labour moving out of agriculture; the larger part of the outflow went to the tertiary sector. This development underlines the low employment elasticity of the manufacturing sector in the Thai growth process, which in turn can be traced to the size distribution in manufacturing skewed to the large enterprises. As we shall see, employment per unit of value added is much smaller in the large enterprises.

Persistence of low relative income in agriculture

There is evidence to suggest that the relative income in agriculture has been deteriorating over the last two decades. Writing at the end of the 1980s, Sussangkarn noted that there was a significant decline in the relative per capita income in agriculture between 1975 and 1980 from 0.43 to 0.35 in 1980 (Sussangkarn 1994, Table 13.2, p. 501). We see from the data presented in Table 5.1 in Chapter 5 that the decline in relative agricultural productivity continued through the rest of the century. In 2000, agricultural productivity was just 20 per

Table 11.1 Macro-economic indicators

	First plan 1961–1966	Second plan 1967–1971	Third plan 1972–1976	Fourth plan 1977–1981	Fifth plan 1982–1986	Sixth plan 1987–1991	Seventh plan 1992–1996
Real GDP growth (% per year)	8.1	7.8	6.5	7.3	5.4	11.0	7.9
Population (millions)	33.1	35.2	42.6	46.1	52.5	56.6	60.0
Nominal per capita income (US$)	147	197	399	757	819	1738	3029
Export growth (% per year)	11.4	4.1	31.5	20.1	9.5	25.7	14.2
Current account (% GDP)	–0.6	–2.7	–1.9	–6.5	–3.5	–5.3	–6.5
Fiscal account (% GDP)	–0.9	–3.0	–2.6	–3.0	–4.2	2.0	2.3
Inflation rate	1.3	0.3	10.9	11.6	2.8	4.7	4.8
Exchange rate (baht per US$)	20.8	20.8	20.4	20.7	26.3	25.5	25.3

Source: National Economic and Social Development Board Data Bank.

cent of the overall GDP per worker—by far the lowest of all the other five Asian countries in the table. It is evident that Thailand has been unable to shed its labour dependent on agriculture at a sufficiently fast rate with the growth in non-agricultural income.

Usually a scenario with declining relative income per worker in agriculture would suggest that the economy has been stagnating, with little development outside the agricultural sector. The agricultural sector has to absorb the bulk of the growing labour force and, since productivity in agriculture cannot keep up with the labour force growth, one observes a declining trend in relative income per worker in this sector. This is indeed what one observes in parts of the Indian subcontinent in the last two or three decades. But the Thai story is different: the startling characteristic of Thailand is that this transformation of production has not been associated with a comparable shift in employment" (Christensen *et al* 1993.). Christensen *et al.* contrast the case of Korea to drive home the point.

Table 11.2 Exports (percentage)

	1985	1990	1996	2003
Agriculture and agro–industry	53.6	34.2	25.6	18.7
Manufacturing	34.4	60.8	65.2	74.5
Mineral and energy	4.9	1.2	0.6	3.6
Others	7.4	3.8	8.6	2.8
Total	100.0	100.0	100.0	100.0

Source: UNCTAD.

Table 11.3 Sectoral production (percentage)

	1960	1970	1980	1985	1990	1996	2001
Agriculture	38.0	27.0	21.0	19.1	13.6	10.6	10.4
Manufacturing	13.0	16.0	22.0	22.5	27.8	31.4	32.0
Services	49.0	57.0	57.0	58.4	58.6	58.0	57.6
Total	100.0	100.0	100.0	100.0	100.0	100.0	100.0

Source: National Economic and Social Development Board Data Bank.

Table 11.4 Sectoral employment (percentage)

	1960	1970	1980	1985	1990	1996	2002
Agriculture	84.0	80.0	70.8	68.8	64.0	54.5	46.1
Manufacturing	3.0	4.0	7.9	7.8	10.2	12.3	14.7
Services	13.0	16.0	21.3	23.4	25.8	32.2	39.2
Total	100.0	100.0	100.0	100.0	100.0	100.0	100.0

Source: Labour Force Surveys, different issues.

Labour share in Korea in 1964 was similar to those of Thailand in 1970. But, as Korea's industry grew, it absorbed labour much more rapidly than Thai industry did. By the late 1980s, Korean industry produced about the same share of GDP as Thai industry, but employed nearly 30 per cent of the labour force, against only 16 per cent in Thailand.

(ibid., p. 6)

The result of the relatively slow absorption of labour outside agriculture has meant that Thailand has followed the classical course of increasing inequality predicted by Kuznets in the first phase of transformation of labour surplus economies. While a small proportion of the labour force achieves high productivity and income levels in the modern developing sector, the continued existence of a mass of low-income workers in the agricultural sector increases the inequality of income over time.

The phenomenon of excess labour being "trapped" in agriculture (which the low relative productivity of labour in the sector suggests) needs explanation. There are two different sets of issues here, with different policy implications. First is a largely labour market problem. Why does the low-income labour not migrate to other sectors and help to reduce income disparities? The second large group of questions surrounds the topic of agricultural development. If there are important labour market problems which slow down the process of reducing the labour force dependent on agriculture, are there obstacles to technological change in agriculture which increases land productivity and thus the relative income of workers in this sector? In this chapter, we concentrate on the first set of issues. (The important problems of agricultural development need to be addressed in depth, but that would carry us well beyond the scope of the study.)

A major factor which has been mentioned as crucial to the phenomenon of labour retention in agriculture is the uncertain property rights in land and the extreme underdevelopment of the market for land sales. Thailand is a country of small landowners, where the proportion of employees (owners of tiny plots or entirely landless workers working for wages) has always been quite small, hovering around 7–8 per cent (see Table 11.5 below).

The extensive margin in Thai agriculture was not a constraint until about 1980 (Sussangkarn 1994, p. 601). Forest areas were readily available for conversion into arable land. A good deal of inter-regional migration in Thailand before the early 1980s was in fact rural-to-rural migration, of which a major subset was the movement of farmers to the forest areas in search of new settlements. While many of these migrants were able to achieve income levels they had not achieved previously, they were often taking possession of the forest land illegally, although it must be admitted that the authorities did not really try to enforce the law. As a result, about 30 per cent of private land is not legally documented (ibid., p. 602). The lack of clear titles to land makes it very difficult for agricultural families to move away permanently from the rural areas of settlement, since this would amount to virtual abandonment of the farm. Apparently, land markets, formal or informal, have not been sufficiently developed in rural Thailand to enable the potential migrant to realize an adequate price for his asset. This seems to be the case also in areas other than those of recent settlement (Feder *et al.* 1988).

The importance of non-permanent migration of labour from agriculture

A second relevant factor in the persistence of the rural–urban income gap is the importance of seasonal migration in the internal migration streams in Thailand. There is much literature on the details of the migration patterns in Thailand. There is a significant decline in the demand for labour in agriculture in the dry season, stretching from January through to March. The regular Labour Force Survey tracks the seasonality of employment by having several rounds of survey during the year. Round I covers the dry season, while Round III (covering the months July–September) tracks the wet season when the demand for labour peaks. The 1977 Labour Force Survey reported that recorded employment in agriculture was around 30 per cent lower in the lean (dry) season than its level in the peak (wet) season, and the 1984 survey reported that the difference was much the same (Sussangkarn 1987, Table 2.1).

The consequence of this large seasonal variation is a combination of labour market changes: a substantial increase in the seasonal rate of unemployment, some decrease in participation rates, and a substantial increase in employment in non-agricultural activities. Associated with the last is the high rate of seasonal migrants flooding the urban labour markets, particularly Bangkok. The detailed data available from the National Migration Survey show that the incidence of seasonal migration is much higher for males. "There are almost 14 percent more men in Bangkok during the dry season compared to the wet season" (Institute for Population Research 1995, p. 39).

The implication of the major importance of seasonal migration for the problem of the rural–urban earnings gap is that seasonal migration is temporary migration. There are substantial reasons (from both the demand and the supply sides of the labour market) why this stream of temporary migrants could have only limited effect on the urban wage levels to bring them into line with the alternative earnings in the rural economy. To take the demand aspect first: temporary migrants are unlikely to compete for jobs in the formal sector. Formal sector employers presumably are inclined to hire workers whose efficiency is not undermined by short periods of service or high rates of turnover. It might be objected that employers would not know in advance which workers are going to stay and which are returning to the villages in the wet season. But given the geographical concentration of the areas of origin of seasonal migrants, and their farming background, it might not be too difficult for a recruiting officer or agent to have a reasonably correct guess about the potential stability of such job seekers. Seasonal migrants would thus generally enter the informal sector of the urban labour markets. Their presence would increase the difference in average earnings between the formal sector and the informal sector, with only a limited impact on the difference between the former and the level of earnings in the rural farm economy.

Turning now to the supply side of the labour market, there is evidence to suggest that there are constraints to seasonal migration so that only a fraction of the potential migrants do participate in labour markets outside the villages. The 1984 Labour Force Survey asked additional questions about the activities of the workers in the rural areas during the lean season. It is possible to use the data collected to throw light on the number of respondents potentially available for migration, how many actually migrated, and the job-seeking experience of those who did migrate. Sussangkarn reports that only 18.02 per cent of the potential seasonal migrants (i.e. excluding those who had a job in the village in the lean season, those who did housework or those who were either too young or too old) actually moved to work outside the village at some point of the season. A majority of those who did not move did not look for a job, but more than a third of this group said they did not know how to look for a job outside the village. The statistic points to the lack of information networks and the associated high cost of temporary migration as important obstacles to job seeking outside the village. In a probit model differentiating the movers from the non-movers, it was seen that the variable "presence of others in the village who moved" had a strong explanatory power predicting the movers (Sussangkarn 1987, p. 24). The detailed analysis of the data by Sussangkarn strongly suggests that seasonal inactivity, far from being a voluntary withdrawal of secondary labour from farm activity, arose from strong obstacles to participation in non-village labour markets.

The role of off-farm employment in household income

The huge relative disparity between agricultural and non-agricultural income per worker estimated from the National Accounts does not mean that the disparity between household incomes in the two broad sectors is as great. Although a household might be registered in a sample survey as having agriculture as the main occupation of its members, generally the earners in peasant households in Asian economies participate in a variety of off-farm activities to generate supplementary sources of income. Sussangkarn (1988) estimated that, according to the data available from the Socio-Economic Surveys, the ratio of the mean per capita income of households in agriculture to that of households in non-agriculture was 2.1 in 1975–76, and increased to 2.3 in 1981, and 2.7 in 1986 (Sussangkarn 1994, Table 13.3, p. 592).

Although agriculture has declined, Thai growth saw a significant increase in non-agricultural employment in the rural sector, in particular in non-farm wage activities (see Table 11.5).

There was a decline of about 18 percentage points in the share of farm households (owners and operators together) over the 14-year period. Most of this was compensated for by an increase in employees of various kinds, and a significant increase in the share of economically inactive, including retirees or senior members of households, whose more active members were part of the temporary migration stream of workers in developing areas in cities and elsewhere.

Table 11.5 Distribution of rural households (%)

	1988	1990	1992	1994	1996	1998	2000	2002
Total population	39.58	40.24	41.77	41.17	42.2	42.11	42.53	42.75
Average household size	4.21	4.25	4.06	3.93	3.84	3.90	3.75	3.63
Farm owners	44.9	44.1	42.0	33.6	32.3	31.9	28.2	26.8
<10 rai	13.5	10.1	10.0	8.8	8.2	8.8	8.2	7.2
>=10 and <40 rai	26.4	28.4	27.0	21.3	20.2	19.6	17.4	16.4
>= 40 rai	5.0	5.6	5.0	3.5	3.9	3.5	2.6	3.2
Farm operators	8.5	7.0	5.9	4.9	5.1	6.0	5.6	5.6
Entrepreneurs, trade industry	9.1	9.2	10.0	10.1	11.3	12.5	12.1	12.3
Professionals	3.6	2.5	3.3	3.9	3.6	3.7	4.7	5.4
Labourers	12.9	12.7	12.5	12.8	11.0	9.2	11.3	11.1
Farm workers	8.5	7.9	7.8	8.6	7.2	7.7	9.3	9.3
General workers	4.4	4.8	4.7	4.2	3.7	1.5	2.0	1.9
Other employees	11.9	15.2	16.1	20.4	21.9	22.1	20.0	20.7
Economically inactive	9.2	9.4	10.2	14.3	14.9	14.7	18.1	18.1

Source: own calculations from the Household Income Consumption Surveys of Thailand.

Table 11.6 shows the rapid growth of rural wage earners in non-agricultural sectors.

The wage sector in the rural area has advanced faster than the national average, so much so that the percentage of rural manufacturing wage earners has increased from only 35.6 per cent in 1988 to 51.5 per cent by 1996. The rural manufacturing sector in Thailand has been mainly concentrated in the central region around Bangkok. However, all the rural regions have expanded their manufacturing sector substantially during this period. It is also interesting to note that at the beginning of

Table 11.6 Distribution of rural wage earners

	1988	1992	1994	1996	1998	2000	2002
% of total wage earners	50.9	52.5	53.0	53.4	51.3	53.4	53.8
By industry:							
Agriculture	44.8	32.4	28.3	21.7	26.5	29.4	27.4
Manufacturing and mining	13.9	22.5	22.8	25.1	23.9	25.0	27.2
Construction	8.4	14.7	17.9	20.2	12.7	11.1	12.6
Commerce	6.4	5.7	6.3	8.7	9.2	8.8	10.2
Transport and utility	3.1	3.2	3.2	3.3	3.5	2.6	2.9
Services	23.7	21.4	21.4	21.1	24.4	23.2	19.7
By occupation:							
Professional and technical	10.2	9.1	8.5	8.8	10.1	10.0	11.6
Managers	1.2	1.5	1.4	1.9	1.8	2.3	1.8
Clerical and sales workers	8.5	6.0	7.8	8.8	10.0	8.9	7.8
Services – transport	8.7	12.2	11.5	11.5	12.7	11.9	14.5
Agriculture and fisheries	44.8	32.6	29.2	22.3	26.9	30.6	26.8
Production workers	26.7	38.7	41.8	46.9	38.5	36.4	37.5

Source: own calculations from the Labour Force Surveys of Thailand.

our period (1988) a sizable portion—nearly 37 per cent—of the wage workers in rural manufacturing was concentrated in small-scale establishments with employment size of fewer than ten workers. The growth period saw a massive shift towards large-scale manufacturing, with the proportion of employment in establishments with over 100 workers exceeding 50 per cent of total rural manufacturing employment in 1996. The subsequent crisis negatively affected rural manufacturing in general. However, the effect was primarily felt in small-scale and particularly medium-scale manufacturing. In fact, the overall employment of large-scale establishments in this period grew rather substantially, reaching more than 60 per cent (which exceeds that of urban manufacturing). Interestingly enough, several years after the crisis by 2002, the total employment of small and medium-scale (fewer than 100 workers) rural establishments was still below that of 1996. It is clear that the infrastructure development in Thailand supported a significant growth of reasonably large factories away from the urban areas.

Although the disparity in incomes between the agricultural and non-agricultural sectors is much smaller than what is suggested by looking at figures of relative GDP per capita, we know that in many countries there is a strong positive correlation between the level of per capita agricultural income and the share of income generated from off-farm sources. Thus, for the lower part of the distribution, the gap between per capita household incomes in the two sectors is likely to be much more than is suggested by the mean values. A second implication of this consideration is that the importance of off-farm income for agricultural households would imply that the distribution of income in the farm sector would be more unequal than otherwise (we address this question in the section below).

III

Enterprise size distribution in manufacturing

The statistics of the size distribution of employment in Thai manufacturing are presented in Table 11.7, separately for the whole kingdom and for the two areas of concentration of manufacturing. The size distribution does not change very much from year to year in any of the regions considered. While the skewed-to-the-right distribution is seen in all these geographical areas, it is most marked in the areas surrounding Bangkok city—which has indeed been the recipient of recent industrial investment.

Policies impacting the SME sector

We can pinpoint some of the problem areas in the specific policies in Thailand which affect the SME sector adversely. The Country Economic Memorandum of the World Bank for 1989 reviewed some of these issues:

- "The most significant bias against SMEs in Thailand arises from the structure of business taxes." Since this tax was levied to gross sales receipts at all levels it tended to threaten a "cascading effect", which encouraged vertical integration. A substantial degree of vertical integration has occurred in many sectors in Thailand, including the important textile industry. The change of the tax system to a value added tax (VAT) was recommended to avoid future disincentives to subcontracting, which the old system implied.

- "The structure of protection within the Thai manufacturing has remained relatively unchanged since 1982 and the dispersion of effective protection rates remains high." The system did try to provide incentives to exporters, but the way of doing this, through tax drawbacks and refunds on inputs, made the incentives of dubious value to SMEs. To the extent that SMEs are less able than large firms to provide initial bank guarantees needed to claim prior exemptions claimed from customs, most of them can only claim their refunds *ex post*. The uncertainty and bureaucratic delays are heavy costs discriminating against SMEs.

- "The Board of Industry's (BOI) investment promotion system has often been criticized for using criteria and procedures that limit the availability of promotional privileges for SMEs." The data show that there has been a steady increase since 1982 in the share of approved projects with investments over

Table 11.7 Percentage distribution of employment by size groups of enterprises in manufacturing

A. 1989

Size groups	Whole kingdom	Bangkok province	Bangkok
1–4	3.7	0.73	3.6
5–9	4.9	1.2	6.6
10–49	17.3	8.4	21.7
50–99	9.3	9.1	10.3
100–299	17.9	20.7	18.6
300–499	10.2	16.1	8.2
500 and above	36.6	43.7	31
Total (th)	1533.3	462.1	636.3

B. 1995

Size groups	Whole kingdom	Bangkok provinces	Bangkok
1–4	2.3	0.4	3.1
5–9	3.9	0.7	6.9
10–49	15	8	22.3
50–99	9.5	9.1	10.5
100–299	20.9	23.4	19.5
300–499	11.5	13.2	9.5
500 and above	36.9	45.1	28.2
Total (th)	3241.7	1075.4	1130.0

Source: own calculations from Establishment Surveys of Thailand.

500 million baht, while ten million baht would more likely be the maximum amount SMEs would be able to invest (ibid., Table 3.9 and pp. 87–89). The minimum size prescribed by the BOI for applications as well as the procedures of the administration of the scheme seem to have ensured that there have been very few applications from SMEs for assistance.

- "The access of SMEs to credit from the formal financial sector, particularly commercial banks, is limited." In June 1983, only about 6 per cent of loans outstanding from commercial banks were for amounts of less than three million baht, "which is probably close to the maximum that could be borrowed by most SMEs". The market structure in banking in Thailand is characterized by high concentration, which has risen since the mid-1960s (World Bank 1983). This is reinforced by the ownership links between the major commercial banks and the largest industrial groups. As far as finance companies are concerned, although they are more involved in lending to SMEs, they have been held back by financial constraints and by their limited branch network.

- "The final source of bias against SMEs arises from the export financing system and applies to firms that are direct or indirect exporters." As in most other Asian countries, the main source of export finance in Thailand is the export credit refinancing system operated by the Board of Trade. The subsidy element in the scheme emerged unintentionally in the 1970s when the interest rates charged to borrowers and the refinancing rate became negative. This form of assistance has been heavily biased to the large firms. "In July 1984, of the 863 exporters that received credit under the scheme, the smallest 482 accounted for only about 4 per cent of the total outstanding while the share of the largest 30 was about 50 per cent" (ibid., p. 90). Apart from the usual factors involving collaterals, contacts, etc., the unwillingness of commercial banks to reach small exporters could be partly explained by the small spreads available to banks, due to the subsidized interest rates on such lending.

Small firms are at a disadvantage vis-à-vis the financial system in most countries. But there are two factors in the Thai scene which make the medium-sized firms face the most adverse environment. First, while very small firms might be able to offset the benefits of non-enforcement of some regulations on the fiscal and other fronts against the lack of incentives, medium-scale firms have high visibility and do not easily escape the attention of the fiscal authorities. Second, while small firms are often located in the central areas of the city, often in the residence of the entrepreneur, alternative sites for location seem to be severely limited for firms growing to the medium scale. The peculiar development of urban Thailand has posed excessive costs of transportation and infrastructure facilities on suitable sites for industrial location. The rising demand for developed sites from foreign firms has been a factor pushing up the price of such areas, and adding to the site constraint for medium-scale Thai firms (ibid., pp. 101–105).

Subcontracting

A few survey-based studies in the 1980s established that the role of subcontracting in Thailand was severely limited. A study by the Institute of Developing Economies of Japan based on a survey in 1984 found that only 8 per cent of the 300-odd firms surveyed had contracting relationships. This compares with 37 per cent in the Philippines and 43 per cent in Singapore, found by similar surveys in those countries.[2] The study also made use of a small survey of 140 SMEs conducted by the Thamasat University of Thailand in 1985. Fewer than half of the SMEs surveyed had any subcontracting relationship. But what is more significant is that most subcontracting relationships seemed to occur among the small firms themselves. Only one of these subcontracting SMEs had a relationship with a large firm. A second revealing finding was that subcontracting was almost entirely confined to the light manufacturing industries, like wood products and textiles. It was not found much in the industries which have developed strong subcontracting relationships in Japan and Taiwan, like machinery, and electrical and transport equipment. Third, the typical subcontracting relationship was not one based on specialized technological transfer or economies in the production of parts and components. Rather, the subcontractors were prone to produce low-quality, low-price items, and in fact were of smaller size in terms of assets, sales, and employment than the sample average.

We conclude that, unlike the East Asian model, subcontracting was not a significant route in the development of small firms.

IV

Trends in inequality

Figure 11.1 presents long-term trends in Thai household income inequality. As can be seen, Thai long-term growth was accompanied by a rather dramatic increase in inequality between 1960 and 1990. Most of the increase seems to have been concentrated in the decade of the 1980s when Thailand experienced its growth led by newly emerging manufacturers. The slight dip in the inequality measures in the early 1990s seems to have been reversed after the Asian financial crisis of the late 1990s.

The increase in inequality affected households in all three groupings—urban, semi-urban (or "s" in the Thai government's terminology), and rural sectors. In the period before the accelerated growth of the 1980s, the index of income inequality increased faster in the rural (and smaller urban areas) but this order was reversed in the growth period of 1986–92. Subsequently, when inequality decreased in the late growth period of 1992–96, the fall in inequality was stronger in the urban sector. Thus in the year before the Asian financial crisis, the inequality index was significantly higher in the rural and semi-urban areas than in the urban communities proper as defined by the Thai Socio-Economic Surveys (see Table 11.8).

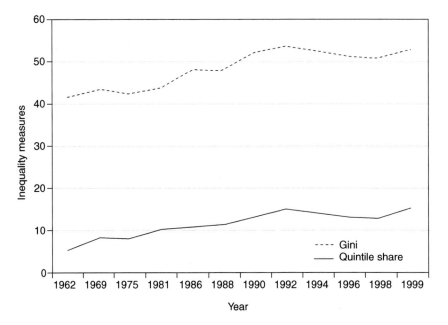

Figure 11.1 Gini coefficient and quintile share measures of inequality (source: Warr (2002, Figure 3)).

In spite of the increase in inequality, poverty was reduced throughout the history of Thai development until the recent post-Asian crisis years. It is, however, interesting to note that the steepest decline occurred in the 1970s. The decline moderated in the 1980s when inequality increased in a more pronounced way. There was an upturn in the headcount ratio after the Asian crisis (see Figure 11.2).

We can begin the discussion of the causes of the increasing inequality with growth in Thailand by recalling the method of dynamic decomposition of the factors affecting inequality trends summarized in Chapter 1. The distinction made of the three elements (the "within-group" change—sometimes called the residual—the "between-groups" trend in inequality, and the labour allocation effect) can be applied to any number of classifications of the labour force. A report by the Ahuja *et al.* (1997) sought to see the difference in the results of this decomposition for several alternative specifications of groups in the Thai economy over the period 1975 to 1992. The Gini increased in this period from 35.74 to 45.39 with E(2), the measure more sensitive to high incomes, increasing from 0.497 to 0.801 (see pp. 38–39 for details).

The results from this model are not able to shed light on the relative importance of the different factors to inequality or its changes over time. Rather, they give for each factor separately the contribution of that factor to the three components of inequality distinguished in the Mookerjee–Shorrocks decomposition.

Table 11.8 Inequality indices by community types

Community type	Year								Growth rates			
	1976	1981	1986	1988	1990	1992	1994	1996	1976–96	1976–86	1986–92	1992–96
Urban	0.244	0.256	0.276	0.284	0.357	0.387	0.321	0.307	6.4	0.32	1.86	–2.00
Semi-urban areas	0.259	0.266	0.356	0.319	0.360	0.388	0.408	0.387	12.7	0.97	0.53	–0.04
Rural	0.220	0.250	0.288	0.295	0.336	0.314	0.358	0.319	10.0	0.68	0.43	0.14

Source: Jeong (2005, Table A.4).

Notes
The indices are Theil-L. Growth rates are total change for 1976–96 multiplied by 100. For the three separate periods, they are annual average change (also multiplied by 100).

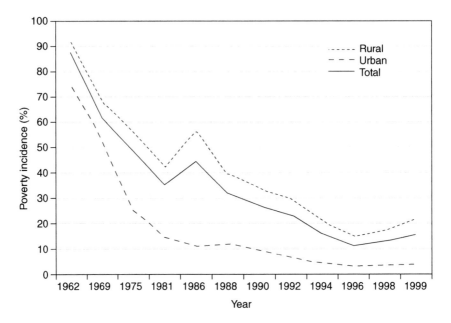

Figure 11.2 Headcount measure of poverty incidence (source: Warr (2002, Figure 2, p. 636)).

Of the several sets of groupings tried,[3] gender and age seem to contribute to inequality only through the "within-group" component. Three attributes (education, location of urban/rural, and region) are at the halfway level, with about half of the change in inequality in each case being explained by the "within-group" component and the other half by "between-group" variations. The attribute "socio-economic class" is the only one of these attributes which can explain a significantly large part of the change in inequality to "between-group" factors. The major part of this explanation (about two-thirds) is due to changes in relative income between the various types of socio-economic groups distinguished, while the other third is due to the population shifts among these types.

It should be emphasized that the socio-economic groupings in fact represent different classes of households within spatial groupings like rural–urban or regions. Thus the results show that the rising inequality in the Thai growth process was driven more by growing income differences between occupational categories than between spatial groups. There are several elements in this story which might be summarized as follows. Increase in inequality in an agrarian economy normally suggests that there is growing imbalance with urbanization— inequality in the urban areas hosting the new non-agricultural activities co-existing with the farm-based rural sector with low income (but much less inequality). This stereotype does not fit the empirics of Thai economic growth. As we have seen, the trend to increasing inequality during the growth process was as strong in the rural as in the urban and semi-urban sectors (Table 11.8 above). At the same time, the flow of labour from the rural to the urban sectors has been slow.

Part of the reason for the slow transfer of labour to the urban sector was the peculiarity of the urban labour markets in Thailand. As we have already discussed, the development of the urban economy in Thailand, and in the concentrated developing region of Bangkok and its environs in particular, the growth of new enterprises was based on utilization of massive flows of seasonal and temporary migrants, particularly from the low-income rural economies of the north and the north-east. The use of this type of migrant labour in the urban economy accentuated the dualism within the latter (particularly the gap in earnings between the formal and the informal sectors), thus accentuating inequality within the urban sector.[4]

We have seen earlier that the relative productivity in Thai agriculture has been unusually low relative to the other sectors throughout the growth process. While Thai agriculture clearly supported a good deal of under-employed labour, the development of non-farm employment within the rural sector was not insignificant. The way this income, as well as the remittances from labour temporarily migrating to the non-rural economy, was distributed among rural households has been crucial to the trend in inequality in the rural sector. We have seen that in some Asian economies, notably Taiwan, the distribution of income from off-farm sources was significantly equalizing for the rural households (see Chapter 8). But the evolution of off-farm sources of income in Thailand seems to have had a different impact.

Table 11.9 gives the sources of different types of income accruing to rural households, across the different deciles of per capita income, for selected years in the rural sector of Thailand. It is clear that the main sources of off-farm income (both wages and salaries, and non-farm profit) were much more unequally distributed than farm profit or income in-kind. It is equally clear that these sources of growing inequality worsened over the period of growth 1988–96, and remained so after the post-crisis recovery.

Quantitative analysis of income components of inequality

It is possible to assess the contribution to overall inequality of different sources of income in the household by applying the technique of pseudo-Gini analysis, which has been used elsewhere in this book. The full results for the rural and the urban areas separately over the phases of the cycle in the period 1988–2002 are set out in the Appendix to this chapter.

The first point to strike us is that the wages and salaries component of household income is the largest contributor to the overall Gini in both the rural and the urban sectors. As expected, the contribution is larger in the urban sector: 50 per cent or more over the period. But the contribution of this component to rural income inequality although less, is still quantitatively the most important component—rising from 33 per cent in the initial year to 40 per cent in subsequent

Table 11.9 Distribution of components of per capita income (rural)

		D = 1	D = 2	D = 3	D = 5	D = 8	D = 9	D = 10
1988	Income components (%)							
	Wages and salaries	17.5	17.5	19.5	18.9	25.8	24.9	34.1
	Non-farm profit	2.6	2.8	2.5	6.6	11.7	12.5	13.9
	Farm profit	15.1	19.1	21.6	26.8	24.3	27.3	20.3
	Income in-kind	61.3	56.3	50.7	41.9	28.9	24.6	16.7
1996	Income components (%)							
	Wages and salaries	18.2	22.7	23.4	29.5	31.8	32.0	35.7
	Non-farm profit	2.3	4.0	4.6	6.8	13.3	15.9	17.7
	Farm profit	17.7	18.9	23.5	21.7	18.9	19.3	17.9
	Income in-kind	53.7	44.1	37.7	29.5	21.4	18.2	12.7
2000	Income components (%)							
	Wages and salaries	17.5	19.7	20.2	25.9	29.3	35.1	39.4
	Non-farm profit	2.3	3.8	4.4	7.9	12.6	15.2	16.4
	Farm profit	14.2	18.7	19.7	19.1	17.9	13.8	15.0
	Income in-kind	58.3	47.9	42.2	34.0	25.1	19.7	12.3

Source: own calculations from the data tapes of the Household Income-Expenditure Surveys (HIES).

years. This is partly because the income share of this component in rural house-hold incomes remains the largest of the various components in most years and surprisingly exceeds the share of each of the other two important components in the rural sector (farm profits or income in-kind).

In the urban sector, non-farm profit replaces farm profit as the second most important source of household income. But surprisingly, non-farm profit continues to remain as important a contributor to overall inequality (Gini) in the rural sector as farm profit. This result underlines the importance of non-farm businesses in the rural economy, along with the significance of wage income in this sector.

The results presented in Tables 11.A1 and 11.A2 in the Appendix also enable us to identify how the different functional components of the household income basket affect changes in inequality over the period studied. In particular, they shed light on the dynamic impact of the different income sources for the cyclical phases witnessed in the 1988–2002 period. Of particular interest is the contribution of different income complements to the increase in the Gini coefficient in the period 1988–92 when the inequality index increased. This period captures the end of the phase of increasing inequality during the export-oriented expansion phase of the Thai economy. The index of inequality declined in the last years of the expansion phase 1992–96, before the Asian crisis ended the boom.[5]

A major difference is seen in the contributions of the income components between the urban and the rural areas. In the urban economy, the Gini index went up during the period by 0.056. Non-farm profit was the biggest contributor to this change at 0.044, followed by property income at 0.013. The contribution of wages and salaries was quite modest at 0.004. By contrast, in the rural sector, where the Gini increased by 0.022, the major contributor was in fact wages and salaries. Its contribution was as much as 0.037 and was offset by the negative contribution of farm profit to the tune of –0.021. The contributions of non-farm profit and property income to the increase in inequality in the rural sector were positive but very modest. The rural–urban difference brings out the contrasting role of the expansion of non-farm activities in the two sectors. In the rural areas, the expansion of new industrial firms had as yet not led to an expansion of profits and property income. Rather, the impact was felt in the increase in wage differentials with respect to unskilled (or agricultural) labour.

To conclude, the contrast between the Taiwan and the Thailand experiences in the contribution of off-farm employment to rural inequality cannot be over-emphasized. In Taiwan, off-farm employment opportunities played a decisive role in the trend to low rural inequality, but the impact has been the opposite in the Thai case. It should be clear that the different patterns of industrialization, specifically with respect to the size structure of manufacturing, were instrumental in this difference. The decentralized pattern of Taiwan's industrial growth and the dynamism of its dispersed small-scale units offered opportunities to low-income rural families to augment their total income. By contrast, non-farm sources (both wages and non-farm profit) contributed disproportionately to the total income of relatively richer households.

The return to education in Thailand

The critical importance of the wages and salaries component to the increase in inequality of household income distribution underlines the role of the relative price of skilled labour during Thailand's expansion. It leads us to another significant aspect of Thai development: the role of education.

The rate of return to education in Thailand during its growth years was exceptionally high. It is well known that the use of educated labour in the public sector is substantial. Thus we calculated the return to education separately for the public and the private sectors. The results of the estimated earnings function for wage and salary earners produced the coefficients for the years of schooling given in Table 11.10.[6]

The values of these coefficients even in the private sector are very high compared to other Asian economies during their periods of growth. In Korea, for example, we have seen that the coefficients of the years of education in a similar earnings function was 0.055 in 1986, falling to 0.036 in 1993 (Fields and Yoo 1998).

Table 11.10 Coefficients of years of schooling in estimated earnings function

Sector	1988	1996	2000	2002
Public	0.095	0.123	0.126	0.119
Private	0.078	0.081	0.069	0.072

Source: Own calculations from the files of the Labour Force Surveys.

Sussangkarn (1994), among others, has pointed out that the wage differentials for the skilled or college educated workers were exceptionally high in the last two decades of the previous century and exceeded by quite a margin the differential advantage of secondary school graduates over primary school graduates (Figure 13.7, p. 607).[7] These high educational differentials are due to both demand and supply factors.

- Supply-side factors: there is no doubt that, on the supply side, the sluggishness in the development of secondary education has been a feature of Thai development which distinguishes it from other East Asian countries in particular. Thailand succeeded in advancing primary education long before most developing countries. A universal education system launched in 1930 all but eliminated illiteracy. The impact of the six-year compulsory education adopted in 1960 should have impacted the education profile of those who were born in the early 1950s. However, even by the early 1960s, only about a third of the labour had at least six years of education. The proportion went up to about 40 per cent of the cohort in the early 1970s, and to only about half of those born between the late 1970s and early 1980s. The supply of upper secondary school leavers was even more scarce, with only a third of those born in the early 1980s finishing this level of education. In the mid-1980s, 75 per cent of the Thai workforce had only primary education. The gross enrolment ratio at the secondary level was only 30 per cent, well below the 90 per cent level of Korea and Taiwan, and even significantly below that of Indonesia (40 per cent) and the Philippines (70 per cent) (Sussangkarn, op. cit., p. 609).
- Demand-side factors: while the supply of educated labour was constrained by the inadequate growth of the post-primary education, the demand for such labour was maintained at a high level by the pattern of growth in Thailand. The growth of manufacturing biased to large firms clearly was a significant factor, but so was the rapid growth of employment in the tertiary sector, and particularly in the leading subsector of business services. The two sectors which demand educated labour more than any other (public/social services and business services) accounted for 16 per cent of total employment in 1988 compared to 8.5 per cent for all manufacturing. This percentage increased to nearly 25 per cent in 2002 as against 15 per cent for manufacturing (Labour Force Surveys). While the role of the public sector in the formal sector of the Thai economy had slowed down after the 1970s, the growth pattern with its heavy dependence on the inflow of foreign capital through the financial system, and its consternation in the Bangkok region, led to a surge in employment in business services.

V

International competitiveness

Industrial development skewed to large-scale units and supported in part by large inflows of capital could lead to high and/or growing inequality of income. At the same time, in some cases it might set in motion forces in the economy which adversely affect the country's competitiveness in export markets and thus undermine the basis of the growth process. In this section, we discuss the empirical evidence of this type of development in Thailand. The first element in the equation determining the trends in the unit cost of labour in foreign markets is the trend in wages relative to productivity in manufacturing (of equation 2, see p. 220 above).

Real wage trends

The increase in the real wages had been relatively modest in Thailand until the late 1980s. Warr (1993) reports a 2 per cent annual increase in the average real wages in the formal sector between 1982 and 1991, followed by a dramatic acceleration to 10 per cent over 1991–94. According to Warr, between 1990 and 1995, real wages increased by around 30 per cent for the workforce as a whole and by 48 per cent in manufacturing. The manufacturing sector saw a much more dramatic increase in real wages, indicating a sectoral bias away from agriculture.

A more detailed analysis of long-term trends in real wages is provided by Pholphirul (2007) and is reproduced in Figure 11.3. The figure illustrates the average real wage rate of the Thai economy, computed as adjusted labour share times the ratio of GDP at factor cost, divided by the reported number of workers. The wage per worker is deflated by the 1988 GDP deflator. From 1980 to 1985, the real average rates grew around 1.8 percentage points per annum, but there was a dramatic acceleration in the subsequent period of 1986 to 1996 to 4.3 per cent.[8]

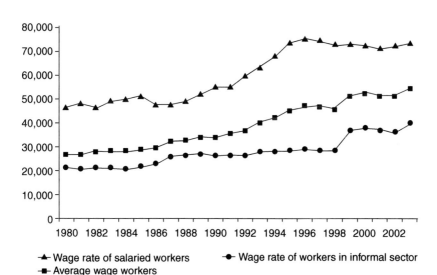

Figure 11.3 Real wage rates (baht per year) (source: Pholphirul (2005, Figure 3)).

Note
What Pholphirul calls "salaried workers" are really formal sector wage and salary earners.

Pholphirul also estimated the real wage rate of workers in the formal and the informal sector on the same basis. The informal sector wage rate is presumably the attributed labour income of all workers in the informal sector (including own-account workers). It is seen that the wage and salary income per worker in the formal sector started to increase in 1986 but showed a dramatic surge in the 1990s before tapering off at the onset of the Asian crisis. As indicated in Figure 11.3, the wages of workers in the informal sector shows only a slight increase from 26,169 baht in 1987 to 28,874 baht in 1998. The significant increase only occurred in the post-crisis era and by 2003 the average computed wage of the informal sector stood at 40,092 baht. As Pholphirul (2005) reports, in 1987, real wages of workers in the formal sector were about 1.8 times higher than those of workers in the informal sector, and this gap widened to 2.6 times in 1996.

A more direct analysis of reported wage differential between the agricultural and non-agricultural sectors is provided by Coxhead and Plangpraphan (1999). As is evident from Figure 11.4, reproduced from their work, the Bangkok Metropolitan Region (BMR) shows the most dramatic appreciation in the real wages. This appreciation started in earnest in the early 1980s but the real acceleration did not happen until the late 1980s. The average of agriculture and non-agriculture shows relatively similar patterns. The picture in these graphs shows that wages in the non-agricultural sector started to pull ahead of the agricultural sector at the beginning of the 1980s after two decades of very mild increase, and really surged ahead in the 1990s.

Movement in wages relative to productivity

Pholphirul (2005) has calculated the trend in real wages relative to labour productivity and has also presented the time-series for the profit rate in the non-agricultural sector, based on the National Accounts statistics. This is reproduced in Figure 11.5. Three phases could be distinguished.

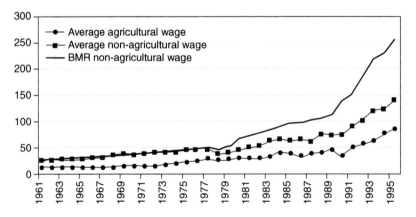

Figure 11.4 Agricultural and non-agricultural wages (baht/day) (source: Coxhead and Plangpraphan (1999)).

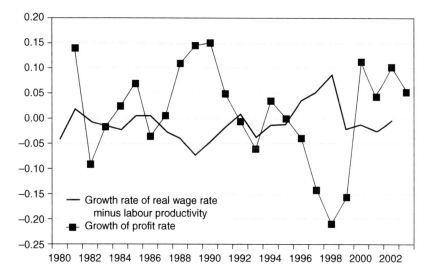

Figure 11.5 Trends in real wage relative to productivity and in the profit rate (source: Pholphirul (2005, Figure 16, p. 28)).

- In the first half of the 1980s, when real wages in the formal sector had been stagnant (although wages in non-agriculture started to increase from the beginning of the decade), the wage–productivity ratio was also roughly constant.
- While wages started to increase in the second half of the 1980s, profit rates took off. Evidently the increase in productivity jumped to new heights far exceeding the trend rate in wage, leading to the significant decline in "wages minus productivity", as seen in the graph.
- Wages accelerated in the 1990s. We now see that this led to the productivity–wage gap falling through the years leading up to the crisis with the consequent downward trend in the profit rate in Figure 11.5. It is clear that the decline in the productivity–wage gap in the 1990s was a significant factor in the loss of competitiveness and the onset of the crisis in 1997.

Pholphirul's trends analysed from the National Accounts are consistent with more specific wage–productivity data available from other sources. Work done from the data files at the World Bank pointed to dramatic change in the growth rate of the average wage, relative to that in labour productivity in manufacturing. The difference in the two trend values was negative for the two periods 1971–77 and 1977–86, at –2.2 per cent per annum and –0.3 per cent, respectively. In the subsequent period of rapid growth, 1986–94, the difference became significantly positive at 1.9 per cent (Mazumdar and Tzannatos 1997, p. 75). This is consistent with the evidence presented above and with a remarkable change in the Thai labour market at the beginning of the manufacturing boom led by exports.

Causes of wage increase in the growth phase

Before 1980, the manufacturing sector in Thailand expanded very much like in the classical Lewis model with a perfectly elastic supply of labour. Average earnings were practically constant over this decade, in spite of a fairly high rate of growth of employment. The turning point seems to have come in the first half of the 1980s. What explains the upward trend in wages in the non-agricultural economy of Thailand coinciding with its period of industrial growth? Clearly there was an increase in the alternative earnings or supply price of labour as revealed by the increase in agricultural earnings. The latter was fuelled by both the rise in agricultural productivity and the larger volume of rural-to-urban migration, fuelled by the expansion of non-agriculture. But as we can see from Figure 11.4 above, the rate of increase of wages was much higher in the non-agricultural sector.

There are at least four important reasons for this:

- The increase in demand for labour was partly for more skilled labour with more formal education. We have already seen that the Thai education system was deficient in ensuring an elastic supply of more educated labour.
- The segmentation in the market for non-agricultural labour played a significant role. While temporary migrants from the depressed rural north were in reasonable elastic supply, the new industries probably had greater need for more committed, stable migrants, whose elasticity of supply is most likely to have been much less.
- The lack of decentralized industrialization was not ideal for increasing the widespread acquisition of skills needed for new occupations. The concentration of employment in non-agricultural activities in Bangkok and its environs reduced the scope of on-the-job training in a large part of the low-income regions of the country.
- The inflation of profits in the rapidly developing large-scale sector in Bangkok and its environs must have been a potent force in employers' willingness to dole out wage increments to labour as they scrambled to increase the enterprise workforce rapidly. Both internal labour market and profit-sharing mechanisms must have played a strong role. It is seen from Figure 11.5 that the profit rate took a spectacular jump in the first half of the 1980s when wages started accelerating in the non-agriculture sector. This wage pressure gathered momentum in the 1990s, even as the profit rate plummeted—a phenomenon which is explained by the persistence of expectations, even after a turning point in the economy might have been reached.

The reader could go back at this point to equation (2) in this chapter. In terms of the equation, determining the trend in the unit cost of labour (and so the international competitiveness of the economy), it is now seen from the analysis above that the rise in the wage–productivity ratio contributed to Thailand's problem in sustaining the export-led boom. A second element in the equation is the movement of the domestic real exchange rate or the ratio of the price of non-tradables relative to that of tradables.

Trend in the value of the domestic real exchange date (DRER)

We have argued that an economy could face a significant problem of the Dutch disease type if the inflation of income due to growth based on exports and capital inflow is spent on domestic tertiary sector goods. Warr has presented convincing statistics on relative prices and related indicators to show that this is what happened in the Thai process of growth leading to the 1997 crisis. The Warr measure of relative prices indexed to begin at 0.7 in January 1988 declined almost continuously from 1990 onwards, reaching a low value of 0.38 in April 1997; a decline of nearly 50 per cent over a seven-year period.[9] This deterioration of the DRER added significantly to the increase in unit labour cost due to the upward wage–productivity trend identified above.

The exchange rate

The third element in the equation (2) defining the rate of change in unit labour cost is the exchange rate. Thailand had adopted a policy of fixed exchange rate for a long time, pegging the baht to the US dollar. The rate hardly deviated from 20 bahts to the dollar over the three decades between 1950 and 1980. The difficulties in the current account following the second oil crisis induced the government to modify its exchange rate policy somewhat. There were two limited devaluations in 1981 and 1984, and from the mid-1980s the currency was pegged to a basket of currencies. But since the weight of the dollar in this basket was about 90 per cent, effectively the Thai regime was back to the fixed exchange regime of earlier years. The tying of the exchange rate to the US dollar implied that the inflation rate in Thailand more or less tracked the course of inflation in the US.

Causes of the crisis

The material surveyed above clearly shows that the type of industrialization pursued by Thailand was leading to a fall in international competitiveness over time. The proximate cause of the 1997 crisis was the slowdown in exports, which indeed materialized in 1996. The rate of export growth, which was more than 20 per cent in each of the two years 1994 and 1995, plummeted to a negative figure of 0.35 per cent. Now a slowdown in exports in a particular year is not likely to trigger a major crisis in the ordinary course of events; the fact that it did in the Thai case was really due to two factors.

First, was the perception among all business observers that Thailand was losing long-term competitiveness for all the reasons discussed above. Because it was being anticipated in the prudent circles of economic observers, the export slump was taken to suggest a change in the long-term expectations about the economy.

Second, the real factors were vastly exaggerated by financial and monetary factors which had become significant in the Thai development history through a combination of policies connected with foreign capital inflow and domestic monetary policies, including the control or lack of it by the Thai banking system. The Thai authorities had sold themselves a vision of Bangkok emerging as a centre of finance capital on the lines of Singapore or Hong Kong, and had decided to relax all controls on capital movement. This had encouraged a massive inflow of short-term capital along with longer-term capital investment. In the years preceding the 1997 crisis, the inflow of short-term capital exploded, far exceeding the rate of growth of longer-term foreign capital. "From 1994 onwards, the stock of short-term capital exceeded the value of reserves and the discrepancy between them increased steadily" (Warr 1999, p. 638 and Figure 2). In early 1997, short-term capital was 80 per cent higher.

What triggered the massive inflow of short-term capital into the Thai economy? The short answer to this complicated question is that it was the bubble economy which had developed with massive demand increase for non-tradable assets, which now was fuelled further by speculative excesses. The big difference with bubbles elsewhere was that, in the case of Thailand, a substantial part of the capital involved in the speculative support of asset creation (shopping malls, residential buildings, etc.) was of foreign origin, which was available on a short-term basis and could be withdrawn with very short notice. The Bank of Thailand seems to have perversely encouraged short-term borrowing by non-bank financial institutions. At the same time, the desire to maintain a fixed exchange rate made the external financial system unsustainable. The inevitable collapse of confidence led to sudden flight of short-term capital, which ushered in the crisis in 1997.

VI

Conclusions

Although Thailand recovered fairly quickly from the depression of 1997 and growth was restored (albeit at a lower level than at the turn of the century), the problems of income disparity remain unresolved and have recently spilled over into serious political instability. The problems of the pattern of growth analysed in this chapter remain as a warning to Asian economies pursuing export-oriented industrialization, spearheaded by large centralized enterprises, and fuelled by uncontrolled capital inflow.

Appendix

The results of the analysis of income inequality follow the technique of pseudo-Gini set out in Chapter 6 (Appendix) above.

Table 11.A1 Inequality decomposition by income components (urban only)

	Income components	Pseudo-Gini	Income share	Factor Gini	Gini correlation	Contribution to Gini (%)
1988	Wages and salaries	0.472	0.477	0.653	0.723	0.225 (51.4)
	Non-farm profit	0.435	0.194	0.845	0.514	0.084 (19.3)
	Farm profit	0.197	0.027	0.967	0.204	0.005 (1.2)
	Property income	0.667	0.009	0.999	0.668	0.006 (1.4)
	Current transfers	0.444	0.081	0.909	0.488	0.036 (8.2)
	Income in-kind	0.363	0.202	0.570	0.638	0.073 (16.7)
	Other money income	0.710	0.011	1.00	0.709	0.008 (1.8)
	Total income	0.437	–	0.437	–	0.437 (100)
1992	Wages and salaries	0.461	0.497	0.644	0.716	0.229 (46.4)
	Non-farm profit	0.586	0.219	0.870	0.674	0.128 (26.0)
	Farm profit	0.376	0.019	0.994	0.379	0.007 (1.4)
	Property income	0.993	0.019	1.02	0.974	0.019 (3.8)
	Current transfers	0.435	0.062	0.923	0.471	0.027 (5.5)
	Income in-kind	0.431	0.172	0.617	0.698	0.074 (15.0)
	Other money income	0.802	0.012	1.01	0.793	0.010 (1.9)
	Total income	0.494	–	0.494	–	0.494 (100)
1996	Wages and salaries	0.458	0.507	0.643	0.712	0.232 (49.5)
	Non-farm profit	0.525	0.220	0.856	0.613	0.116 (24.6)
	Farm profit	0.371	0.021	0.985	0.377	0.008 (1.7)
	Property income	0.890	0.017	1.02	0.869	0.015 (3.2)
	Current transfers	0.349	0.062	0.916	0.381	0.022 (4.6)
	Income in-kind	0.440	0.164	0.617	0.713	0.072 (15.4)
	Other money income	0.622	0.008	0.993	0.627	0.005 (1.1)
	Total income	0.470	–	0.470	–	0.470 (100)

continued

Table 11.A1 continued

	Income components	Pseudo-Gini	Income share	Factor Gini	Gini correlation	Contribution to Gini (%)
2000	Wages and salaries	0.491	0.522	0.653	0.752	0.256 (55.6)
	Non-farm profit	0.469	0.200	0.852	0.550	0.094 (20.3)
	Farm profit	0.196	0.014	0.980	0.200	0.003 (0.6)
	Property income	0.654	0.017	0.962	0.680	0.011 (2.4)
	Current transfers	0.393	0.085	0.900	0.437	0.033 (7.2)
	Income in-kind	0.376	0.152	0.577	0.651	0.057 (12.4)
	Other money income	0.680	0.010	1.05	0.647	0.007 (1.5)
	Total income	0.461	–	0.461	–	0.461 (100)
2002	Wages and salaries	0.495	0.512	0.664	0.746	0.253 (54.0)
	Non-farm profit	0.451	0.212	0.839	0.538	0.096 (20.4)
	Farm profit	0.195	0.013	0.980	0.199	0.003 (0.5)
	Property income	0.904	0.025	1.02	0.886	0.023 (4.8)
	Current transfers	0.449	0.093	0.902	0.497	0.042 (8.9)
	Income in-kind	0.358	0.135	0.573	0.626	0.048 (10.3)
	Other money income	0.526	0.009	0.979	0.537	0.005 (1.0)
	Total income	0.469	–	0.469	–	0.469 (100)

Note
All the variables defining the columns in Tables 11.A1 and 11.A2 are as defined in the Chapter 6 Appendix.

Table 11.A2 Inequality decomposition by income components (rural only)

	Income components	Pseudo-Gini	Income share	Factor Gini	Gini correlation	Contribution to Gini (%)
1988	Wages and salaries	0.570	0.263	0.805	0.708	0.150 (33.8)
	Non-farm profit	0.677	0.105	0.933	0.726	0.071 (16.0)
	Farm profit	0.414	0.234	0.750	0.551	0.097 (21.8)
	Property income	0.690	0.011	0.992	0.695	0.008 (1.7)
	Current transfers	0.653	0.083	0.928	0.704	0.054 (12.2)
	Income in-kind	0.200	0.295	0.369	0.544	0.059 (13.3)
	Other money income	0.583	0.009	0.994	0.587	0.005 (1.2)
	Total income	0.444	–	0.444	–	0.444 (100)
1992	Wages and salaries	0.603	0.310	0.799	0.755	0.187 (40.1)
	Non-farm profit	0.648	0.116	0.921	0.704	0.075 (16.1)
	Farm profit	0.372	0.203	0.763	0.487	0.076 (16.2)
	Property income	0.832	0.013	1.03	0.806	0.011(2.3)
	Current transfers	0.556	0.081	0.912	0.609	0.045 (9.7)
	Income in-kind	0.232	0.261	0.400	0.579	0.061 (13.0)
	Other money income	0.772	0.015	1.1	0.722	0.012 (2.5)
	Total income	0.466	–	0.466	–	0.466 (100)
1996	Wages and salaries	0.521	0.315	0.764	0.682	0.164 (36.1)
	Non-farm profit	0.672	0.130	0.920	0.731	0.087 (19.2)
	Farm profit	0.417	0.194	0.790	0.528	0.081(17.8)
	Property income	0.783	0.012	0.990	0.791	0.009 (2.1)
	Current transfers	0.453	0.110	0.864	0.524	0.050 (11.0)
	Income in-kind	0.209	0.217	0.391	0.534	0.045 (10.0)
	Other money income	0.792	0.022	0.992	0.799	0.017 (3.8)
	Total income	0.454	–	0.454	–	0.454 (100)

continued

Table 11.A2 continued

	Income components	Pseudo-Gini	Income share	Factor Gini	Gini correlation	Contribution to Gini (%)
2000	Wages and salaries	0.578	0.329	0.785	0.736	0.190 (39.9)
	Non-farm profit	0.661	0.128	0.921	0.718	0.085 (17.7)
	Farm profit	0.452	0.162	0.829	0.546	0.073 (15.4)
	Property income	0.918	0.016	1.01	0.909	0.015 (3.1)
	Current transfers	0.463	0.116	0.859	0.538	0.054 (11.3)
	Income in-kind	0.204	0.229	0.384	0.531	0.047 (9.8)
	Other money income	0.712	0.020	0.981	0.726	0.014 (3.0)
	Total income	0.477	–	0.477	–	0.477 (100)
2002	Wages and salaries	0.542	0.331	0.766	0.708	0.179 (38.9)
	Non-farm profit	0.619	0.128	0.913	0.678	0.079 (17.2)
	Farm profit	0.461	0.180	0.821	0.562	0.083 (18.0)
	Property income	0.691	0.011	0.971	0.712	0.008 (1.6)
	Current transfers	0.424	0.126	0.840	0.504	0.053 (11.6)
	Income in-kind	0.204	0.197	0.390	0.523	0.040 (8.7)
	Other money income	0.705	0.026	0.968	0.728	0.018 (4.0)
	Total income	0.462	–	0.462	–	0.462 (100)

12 Size structure of manufacturing industry in Bangladesh and implications for growth and poverty

Nazneen Ahmed, Zaid Bakht, and Md. Yunus

I Introduction

The developmental odds faced by Bangladesh at the time of independence in 1971 were formidable. The challenges of high population growth, constant food shortages, recurring natural disaster, high aid dependence, limited production of tradable goods, widespread poverty, and low levels of human development were compounded by the dislocations caused by the war of liberation. Against that backdrop, the prospects for the Bangladesh economy appeared rather bleak.

However, Bangladesh's achievements over the past four decades negated considerably that pessimistic outlook. Against the benchmark trend GDP growth rate of 3.2 per cent during 1950–70, Bangladesh achieved a reasonably steady annual rate of growth of over 4 per cent during the first two decades of independence and moved into the higher growth trajectory of nearly 5 per cent during the 1990s. The economy achieved a trend growth rate of 5.9 per cent during 2000–10.

The boom in export and remittance earnings, with yearly compound growth of more than 12 per cent during 1980–2010, coupled with the decline in population growth rate from the post-independence peak of 2.7 per cent to 1.2 per cent in recent years, helped raise average yearly per capita gross national income (GNI) growth to more than 5 per cent during the past three decades. This was more than twice the global median for per capita growth during the same period.

The acceleration in the pace of growth started in the early 1990s, when Bangladesh returned to a democratic government after almost a decade of autocratic rule. This coincided with the stepped-up phase of wide-ranging policy reforms involving deregulation of investment, trade liberalization, and exchange rate, fiscal, and financial sector reforms.

On the face of it, the rise in per capita income seems to have ushered in a significant decline in the level of absolute poverty. Household income surveys showed the incidence of income-poverty to be around 31 per cent in 2010 against 58.8 per cent in 1991–92. Bangladesh also achieved impressive successes in the broad area of human development, as reflected in the aggregate measure of the human development index and human poverty index.

However, despite these impressive records of growth and poverty reduction, Bangladesh continues to remain at the bottom of the income scale, with per capita GNI of only US$750. There has been concern in recent years that economic growth in Bangladesh has not been sufficiently pro-poor and the low employment content of the growth achieved has been suggested as a reason behind this (Islam 2006). Agriculture has continued to account for nearly 50 per cent of employment, although its share in GDP has been steadily declining. There has also been the disturbing evidence of widening social inequality as reflected in the rising Gini coefficient of income distribution (Government of Bangladesh 2009). The incidence of spatial inequality has also been high in Bangladesh.

In a labour surplus economy like Bangladesh, the nexus between growth and equity is largely determined by the evolving pattern of structural changes of the economy. The pace at which surplus labour from agriculture is siphoned off depends on how labour-intensive the growth outside agriculture is, particularly in the manufacturing sector, which often shoulders key responsibility in carrying the economy forward.

Again, the employment intensity of manufacturing growth and its spatial attributes are expected to be closely linked with the size structure of the sector. Faced with factor prices closer to their social opportunity costs, smaller enterprises are often more efficient users of resources and tend to be more labour-intensive in labour surplus economies. Low capital, skill, and technology content also enable the smaller enterprises to be geographically more dispersed. These attributes thus render these enterprises more supportive of poverty-reducing development strategies. The issue of size structure has generated considerable research interest in recent years (Mazumdar 2003).

This chapter explores the evolving pattern of size structure in the manufacturing sector of Bangladesh and its implications for growth and equity. It looks at the structural transformation of the Bangladesh economy during the past three decades, the changing pattern of size structure in the manufacturing sector, productivity and wage differentials across different size groups, and the factors contributing to the structural change in the manufacturing sector.

II Structural transformation of the Bangladesh economy

The Bangladesh economy remained predominantly agrarian during the first two decades of independence, with agriculture (including fishery, livestock, and forestry) accounting for almost 37 per cent of GDP in 1988–89 (Table 12.1). During this period, the moderate decline in the share of agriculture was made up by growth in the service sector, particularly transport and communication. The decline in the share of agriculture accelerated during the 1990s, which coincided with the intensified phase of policy reform. During this and the subsequent decade, the decline in agriculture's share was matched by an increase in the share of industry (which includes manufacturing, utility, construction, and mining), with the share of the service sector remaining virtually unchanged. Thus, in terms of composition of GDP, the structural transformation of the Bangladesh economy since the early 1990s seems like a transition from agriculture to

Table 12.1 Sectoral composition (%) of GDP

Year	Agriculture	Industry	Service	All
1978–79	44.9	18.2	36.9	100
1988–89	37.1	17.1	45.8	100
1998–99	25.3	25.7	49.0	100
2008–09	20.6	29.7	49.7	100

Source: BBS National Account Statistics.

industry, rather than to service. As mentioned earlier, this has also been the period when Bangladesh moved into a higher growth trajectory.

The evidence with respect to employment, however, presents a different picture (Table 12.2). There has been some decline in the share of agriculture in employment and the consequent increase in the share of industry and service sectors between 1985 and 1995, but beyond 1995 agriculture's share in employment declined only marginally, with modest growth in the share of industry. Agriculture has thus continued to be the mainstay of employment, accounting for as much as 48 per cent of employment in 2005–06. Clearly, the employment content of the observed growth in industrial and service output has not been strong enough to reallocate surplus labour out of agriculture, although some components of the service sector, such as health, education, public administration, real estate, and transport experienced quite high growth in employment. As shown in Table 12.2, the overall yearly growth in employment during 1995–2006 was a paltry 3.1 per cent, while growth in the labour force during the same period was estimated to be nearly 3.2 per cent. The picture becomes even more worrisome when the incidence of under-employment is taken into account, which stood at nearly 25 per cent in 2005–06.

A second major structural change in the Bangladesh economy has been the transition to a more open economy, particularly following the liberalization measures undertaken during the early 1990s. Exports rose from US$1718 million in 1990–91 to US$6467 million in 2000–01, indicating a yearly compound growth of 14.2 per cent. Similar trends are observed with regard to imports and remittance. The openness of the economy shown by total external trade as a percentage of GDP increased from 21 per cent in 1980–81 to 42.6 per cent in 2008–09.

Table 12.2 Sectoral composition (%) of employment

Year	Agriculture	Industry	Service	Total
1985–86	57.1	12.1	30.7	100
1995–96	48.9	13.3	37.8	100
2005–06	48.1	14.4	37.5	100
Yearly growth in employment 1995–2006 (%)	3.0	4.1	2.5	3.1

Source: BBS Labour Force Surveys.

The composition of the export basket has also undergone significant changes during this period (Table 12.3). In 1981–82, raw jute and jute goods were the dominant export items, accounting for 16.2 per cent and 46.5 per cent respectively of total exports. In 2008–09, one finds a very different picture, with knitwear accounting for 41.3 per cent of exports, followed by woven garments accounting for 38 per cent of exports. The combined export of raw jute and jute goods stood at less than 3 per cent of total exports. During this period, the share of manufactured goods in total exports rose significantly, while that of primary goods registered commensurate decline. Bangladesh thus seems to have made a successful transition from resource-based exports to process-based exports, although exports remain precariously dependent on one item, namely, ready-made garments.

A third aspect of structural change in Bangladesh has been the relative role of the public and private sector. Policies towards private sector development underwent significant changes during the first three decades of independence. These changes were often closely associated with political changes in the country.

The development philosophy of the government at the time of Bangladesh's independence in 1971 was to confer on the state the leading role in the development process. Accordingly, immediately after independence, the government took over all industrial units abandoned by non-Bengali entrepreneurs and nationalized all Bangladeshi-owned banks, insurance companies, and industrial enterprises in the large and medium category. The scope of domestic private investment was limited to small and cottage enterprises.

The strategy of public sector-led industrialization was abandoned after the political change in 1975 and the stage was set for a mixed economy strategy, with simultaneous emphasis on public and private sectors. Between 1975 and 1981, a number of policy changes were made to give more room to the private sector. These included elimination of ceilings on private investment, amendment of the Constitution to allow denationalization, and divestiture of a number of public enterprises.

After the political change in 1981, the New Industrial Policy was announced in 1982, which marked a clear shift towards a private sector-led industrialization strategy. All subsequent governments adhered to this strategy of letting the private sector play the leading role in industrialization. In line with this strategy, privatization of public enterprises has been pursued and

Table 12.3 Share of major export items (% of total)

Year	Jute goods	Raw jute	Frozen food	Woven garments	Knitwear	Primary commodity	Manufactured goods
1981–82	46.5	16.2	8.4	1.1	0.0	35.0	65.0
1991–92	6.4	4.3	7.3	53.4	5.9	15.0	85.0
2008–09	1.8	1.0	3.0	38.0	41.3	5.6	94.4

Source: Government of Bangladesh, Ministry of Finance, Economic Review.

policies have been reformed to facilitate private sector growth, resulting in secular decline in the share of public enterprises in industrial value added and employment (Table 12.4).

There have also been some changes in the composition of the industrial sector. Manufacturing has all along been the dominant component of the industrial sector and its share in GDP increased from about 10 per cent in 1988–89 to nearly 18 per cent in 2008–09. However, its share in the *secondary sector* registered some decline as mining, construction, and utilities experienced significant gains following deregulation of investment and inflow of foreign investment in some of these subsectors. A similar picture is seen with regard to the employment share.

Manufacturing employment increased from 3.5 million in 1995–96 to 5.2 million in 2005–06, registering a yearly compound growth of 4 per cent. According to the national income data, manufacturing value added increased at an annual compound rate of 6.6 per cent during the same ten-year period. This would imply an employment elasticity of nearly 0.61 with respect to value addition, which suggests that recent manufacturing growth in Bangladesh has been moderately employment-intensive. A different data set, the Economic Census (which is undertaken less frequently), however, suggests that the manufacturing industry seems to have lost some ground to the service sector with regard to share in non-farm employment during 1986–2002, from 42.9 to 31.1 per cent (Table 12.5)

Table 12.4 Declining share of public enterprises in industrial value added and employment

Year	Share in VA (%)	Share in employment (%)
1976–77	55.1	78.3
1986–87	44.1	45.9
1991–92	23.1	21.1
1995–96	11.4	10.6
2001–02	6.9	5.6
2005–06	1.6	2.7

Source: BBS Census of Manufacturing Industries 2005–06.

Table 12.5 Share of manufacturing in non-farm employment

Year	Share in non-farm employment (%)			All
	Manufacturing	Wholesale and retail trade	Other services	
1986	42.9	33.0	24.1	100
2002	31.1	35.4	33.5	100

Source: BBS Economic Census 1986 and 2001–03.

The formal manufacturing sector in Bangladesh remained quite narrowly based during the 15-year period of 1990–2005. The top ten four-digit industries in terms of value added accounted for about 53 per cent of establishments, 62 per cent of manufacturing value added, and 73 per cent of manufacturing employment in the ten or more workers size category in 2005–06. In fact, the top two industries accounted for 33 per cent of value added and as much as 54 per cent of employment. There was little change in the degree of narrowness over the 15-year period. The only change is that knitwear replaced jute textiles as one of the two top industries, the other one being woven garments in both years.

III Size structure of manufacturing enterprises in Bangladesh

Official data pertaining to the manufacturing industry in Bangladesh are available from several sources, including: the Labour Force Survey (LFS), the Economic Census (EC), the Annual Establishment and Institution Survey (AEIS), and the Survey of Manufacturing Industries (SMI) (formerly the Census of Manufacturing Industries). These censuses and surveys are all carried out by the Bangladesh Bureau of Statistics (BBS). However, the reference period of the latest manufacturing data is not the same in all cases. There are also differences with regard to coverage, definitions, and methodology, both between data sources and also within each source at different points in time.

The manufacturing employment data from the LFS have already been reported. Unfortunately, the LFS does not provide employment data by size classes. Hence in this section, we examine data from the remaining three sources only.

Economic Census (EC)

The first census of non-farm economic activities in Bangladesh was carried out by the BBS in 1986. The census was repeated in 2001 but was limited to the urban areas. Enumeration of the rural undertakings was done in 2003. The main limitation of the EC data is that information for the fewer than ten workers category is not available broken down by smaller size groups, for example, 1–5 workers and 6–9 workers categories. Similarly, beyond 100 workers, the information is not broken down by disaggregate size groups such as 100–299 workers and 300–499 workers. The EC data also do not provide value added information.

Table 12.6 shows distribution of manufacturing employment by size classes in the two census periods. The table shows a U-shaped distribution with the size groups at the two ends accounting for the bulk of employment. However, one notices significant change in the size distribution of the manufacturing undertakings between 1986 and 2001–03. In 1986, micro manufacturing units (fewer than ten workers) accounted for nearly 61 per cent of all manufacturing employment. A large part of these micro units consisted of household-based cottage industries that are operated wholly or mainly with family labour. These are mostly

Table 12.6 Changes in the size distribution of manufacturing employment according to economic census data

Year	Share in manufacturing employment (%)				Total
	Fewer than 10 workers	10–49 workers	50–99 workers	100 or more workers	
1986	60.5	9.3	3.3	26.9	100
2001–03	40.4	13.1	4.2	42.3	100

Source: BBS Economic Census Report.

residual-type activities using traditional technologies where factor productivity and rates of return are abysmally low, often lower than the wage rate of agricultural labourers. People are usually driven to these activities when more productive employment is not available. During the inter-census period, both the absolute level of employment and share in total manufacturing employment declined significantly for this smallest size group.

In contrast, small (10–49 workers) and large (100 and more workers) enterprises demonstrated a more vibrant situation. Employment share of small enterprises went up by nearly 4 percentage points from 9.3 per cent to 13.1 per cent, while the employment share of large enterprises went up by nearly 15 percentage points from 26.9 per cent to 42.3 per cent. In contrast, medium (50–99 workers) enterprises experienced growth in employment share of less than 1 percentage point. However, significant inter-industry variations were also observed amongst enterprises in the 10–99 employment size group with respect to employment growth. Of the top 25 industries in terms of employment share in 2001–03, 14 experienced yearly employment growth of more than 5 per cent. This means that there has been a fairly dynamic component within the 10–99 workers size category, although, on the whole, this size group has registered only moderate growth in employment. The industries with a particularly high growth rate (more than 8 per cent) include wearing apparel, plastic products, footwear, and paper products.

Annual Establishment and Institution Survey (AEIS)

The AEIS is a sample survey of non-farm economic activities. Its coverage includes the following six subsectors:

- manufacturing establishments with fewer than ten workers
- all household-based manufacturing activities
- wholesale and retail trade (all employment sizes)
- hotels and restaurants (all employment sizes)
- establishments providing business, community, social, cultural, and personal services (all employment sizes)
- household-based non-manufacturing service activities.

Table 12.7 presents evidence on employment and value added at constant prices for the manufacturing segment of the AEIS during 1992–93 and 2002–03. As can be seen from the table, the evidence reaffirms the Economic Census findings that household-based manufacturing activities have been on a decline since the early 1990s. Non-household based manufacturing establishments with fewer than ten workers also stagnated with about 2.5 per cent yearly growth in employment during the reference period. The only silver lining in the case of non-household based manufacturing is the improvement in labour productivity, which rose from Tk.37,661 in 1992–93 to Tk.42,667 in 2002–03 at constant 1995–96 prices.

Survey of Manufacturing Industries (SMI)

The SMI, which until recently was known as the Census of Manufacturing Industries (CMI), is a sample survey of manufacturing enterprises with ten or more workers. To get a complete picture of the size distribution of non-household manufacturing, we need to combine AEIS data with CMI data. But AEIS data are available only for 1992–93 and 2002–03, while the comparable disaggregate CMI data are available for the years 1995–96 and 2001–02. Hence, to present employment and value added share of different size categories in the total non-household sector, we have estimated employment and value added in the fewer than ten workers non-household manufacturing category for the same years as CMI data (1995–96 and 2001–02) on the basis of available AEIS data using inter-survey growth rates (Table 12.8). Although SMI data for 2005–06 are now available, we have left them out of this calculation for comparability with available AEIS data.

The evidence again presents a U-shaped distribution, particularly during 1995–96, with large enterprises (500 and more workers) dominating the scene. The bottom end of the manufacturing spectrum, however, seems to be losing ground over time. Clearly, growth in non-household manufacturing in Bangladesh during the 1990s has been overwhelmingly led by large enterprises.

As discussed already, garments are the major export industry of Bangladesh and spearheaded the growth of its manufacturing sector in recent years. The large firms in this industry accounted for the bulk of the remarkable increase in the share of large firms in the manufacturing sector in the last decade of the past century. The share of ready garment firms in the total number of enterprises with 500 or more workers tripled (from 22 to 62 per cent), while its share in all other size groups increased only marginally (BBS Census of Manufacturing).

IV Employment, wages, and productivity trends

The AEIS-based evidence presented in the earlier section showed that employment in the "fewer than ten workers" non-household manufacturing category increased at a yearly rate of 2.5 per cent during the ten-year period of

Table 12.7 Employment and value added in manufacturing units covered by the AEIS

Description	Household-based manufacturing			Non-household based manufacturing with <10 workers		
	1992–93	*2002–03*	*Growth (%)*	*1992–93*	*2002–03*	*Growth (%)*
Total persons engaged	1,166,085	1,082,957	Negative	495,653	631,800	2.5
Value added at 1995–96 prices (million Tk.)	25,521	24,896	Negative	18,667	26,957	3.7

Source: BBS Annual Establishment and Institution Survey.

1992–2002, while the rate of growth of value added during the same period was 3.7 per cent. This implies an employment elasticity of 0.68 with respect to value added for this size group of manufacturing establishments. The evidence also shows that labour productivity for these enterprises increased from about Tk.37,700 in 1992–93 to about Tk.42.700 in 2002–03 in constant 1995–96 prices, indicating a yearly growth in productivity of 1.3 per cent only. The contrasting picture with regard to the formal manufacturing sector employing ten or more workers based on CMI data for 1991–92, 2001–02, and 2005–06 is shown in Table 12.9.

The evidence presents a much more vibrant picture of the formal manufacturing sector for the same period (1991–2001) with employment growth estimated at 7.9 per cent, while value added growth is estimated at 11.2 per cent, indicating an employment elasticity of nearly 0.71. As can be seen, labour productivity in formal manufacturing (employing ten or more workers) was nearly double that in non-household manufacturing (employing fewer than ten workers) in the early 1990s. During 1991–2001, labour productivity in the former group increased at a yearly rate of about 3.1 per cent, which though modest was higher than that observed for the latter group. As a result, productivity differential between the two groups widened further and in 2002 stood at 2.4 : 1. The formal manufacturing sector experienced even higher growth in labour productivity during 2001–05.

However, productivity differentials between different size groups within the formal sector (employing ten or more workers) show a somewhat different trend. Table 12.10 depicts indices of fixed assets per worker (K/L), value added per worker (VA/L), and wage rate for different size groups of enterprises, with values for the largest size group (500 or more workers) equal to 100. The indices have been presented for two years, 1995–96 and 2001–02. The evidence clearly shows a narrowing of the spread between the large enterprises (500 or more workers) and small and medium enterprises (10–199 workers) with respect to all three parameters.

Table 12.8 Percentage distribution of employment and value added by size groups of non-household manufacturing enterprises

Size groups (no. of workers)	Employment share (%)		Value added share (%)	
	1995–96	*2001–02*	*1995–96*	*2001–02*
<10 non-household	21.1	18.1	10.1	9.6
10–49	13.9	9.3	8.0	4.8
50–99	5.0	5.8	4.9	5.6
100–199	9.5	7.4	8.0	6.4
200–499	20.6	22.4	21.3	23.7
500 or more	29.9	37.0	47.6	49.9
All	100	100	100	100

Source. BBS, Annual Enterprise and Establishment Survey, and Census of Manufacturing Industries.

Table 12.9 Labour productivity trends in formal manufacturing in Bangladesh (all values are in constant 1995–96 prices)

Description	1991–92	2001–02	2005–06	Yearly rate of growth (%) 1991–2001	Yearly rate of growth (%) 1991–2005
No. of employees (000 persons)	1156	2466	3335	7.9	7.9
Value added (million Tk.)	85,272	247,520	491,820	11.2	13.3
Value added per employee (Tk.)	73,765	100,385	147,466	3.1	5.1
Employment cost (million Tk.)	30,235	66,500	121,187	8.2	10.4
Annual wage rate (Tk.)	26,155	26,970	36,336	0.3	2.4
Fixed capital per employee (Tk.)	103,118	115,995	189,956	1.2	4.5

Source: BBS, Census of Manufacturing Industries.

Growth of large manufacturing enterprises (500 or more workers) has been spearheaded mainly by ready-made garments and knitwear industries, which are highly labour-intensive activities, and this has brought about a drop in capital intensity and labour productivity in this size group. At the same time, the evidence also supports the notion that significant capital deepening has taken place amongst the small manufacturing enterprises in Bangladesh during the 1990s. Although, as indicated by the Economic Census data, a number of traditional small industries such as grain mill, saw mill, handloom, etc. either stagnated or experienced a decline in employment, there were the more dynamic components of the small and medium industry group who, by taking advantage of the liberalized trade regime, upgraded their technology and catered to both domestic and export markets. According to the Economic Census data, this group included plastic products, footwear, miscellaneous food products, job printing, apparel making, knitted wear, and chemical products.

A case study of the leather footwear industry in Bangladesh carried out in connection with the present study has presented the evidence that side by side with the growth of the modern leather footwear industry catering to both domestic and export markets, there has been very significant expansion of domestic market-oriented small leather footwear enterprises with 10–49 workers, which now produce quality leather footwear, taking advantage of easier access to imported raw materials. However, these enterprises seem to have remained largely outside the coverage of the Survey of Manufacturing Industries.

Similarly, a case study of the knitwear industry in Bangladesh has shown that rapid growth of the export-oriented knitwear industry of large and medium-sized enterprises has heralded the growth of a fairly large number of small knitwear enterprises who mainly perform subcontracting jobs for the larger enterprises under a somewhat flexible production arrangement.

The improvement in product quality and technology has contributed to higher labour productivity and wages to workers in small enterprises. As can be seen, in 1995–96, the wage rate in small enterprises was only 41 per cent of the wage in the large enterprises. But the wage spread seems to have declined over time. However, wage as a proportion of labour productivity has remained higher in the

Table 12.10 Factor intensity and labour productivity indices by size groups

No. of workers	1995–96				2001–02			
	K/L	VA/L	Wage	Wage as % of VA/L	K/L	VA/L	Wage	Wage as % of VA/L
10–49	23	36	41	30.4	64	38	65	38.8
50–99	38	62	50	21.5	47	72	74	23.5
100–199	32	53	54	27.2	69	64	90	32.2
200–499	32	65	77	31.8	44	79	95	27.9
500 or more	100	100	100	26.6	100	100	100	23.0

Source. BB3, CMI unit level data.

case of small enterprises and the gap seems to have widened during the reference period. This means that the growth of the ready-made garments industry (despite being labour-intensive) has not been sufficiently poverty-reducing because of low productive employment generated. As an illustration, it may be mentioned that, in 2005–06, labour productivity in ready-made garments (woven and knit) was Tk.120,000 in current prices, which was only 43 per cent of labour productivity of Tk.279,000 in the rest of the manufacturing sector (with ten or more workers).

Another manifestation of the overwhelming contribution of the ready-made garment industry in the employment generated in the manufacturing sector is the fact that employment elasticity of the formal manufacturing sector (ten or more workers) excluding ready-made garments was estimated to be around 0.50 during 1995–2001, while the employment elasticity of value added in the sector inclusive of the ready-made garment industry was estimated to be as high as 1.2 during the same period.

V Factors contributing to structural change in the manufacturing sector

The structural change in the manufacturing sector of Bangladesh witnessed during the past three decades was the outcome of the interplay of several factors. Of these, the role of public policy, particularly that relating to private sector promotion and external trade, was critically important. A brief account of the major contributing factors behind the observed structural change in the manufacturing sector of Bangladesh is presented below.

Public vs. private sector-led growth strategy

As mentioned earlier, Bangladesh started with a public sector-led industrialization strategy under which private manufacturing investment was restricted to small and cottage industries. But within a few years, the ceiling on private manufacturing investment was relaxed and eventually fully removed. Finally, Bangladesh shifted to a private sector-led industrialization strategy and, in that context, the regulatory regime governing private manufacturing investment was relaxed and wide-ranging policy incentives were put in place. Bakht (1993, 2001), Ahmed and Bakht (2010), Ahmed and Yunus (2010), and Rahman and Bakht (1997) provide a detailed account of these policy shifts.

Historically, public manufacturing investment was channelled into large and capital-intensive industries. Even after substantial privatization and reduction in manufacturing investment during the past two decades, per capita fixed assets in public manufacturing enterprises in 2005–06 remained significantly above the per capita fixed assets level in all enterprises of comparable size. Average employment size in public manufacturing enterprises in 2005–06 was 848, while fixed assets per worker in current prices was Tk.650,000. In contrast, the average fixed assets per worker for all enterprises in the 500+ workers size group was only Tk.23,000 (BBS, Report on Bangladesh SMI 2005–06). Clearly, the shift from public to private sector-led industrialization strategy was partly responsible for the declining trend in capital intensity in the large manufacturing enterprises in Bangladesh during the reference period.

Liberalization of the trade and exchange rate regime

Historically, Bangladesh, like its neighbours in South Asia, pursued a development strategy that was based on import-substituting industrialization. The economic case for this inward-looking strategy was built around the arguments of conservation of scarce foreign exchange and the need to create an industrial base through the provision of a protected domestic market. The policy was pursued with the use of high tariff walls and extensive use of quantitative restrictions (QRs) and other non-tariff barriers. All foreign exchange earnings accrued to the government were then allocated to competing uses through a discretionary mechanism of import licensing.

The main limitation of this autarkic strategy, however, was that it created a distorted incentive structure, resulting in allocative and productive inefficiency. The policy also gave rise to anti-export bias and discouraged growth of exports.

The outcome of this policy has been disappointing in terms of industrialization, export development, the balance of payments situation, and development of the overall economy in sharp contrast to the rapid growth of the East Asian economies that followed a more outward-oriented development strategy. Disenchanted with the import substitution strategy and pursued by donor conditionality, the policy makers in Bangladesh, as in other South Asian economies, began to tilt towards a more open economy policy from the late 1970s.

Trade policy reforms in Bangladesh covered both tariff and non-tariff barriers (NTB). Under non-tariff barriers, the focus has been on deregulation of the import procedure and elimination of QRs. With regard to tariff barriers, the attempt has been to rationalize the tariff structure, reduce the number of duty slabs, and bring down tariff rates and their dispersion amongst similar commodities.

Extensive use of quantitative restrictions was a standard feature of Bangladesh's import control mechanism during the 1970s and early 1980s.

Since the mid-1980s, Bangladesh has come a long way in terms of dismantling its non-tariff barriers. The system of import license has been virtually eliminated and the control list of banned and restricted items has been pared down to a minimum.

Rationalization of the tariff structure has been one of the key elements of trade policy reforms in Bangladesh. The government attempted to reduce the wide variations in tariff rates and ensure that statutory and actual rates do not vary much. The number of *ad valorem* custom duty rates has been reduced gradually (from 18 in 1991–92 to seven in 1995–96). Preferential rates of duties applicable to public sector enterprise were eliminated in 1989. Tariff reform was accelerated significantly in the fiscal year 1992–93 by the compression of custom duty rates into a narrower range for most products, accompanied by the removal of many end-user defined distinctions. As a part of the rationalization measures, a maximum tariff rate was reduced from a level of 350 per cent in 1991–92 to 50 per cent in 1995–96 and then further down to 37.5 per cent in 2000–01. The import-weighted tariff rate declined from 42.1 per cent in 1990–91 to 20.9 per cent in 1994–95, to 15.1 per cent in 2000–01, and to 11.48 per cent in 2003–04 (Bangladesh, Ministry of Finance, Economic Review).

At inception in 1971, Bangladesh pegged its currency to the pound sterling. In support of its import substitution strategy, Bangladesh maintained an overvalued exchange rate. All foreign exchanges accrued to the government were then allocated to competing uses through a discretionary and cumbersome mechanism of import licensing.

To attract remittance and to provide incentive for exports, a secondary exchange market (SEM) was also in operation from the mid-1970s. Bangladeshi wage earners residing abroad could sell their remittance at a higher rate in the SEM. The exporters were also allowed to convert a part of their export earnings through the SEM. Thus, Bangladesh maintained a system of dual exchange rates for quite some time. In 1980, the fixed exchange rate regime was replaced by a system of "managed float" and the taka was pegged to a basket of currencies of the country's major trading partners. The intervention currency was changed from the pound to the US dollar. In 1992, the government abandoned the system of dual exchange rates by unifying the official exchange rate and the SEM rate. Bangladesh made its currency convertible on current account as of 1993.

The system of managed float continued up to 2003 when the country moved to a free-floating system. Between 1980 and 2003, the nominal exchange rate was devalued in small amounts, keeping pace with inflation. In 1979–80, the exchange rate stood at Tk.15.47/$. By 2001–02, it rose to Tk.53.96/$, implying an annual depreciation rate of about 5.8 per cent. The Consumer Price Index (CPI) in 2001–02 stood at 245.92 with 1985–86 = 100, which implies an annual inflation rate of about 5.79 per cent during this period.

After Bangladesh embarked on a free-floating exchange rate system on 31 March 2003, the exchange rate depreciated moderately in the initial years. There was sharp depreciation in 2005–06 that may have been linked to capital flight prior to elections. After that, the yearly depreciation became moderate again. Between 2002–03 and 2006–07, the yearly rate of depreciation was estimated to be about 4.7 per cent.

The liberalization of the trade regime and the pursuit of a market-oriented exchange rate policy substantially reduced the anti-export bias that existed in the trade and exchange rate policy of Bangladesh in the initial years. The reform measures thus provided a favourable policy environment for the growth of export industries.

At around the same time, the international intermediaries, faced with binding quota restrictions of the Multi-Fibre Arrangement (MFA) in their own country, were trying to relocate the ready-made garments industry to some other labour-surplus country and Bangladesh became an obvious choice as it was still free from quota restriction and had very low wages. Thus, the initial investment in this export industry was made under joint venture with the South Korean Daewoo Company. But Bangladeshi entrepreneurs realized the potential of this industry and were quick to seize the opportunity by rapidly investing in the industry. In fact, with the take-off of the local ready-made garments industry, foreign direct investment (FDI) was initially barred from entering into the ready-made garments industry. Later, FDI was allowed in the ready-made garments industry only in the export processing zones. Thus, unlike the case of Sri Lanka and Vietnam, FDI has not been a very important factor behind the rapid growth of the ready-made garments industry in Bangladesh.

Although the trade regime was quite restrictive during the early years of the growth of the ready-made garments industry in Bangladesh (late 1970s and early 1980s), the industry was provided duty-free access to imported raw materials under the bonded warehouse system, which was important in ensuring external competitiveness of the industry as Bangladesh had to import the bulk of the raw materials for this industry. This system was also helpful in supporting the growth of a number of backward linkage industries, such as printing and packaging, plastic accessories for ready-made garments, and textile spinning and weaving. Other export industries that have benefited from liberalized trade and exchange rate regime include fish and seafood processing, leather and leather products, and light engineering.

Easier access to imported raw materials has also facilitated the growth of a number of domestic market-oriented industries. These include pharmaceuticals, plastic products, leather footwear, and processed food products.

Access to finance

The export industries which grew because of liberalized trade and exchange rate policy belonged mostly to medium and large-scale industries. In the case of the knitwear industry, the growth of large-scale export units also facilitated the growth of smaller-sized knitwear units because of the scope of subcontracting. The incidence of such subcontracting was less significant in the case of other export industries. Some of the enterprises in backward linkage industries, particularly in printing and packaging, were also smaller.

By contrast, most of the domestic market-oriented industries (such as plastic products and leather footwear), which grew due to easier access to imported raw materials, had a significant share of enterprises of relatively smaller size. One factor that has contributed to this divergent growth of size groups in domestic and export industries is differential access to finance. The rapid growth of export-oriented, large-scale ready-made garments, knitwear, leather, and leather products industries was largely facilitated by the system of back-to-back LC and working capital financing under which exporters could obtain financing for import of raw materials and other working capital needs at concessional rates against confirmed export LC. This facility was also extended to deemed exporters who supplied manufactured inputs to export industries, but domestic market-oriented industries remained outside the scope of this facility. The implied segmentation of the capital market thus influenced the size structure of the export industries in favour of larger enterprises.

Lack of access to institutional finance has been a persistent constraint to the growth of small industries. In the past, government attempted to provide small enterprises with access to finance through targeted lending. But the actual delivery of institutional credit to this sector remained grossly inadequate and stagnant at around 2 per cent of total bank credit disbursement during 2001–05. A similar situation also existed prior to 2001.

In 2003–04, a refinancing scheme for credit to small and medium enterprises was set up under the central bank. Under this scheme, the central bank charges participating institutions at the bank rate (5 per cent), while the lending institutions decide on the lending rate. This provides these institutions with the scope to lend to small and medium enterprises without real estate-based collateral, as their risks will be covered through the refinancing facility and they can accommodate any additional cost of loan administration through an appropriate spread between the borrowing and the lending rate. So far, the scheme appears successful in extending collateral-free loans to small and medium enterprises, although a disproportionately large proportion of the loan recipients are seen to belong to trading rather than manufacturing.

Market access and fiscal incentives

Before its phasing out on 1 January 2005, the MFA acted as a trade-restrictive quantitative measure. However, for Bangladesh, the MFA was a blessing as it provided market access for its ready-made garments for the first time in history, thus allowing Bangladeshi apparels to get a foothold in the export market. The subsequent rapid growth of the ready-made garment industry in Bangladesh also owes a great deal to the MFA. Eventually, the quota became binding and restrictive for Bangladesh. However, by then, Bangladesh had attained competitive advantage in the export of ready-made garments so that it could sustain its ready-made garments exports even after the phasing out of the MFA.

Another important aspect of market access facilitating the growth of the ready-made garments industry in Bangladesh was the Generalized System of Preferences (GSP), under which Bangladesh as a developing country is granted duty-free access to selected developed country markets subject to conditions relating to rules of origin, while the duty on comparable import from other developing countries stood at around 12 per cent. The rules of origin for the GSP in the European market required two-stage value addition, that is, the ready-made garment and the fabric input must be of Bangladesh origin. At one point, the rules of origin required three-stage value addition, which meant that the yarn used in the fabric input also had to be of Bangladesh origin.

This provided the incentive for the setting up of backward linkage industries, strengthened further with the fiscal incentive of a 20 per cent cash subsidy for ready-made garments exported with fabric of local origin (introduced in early

1990). This means that for every $100 worth of ready-made garments exported, the government provided a $20 cash subsidy to the exporter if the fabric used was of local origin.

The market access granted through the GSP and the fiscal incentive in the form of the cash subsidy together sparked rapid growth in large-scale composite knitwear mills, which produced all three products (yarn, knit fabric, and knit garments). This also facilitated the setting up of large independent spinning and weaving mills. Given that the production of knit fabric requires less lumpy investment than woven fabric, the backward linkage expanded more rapidly for knit garments. As a result, the export of knitwear in the European market grew very rapidly and ultimately knitwear surpassed woven garments as the country's top export earner.

The export-oriented processed fish and seafood industry also grew rapidly, benefiting from the European GSP facility.

Growth in domestic demand

As mentioned earlier, the Bangladesh economy experienced a steady increase in GDP growth from about 4 per cent during the 1980s to about 5 per cent during the 1990s and then to about 6 per cent during the 2000s. The economy got a further boost through a significant increase in remittance income. The consequent growth in domestic demand contributed to rapid expansion of many domestic market-oriented consumer goods industries, such as plastic, leather footwear, and processed food products. As an illustration of growth in domestic demand, it may be mentioned that, during the 1980s, Bangladesh exported most of the tea it produced. Currently, the bulk of the tea produced is consumed domestically.

One sector experiencing significant growth due to the increase in domestic demand in remittance income is construction. During the 1990s, the construction sector grew at a trend rate of nearly 9 per cent, so industries supplying input to the construction sector experienced rapid growth. These included bricks and tiles, iron and steel re-rolling, cement, and wooden furniture. Easier access to imported raw materials also supported the growth of iron and steel re-rolling, cement, and wooden furniture industries. The cement industry also benefited from substantial inflows of FDI.

Of these construction-related activities, bricks and tiles and wooden furniture are labour-intensive industries, while iron and steel re-rolling and cement are capital-intensive industries. Except wooden furniture, all other industries belong to the medium and large size categories. Wooden furniture has a mix of both large and small enterprises.

VI Concluding remarks

The evidence presented has shown that non-household manufacturing enterprises employing fewer than ten workers and those employing 10–49 workers accounted for a significant proportion of manufacturing establishments and employment during the early 1990s. At the other end, enterprises with 200 or more workers constituted the other major component of manufacturing establishments and employment, and accounted for the bulk of manufacturing value added. This conventional dualistic look of the manufacturing sector with a missing middle, however, seems to be on the decline in Bangladesh.

During the 1990s, non-household manufacturing establishments employing fewer than ten workers stagnated, with low employment and value added. Growth in manufacturing during this period was spearheaded by large enterprises employing 200 or more workers. The disaggregate picture shows that growth of large manufacturing enterprises was again dominated by a single industry, namely, ready-made garments.

Given the high labour intensity and low labour productivity of the ready-made garments industry, the contribution of the industry to large manufacturing ushered in a decline in capital intensity and labour productivity in the largest size group of enterprises (500 of more workers).

At the same time, a core dynamic component in the small industry group (10–99 workers) seems to have undergone considerable modernization (taking advantage of trade liberalization measures) and raised both fixed assets per worker and labour productivity. This has been successful in bringing under its fold a larger segment of the domestic market and establishing a foothold in the export market. This has narrowed the spread of capital intensity and labour productivity between small and large industry, reflecting upward mobility on the part of the modern component of the small industry group. The formal manufacturing sector as a whole (employing ten or more workers) experienced moderate growth in capital intensity and labour productivity during the 1990s. The picture improved somewhat during 2001–05.

An analysis of the factors contributing to structural change in the manufacturing sector of Bangladesh shows that a shift in public policy with regard to the relative role of the public and the private sector, reforms in trade and exchange rate policy, differential access to institutional finance, preferential market access, fiscal incentives, and growth in domestic demand shaped the pattern of structural change in the sector during the past three decades.

On the whole, however, the quality of manufacturing employment growth in Bangladesh seems to have been low, reflected in low growth of labour productivity and real wages with a consequent low impact on poverty reduction and equitable growth. This has happened because manufacturing growth in Bangladesh has been too narrowly based on the low productive ready-made garments industry alone.

13 The case of Vietnam[1]

Paul Shaffer and Le Dang Trung

I Introduction

Vietnam's economic transformation since the period of reforms, or *doi moi* (renovation), initiated in the mid-1980s, is quite remarkable. There have been dramatic changes in virtually all facets of social and economic life. Economic policies and institutions have evolved from those of a centrally planned economy towards those of a market-based economy. A shortlist of some of the most important reforms includes: domestic price liberalization for most agricultural products, liberalization of the trade regime culminating in World Trade Organization accession in 2007, encouragement of foreign direct investment, and ongoing legal reform aimed at strengthening property rights and contracts.

In terms of economic performance, growth averaged around 8 per cent throughout much of the 1990s and over 7 per cent since 2000. The consequences for poverty reduction have been even more impressive. According to household survey data, poverty incidence has fallen from around 58 per cent in 1993 to around 19.5 per cent in 2004 (VASS 2006). Most social indicators have seen quite rapid improvement as well, including child mortality, which has fallen dramatically (Social Watch 2008). Overall, Vietnam's record with respect to both growth and equity has been impressive, despite concerns about rising inequality.

In light of the commitment to equity and growth in Vietnam, it is surprising that limited attention has been devoted to the question of the size structure of enterprises in terms of employment.[2] In the context of Vietnam, the size structure of enterprises has bearing on at least three issues of major concern to policy makers: employment, internal migration, and income distribution. Employment has been a longstanding preoccupation of policy makers, given the sizable annual number of new entrants into the labour force and the potential for unrest associated with urban unemployment (Dapice 2006). The size distribution of firms is often closely related to the labour intensity of production and, in the aggregate, employment elasticities of growth.

Internal migration, in particular to large urban areas, is a sensitive issue given the illegal status of many migrants. It appears to be a quite sizable phenomenon (JDR 2008, pp. 22–24) and an important source of income for the poor (VASS 2006, pp. 38–42). It is likely to increase in importance over time, in the absence of policy measures that promote a more spatially balanced pattern of industrialization.

Income distribution remains a central concern of policy makers in the context of Vietnam's rapid economic growth. The prospect of large and increasing gaps in living standards between population groups is a potential source of social unrest and anathema to the ideologies of senior decision makers.

This chapter reviews the size distribution of manufacturing firms with respect to employment, number of firms, and productivity. It presents explanations for the size distribution, drawing on historical factors, factor-price distortions, productivity catch-up, globalization, ownership types, categories of manufacturing, and export orientation. It also reviews data on levels, trends, and sources of inequality in Vietnam since *doi moi*.

There is one preliminary point to note. The analysis in this chapter does not include the household sector, that is, household enterprises. This excludes most of the bottom end of the distribution and leads to a number of different conclusions than found elsewhere in the literature (JDR 2006). Nevertheless, this exclusion allows for comparability with the other chapters in this volume and is in keeping with the broader literature (Mazumdar 2003).

II Vietnam's economy

There are four salient features of Vietnam's experience: (i) unlike China, consumption represents a significant share of GDP and of GDP growth since 2000, equalling or exceeding the Asian average; (ii) similar to China and India, investment has played a very significant role in recent years, contributing over half of GDP growth since 2000 and standing well in excess of the Asian country average; (iii) exports have been central to Vietnam's growth strategy, accounting for around three-quarters of GDP in 2008, though net exports have been consistently negative (Table 13.1); (iv) employment/GDP growth elasticities, as well as employment growth rates, have exceeded those of China by a wide margin, which is reflected in

Table 13.1 GDP decomposition, select Asian countries (in per cent)

	1995			2000				2008			
	C^a	I^b	Net X^c	C	I	X^d	Net X	C	I	X	Net X
Vietnam	81.3	27.2	−9.1	73.4	30.5	55	−3.7	74.7	44.1	76.8	−20.8
China	58.2	40.3	1.6	62.3	35.3	20.8	2.4	48.6	43.5	33	7.9
India	77.4	24.6	−1.5	77.1	25.9	13.2	−1.9	67	36.2	24	−4.3
All*	76.6	25.9	−7.6	74.8	25	45.4	−1.4	67.7	23.6	45.4	2.9

Source: Prasad (2009, Tables 1 and 3).

Notes
a Total consumption (private + government).
b Investment.
c Exports – imports.
d Exports.
* Unweighted median of Bangladesh, Cambodia, China, Hong Kong, India, Indonesia, Korea, Malaysia, Pakistan, Philippines, Singapore, Sri Lanka, Taiwan, Thailand, and Vietnam.

the importance of consumption in Vietnam's GDP (Table 13.2). The rapid consumption growth is also reflected in the dramatic fall in the food share in household expenditure across all consumption quartiles, as shown in Table 13.3. In summary, Vietnam represents a hybrid model which incorporates the high investment and export growth of the Chinese model along with high levels of consumption and solid employment growth (since 2000) found elsewhere in Asia.

Table 13.4 presents data on the structural transformation of Vietnam's economy.[3] There has been a progressive decline in the economic importance of agriculture, forestry, and fishing, which accelerated markedly after *doi moi*. Their share of GDP fell from around 39 per cent to 27 per cent between 1990 and 1995 and subsequently dropped to 21 per cent in 2005. Between 1990 and 2005, the economic shares of manufacturing and construction increased from 12 per cent to 21 per cent and 3.8 per cent to 6.4 per cent, respectively, while that of services stayed relatively constant over this time period at around 38 per cent. The breakdown within the service sector also remained relatively constant over time with the biggest share increase going to distributive services (trade/transport/storage/communications). The Vietnamese experience follows the so-called South-East Asian pattern of structural transformation, whereby industrialization, in particular the growth of manufacturing, has played a very significant role in the process of economic growth (Ocampo and Vos 2008, Ch. 2).

Table 13.2 GDP and employment growth, Vietnam and select Asian countries, 2000–08

	GDP growth	C	I	Net X	Employment growth rate	Employment/GDP growth elasticities
Vietnam	7.5	0.71	0.57	−0.32	2.3	0.31
China	10.2	0.40	0.49	0.11	0.9	0.09
India	7.2	0.57	0.50	−0.04	1.9	0.26
All*	5.2	0.71	0.27	0.08	1.9	0.37

Source: calculated from Prasad (2009, Table 2).

Note
* Unweighted median of Bangladesh, Cambodia, China, Hong Kong, India, Indonesia, Korea, Malaysia, Pakistan, Philippines, Singapore, Sri Lanka, Taiwan, Thailand, and Vietnam.

Table 13.3 Food shares in household consumption

	1993	1998	2002	2004	2006
Poorest	73.25	70.6	67.47	66.36	64.98
2	68.63	64.7	59.44	57.04	55.53
3	64.46	59.88	54.34	51.4	50.49
4	59.03	54.84	48.2	45.68	44.31
Richest	49.58	43.43	38.87	36.81	36.83
All	62.43	56.85	53.42	51.42	50.33

Source. Vietnam Household Living Standards Surveys.

Table 13.4 Sectoral composition of GDP

	1990	1995	2000	2005	Growth rates (of shares)		
					1990–2000	2000–05	1990–2005
Primary	43.94	31.99	34.18	31.56	−22	−8	−28
1 Agriculture, forestry, fishing	38.73	27.18	24.53	20.97	−37	−15	−46
2 Mining and quarrying	5.21	4.81	9.65	10.59	85	10	103
Secondary	17.47	23.94	27.08	30.43	55	12	74
3 Manufacturing	12.26	14.99	18.56	20.63	51	11	68
4 Utilities (electricity, gas, water)	1.37	2.05	3.17	3.45	131	9	152
5 Construction	3.84	6.9	5.35	6.35	39	19	65
Tertiary	38.59	44.06	38.74	38.03	0	−2	−1
6 Distributive services[a]	16.46	20.36	18.16	17.92	10	−1	9
7 Producer services[b]	7.85	8.03	6.71	6.44	−15	−4	−18
8 Personal services[c]	4.69	4.32	3.83	3.99	−18	4	−15
9 Public, social and community services[d]	9.59	11.35	10.04	9.68	5	−4	1

Source: GSO Statistical Yearbooks.

Notes

a Trade and repairs; transport, storage and communications.
b Financial intermediation; science and technology; real estate, renting and business.
c Hotels and restaurants; recreation, cultural and sporting activities.
d Public administration and social security; health and social work; education and training; activities of party and membership organizations; community, social and personal service activities.

Table 13.5 presents data on the sectoral composition of employment between 1990 and 2005. In terms of manufacturing, two distinct time periods are discernable. Between 1990 and 2000, manufacturing's share of employment remained quite stable, increasing from 10 per cent to 11.5 per cent. Over the period 2000–05, however, it jumped sharply, from 11.5 per cent to 17.4 per cent. Likewise, for agriculture, forestry, and fishing, the period 1990–2000 is characterized by a relatively slow decline in employment share from 73 per cent to 68 per cent, which then falls sharply to 57 per cent by 2005. For services, the employment share increased steadily over the entire time period, but more rapidly after 2000. The distributive services, (trade/repairs/transport/storage/communications) accounted for most of the share increase in the tertiary sector. In summary, the transfer of labour from primary to secondary and tertiary sectors was extremely modest throughout the 1990s and accelerated rapidly after 2000.

A further key structural change in Vietnam's economy has been associated with the role of the state in economic life. As discussed above, this is not surprising given the transition from a command to a market-based economy. The state share of GDP actually increased since 1990 and still stood at around 38 per cent in 2005. The state share of employment fell between 1985 and 2005, as did the state share of industrial output. The latter fell quite precipitously between 1995 and 2005 from 50 to 25 per cent (Table 13.6).

In terms of their contribution to output, "light industries" dominated the scene as late as 2005, machinery and transportation equipment accounting for only 15 per cent of output. Food and beverages was the largest contributor to value added (26 per cent), but otherwise output was evenly spread over a range of light industries. With respect to employment, the most important subsectors are leather products (18 per cent); garments (16 per cent); food, beverages, and cigarettes (14.5 per cent); and manufacturing of wood and wood products (11.9 per cent). It is worth noting that textiles, garments, and leather products are the major export industries in the Vietnamese economy, accounting for 22 per cent of total export turnover in 2008 (GSO, Statistical Yearbook 2008).

III Size structure of manufacturing enterprises in Vietnam

Data sources and definitions

There are three main databases with detailed information on, and wide coverage of, enterprises in Vietnam. First, there are the Vietnam Living Standard Surveys (VLSS) of 1993 and 1998, and subsequent Vietnam Household Living Standard Surveys (VHLSS) of 2002, 2004, and 2006. These survey instruments contained modules on household enterprises and have been used to analyse their various features.[4] These data will not be used in the present analysis given its focus on the non-household sector. It should be made clear, though, that the vast majority of firms in Vietnam are household enterprises, which tend to be very small. As mentioned above, their exclusion from the analysis has the effect of leaving out the bottom end of the combined distribution of household and non-household enterprises.

Table 13.5 Sectoral composition of employment

	1990	1995	2000	2005	Growth rates (of shares)		
					1990–2000	2000–05	1990–2005
Primary	73.9	72.0	68.8	57.9	–7	–16	–22
1 Agriculture, forestry, fishing	73.0	71.3	68.2	57.1	–7	–16	–22
2 Mining and quarrying	0.9	0.7	0.6	0.8	–33	34	–11
Secondary	10.3	10.6	11.5	17.4	11	51	68
3 Manufacturing	7.8	8.0	8.7	12.3	12	41	58
4 Utilities (electricity, gas, water)	0.3	0.2	0.2	0.4	–16	85	56
5 Construction	2.3	2.4	2.6	4.7	12	84	106
Tertiary	15.7	17.4	19.8	24.7	26	24	57
6 Distributive services[a]	6.8	8.2	9.9	13.2	46	33	94
7 Producer services[b]	0.5	0.5	0.6	0.7	18	21	43
8 Personal services[c]	1.5	1.8	2.0	1.9	32	–7	23
9 Public, social and community services[d]	6.9	6.9	7.3	8.9	6	22	29

Source: GSO Statistical Yearbooks.

Notes

a Trade and repairs; transport, storage and communications.
b Financial intermediation; science and technology; real estate, renting and business.
c Hotels and restaurants; recreation, cultural and sporting activities.
d Public administration and social security; health and social work; education and training; activities of party and membership organizations; community, social, and personal service activities.

Table 13.6 State share of GDP, employment, and industrial output

Year	GDP	Employment	Industrial output
1985	35.74	14.86	57
1990	32.50	11.28	59
1995	40.18	8.83	50
2000	38.52	9.31	34
2005	38.40	9.50	25

Source: GSO Statistical Yearbooks.

A second data source is composed of four surveys of small and medium enterprises conducted in Vietnam in 1991, 1997, 2003, and 2005 by the Institute of Labour Sciences and Social Affairs (ILSSA) and the Stockholm School of Economics (SSE).[5] The first three of these surveys were not national in scope and were restricted to firms with fewer than 100 employees. Accordingly, they do not provide information on the overall size distribution of enterprises.

The final data source, which will be relied on heavily, is the Enterprise Census, conducted annually since 2000 by the General Statistical Office of Vietnam (GSO 2008).

In terms of definitions, a distinction is maintained between state, non-state, and foreign direct investment (FDI) enterprises. State enterprises comprise enterprises with 100 per cent of state capital, including limited liability companies, as well as stock companies with public shares greater than 50 per cent. Domestic non-state enterprises are enterprises set up by domestic capital, with public shares of less than 50 per cent, including cooperatives, private companies, private limited liability companies, private stock companies, and stock companies with a less than 50 per cent public share of registered capital. FDI enterprises are firms with 100 per cent of capital invested by foreigners as well as joint ventures.

Size distribution and employment

Table 13.7 presents data on the distribution of employment by firm size group in manufacturing between 2000 and 2006. There are a number of interesting features of this distribution.

Table 13.7 Percentage distribution of employment by size group in manufacturing

Size group	2000	2001	2002	2003	2004	2005
5–9	0.95	0.88	0.95	0.92	0.95	1.08
10–49	5.69	5.91	6.14	6.05	6.50	7.04
50–99	5.55	5.44	5.59	5.34	5.53	5.85
100–199	9.40	9.01	9.28	8.59	8.48	8.64
200–499	20.00	19.23	19.66	18.23	17.70	17.48
500 and over	58.40	59.54	58.37	60.87	60.84	59.91

Source: Vietnam Enterprise Censuses 2000–05.

First, there is a pronounced skew in favour of firms with 500 or more employees. Such firms account for almost 60 per cent of total employment. By comparative standards, the skew is extremely large, in excess of that found elsewhere in Asia (Mazumdar 2003). For example, the share of employment generated by firms with 500 or more employees in three countries characterized by large enterprises, Korea (1986), Thailand (1989), and Malaysia (1981), was 35 per cent, 37 per cent, and 30 per cent, respectively.

Second, the bottom end of the distribution, that is, firms with between five and nine employees, is extremely small, accounting for around 1 per cent of employment. The relevant figures for Korea, Thailand, and Malaysia are between 3 per cent and 5 per cent. It should be noted that all of these comparisons exclude the household sector, which accounts for most small enterprises. From the point of view of non-household firms, Vietnam is characterized by a "missing low end" along with an "undersized middle".

Third, despite significant changes in the legal and policy climate since 2000, there is little change in the overall structure of the distribution. The main size categories which lost relative share are in the middle, namely the 100–199 and 200–499 groupings, which declined by 10 per cent and 13 per cent, respectively. The main category which gained is the 10–49 grouping, which increased by around 24 per cent, though from a very low level.

Size distribution and productivity

Table 13.8 presents estimates of labour productivity (value added per worker) for the different size groups of firms in 2003 and 2005, the only two years in the dataset for which such information exists. One preliminary point concerns the labour productivity estimates. We have used two methods to calculate value added, heretofore labelled "actual" and "calibrated" value added. The first approach relies on the detailed cost modules in the questionnaire to calculate the value of intermediate inputs, which are then subtracted from total revenue. An outlier correction algorithm has been applied to these data as the cost structure in a number of observations seems quite unrealistic, resulting in large negative value added estimates for certain size categories of firms. The second approach takes the difference between total revenue and profits declared by firms to calculate total costs. It then uses the ratio between intermediate costs and total costs, found in the cost section of the questionnaire, to estimate intermediate costs. In light of the apparent anomalies in the cost data in the questionnaires, it is probable that estimates of calibrated value added are more reliable than actual value added. In Table 13.8, we present results of both.

There are two important points about the data in Table 13.8. First, labour productivity differences between extreme size groups are smaller than in other countries, with a similar skew in favour of larger firms. For example, labour productivity differences between the smallest and largest firms in Korea were 0.3 : 1 (Mazumdar 2003). Second, according to the data, labour productivity is highest among firms in the middle of the distribution.[6] The finding holds in both 2003 and 2005 and is

Table 13.8 Value added per worker by size group in manufacturing

	2003						2005					
	Calibrated value added		Actual value added*				Calibrated value added		Actual value added*			
	Million VND/ worker	Index value (500+ = 100)	Million VND/ worker	Index value (500+ = 100)			Million VND/ worker	Index value (500+ = 100)	Million VND/ worker	Index value (500+ = 100)		
5–9	31.9	50.3	25.4	54.2			39.38	58	27.8	34.1		
10–49	44.2	69.7	31.8	67.8			67.97	64	55.9	68.6		
50–99	61.7	97.3	41.6	88.8			106.78	80	74.9	91.8		
100–199	76.7	120.9	50.2	107.1			133.71	131	87.0	106.6		
200–499	83.3	131.4	55.0	117.5			101.80	112	91.0	111.6		
500 and over	63.4	100.0	46.9	100.0			90.87	100	81.6	100.0		

Source: Vietnam Enterprise Census 2005.

Note
* Outlier corrected.

robust to the method of value added estimation. It is interesting to note that these are the same size groups which have grown more slowly than the others, as shown in Table 13.7 above. Together, these points suggest that, overall, the size distribution of firms may not be driven primarily by efficiency-related considerations relating, say, to economies of scale. Further, they raise two key questions: (i) what is the reason for the pronounced skew in favour of very large firms in terms of total employment?; and (ii) why have mid-sized enterprises not grown at a faster pace, given that they appear to have the highest labour productivity?

IV Historical/policy context

The evolution of industrial policy and the organization of industrial production prior and subsequent to *doi moi* provide a *prima facie* explanation of the skew in favour of large enterprises and the slow growth of medium-sized firms in manufacturing. There are two main issues. The first concerns the emphasis on state-owned enterprises (SOEs), and subsequently on FDI firms, which have tended to be more capital intensive (Mekong Economics 2002, p. 6) and larger than domestic non-state enterprises, as evidenced by Figure 13.1.

The second aspect concerns the quite complex development trajectory of the non-state sector with implications for the current situation of private sector enterprises. The present discussion provides broad historical context about these issues with emphasis on the changing policy environment.

The initial period of reform was characterized by official pronouncements in support of the non-state sector and its increasing importance to the economy. Vietnam's industry, however, was still dominated by the state sector, which

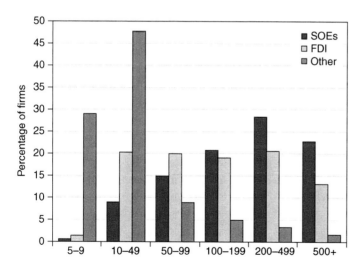

Figure 13.1 Size distribution of firms by ownership type, 2000 (source: GSO, Vietnam Enterprise Survey (2000)).

tended to be larger and more capital intensive. Following the Sixth Party Congress, a number of decrees were promulgated in support of the private sector; notably, the Decree of March 1988 (*On Policies Toward the Individual Economy, Private Industrial Production and Business*), which affirmed the state's guarantee of the "rights to property, inheritance, and income of units and individuals in these sectors" (Fforde and De Vylder, 1996, p. 155). Furthermore, one of six targets agreed by the Fourth Plenum of the Communist Party of December 1987 affirmed the commitment to "create work for the millions of workers who do not have stable employment by ... absorbing labor into small-scale industry[7] in both the towns and the cities..." (ibid., p. 150).

SOE-led industrialization and FDI promotion: 1990s

A striking feature of most of the 1990s was the continuing importance of the state sector in the economy. The state share of GDP increased from 32.5 per cent in 1990 to 38.5 per cent in 2000. The state share of industrial output remained at or above 50 per cent until the latter years of the decade, when the effects of rapid inflows of FDI became apparent (see below). A number of factors contributed to the centrality of SOEs in the industrialization process, including: the economic crisis of 1989–91, when aid from the Soviet Union plummeted, and SOE revenue became increasingly important to secure a tax base (Fforde 2007, Ch. 8); the increase in the relative importance of industries in which the state sector dominated, including power, building materials, and telecommunications; the influx of FDI and aid, which bolstered SOEs in water supply, power, construction, and construction materials; preferential access to export quotas afforded SOEs in lighter industries, such as garments, which served to perpetuate their dominance (van Arkadie and Mallon 2004). In general terms, the less than favourable attitude towards the domestic private sector by authorities may have contributed to the so-called "tall poppy syndrome", whereby "private companies in Vietnam are reluctant to grow relatively large for fear of attracting too much negative attention from authorities and regulators" (Steer and Taussig 2002, p. 9).

A second major development in the 1990s was the influx of FDI, which expanded rapidly throughout the decade. A number of policy measures were enacted to promote foreign investment, most notably the Foreign Investment Law in 1987. The FDI share of total industrial output increased from less than one-tenth in 1990 to around one-third in 2000, reflecting a very high rate of growth (Van Arkadie and Mallon 2004, p. 199). In fact, in the mid-1990s, Vietnam was the top recipient of FDI per GDP of all developing and transition countries (JDR 2006, p. 12).

Private sector promotion: post-2000

The post-2000 period has been characterized by two key trends. First, the process of SOE reform has gathered steam. Second, efforts to promote the domestic private sector have accelerated with a number of palpable effects.

The three rounds of SOE reform undertaken in the 1990s paved the way for an accelerated pace of reform. The process of equitization is of particular note, in this regard. The pace sped up from around 100 SOEs in 1998 to close to 500 per year in the mid-2000s (JDR 2006, p. 10). Recently, Vietcombank, one of the six largest state-owned banks, has been equitized. Given that SOE creation effectively ended in 2001, the number of state-owned enterprises and the employment share of SOEs have steadily declined since this period. Table 13.9 shows the trends in employment by types of firms in the manufacturing sector.

The promotion of the private sector gained symbolic and substantive support through the passage of the Enterprise Law of 2000. The key effects of the Enterprise Law were to simplify the procedures for formal registration of businesses and reduce the associated time and financial costs. Other important effects were to: lessen uncertainty about the legal status of various activities, reducing the scope for corruption and petty harassment; clarify mechanisms for investor protection; and consolidate and unify the fragmented regulatory framework, adding consistency and clarity, etc. (van Arkadie and Mallon 2004, p. 165). Other important policy developments include the 2001–10 Socio-Economic Development Strategy (SEDP) endorsed at the Ninth Party Congress in 2001 and the resolution of the Fifth Party Plenum in 2002. The SEDP laid out the commitment of equal treatment of enterprises regardless of their ownership type and emphasized the importance of SMEs for employment generation and poverty reduction. The 2002 resolution stressed the importance of the private sector to the economy as a source of employment creation, growth, and public revenue. One further policy initiative of note is the SME Five Year Plan 2006–2010 (Ministry of Planning and Investment 2006). The document reflects high-level commitment to SME promotion, recognizing both the importance of SMEs for pro-poor growth as well as obstacles to SME development.

V Factor-price and factor-access issues

As discussed elsewhere in this volume, it is often maintained that factor-price ratios are a key determinant of the size distribution of enterprises in a given industry. Specifically, differences in the relative price of capital and labour across size categories of firms may lead to the adoption of different technologies and production techniques. In Vietnam, this argument has particular force when applied to

Table 13.9 Employment shares of manufacturing firms by type of ownership, 2000–05

	2000	2001	2002	2003	2004	2005
SOEs	44	43	36	32	28	22
FDIs	26	26	27	30	32	35
Other	30	30	37	38	40	43
Domestic non-state	100	100	100	100	100	100

Source: Vietnam Enterprise Census.

the price of, and access to, capital. An additional factor to consider is the differential access to land across size and ownership categories of enterprises.

Labour

It should be noted that, in Vietnam, it is unlikely that labour market imperfections are a major contributor to firm size differentials between categories of enterprises. Specifically, there are a number of reasons to doubt that wage premiums in the state sector account for the size distribution of firms by ownership type, shown in Figure 13.1. First, econometric evidence does not show a large enough public sector premium to account for the very marked skew in the size distribution of SOEs. The 1990s data suggest that public and private sectors have similar wage rates, though the former offers a 20 per cent premium for total compensation due to the greater number of hours worked (Bales and Rama 2001). While public sector wages increased after 2000, the share of large SOEs fell precipitously during this same period. Second, and more importantly, some data suggest that SOEs are overstaffed by around 50 per cent relative to the private sector (Belser and Rama 2001), despite the significant downsizing of the 1990s. As such, it seems unlikely that higher public sector compensation levels triggered a process of capital for labour substitution with the effect of increasing firm size. Third, in general terms, labour markets in Vietnam function quite well. Minimum wage rates do not tend to be binding constraints on hiring. Further, remuneration gaps according to gender, geography, and registration status of the enterprise have narrowed significantly over time (JDR 2006, 89).[8]

Capital

There is considerable evidence in Vietnam of capital market segmentation between SOEs and privately owned firms and among firms of different sizes. While access to capital by the private sector has improved steadily over time, lack of credit remains a major impediment to the growth of privately owned, smaller enterprises. It is among the most frequently cited constraints on expansion by firm managers and owners.

Prior to reforms, the banking sector served the primary function of allotting credit to state institutions to help them reach their production quotas specified in the plan (van Arkadie and Mallon 2004). Lending was not based on commercial criteria, nor were the respective roles of central and commercial banking distinguished. In the early years of *doi moi*, the formal structures of a modern banking system began to appear with the introduction of a two-tier banking system, the issuance of guidelines requiring the four state-owned commercial banks to operate according to commercial criteria, the emergence of a number of joint stock banks, etc. In practice, the banking system faced numerous political and technical challenges, resulting in a significant proportion of non-performing loans and continued lending to state-owned enterprises on the basis of administrative directives.

Despite these difficulties, progress has been made in the allocation of credit between the state and non-state sectors. Total credit allotted to state enterprises has fallen significantly from 90 per cent to around 30 per cent as the private sector's share has increased to around 70 per cent. Likewise, the share of credit extended by the state-owned commercial banks has fallen from around 80 per cent to around 60 per cent (Table 13.10). These changes in the allocation of lending have occurred together with rapid and significant financial deepening, whereby total credit has expanded to over 60 per cent of GDP from much lower levels (JDR 2006, Ch. 5).

Other data suggest that capital market segmentation persists. Evidence of segmentation is provided when contrasting the source of loans between SOEs and private firms. Drawing on survey data of around 750 private and state-owned enterprises in Vietnam, Tenev *et al.* (2003) found significant differences in borrowing patterns between state and non-state enterprises. The latter were more likely to borrow from family friends, money lenders, and private joint stock banks. State enterprises rely much more extensively on state-owned commercial banks and (to a lesser extent) investment funds. The authors conclude that "firms face a segmented financial market with differential access to and preferences for various sources of loan financing" (ibid., pp. 61–62).

When enterprise survey respondents are asked about the main obstacles to growth, it is striking that the lack of credit invariably figures prominently in their responses. One example involves the aforementioned surveys of SMEs conducted by the Institute of Labour Sciences and Social Affairs and the Stockholm School. In these surveys, shortage of capital was the main problem identified, cited by 50–60 per cent of respondents. Interestingly, these figures did not decline over time (Kokko and Sjöholm 2006, p. 172). In the abovementioned survey by Tenev *et al.* (2003, p. 5), around half of private enterprises cited access to financing as a major or severe obstacle. Other surveys have come to similar results (Riedel 1997, p. 15; Steer and Taussig 2002, p. 32; Webster and Taussig 1999).

Table 13.10 Allocation of credit (percentages)

Total credit	1990	1995	2000	2005	2007
State enterprises	90	56.9	44.9	32.8	31.4
Other sectors	10	43.1	55.1	67.2	68.6
Of which:					
SOCB[a]	–	79.6	73.3	69	61.9
State enterprises	–	49.3	39.4	28.4	24.7
Other sectors	–	30.3	34	40.4	37.4
Other banks[b]	–	20.4	26.7	31	38.1
State enterprises	–	7.6	5.6	4.2	6.7
Other sectors	–	12.8	21.1	26.8	31.4

Source: van Arkadie and Mallon (2004, p. 100), IMF (1999, 2003, 2007).
Notes
a Four large state-owned commercial banks.
b Mainly joint stock and joint venture banks and foreign banks.

The twin facts of increasing expansion of credit to the non-state sector and persistent concerns among private sector firms about the lack of credit direct attention to the issue of size. These twin observations would be consistent with a disproportionate allocation of credit to a smaller number of larger firms. It has been argued that both very large and very small firms have privileged access to credit at the expenses of small and medium-sized firms (JDR 2006, p. 59). There are a number of econometric results in the literature which are consistent with this interpretation. [9]

Land

Access to land is a second obstacle to private sector growth with disproportionate effects on small and medium-sized firms. Vietnam has undertaken quite far-reaching reforms in the legal status and administration of land over its transition period. The biggest issue, from the point of view of private SMEs, concerns formal tenure over, or access to, urban or peri-urban land for commercial purposes. Lack of official tenure had implications for credit access and long-term investment decisions, whereas lack of access is a constraint on expansion.

The legal status of land changed markedly in 1988 with Resolution 10 on the "Renewal of Economic Management in Agriculture", whereby land use rights were allotted to farm households for periods of 15–40 years. The watershed Land Law of 1993, as well as revisions in 1998 and 2004, introduced a number of important changes, most importantly the right to exchange, transfer, lease, inherit, and mortgage land use rights (Akram-Lodhi 2005, pp. 110–112). Progress in issuing land use rights via so-called "Red Books" has made considerable headway in rural areas, though less so in urban areas (JDR 2006, pp. 73–74).

There are three main mechanisms by which firms can access land for commercial purchases: direct allocation from government (usually People's Committees), transfer from holders of Certificates of Land Use Rights (CLURs), and auctions, though this last mechanism is quite recent and has not been widely used. The first mechanism is mainly restricted to larger firms, in particular SOEs, and is uncommon for SMEs (ibid., p. 75).

The second mechanism has limited effectiveness due to the limited allotment of CLURs, especially in urban and peri-urban areas. Accordingly, some estimate that 70 per cent of transactions involving land use rights take place informally and involve businesses leasing directly from SOEs and households (Tenev *et al.* 2003, p. 68). Survey data reveal a non-negligible and statistically significant difference in the possession of CLURs by private firms and SOEs, 62 per cent versus 70 per cent, respectively. For those who do engage in the informal market for land rights, however, administrative penalties can be levied by authorities (Harvie 2008, p. 210). Further, security of tenure is less than optimal, with negative implications for longer term investment decisions.

The limited effectiveness of these transfer mechanisms, combined with the historical legacy of a command economy, result in a quite skewed distribution of available land in favour of SOEs. According to data from the World Bank's Investment Climate Survey, SOEs possess on average five times the available land of non-state firms with more than 250 employees (JDR 2006, p. 79). The situation in Hanoi is particularly skewed: over 95 per cent of land leased to enterprises is in the hands of SOEs (ibid., p. 81).

There are two main implications of limited land access for SMEs. First, many are unable to use land as collateral for access to credit. This is a longstanding problem which persists (Hill 2000, p. 293). The negative effects on access to finance are magnified by the heavy emphasis on physical collateral in bank lending decisions to the private sector (Malesky and Taussig 2008). The issues of security of land tenure and credit access are closely intertwined.

Second, firm growth is constrained. Survey data, drawing on perceptions of CEOs, suggest that the land constraint may be quite significant (Tenev *et al.* 2003, pp. 69–70). Some 82 and 35 per cent of respondents said they would expand plant size or diversify into new activities, respectively, with improved land access. As discussed above, this problem more severely affects smaller and medium-sized private firms.

VI Productivity catch-up and globalization: explaining the slow growth of medium-sized firms

In addition to land and capital constraints, other factors have limited the growth of small and medium-sized enterprises in Vietnam.

The limited employment elasticities of growth in Vietnam throughout the 1990s, in particular for manufacturing, have received considerable attention in the literature. It has been estimated that every percentage point of GDP growth in the late 1990s increased employment by around 0.22 per cent, a very low figure by South-East Asian standards (Thoburn 2004, p. 133). A number of explanations have been offered for the relatively limited employment response, many relating to policy distortions affecting the economy. Some, like Jenkins (2004), have argued that slow employment growth in industry is due to rapid productivity growth on the part of firms in Vietnam, responding to the imperative of increasing labour productivity to survive in increasingly competitive market conditions. These productivity gains were more the result of capital upgrading than of labour shedding, given that assets per worker increased markedly.

The importance of productivity growth for firms with fewer than 100 employees comes out forcefully in the results of the ILSSA/SSE surveys of the 1990s. There were large increases in capital intensity and labour productivity between 1991 and 1997. Employment elasticities for total employment were low, varying between 0.17 per cent and 0.24 per cent in urban and rural areas respectively (Ronnås 2001, p. 214).These changes were due to very rapid upgrading by firms set up in the earlier period, as well as by the entry of new, more capital-intensive firms. A critical determinant of the success of surviving firms was their ability to generate profits and accumulate capital at a very high rate (Ronnås 1998, p. 42).

The second major issue concerns barriers to small and medium-sized firms as they attempt to integrate into global value chains. This has particular relevance for textiles, garments, and footwear, which have all experienced rapid growth as merchandise exports. There are three main issues. First, what is the relationship between firm size and export orientation? Second, what are the factors limiting integration of SMEs in value chains? Third, what factors restrict the entry of firms into higher value-added activities?

As shown in Table 13.11, the percentage of exporting firms increases monotonically with firm size for the three years (2000, 2003, 2004) in which data on exports were collected. In 2004, there remained a significant gap between the percentage of medium and large-sized firms which export, with the latter figure exceeding 70 per cent and the former between 44 and 58 per cent. It should be noted, however, that this gap fell between 2000 and 2004, though at an insufficient rate to affect the overall skew in favour of large firms.

The second set of factors attempts to explain the gap between the export orientation of SMEs and large-sized firms. Drawing on interviews with global buyers and firms, as well as secondary evidence, Nadvi and Thoburn (2004a, 2004b) argue that SMEs in Vietnam face a range of difficulties when attempting to insert themselves in international value chains.[10] Pressures to meet international labour standards along with demands for higher quality products with shorter lead times have proved particularly difficult. In the case of labour standards, small firms complained of difficulties in meeting health and safety regulations related to ventilation and working space. Full compliance would require redesigned plant layouts or entirely new factory premises (Nadvi and Thoburn, 2004a, p. 259).

In a dynamic sense, increasing value added in production is critical to the success of industrialization. In the context of the garment industry, this involves the shift from cut-make-trim (CMT) activities, for which firms are assigned a processing fee, to free-on-board (FOB) tasks, whereby firms provide the fabrics and charge a price for the final garment. Critical here is the ability to source high-quality fabric domestically or abroad, to take on large orders, and to supply a diverse range of products. In their interviews, Nadvi and Thoburn (2004b, p. 119) found a decided bias in favour of large SOEs for FOB-type tasks:

Table 13.11 Percentage of exporting firms by firm size group in manufacturing

Size groups	2000	2003	2004
5–9	2.1	3.23	3.82
10–49	9.76	11.76	12.31
50–99	27.62	29.67	32.39
100–199	30.52	40.52	44.36
200–499	42.81	49.6	58.6
500 and over	63.46	53.54	71.83

Source: Vietnam Enterprise Censuses 2000–05

Such firms are able to take on large orders, to manufacture a relatively diverse product range, and to easily meet demands on compliance with global standards, especially labour codes ... small private firms often supply smaller regional traders [and] ... are unable to access the higher quality and higher value chains.

Harvie (2008, p. 221) has suggested a number of additional factors constraining the access of SMEs to export markets. He argues that lack of understanding of foreign markets due to limited experience with trade has been a major barrier to entry. The specific informational gaps relate to "management accounting, technical requirements, marketing skills, import regulations, and consumer preferences".[11] Lack of foreign language skills has served as an additional barrier.

A related issue concerns technology. Insofar as the optimal technology mix differs by the size of firms, the lack of appropriate technology may be a serious handicap to SME growth (Lall 2003). SMEs may be unable to invest in the development or adaptation of optimal technology given credit market failures, discussed above. In addition, public support for research and development has not favoured SMEs in Vietnam. Accordingly, it has been remarked that there are no specific policies for SMEs related to technology, no SME-specific research institutions have been created, and existing scientific, technology, and training organizations are not strong enough to meet SME needs (Harvie 2008, p. 213). Further, 2005 survey data from 100 garment/textile and chemical enterprises reveal that most firms have no long-term investment plan for technological innovation, despite the fact that most accepted the need for technological innovation to improve competitiveness (Hakkala and Kokko 2007, p. 27).

VII Ownership type, manufacturing category, and exports: explaining the persistence of large firms

As discussed, a key characteristic of the size distribution of manufacturing enterprises is the heavy skew in favour of large firms, which remained constant from 2000 to 2005. The present section examines three potential explanations for this skew: SOE bias, economies of scale, and export orientation. It concludes that only the last explanation is persuasive.

SOEs have historically been favoured in terms of access to capital and land. But in fact recent years have seen quite a precipitous decline in the relative importance of large SOEs. The SOE share of total employment for the largest firms has fallen from around a half to a quarter from 2000 to 2005. Likewise, the number of large SOEs has stayed relatively constant, while that of FDI and domestic non-state enterprises[12] has increased by 168 per cent and 220 per cent, respectively. Virtually all of the doubling in the number of large manufacturing firms is attributable to growth in the non-state sector. In short, there has been quite a dramatic reconfiguration of the top end, with SOEs losing relative share to both FDI and domestic non-state firms (Table 13.12).

Table 13.12 Number of firms with 500+ employees by type of ownership

	2000	2001	2002	2003	2004	2005	Rate of growth
SOEs	342	413	402	422	433	356	4
FDIs	175	202	229	323	410	469	168
Others	137	167	243	329	371	439	220
Total	654	782	874	1074	1214	1264	93

Source: Vietnam Enterprise Censuses 2000–05.

A second potential explanation concerns the dominance within manufacturing of industries with high fixed costs where economies of scale in production may be particularly important. In Vietnam, this involves capital-intensive industries such as chemicals, rubber and plastic products, and transportation equipment. Manufacturing in large firms is dominated by leather and footwear, garments, and food/beverages/cigarettes. As evidenced by Table 13.13, over time, the biggest gains in relative shares of employment, and the highest growth rates of number of large firms, has occurred in garments and manufacturing of wood and wood products. Overall, economies of scale do not seem to be the main factor explaining the skew in favour of large firms.

While economies of scale in production may not explain the skew in favour of large firms, it is important to examine whether labour productivity differences, for any number of reasons, may be driving the size distribution. In particular, is value added per worker higher in the largest firms across the major sub-categories of manufacturing? To recall from Table 13.8, *overall* labour productivity levels appear higher in mid-sized firms with between 100 and 499 employees than in firms with over 500 workers.

Disaggregated data (Table 13.14) present a more mixed picture. Large firms have the highest levels of labour productivity in garments, which is consistent with the argument presented in the previous section about the product quality and diversity advantages of large exporting firms. Mid-sized firms

Table 13.13 Number of firms with 500+ employees by category of manufacturing

	2000	2001	2002	2003	2004	2005	Rate of growth
Food, beverages, cigarettes	135	158	173	193	208	217	61
Textiles	57	67	69	68	74	77	35
Garments	112	135	161	227	267	277	147
Leather and footwear	127	133	142	164	170	169	33
Manufacturing of wood and wood products	51	60	71	100	127	152	198
Other	194	253	285	349	406	404	108
Total	654	782	874	1074	1214	1264	93

Source: Vietnam Enterprise Censuses 2000–2005

Table 13.14 Calibrated value-added per worker by size group and category of manufacturing, 2005

	Food, beverages, cigarettes		Textiles		Garments		Leather and footwear		Manufacturing of wood and wood products		Other	
	Million dong/ worker	Index value (500+ = 100)	Million dong/ worker	Index value (500+ = 100)	Million dong/ worker	Index value (500+ = 100)	Million dong/ worker	Index value (500+ = 100)	Million dong/ worker	Index value (500+ = 100)	Million dong/ worker	Index value (500+ = 100)
5–9	42.91	33.45	158.04	249.94	11.69	35.76	n.a.	n.a.	16.91	38.22	26.41	23.13
10–49	72.71	65.16	222.14	351.32	17.25	52.77	53.35	180.24	34.29	77.51	64.79	56.74
50–99	75.88	68.00	65.13	103.00	13.82	42.28	26.32	88.92	33.99	76.83	137.13	120.09
100–199	96.2	86.21	37.35	59.07	18.99	55.34	53.89	182.06	33.21	75.07	178.57	156.38
200–499	120.16	107.68	62.45	98.77	30.8	94.22	36.79	124.29	66.57	150.47	119.81	104.92
500 and over	111.59	100.00	63.23	100.00	32.69	100.00	29.6	100.00	44.24	100.00	114.19	100.00

Source: Vietnam Enterprise Censuses, 2005.

(100–499 workers) have high productivity in leather and footwear, while firms with between 200–499 workers dominate in food, beverages, and cigarettes and manufacturing of wood and wood products. Smaller firms in textiles appear to have the highest productivity levels. These data show that the relationship between productivity and firm size across sub-categories of manufacturing is varied. The core conclusion still holds, however, that the predominance of large firms is not due, in general, to their superior labour productivity.

The third explanation for the persistent skew is that the same forces which limit the entry of SMEs into export markets favour large firms. Tables 13.15 and 13.16 present preliminary evidence in support of this position.[13] It is striking that all of the increase in the employment share of FDI and domestic non-state firms is due to the increasing employment share of exporting firms. These findings are paralleled by the growth rates in the number of exporting FDI and domestic, non-state firms. For the latter, the rate of growth of large exporting firms is almost double that of all domestic, non-state firms.

This last point is significant, given the widely held view that the large-scale domestic private sector has been slow to develop. For example the JDR (2006, p. i) maintains that "only a handful of domestic private firms have made it to the top". As shown below, the number of large, domestic, non-state firms almost tripled from 137 to 371, while the number of large, domestic, non-state exporting firms more than quadrupled from 65 to 276. Part of the explanation may lie with the acceleration of the equitization process, whereby private domestic interests have increased their stake in formerly state-owned corporations. This cannot be the entire story, however, given the very rapid increase in the number of private firms and the fact that the absolute number of SOEs has not declined. Further, it is unlikely that the increasing tendency for FDI firms to partner with domestic non-state ones could account for this trend, given that joint ventures fall under the FDI classification, not domestic non-state. Panel data could shed additional light on this question, though inconsistent firm-level identifiers have precluded exploiting the panel dimension of the census data at the present time.

While a number of reasons have been offered for the failure of SMEs to *directly* access export markets, the question remains as to why large exporting

Table 13.15 Employment shares for firms with 500+ employees by type of ownership and export status

	2000	2004	Share change
SOEs	52.0	35.8	−16.2
of which exporting firms	*34.4*	*20.7*	*−13.7*
FDIs	28.4	38.8	10.4
of which exporting firms	*25.8*	*36.2*	*10.4*
Domestic non-state	19.6	25.4	5.8
of which exporting firms	*11.5*	*20.6*	*9.1*

Source. Vietnam Enterprise Censuses.

Table 13.16 Number of firms with 500+ employees by type of ownership and export status

	2000	2004	Growth rate
SOEs	342	433	26.6
of which exporting firms	*197*	*224*	*13.7*
FDIs	175	410	134.3
of which exporting firms	*153*	*372*	*143.1*
Domestic non-state	137	371	170.8
of which exporting firms	*65*	*276*	*324.6*

Source: Vietnam Enterprise Censuses.

firms have not made greater use of subcontracting arrangements with smaller firms. As discussed elsewhere in this volume, the growth of SMEs in both Japan and Taiwan was facilitated by the expansion of just such subcontracting arrangements. One explanation concerns geography, namely the proximity of manufacturing enterprises in South East Asia and China, coupled with the significant distances between industrial hubs in the north and south of the country. Another reason, more generally, may relate to the increasing importance of transnational supply networks in global value chains. Whatever the reason, as the JDR (2006, p. 36) remarks, "unlike other East Asian countries at an early stage of their industrialization, it would appear that Vietnam has not integrated well its exporters with its local producers".

VIII Distribution of income

As discussed in the introduction, the size structure of manufacturing has potentially important implications for distributional patterns in the economy. Some of the transmission mechanisms linking the size structure and distributional outcomes include the nature of technology used in production, patterns of employment generation, productivity, and wages (Berry 2010, p. 289), and, on the consumption side, the price and quality of consumption goods produced. The salience of these types of issues will only increase as Vietnam's economy shifts from primary to secondary and tertiary production.

Table 13.17 presents a number of indicators of relative inequality, based on consumption expenditure data from the Vietnam Household Living Standard Surveys.[14] The Gini coefficient has increased moderately since the 1990s but stayed relatively constant through the 2000s. In terms of levels, the Gini value of 0.36 reflects a moderate degree of inequality, which places Vietnam near the middle of the pack of Asian countries (ADB 2007, p. 3). If one focuses on the top and bottom deciles of the distribution, the average consumption of the former has increased from around 7.5 to 9.5 times that of the latter between 1993 and 2006. The consumption share of the bottom decile has dropped somewhat over this period from 3.51 per cent to 2.90 per cent. In general, these findings are consistent with the depiction of Vietnam's economy as a hybrid model which has

Table 13.17 Levels and trends of consumption inequality

Gini	0.34	0.35	0.37	0.37	0.36
Decile dispersion ratio	7.66	8.58	9.42	9.91	9.57
Consumption expenditure (CE) share of poorest decile	3.51	3.33	3.17	2.91	2.90

Source: authors' calculations based on VHLSS 1993–2006.

not witnessed the dramatic spike in inequality as, say, China, but has seen a modest increase in relative inequality associated with the high investment shares of national income.[15]

In assessing the relationship between inequality and size structure, a first step involves an examination of levels and trends of wages and employment by size. Table 13.18 reviews the relationship between firm size and average wages. Two points are particularly striking. First, the dispersion of wages across the size categories has fallen considerably over time. Average wages in the smallest firms rose from around 55 per cent to 70 per cent of wages in the largest firms between 2000 and 2005. Second, the dispersion is quite low by comparative standards. Average wages in medium-sized firms are very close to those in the largest firm size categories. These data are not surprising in light of the finding that higher levels of labour productivity are found in medium than large-sized firms.

In terms of employment, a similar pattern emerges. Medium-sized firms are more capital-intensive than large-sized firms. Further, as discussed, the sluggish employment growth in manufacturing in the 1990s was reversed after 2000. Over the period 2000–05, manufacturing's share of GDP rose by 11 per cent, while its share of total employment increased by 41 per cent. Over the entire period, 1990–2005, the growth rates of manufacturing's share of GDP and employment were similar at 74 per cent and 68 per cent, respectively. In summary, the employment intensity of manufacturing growth has been quite impressive since 2000, which reflects, in part, the relatively high labour intensity of large-sized manufacturing firms. These data do not suggest that the size structure of manufacturing firms has had a perverse impact on inequality in Vietnam.

Another important finding is in the performance of the service sector with respect to GDP and employment growth. As shown above, employment share

Table 13.18 Average wages by size group in manufacturing (index value)

Size group	2000	2001	2002	2003	2004	2005	2006
5–9	54	60	60	67	68	70	68
10–49	64	70	70	73	74	73	73
50–99	87	91	86	87	87	86	84
100–199	93	97	95	92	94	93	94
200–499	100	105	101	99	97	96	94
500 and over	100	100	100	100	100	100	100

Source: Vietnam Enterprise Censuses

growth in the tertiary sector has been very high over the entire period of 1990–2005, despite falling GDP shares over this same period. In certain contexts, the rapid growth in employment in the tertiary sector has been a major contributor to inequality, in that wages tend to be more dispersed in this sector (see Chapter 6 on the Indian evidence).

To provide an indication of the sectoral contribution to inequality change in Vietnam, we present a decomposition of the Gini coefficient by source of income.[16] The Gini decomposition draws on the earlier work of Lerman and Yitzhaki (1985), who demonstrated that the Gini coefficient may be represented as:

$$G = \sum_{k=1}^{K} S_k G_k R_k$$

where S_k and G_k are income source k's share of income and its Gini coefficient, respectively. R_k is the Gini correlation between income source k and the entire distribution. Intuitively, the decomposition states that the contribution of any income source to total inequality is a function of its: (i) importance to total income, (ii) internal distribution of income, and (iii) relationship to the overall distribution.

A useful feature of the decomposition is that it can be used to estimate the marginal effects on the Gini coefficient of a 1 per cent change, e, in income source k, holding all else constant. It has been shown (Stark *et al.* 1986) that the partial derivative of the Gini, G, with respect to a percentage change in income, e, from source k equals:

$$\frac{\partial G}{\partial e} = S_k (G_k R_k - G)$$

By rearranging, and expressing in percentage terms, we have:

$$\frac{\partial G/\partial e}{G} = \frac{S_k G_k R_k}{G} - S_k$$

whereby a percentage change in the total Gini, G, due to a percentage change in income, e, from source k, equals the contribution of source k ($S_k G_k R_k$) to total inequality, that is, the Gini share, minus its share of total income (S_k). Alternatively, the relationship may be expressed as:

$$\frac{\partial G/\partial e}{G} = \frac{S_k G_k R_k}{G} - S_k = S_k (\eta_k - 1)$$

where

$$\eta_k = \frac{G_k R_k}{G}$$

which represents the Gini income elasticity (GIE), η_k, for source k. The key intuition is that the product G_k*R_k, or the pseudo-Gini coefficient, not the source Gini coefficient, provides the most critical information in the overall Gini coefficient decomposition. It is relevant to note also that, if the pseudo-Gini for source k exceeds the value of the overall Gini, such that η_k is greater than 1, then overall inequality will increase for any percentage increase in income source k.

Table 13.19 below presents results of the above exercise for three main categories of income: primary, manufacturing, and other. The latter two are distinguished by strata (rural, urban). The "Other" category includes tertiary income plus three income sources, which generally fall under secondary income: mining/oil/gas, utilities, and construction. Data are presented for two rounds of the VHLSS surveys, which allowed this categorization of income.[17]

There are two key results which bear on the discussion about the sectoral contribution to inequality. First, urban-based manufacturing has the highest pseudo-Gini, and GIE, of all income sources in both years. Its marginal contribution to overall inequality is small (2 per cent to 3 per cent), however, given its low share of total income (S_k). Second, the pseudo-Ginis of urban and rural manufacturing are higher than that of urban and rural services, respectively. Unlike certain contexts, such as India, the tertiary sector is not more unequal than manufacturing, as evidenced by their respective Ginis, nor more unequalizing, as evidenced by their respective pseudo-Ginis. It is a greater contributor to overall inequality, however, given its much larger share of total income. It is possible that the relatively more equal, and equalizing, character of the service sector in Vietnam is due to its composition. As was shown in Table 13.4, distributive, public, social, and community services are strongly represented, while producer services, which comprises financial intermediation, science and technology, real estate and renting, and business, make up a very small share of this sector.

IX Conclusion

Data from six rounds (2000–05) of the enterprise census in Vietnam reveal two striking features of the size distribution of enterprises with respect to employment. First, the distribution is heavily skewed in favour of firms with 500 or more employees. Such firms account for almost 60 per cent of total employment. By comparative standards, the skew is extremely large, in excess of that found elsewhere in Asia. Second, firms with fewer than 100 employees are the fastest growing category of enterprises, while those between 100 and 499 are the slowest. The latter happen to be the firms with the highest labour productivity. The preceding analysis has attempted to address two questions which these findings raise: What is the reason for the pronounced skew in favour of very large firms in terms of total employment? Why have mid-sized enterprises not grown at a faster pace, given that they appear to have the highest labour productivity?

The first set of explanations concern factor-price distortions, specifically capital market segmentation and differential access to land. Evidence suggests that SOEs, which tend to be larger, have enjoyed preferential access to finance

Table 13.19 Gini decomposition by sources of income

	2002							2006						
	Sk	Gk	Rk	Gk*Rk	GIE (η)	Gini share	%Δ	Sk	Gk	Rk	Gk*Rk	GIE (η)	Gini share	%Δ
Primary	0.32	0.61	0.37	0.23	0.56	0.18	−0.14	0.38	0.66	0.53	0.35	0.83	0.31	−0.17
Manufacturing (urban)	0.02	0.99	0.74	0.73	1.83	0.04	0.02	0.06	0.96	0.68	0.65	1.55	0.09	0.03
Manufacturing (rural)	0.04	0.96	0.49	0.47	1.18	0.04	0.01	0.06	0.91	0.44	0.40	0.95	0.06	−0.00
Other (urban)	0.31	0.87	0.77	0.67	1.67	0.51	0.20	0.26	0.87	0.71	0.62	1.47	0.37	0.11
Other (rural)	0.31	0.67	0.44	0.29	0.74	0.23	−0.08	0.24	0.71	0.44	0.31	0.74	0.17	−0.07
Total income	–	0.40	–	–	–	100	–	–	0.42	–	–	–	100	–

and that lack of credit remains a major impediment to the growth of privately owned, smaller enterprises. Limited access to land constrains SME growth directly, through its impact on the physical expansion of facilities, and indirectly, by limiting collateral for access to credit.

In addition to factor-price distortions, two other explanations have been offered for the slow growth of SMEs. In the 1990s, employment growth in SMEs was limited by the process of productivity catch-up, which involved the substitution of capital for labour in production. This limited the graduation of smaller firms into the mid-sized categories. Second, specific barriers to entry in global value chains have limited the present-day growth of small and medium-sized firms and constrained their insertion into higher value-added activities. The last set of issues is also the primary explanation for the continued predominance of very large firms in the size distribution of employment since 2000, a phenomenon which is not persuasively explained by SOE bias or by economies of scale in general.

The size structure of manufacturing has bearing on at least three policy relevant issues in Vietnam: employment, internal migration, and income distribution. In terms of the latter, Vietnam has witnessed a moderate increase in relative inequality since the onset of reforms and constant inequality between 2000 and 2005. It is unlikely that the size structure of manufacturing firms has been a major contributor to inequality in that wage dispersion between different firm size categories is very modest and employment growth has been rapid since 2000, which reflects the relatively high labour intensity of large-sized manufacturing firms. Further, the sectoral decomposition suggests that manufacturing, and in particular urban manufacturing, is more unequal and more unequalizing than services, though its marginal contribution to total inequality is small due to its small income share. Accordingly, the inability of the manufacturing sector to absorb additional supplies of labour, which are subsequently pushed into services, does not appear to have been as unequalizing as in, say, India. In summary, these data do not suggest that the rightward skew in the size structure of manufacturing firms has had adverse effects on inequality in Vietnam.

As discussed above, the issue of SME promotion has not been ignored by policy makers. The 2001–10 Socio-Economic Development Strategy emphasizes the importance of SMEs for employment generation and poverty reduction. Likewise, the SME Five Year Plan 2006–2010, approved in 2006, outlines a number of measures designed to facilitate SME development. The recognition of the imperative of SME growth is not surprising given the importance of manufacturing in Vietnam's economy, as well as the necessity of improving the employment intensity of industrial growth in the years ahead. It remains to be seen if policy measures such as those above will succeed in addressing some of the constraints to SME development outlined above.

14 Conclusions

This book offers an interpretation of the different trajectories of growth in Asian economies in recent decades based on their differing size structure of manufacturing. Three basic patterns can be discerned in the recent Asian economic development. First is the pattern of India with its bi-modal distribution and a conspicuous missing middle. Second, we have the classic East Asian model of a rather even size distribution in which SMEs participate in manufacturing growth as much as the larger enterprises. Last, we have the pattern followed by some of the more recent developing countries of Asia which depend very much on a size distribution skewed to large firms that spearhead the development of their manufacturing sector. China is of course the major example of this type of development. But since we do not have the expertise to do basic research on China from this point of view (and the secondary sources are somewhat deficient in the adequate treatment of this topic), we have relied in this book on an account of the early example of Thailand, and two contributions by experts on Bangladesh and Vietnam. A short reference to the Chinese case is made at the end of this chapter.

Chapter 1 offers a brief theoretical discussion of the consequences for growth and equity of the three major types of size distribution found in Asian development. It makes the point that the even size distribution found in East Asian growth is indeed the most likely pattern to produce the kind of growth with equity for which these economies have been applauded in the literature. The major reasons why the size distribution with the missing middle nor the one skewed to the large firms are not likely to produce this result are explored. Chapter 2 gives a comprehensive picture of the size distribution in manufacturing, and its evolution over time, for the different Asian economies (including China). It also contrasts the Asian experience with the more recent trends in developed countries.

I

Part II of the book is a detailed study of the Indian case of the missing middle. The manufacturing sector has been characterized by a pronounced dualism with strong modes at the low and high size groups, a conspicuous missing middle and an unusually large productivity gap between the two. It is argued that it is this problem in the manufacturing sector which has led to relatively low productivity in manufacturing. This in its turn has slowed down the growth rate of manufacturing, in both the domestic and export markets, and has produced the unusual pattern of growth led by the tertiary sector. The problem of inequality in the growth process is also partly due to relatively faster development of the tertiary sector, and to dualism in manufacturing itself.

The market for manufactured goods has in fact been segmented, with the low-end sector catering to the needs of poor consumers with low quality cheap goods, while the large-scale sector has produced high-end consumer goods for the upper middle classes as well as intermediate goods. The recent growth of the middle class, touted in the popular press, is, on examination, not found to be as important in relative terms as other strongly developing Asian economies like China (Chapter 6). The phenomenon of the missing middle is also responsible for slowing down the growth of skilled labour. In East Asian development, it is precisely the growth of SMEs that has ushered in the wide diffusion of technology and labour skills demanded by modern enterprise—often facilitating the process emanating from large firms through the elaborate system of subcontracting.

The bi-modal structure in manufacturing has also been a major factor driving the increase in inequality in the Indian growth process. First, the dualistic structure itself creates inequality in the distribution of earnings within manufacturing. Second, the growth process driven by the tertiary rather than the manufacturing sector (and which is partly a consequence of the peculiar size structure of the latter) compounds inequality. It has been shown that the earnings distribution is more unequal in the tertiary sector, since it contains a juxtaposition of high-income business and financial services and low-earning trade and services (Chapters 3 and 5).

Causes of dualism in manufacturing

The dualistic structure with its missing middle was a direct consequence of the small-scale industry policy of the post-independence years. Under the policy, a long list of industries was specified for production in small-scale units and license to produce was not available for firms larger than the specified size. This policy led directly to the regime of product market segmentation in which low-quality consumer goods were produced for the mass of domestic consumers, while capital-intensive and intermediate goods were produced by large units. But the structure has survived the dismantling of the protection system and has continued to prosper two decades after the reforms. The central root for this persistence is discussed in Chapter 7. In many discussions, the critical finger has been pointed to labour legislation which discourages the expansion of employment in enterprises above a certain size (see, for example, World Bank 2010). But to single out labour laws among a host of other legal restrictions is probably not realistic. In our field investigations, other regulations—for example, those relating to land and fiscal regulations—have been mentioned as more critical by many of the respondents. The lack of infrastructure, adequate supply of electricity, and the lack of decentralization have been important factors in perpetuating the phenomenon of the missing middle.

An important issue is the bundle of factors coming under the general description of "hysterisis", which is such an important phenomenon in the economy. It means that once a policy of such critical importance as the reservation policy has been in operation for a long period, it creates economic relationships and institutions which support the existing structure, even after the original cause which created the structure has disappeared. In the Indian manufacturing context, important groups of factors coming under this heading would be the structure of trade with its widespread dependence on small retail outlets, and the nature of entrepreneurship, which might be as segmented as the product market. The business acumen and culture of the entrepreneurial class which have dominated the small-scale enterprises might not be suited to the requirements of larger-scale modern industry.

II

Part III of the book turns to a discussion of the pattern of development in which size distribution in manufacturing has been more even—with small and medium enterprises contributing as much to the growth as the large ones. A second feature of this type of size structure is that the economic distance between the small and large units (in terms of labour productivity and wage difference) is much smaller than in the missing middle case discussed in Part II. The Japanese model of development in the first three decades of the twentieth century spearheaded this pattern of development. It was followed by Taiwan and Korea after the Second World War.

In all three cases, modern industrialization was started by large enterprises, with the new manufactured products going disproportionately into exports. But very soon the small and medium enterprises started playing a much more important role, in terms of both employment and value added and, although exports continued to be important in the demand expansion for manufacturers, a large share was accounted for by the increase in the size of the domestic market for such goods. In the Japanese case, it was possibly the impetus provided by the disruption of the world market during the First World War that led to a relatively greater importance of the domestic market. For Taiwan, the experiment with large-scale export-oriented firms was short-lived. We discussed, in Chapter 9, the special characteristics of the Taiwan entrepreneurs and the political economy of the country which encouraged this turn towards small and medium enterprises. Korea, as discussed in Chapter 10, was unique in having a deliberate and successful government policy, adopted in the mid-stream of its industrialization (around 1975), which shifted the size structure towards greater participation of SMEs.

Unlike in the Indian case, all three East Asian developments were led by the manufacturing sector, not the tertiary. Exports, although a significant part of the manufacturing growth, were not dominant. The domestic market for manufactured goods expanded at a significant rate partly because the pattern of development distributed the gains of growth over a wide section of the population. In fact, the equitable distribution and growth of manufactured consumer goods fed on each other. The East Asian scenario contrasts with that of India where, as we have seen, growth led by the tertiary rather than the manufacturing sector and increased inequality reinforced *each other.*

G.C. Allen (1940) drew attention to another feature of Japan's growth of manufactured goods—the cultural preference of the growing middle-class for consumer goods catering to local tastes, which were best produced by small-scale units. It is important to realize that there is segmentation in the product markets between the small and large firms in India as well, but the difference is that the small manufacturing enterprises in India specialize in low-quality goods and services which can cater to the demand of low-income consumers. Quantitatively, the importance of small-scale consumer products in the Indian economy demanded by the higher income groups would seem to be much less than in the Japanese economy during its period of industrialization before the Second World War.

An important feature of East Asian growth which supported both the markets for manufactured goods and equitable growth was the increase in labour productivity in agriculture. The East Asian economies were as agrarian as India at the beginning of their industrialization. Thus a substantial growth rate of labour productivity in this sector would pull up the growth rate of the whole economy. Labour productivity growth in agriculture is determined partly by growth in land productivity and partly by the reallocation of labour from agriculture as surplus labour is transferred to non-agricultural activities. The East Asian economies benefited from progress on both fronts over the course of their economic development. Land productivity in Taiwan and Korea in particular was enhanced by sweeping land reforms after the Second World War. This was aided by a higher rate of reallocation of labour to non-agriculture than India. At least part of this difference could be attributed to the pattern of growth in manufacturing, and more specifically to the difference in its size distribution. We recall from Chapter 5 that the rate of reallocation of labour from agriculture in India was at the rate of 0.7 per cent per annum in 1985–2004. This contrasts with Taiwan's 2.0 per cent in the 1960–75 period, and Korea's 1.5 per cent over the years 1965–88. Agricultural productivity per worker relative to GDP per worker can be expected to decline with industrialization, since labour productivity is so much higher in industry. But as can be expected from the record of reallocation of labour, the decline was much sharper in India than in either of the other two.

If the reallocation of surplus labour from agriculture was so much larger in the two East Asian economies during their post-war industrialization, why do we not see inequality growing more in these economies than in India? The Kuznets hypothesis had predicted that, with reallocation of labour to the high-productivity sector, we would expect inequality to increase. In fact, both Korea and Taiwan might have had some trend to increasing inequality in the early years of development, but this period was extremely short. Inequality declined sharply in the later decades of growth in both economies, while in India we have the picture of rising inequality as the growth rate has increased.

The outcome in the dynamic process of growth and equity depends on the relative strength of two broad groups of factors, as discussed in the opening chapter. While an increase in income differences "between sectors" can be expected to increase inequality, it could be offset by the opposite effect of decline in income differences "within sectors". The more even size distribution of enterprises in the manufacturing sector produced a significantly smaller degree of "within sector" inequality relative to the bi-modal size structure in Indian manufacturing. This applied both to wage and entrepreneurial earnings. Further, the more equal distribution of income in manufacturing could be expected to induce a less unequal distribution in the tertiary sector as well because the pattern of demand for low- and high-income services would be less bi-modal than in the Indian case. We have seen already that, although the income difference between agriculture and the other sectors increased over the period of growth both in Taiwan and Korea, the relative decline was at a significantly slower rate than in the case of India. Thus the diminishing "within sector" inequality within the individual sectors was strong enough to overwhelm any increase in "between sector" inequality in the East Asian economies.

There are some important factors which strengthened the development of the even size distribution in East Asian manufacturing and paved the way for its record of growth with equity.

1 Foremost among these is the development of subcontracting in a way which helped the smaller subcontractors to have a creative and competitive relationship with larger manufacturing firms and trading units. It was a relationship which allowed them to grow, not only in market shares but also with technological sophistication. It is this which enabled small enterprises to participate in exports, and combine the marketing advantages of large units with the flexibility and lower costs of small ones. The Japanese case was the first one to become important in the inter-war years, but we have seen in Chapters 9 and 10 that Taiwan and Korea (the latter after 1975) also developed this type of inter-firm relationship successfully.

2 Decentralized industrialization was a major factor in promoting growth of smaller firms. Of course the relatively small size of these countries helped in this process, but the growth of manufacturing in smaller towns and rural areas was significantly supported by government policies relating to infrastructure and the development of electricity. The development of high productivity non-farm activities helped the promotion of small units as well as the trend to equality in the farm sector. We have quoted statistical evidence in Chapter 9 to suggest that this seems to have been particularly important in the Taiwan case.

3 The rapid growth of education, particularly at the post-primary level, supported both SME development and growth with equity. Several avenues

through which educational development contributed might be noted. First, it reduced the rate of return to post-primary education, which is remarkable considering the high rate of growth of modern activities with their requirements for educated labour. Second, it was instrumental in enhancing the ability of new entrepreneurs to acquire industrial skills and set up small businesses. Third, the strong relationship between larger firms and SMEs, which was important in the widespread growth of the subcontracting system (including in particular the transfer of technological knowledge to small entrepreneurs), was facilitated by the spread of education. We have noted that, in the Indian case, one of the major factors which prevents small enterprises from graduating to larger units is that entrepreneurship is culturally non-homogeneous. The difference between India and the East Asian economies on this point might be due to many factors, including the historical development of these societies. But the weaker development of education must be one of the factors compounding historical and sociological factors.

III

Part IV of the book deals with the case of industrializing economies which have showed a bias in the size distribution of their manufacturing enterprises towards large enterprises. The classic case of industrialization with this type of bias was Thailand, which had a remarkable period of export-led manufacturing growth extending from the mid-1980s until 1996 when the growth process was suddenly interrupted by the financial crisis (which spread outside its borders affecting a few other Asian economies).

The case shows how a rapid growth in this type of an agrarian economy could increase inequality in income during the growth process, even though it had significant success in the reduction of poverty. The process through which this mechanism is examined with the Thai data supports the hypothesis set out in Chapter 1. It is shown that the factors causing inter-sector inequality (between agriculture on the one hand and industry and the leading tertiary sector on the other) are seen to be as important as the growth of "within sector" inequality. Several other factors in such an economy help to strengthen the forces producing the trend to increasing inequality. At the top of this list is the behaviour of the labour market. Labour absorption outside the agricultural sector was not fast enough to pull up the relatively low income per worker in the sector (which is partly the result of a significant incidence of under-employment or surplus labour). Second, the spatial centralization of growth of both the manufacturing and the tertiary sectors, and the absence of subcontracting relationships which were so important in East Asian economies, leads to a fragmented labour market. While wages tended to take off at the points of non-agricultural growth (Bangkok and the surrounding regions in Thailand), low-income labour remained in the less developed regions. Labour migration was dominated by temporary or seasonal migrants who fill the demand for unskilled labour in the growth poles.

This pattern itself is not conducive to widespread skill formation in the labour force and is accentuated by the under-development of the education system. We saw in Chapter 11 that the rate of return to education was extremely high and showed no sign of declining, in marked contrast to the economies of Taiwan or Korea. While the supply side of the skilled labour force is partly the result of government education policies, a significant part of the labour market developments could be traced to the large firm-oriented industrialization.

The Thai type of development is dependent on the growth of manufacturing exports. It has been shown in Chapter 11 that this model contains the seeds of the development of Dutch disease, which undermines international competitiveness and threatens to weaken the major factors which had supported the growth process. The growing inequality which had accompanied this type of growth causes the pattern of demand to shift disproportionately to the high-end service industries and the construction sector. This tends to cause the price of non-tradables to increase relative to the price of tradables—leading to a loss in competitiveness with an exchange rate tied to the dollar. The process is helped along with inflation in wage rates in the developing sectors.

In the Thai case, the role of the banking system was an added factor specific to the country's history. Foreign capital inflow was heavily biased to short-term funds increasing the banks' liquidity rather than the form of long-term direct investment. Thus with the change in expectations about the stability of the exchange rate, capital flight from Thailand was easy and immediate, ushering in the financial crisis of 1997.

Although the Thai economy recovered significantly in the first decade of the century from the aftermath of the crisis, the problems of the pattern of development was endemic. The unequal distribution of the fruits of growth has fuelled the political instability of recent months. The Thai case remains a warning for countries pursuing a type of rapid industrialization concentrated in large geographically centralized firms.

Limited industrialization: the case of Bangladesh

Chapter 12 is a contribution on Bangladesh, a case of development of manufacturing with its size structure skewed to large enterprises, but unlike Thailand the growth did not proceed on a wide spectrum of industries. It is the case of industrialization (which has been typical of several low-income countries round the world) in which a single industry, garments in this case, has spearheaded growth based on exports. Although the country started with a state-oriented, autarkic approach to development, it soon embraced the philosophy of export-led growth spearheaded by the private sector. While external trade as a percentage of GDP doubled over the three decades ending in 2008–09, the composition of exports also changed dramatically, woven garments and knitwear together accounting for 80 per cent of all exports, displacing jute and jute goods as the mainstay of exports in 1980–81. This upsurge of garments-led growth of exports was accompanied by a growth rate of GDP which accelerated to 5 per cent per annum in the

1990s and further to nearly 6 per cent in the first decade of this century. This healthy growth has enabled Bangladesh to be regarded as a rather successful case of development among the group of low-income countries—achieving a significant rate of poverty reduction.

A feature of the growth of the export-oriented manufacturing sector was its domination by large-scale enterprises. In Chapter 12, Ahmed, Bakht, and Yunus report statistics from the *Census of Manufacturing Industries* of Bangladesh showing that, while in 1995–96 there was hint of a U-shaped distribution of employment by size of firms in non-household manufacturing, the size structure was dominated by large 500+ enterprises, and later data for 2000–01 showed that the smaller firms were losing ground. While the growth in non-household manufacturing was clearly led by large firms with 500+ workers, other data showed that during the decade of the 1990s the share of this group in the garments industry (in terms of number of firms) increased at a rate of five or six times that of the total of all manufacturing firms.

It would, however, be wrong to conclude that the rather satisfactory growth of GDP in Bangladesh and the poverty reduction was primarily due to the export-oriented growth of garments produced in large factories. The manufacturing sector in 2008–09 constituted just 18 per cent of GDP (increasing from 1 per cent 30 years ago), and garments were somewhat more than a *third* of value added in this sector. Bangladesh was able to attain a very reasonable growth rate in its large agricultural sector. It was also helped by a strong growth of remittances from international migrants, who in fact partly fuelled the growth in construction and the services sector.

The model of export-led industrialization dependent on a single major industry, on the other hand, could be seen to have had some serious problems, which might indeed become more serious in the future.

First, the impact through linkages on other manufacturing sectors has been limited. Backward linkages to other ancillary industries were indeed encouraged by government policies. Thus subsidies were provided to garment firms which made use of domestically produced inputs like yarn. These measures, however, encouraged the establishment of large integrated factories and might have discouraged the development of small enterprises. The larger effect through the growth of higher income and consumer demand seems to have been limited. Some factories depending on the expansion of demand were indeed established in such industries as plastics, leather footwear, and food processing. In fact, the growth rate of number of firms in these industries in the small-medium range was well above those for garments. But the relative size of these developments was not great. Ahmed *et al.* report that in 2005–06 the largest industry after garments at the four-digit level (in terms of the share of value added) was bricks and tiles, followed by pharmaceuticals and cigarettes (each of which contributed no more than 3–7 per cent).

One reason for the limited development of the domestic market for manufactured goods, in spite of the rather significant protective barriers existing in the economy, is the pattern of development which this particular type of growth encouraged. The manufacturing growth in the formal sector was reasonably labour-intensive, and real wages in the sector also increased at 2.4 per cent per annum during 1991–2005. But total employment in the sector was too small, at no more than 10 per cent in 2004–05. Construction, which is classified under "industry" at the three-sector level in Bangladesh, added another 2.5 per cent. All industry, including construction and unorganized (or household) manufacturing, grew at the rate of 4.1 per cent over this period—only slightly above agriculture (3 per cent) and services (3.1 per cent). Thus the reallocation of surplus labour from agriculture was quite small.

Added to the problems of slow increase in consumer demand was the growing inequality in the distribution of income. Ahmed *et al.* do not deal with this topic in their contribution, but other studies show that the degree of income inequality is high by Asian standards and increasing. Khan (2009) reviewed the data from the successive Household Income and Expenditure Surveys (HIES).[1] He estimated that the Gini coefficient for household income per capita increased in the rural areas from a low of 0.196 in 1991–92 to 0.344 in 2005, and in the urban areas from 0.578 to 0.610.[2]

Looking at the trends in inequality for the various socio-economic groups, Khan reports that the latter could be divided into two types: farming and wages (both agricultural and non-agricultural) are the two major "equalizing" types; while salaries, non-farm entrepreneurial income and remittances received from abroad are the strongly "unequalizing" types. Over the period studied, the former types have dwindled in importance, while the latter have increased their share in Bangladesh GDP. Thus the two major features of the Bangladesh growth pattern—manufacture's bias to large-scale firms which increased the incidence of entrepreneurial income and salaries, and the inflow of remittance—have been instrumental in increasing inequality.

As with the Thai case of development, the pattern of development has led to a disproportionate growth of services and construction. As we have seen, inequality and the growth of these two sectors feed on each other in a vicious circle. Another point of similarity with the Thai case is the centralized nature of growth. The importance of the capital city and three other major towns relative to the rest of the economy has been conspicuous in terms of both employment and income generated.

The growth of the exports of manufactured garments was not financed primarily by foreign direct investment but by domestic sources of capital. Thus Bangladesh has avoided the risk of sudden capital outflow, which was critical in the interruption of the Thai growth process. But the concentration on a single area of exports has its risks and might be a source of trouble in the future.

The case of Vietnam

Vietnam presents a case of size distribution skewed to the large size group, but it does not show a pronounced trend to increasing inequality like China. Its level of consumption inequality, as measured by the Gini coefficient, increased slightly from 0.34 in 1993 to 0.37 in 2003 and stayed at more or less the same level at 0.36 in 2006. This level of inequality is in fact rather lower than in the other Asian economies where the size distribution in manufacturing has been markedly skewed to the right. For example, Thailand had a Gini which seems to have exceeded 0.50 in the 1990s, according to some measures of income inequality, and was 0.41 in terms of expenditure inequality. It was also well below the Chinese level, where in 2004 consumption inequality was estimated to be 0.47 (ADB 2007, Table 4.1). The degree of inequality was, however, significantly higher than in the countries of the East Asian model discussed in Part III, and Vietnam did not have the decline in inequality which Taiwan and post-1975 Korea did in their periods of rapid growth.

The limited problem of inequality experienced by Vietnam, in spite of the large-scale oriented industrialization, needs explanation. The first point in our analytical model of this type of growth was that, since the expansion of the domestic markets would be constrained by slow growth of the wage sector, the transfer of labour from agriculture might be slow and the tertiary sector with its more dualistic wage distribution would lead the increase in non-agriculture employment.

Chapter 13 does show that export expansion was a major factor in Vietnam's industrialization, and this certainly accounts for the skewed distribution of employment to the very large enterprises. But Schaffer and Dang Trung did not have the data to examine the proportion of manufacturing growth which could be accounted for by the expansion of domestic consumer demand. There are important indirect suggestions coming from the analysis presented. The authors point out that Vietnam represents a "hybrid model", "which incorporates the high investment and export growth of the Chinese model along with high levels of consumption and solid employment growth (since 2000) found elsewhere in Asia". The share of consumption in GDP was already high at 81 per cent in 1995, and fell rather gently to 75 per cent. It was much higher than China's and substantially higher than India's. The high consumption share obviously supported a significant expansion of demand for manufactured goods at the growth rate of GDP in excess of 7 per cent per annum. We thus see that, as with the East Asian countries, manufacturing was the lead sector in the growth process both in terms of value added and employment (Tables 13.4 and 13.5).

It appears that there are differences in key aspects of the growth trajectory even within the subset of Asian countries with a markedly skewed size distribution of manufacturing employment resulting from a vigorous export orientation. The special experience of Vietnam with its high share of consumption, and its contrast with China on this critical point, needs special research and is beyond the scope of this study. But certain important points can still be gleaned from the material presented in Chapter 13 and elsewhere.

It will be recalled that an important factor contributing to inequality in developing economies of Asia is the extent of the productivity differential between agriculture and non-agriculture. Vietnam has been distinguished by having one of the smallest productivity gaps between the two broad sectors. Table 5.1 (in

Chapter 5) based on ADB data shows that the relative productivity in agriculture increased over the period since 1980—and in 2007 was at 67, the highest in Asia (at the same level as Malaysia). This upward trend in relative agricultural productivity seems to be unusual in the Asian context. Even if the less dramatic figures of Schaffer and Dang Trung in Chapter 13 are to be considered to be nearer to the correct situation, the fact that agriculture was able to hold its relative productivity at a high enough level at 0.53 over the period 1990–2005 is remarkable in the comparative context. China was also able to hold the relative agricultural sector constant but at a lower level of 0.41 (see Chapter 5). The unusual performance in Vietnam's agriculture is particularly surprising because the large-enterprise-oriented development of manufacturing could ordinarily be expected to be a factor in a large productivity gap between the manufacturing and agricultural economies. In 2005, the productivity of manufacturing does not seem to have been unusually higher than that in the tertiary sector. It is only 15 per cent higher, although it does seem to have increased remarkably, from being a third lower in 1990.[3]

The relative productivity in agriculture could improve if there is a substantial transfer of surplus labour from the peasant sector. But this is probably not the case in Vietnam. The rate of reallocation of labour since 1990 has not been higher than in China, Indonesia, and even India (Table 5.1). We then have to look at the rate of increase in land productivity. Benjamin and Brandt (2003) produced data on growth rates for different components of income for households. For rural households, the growth rate of income per capita originating in the crop sector did in fact grow at a high rate of over 5 per cent per annum in the 1993–2006 period, which supported the overall growth rate of 8 per cent; much of this high growth seems to have been concentrated in the initial period of 1993–98. It is tempting to suggest that the severe disruption of the civil war had created disruptions which could be dealt with in the early growth period. Land was distributed much more unequally in the south, but Craig *et al.*'s data suggest that the growth of the crop sector was in fact substantially higher in the south (ibid., Table 12).

There are other important factors in Vietnam's limited trend to increasing inequality. A significant contrast with the experience of China (see below) could be the regional aspects of development. In a smaller country, we would expect that, in spite of the development of large-scale industry with the bias to large enterprises, there might be less concentration of industrial employment in particular regions or urban concentrations. Craig *et al.* have made an attempt to look at the contribution of regional variations to inequality (measured by the log variance of incomes) (op. cit., p. 34 and Table 16). Their conclusions from the results reported are as follows:

> First, location plays a relatively small role in overall inequality. North-South differences contribute no more than a few percent. Regional and provincial effects are more pronounced; provincial differences however still account for no more than 20 percent. Far more important are differences among

households, within provinces. Second, urban–rural differences which were around a factor of 2 in the early 1990s also explain a relatively small percentage of overall inequality. Combined, locale plus urban–rural explains about 15 percent more of the inequality than locale alone.

A second important factor in Vietnam's limited trend towards inequality is revealed in the analysis of the functional distribution of income. The results of the Shorrock decomposition of the contributions of the components of household income (by type of income) show that the most equalizing of the several income sources considered is crop income followed by wage income. Growth of these types of income in both rural and the urban areas, and in the south as well as the north, tends to reduce inequality. The income sources contributing most to inequality are family business income and remittances (ibid., Table 12). In the rural areas, the more rapid growth of wages and farming income helped to offset the influence of family business income on overall inequality. Wages performed a similar role in the urban areas, and played a prominent role in reducing inequality up until 2002. After 2002, the equalizing role of wages became less strong, while other sources of income exerted upward pressure on inequality. Growth no longer disproportionately benefited the lower income households, so that the level of inequality stabilized at the 2002 level.

This record of the equalizing role of wages in Vietnam is unusual in the process of growth. We have seen in the case of Thailand in Chapter 11 that the single most important source of inequality was wages and salaries and in fact the high return to more skilled and educated labour was indeed the major factor driving the relatively high level of inequality. The contrary experience of Vietnam is closer to the East Asian model analysed in Part III of this study. In the study of international comparison of rates of return to education by Psacharopoulos and Patrinos (2002), the rate of return to higher education was one of the lowest in the sample.

While the factors discussed in the last paragraphs have mitigated inequality in Vietnam and even reduced it somewhat in its early period of growth, the high inequality associated with the industrialization oriented to large firms remains prominent. It is not only that the level of inequality is higher and not on a declining trend as in the East Asian countries in their period of growth, but the potential for stronger trends to inequality remains significant. The analysis of Shaffer and Dang Trung of the contribution to inequality of the three major sectors of economic activity in Vietnam is relevant here. Their result is that the "pseudo-Gini" of manufacturing is the highest of the three sectors, in both the urban and the rural sectors, several times higher than in the primary sector, and marginally higher than in the tertiary (other) sector (Chapter 13, Table 13.19). This implies that, although the current contribution of manufacturing to overall inequality is small because the share of manufacturing in total employment is small, the overall inequality will increase as the share increases (if the parameters of the income distribution function remain the same).

The case of China

We have not included a separate chapter on the interesting and complicated case of China—with its strong manufacturing growth tilted towards large enterprises—because we felt we did not have the expertise and knowledge of the data sources to do justice to the topic. But discussion of size of firm and Asian industrialization would be seriously incomplete without some reference to this very important case. The following discussion is in the form of tentative notes gathered from the secondary sources in English. It is hoped that Chinese experts will fill up a significant gap in the literature with a thorough treatment of this topic in the near future.

We have reviewed the broad outlines of the size structure of manufacturing in China in Chapter 2. As with Vietnam, the importance of the state sector in the size structure skewed to the right is to be emphasized. But in the Chinese case, it is complicated by the importance of town and village enterprises (TVEs) and of foreign-invested enterprises (FIEs). Overall, the dominant feature is the prevalence of large firms, though mid-sized firms are also of some importance because of the recent developments of private enterprises, both in and out of the coverage of TVEs.

Along with the exceptionally high growth rate of the Chinese economy, there is indisputable evidence that inequality in the rural and the urban areas has increased over the years. This trend to inequality has been accompanied by a strong reduction of poverty, partly because the growth rate in the rural and agriculture sector has been strong as well as in the urban sector. Benjamin *et al.* give the results from the household sample survey data for the years 1987–2001; they conclude that the "increase in inequality has been quite steady over this period with no evidence of a slowing trend" (Benjamin *et al.* 2008, p. 742, and Figure 18.2). The authors comment; "Most of our estimates also suggest that the official estimates of inequality are probably too low, with the true Gini probably in the 0.40–0.50 range for both rural and urban areas" (ibid., p. 729). A more recent estimate by the Chinese Academy of Social Sciences from the 1 per cent Population Sampling Survey of 2005 produced numbers for the working population above 16 years of age. This restricted sample was necessary in order to identify the migrants into the urban areas as a separate entity.[4] The results showed that the Gini for urban workers was 0.424, for the rural 0.426, and for migrants 0.310. If the migrants are included along with the other two groups, the inequality increases to 0.47 (OECD 2010, Chapter 3, p. 120).

The increase in inequality has gone hand in hand with a substantial relative increase in employment and output in the secondary (industry) sector. It is tempting to conclude that the size structure in manufacturing favouring large firms has been a major factor in this increase in inequality. While a detailed analysis of this relationship is not possible here, it is probably appropriate to point to some of the major areas through which such a relationship could have worked itself out.

The first question is the extent to which the reallocation of labour from agriculture to the developing sectors increased the "between sector" inequality. Chinese growth in the non-agricultural sector had a decisive change in the second period of reforms. In the 1980s, the tertiary sector increased its share of GDP more than manufacturing. But after 1990 the secondary sector increased its share significantly more than the tertiary, even as the decline in the primary sector share accelerated. An important point to emphasize is that this increasing share of the secondary sector in GDP was achieved with hardly any change in its employment share. Thus labour productivity in the secondary sector had a substantial jump in the 1990–2005 period relative to agriculture and the tertiary sectors (Naughton 2007, Figures 6.3 and 6.4, pp. 151–154). Table 14.1, based on the data derived from the Naughton graphs, shows the relative labour productivity (relative to overall GDP per worker).

The data show the rising productivity gap of manufacturing which dominates the secondary sector, in comparison not only with agriculture but also with the tertiary sector. This rising productivity differential is clearly related to the pattern of development and in particular the growth of large capital-intensive firms. This might appear to some as perplexing, as Chinese manufacturing growth is based rather extensively on the exports of what are regarded as labour-intensive products. But the difference with the experience of East Asian economies is that the very limited participation of small firms in the industrial (and export) development meant that the techniques of production, even in "light" industries, required technologies which needed a substantial use of capital per worker and high labour productivity. The downsizing of the SOEs clearly meant that capital was used much more efficiently in the newer firms which led the growth process, but we can see from the data given in Chapter 2 that, although the capital–labour ratio in the newer, foreign-invested (OECD) and joint public–private firms (SHRs) was 50 per cent lower than in SOEs, it was four times the mean value in the smaller private firms. Statistical work done by Bosworth and Collins (2007) produced figures which show that, as the rate of growth of output per worker in the 1993–2004 period doubled from that of their previous 1978–93 period, the contribution of physical capital also doubled along with that of factor productivity (reproduced in Bardhan 2010, Table 1, p. 23, which also gives comparable data for India).

Let us now turn to "within sector", inequality which in Asia is generally higher than "between sector" inequality. As far as productivity differential by firm size is concerned, the figures given in Table 2.1 suggest the extent of

Table 14.1 Relative labour productivity (relative to overall GDP per worker)

	1978	*1990*	*2005*
Primary	0.58	0.48	0.27
Secondary	1.53	1.79	2.24
Tertiary	2.64	1.85	1.33

disparity in labour productivity and wages per worker in manufacturing between small and large firms in China is much less than in other Asian economies, including East Asian ones. On the other hand, there are two routes along which the "within sector" inequality in non-agriculture could have a substantial impact.

The first is the share of wages in value added. We refer here to the point made in Chapter 12 that China had an exceptionally low share of consumption in GDP compared to India and even Vietnam. It stands to reason that this would be reflected in the exceptionally low share of wages in the non-agricultural sector, which accounts for the bulk of wage employment. Aziz and Cui (2007) have estimated that the wage share declined more or less continuously as a percentage of GNP from 67 per cent in 1980 to 56 per cent in 2005 (p. 6). In fact, the authors suggest that, since the Chinese statistical system includes self-employed income in their wage share estimates and the former contains a component of capital income, the decline has actually been underestimated. Wage earners have grown at the expense of the self-employed, and *ceteris paribus* this would have caused the wage share to increase in the Chinese data. Aziz and Cui argue that the decline in wage share played a more important role in the decline in the share of consumption than an increase in household savings. We can extend this finding to the concerns of our present enquiry to suggest that the size distribution of firms in manufacturing skewed to the larger sizes and ownership groups with a high capital–labour ratio has been a major cause of the declining and low share of wages.

While the share of wages in manufacturing firms is low and possibly declining in China, a second significant factor contributing to inequality is the high degree of inequality within the group of wage and salary earners. Benjamin *et al.* (2008) report on results of decomposing inequality by the components of household income—consisting of wage income, family business income, pensions, transfers, and other sources. Their work on household survey data from two different sources show that: (i) wage income, both in the urban and the rural sectors, has the largest contribution to income inequality among households; (ii) this contribution has been increasing over time (Brandt and Rawski, Chapter 18, Table 18.8, p. 763). The most obvious component of this inequality is the high return to formal education. Cai *et al.* (2008) have calculated the rate of return to years of schooling using urban household survey data. Their results show that the rate of return to education (from a Mincerian equation) increased from 4.0 per cent in 1988 to 10.1 per cent in 2001—a massive increase, much of it happening in the 1990s. There is clear evidence of increasing returns to education, with the rate of return for successive grades increasing from 13.8 per cent in junior high, to 21.4 per cent in high school, and an astonishing 37.3 per cent for college and above. This experience of high and rising return to education is like the experience of Thailand and India reviewed in earlier chapters in the book, but very different from the experience of the development of other countries in the East Asian group. The different size structure of manufacturing in the former as contrasted with the experience of the East Asian countries (and even Vietnam) must surely be one of the significant factors in the difference—particularly in the demand-side factors affecting the labour markets. The percentage of college employees in Chinese manufacturing firms in 2004 increased from 2.6 per cent for the size group of less than nine workers, to 3.8 per cent for the 9–19 workers group, to 20.9 per cent for the 500–2000 size group and 29.6 per cent for firms with more than 2000 workers (ADB 2010b, Table 1 of the China Report).

Finally a reference must be made to the role of the tertiary sector in the process of growth and inequality. We have seen in the earlier chapters of this book that the large tertiary sector in both Thailand and India contributed in a major way to the increase in inequality. We have also suggested that a major reason for this role played by the tertiary sector is the dualistic nature of this sector including both low- and high-income activities, which in its turn can be traced to the pattern of development of manufacturing. It is likely that the tertiary sector in China has played a lesser role, at least not to the same quantitative extent. Emerging from the planned socialist state, China had very limited development of tertiary activities. At the start of the reform process in 1980, the tertiary sector had about 12 per cent of total employment. This share increased gradually and, around 1993–94, it started to exceed the share of employment in manufacturing. In 2004, its share had climbed to 30 per cent and was now significantly more than manufacturing. But as a proportion of GDP it was still close to 10 per cent below manufacturing (Naughton 2007). The growth of the tertiary sector has been propelled partly by the rapid increase in business and financial services which accompanied China's export and large-scale oriented industrialization.

While this development, and the demand it makes on the use of educated labour, must have contributed to the rising inequality, an offsetting factor has been the lower incidence of dualism in the Chinese economy. The lower pace of development of the informal sector, which in India and Thailand is a significant part of tertiary employment, has probably been a factor working against further inequality. Clearly, the downsizing of the state enterprises in the second half of the 1990s, and the lay-offs it brought in its wake, has increased the size of the tertiary sector, as displaced employees as well as rural migrants have sought to make a living in the urban informal sector. But it is likely that, in spite of this more recent growth, the importance of this sector is less than in countries like India and Thailand, which have large informal sectors of long standing.

China has not suffered from the problem of risky industrialization, like that of Thailand, based on manufacturing development led by large enterprises oriented to the export market because inflow of foreign capital is more firmly based on long-term FDI rather than short-term financial flows. But experts are already beginning to articulate their worries about the limited development of the domestic markets, partly caused by a very low share of consumption in the macroeconomic balance of the economy, which limits the growth of domestic markets for manufactured goods. More research also needs to be done on the apparent lack of participation of small enterprises in manufacturing, which has been such an important element in growth with equity in the East Asian model.

Notes

1 Introduction

1 There are some minor variations among countries. The Indian statistical system defined the directory manufacturing establishments (DME) sector as starting with six workers. Details are given in Chapter 4.
2 There is a large body of literature on the sources of the persistence of this wage ladder: it is partly due to the non-homogeneous quality of labour and partly due to institutional factors. See, for example, Mazumdar (1983).
3 We will see in Chapter 4 that, in the Indian case, the rate of growth of value added has been quite high in large-scale manufacturing in recent decades, but the contribution of this subsector to the increase in manufacturing employment has been small. This is partly because employment elasticity has been low, and partly because the total share of this sector in all manufacturing employment started from a low base.

2 An international comparison of the size structure of manufacturing firms

1 We are very thankful to Rana Hasan of the Asian Development Bank, who organized the data collection and made it available to us.
2 Mazumdar and Sarkar (2008, p. 205). See also the reference cited there.
3 There has, however, been an increase in the relative labour productivity of the largest size group (500+) such that the productivity indices (with the 500+ group as base) of all other size groups are lower.
4 The Swedish case is discussed by Carlsson (2006, section 4).

3 Salient features of the growth pattern in India

1 Not all of the NSS and NAS difference in consumption estimates is due to the estimation problems. There is a more substantive reason for part of the difference because of changes in macro-economic aggregates over time. The contribution of consumption expenditure (both private and government) in GDP at market prices fell substantially from 79 percentage points to 70 during the decade from 1993–94 to 2004–05, but thereafter it has been able to hold its share in GDP (until 2008–09).
2 It is usual to date the period of reform from the devaluation of the rupee in 1991, but Rodrick and Subramanian (2004) have pointed out convincingly that the acceleration in growth in the Indian economy can be traced to the early 1980s and coincided with the pro-growth and pro-business policies gradually adopted by the second era of the Indira Gandhi government, and pursued more deliberately by Rajiv Gandhi after the assassination of his mother.

3 Sarkar and Mehta (2010) presented the data of real wages separately for the rural and urban areas by deflating the reported money wages by the index of the cost-of-living for agricultural workers (CPIAL) for rural areas, and the consumer price index for industrial workers (CPIIW) for the urban areas. Their results show that the real wage of casual labour increased at the rate of nearly 3 per cent per annum in both areas, up from 2 per cent in 1983–93, but still considerably below the growth rate of GDP per workers. The wage increase is nearer the rate of consumption per capita.

4 Based on the observed consumer behaviour in 1973–74, it was estimated that, on average, consumption expenditure of Rs.49.09 per capita per month was associated with a calorie intake of 2400 per capita per day in rural areas and Rs.56.64 per capita per month with a calorie intake of 2100 per capita per day in urban areas. Thus, the concept of poverty line was partly normative and partly behavioural. Such measures focus on the purchasing power needed to meet the specific calorie intake standard with some amount for non-food consumption need as chosen by consumers in the year 1973–74.

The poverty line has been updated over the years to allow only for changes in the prices with reference to the consumption basket associated with the poverty line in the base year (1973–74). This procedure of updating the poverty line did not allow for adjustments in the consumption basket over time to meet the calorie norm. The calorie norm was not considered important; rather emphasis was given on comparability across time (Hashim and Sarkar 2011).

5 There is a large body of literature on this topic. One useful reference is Kuznets (1966, Chapter 3).

4 The non-household sector in Indian manufacturing

1 This can be seen from the data collected during the field study of the unorganized sector units in footwear production in Calcutta. Tiny units employing up to six workers constituted half of the units in the peak season and four-fifths of the units during the slack period. The unorganized manufacturing survey of NSSO asked questions on the economic activity of enterprises in the last month before the survey and the projection is made for the whole year on the basis of the activity for this one month and the number of months for which the particular enterprise operates. Our own survey suggests that units which operated year-round constituted less than half of the total units, even among the larger ones (employing more than six workers) (Sarkar 2011, Table 9).

2 The data from the NSS on the informal sector establishment survey and the ASI on the formal sector factories have been recently analysed to shed light on the nature of production functions in the two types of firms (Kathuria *et al.* 2011). The measurement of capital is a problem in these surveys.

3 The data presented in the table, of course, lump together all non-ASI categories to include three subgroups of the unorganized sector (Table 4.1 above). Separate figures on the DME sector are not available.

4 The Third Census of the Small Medium Enterprises in Manufacturing of 2003–04 reported that the number of workers in the unregistered sector of manufacturing (in units using electricity) was 19 lakhs in the 1–9 size group, but another eight lakhs were in the 10+ units.

5 However, a detailed study of wages has shown that there is a hierarchy of wage levels even within the organized sector establishments. (i.e. study from the World Bank in 1978–87: Little *et al.* 1987). Significantly lower wage differences are found not only for uncovered workers but also for workers employed in smaller factories within the covered sector. These wage differences most likely reflect differences in labour productivity, and are of critical importance to the analysis of Indian labour markets.

5 The impact of the missing middle on the growth rate

1 The ADB report discusses one of the main factors, the level of development of rural industrialization. Town and village enterprises (TVEs) in China have played a very important role in its economy, particularly in making it the manufacturing hub of the world. TVEs are involved in processing and marketing of agricultural products, their contribution to national industrial output in 2008 was 45.5 per cent, and their share in foreign exchange earnings was 40 per cent in 2007.

TVE development helped the growth of the rural middle class in multiple ways. First, the value added share of rural TVEs in the rural economy is 71 per cent and they employ only 29 per cent of the rural labour force. This reflects much higher labour productivity in TVEs compared to even the highly productive Chinese agriculture. TVE development has enabled the creation of a large rural middle class. Second, the TVE sector is also a major source of local government revenue that funds local infrastructure and social development, which are crucial to the expansion of the middle class. Last, the growth of TVEs has invigorated the growth of service industries in nearby rural towns and small cities and led to further growth of the middle class in small towns as well.

2 Government of India, *Economic Survey 2011*, Chapter 6, Table 6.1.

6 The missing middle in manufacturing

1 The evidence on the contribution of the tertiary sector to the growing inequality in recent Indian development has been documented in the last chapter.

2 See the Appendix to this chapter for detail of the calculation of the pseudo-Gini by sectors of activity.

3 Topalova includes the 1987–88 round of the NSS in addition to the three rounds used by us in the chapter.

4 See Appendix 1 for a summary of the method used. First, an earning function is estimated for hourly earnings. Second, the coefficients of the significant explanatory variables, together with the other relevant statistics of covariance and correlation coefficients, are used to calculate the factor inequality weights (i.e. the share of the inequality measure accounted for by each of the different explanatory variables).

5 The results are given in Mazumdar (2010, Table 4.5).

6 ADB (2010b) applies the Fields (2003) equation to calculate the shares of the different explanatory variables (the factor inequality weights) to the change in the inequality measure over the period 1993–2004. While the increase in the Gini coefficient was quite small over this period, increasing from 0.2851 to 0.2950, the ADB calculated that the share of the level of education accounted for fully 47 per cent of the increase. Occupation, used as a three-group variable (skilled, semi-skilled, and unskilled) was also important at 22 per cent, but production sector accounted for a paltry 2 per cent. In this exercise, the individual state dummies also played an important role, accounting for 37 per cent of the increase.

7 Causes of dualism in Indian manufacturing

1 Some of these points have been made by Dsouza (2009) and Bhattacharjea (2006).

2 Deepita Chakravarty (2010) describes the evolution of the policies of CITU—the trade union affiliated with the ruling party, which had as its members both the formal and the informal sector workers. In the 1960s and the 1970s, its policy was that of militancy directed at the large factories, which resulted in a serious decline of the formal sector. In subsequent decades, it continued to press for high wages and job security for workers in this subsector, but also was open to the use of contract labour and subcontracting. The net result was that the high-wage permanent core of workers in the

large-scale units was much reduced, but it was matched by a significant increase in employment of the informal type, both contract labour working alongside the permanent core in large enterprises and workers in subcontracted small enterprises. Both types of workers were members of CITU. The union policies were to serve the interests of both. The patron–client relationship developed by the union with the informal workers meant that their employment was controlled by the union, which also provided their votes to the ruling party at election time.

3 The customary measure of labour flows is built upon the basis of plant-level longitudinal data. The data from the ASI are, however, not available for individual plants. The OECD study thus had to be satisfied with industry-level longitudinal data for the period 2000–04 (both three-digit and five-digit industries were considered).

4 Since Tirupur never went in for large-batch export production, the scope for economies of scale on the Chinese model has not been a major concern. Chari (2004) found that "neither vertical nor horizontal integration correlates with business volume. ... What is clear is that contracting reduces entry costs for all firms, large and small, while providing a means for providing the labor problems of large factory establishments" (p. 78).

8 The role of small-medium enterprises in manufacturing and economic development: the case of Japan

1 Fortunately the English-language literature on Japanese growth in the period we are considering, and on the size distribution of manufacturing, is quite extensive.

2 See Chapter 2 above.

3 Cf Broadbridge (1966, Tables 13 and 14, p. 5). The productivity in Japan (1960) in the 10–19 size class was 29 per cent of the 1000+ plants, while it was 70 per cent in the USA (1958) and 90 per cent in Britain (1949).

4 Comparative data for India and Japan for the year 1987 are to be found in Mazumdar and Sarkar (2008, Chapter 9).

5 The literature on this topic in English is small. Thus our account in this section depends heavily on Minami (1976).

6 We cannot maintain this conclusively and certainly cannot imply that the degree of inequality fell proportionately to the same extent as the share of wages, since it is always difficult to estimate the contribution of labour share in self-employed enterprises from available wage-productivity data.

9 The role of small-medium enterprises in manufacturing and economic development: the case of Taiwan

1 Tien-Chen Chou (1995), especially Chapter 4.

2 It is not easy to quantify the rise in the female participation rates. The data from the household registers show the rate increasing from 23 per cent in 1966 (after falling from around 28 per cent in the early 1950s) to 40.7 per cent in 1975. The labour force surveys report a much more modest increase from 34 per cent in 1966 to 38.6 per cent in 1975. See Galenson (1979, Table 6.1, p. 385 and the footnotes to the table).

3 Levy pointed out that the Taiwan–Korean difference, with the former having a more even size distribution emerged only in the second phase of development distinguished in Section II, when Taiwan developed from an IS policy to export-oriented development. In 1966 (when indeed Korea was just starting its industrial development but Taiwan was already on the way), the share of employment in 500+ firms in Korea was at a substantially lower level than Taiwan's (25 against 36 per cent) but only ten years later the pattern had more than reversed itself.

4 See Fei *et al.* (1978), p. 23, equations 2.8 through 2.9. This is an earlier version of the type of analysis using the technique of "pseudo-Gini" used in Chapter 3 (India), Chapter 11 (Thailand) and Chapter 13 (Vietnam).

5 Ibid., footnote 16. Real wage rates in agriculture did not begin to rise until 1966 or 1967, although agricultural output increased at a rate of over 4 per cent per annum. There is no evidence of widespread mechanization in the period of growth 1952–66. At the same time, practically all the increase in the labour force was being absorbed in non-agriculture. Hence the labour resources needed to support agriculture growth came from increased flow of labour days from a more or less constant stock. Thorbecke (1979) has presented data to show that the man-days per agricultural worker was 111 days just after the Second World War but increased consistently in the post-war growth period to reach 200. Because of the general prevalence of under-employment in the first two decades after the war, such an increase in man-days per worker could take place without any pressure on the daily wage, until the turning point was reached at the end of the 1960s.

6 See Thorbecke and Wan (1993), especially Table 12.1.

7 In particular, the net entrants to the labour force, mostly women, belonged to the upper part of the household income distribution.

10 The case of Korea

1 President Park was assassinated in October 1979.

2 Bai (1982) estimated that the marginal productivity of labour in the agricultural sector was below the real wage until 1969 but that it rose above this level thereafter. Richardson and Kim (1986) pointed out that the relationship between changes in wages and changes in employment in manufacturing strengthened in the late 1960s. They estimated that, in the 1966–1975 period, a 1 per cent increase in employment in manufacturing led to a 0.67 per cent rise in real wages (ibid., p. 20).

3 See on this point the discussion, for example, in Jong-il You's Chapter 5 in Rodgers (1994).

4 The problem of wage pressure and inflation became severe again in the last years of the 1980s following the "democratic" liberalization measures and assertion of labour rights following the changes in industrial relations law in 1987. But this new period is outside the scope of this chapter.

5 Export sales ratio is the ratio of export sales (including indirect sales) to total sales.

6 Abe and Kawakami's data show that in 1982–83 the sales ratio for Taiwan SMEs was around 73 per cent compared to 25 per cent for Korea. (op. cit., Table VIB, p. 396). But see the data problems for Taiwan mentioned by the authors in the footnote.

7 The apparent anomaly in the sharp increase in the *decile ratio* for the employees between 1976 and 1982 is easily explained when we remember that this period saw the beginning of the restructuring of the Korean industry towards more skill-intensive sectors with their higher demand for highly educated labour. The increased employment of highly educated labour could increase the decile ratio even when the distribution of earnings within the group of less educated workers could drive the overall *Gini* to lower levels.

8 For the period 1967–1980, the ratio of earnings of workers in 500+ enterprises to those in 10–20 enterprises fell from 1.71 to 1.16 for university graduates and from 2.02 to 1.33 for elementary or middle school graduates (Mazumdar 1990).

11 The case of Thailand

1 A large proportion of the manufactured goods produced in these economies are exported, so the index of manufactured goods prices would indeed be the index of traded goods. Non-traded services, transport, and housing costs (as determined by the cost of land and building) have a dominant place in the consumer budget. The only major item of consumption which is generally a traded good is rice, an important staple item in the Asian diet. But most Asian economies maintain an administered price of

rice. It is insulated from the world trading price of rice through the operation of a public marketing agency which is funded to accumulate and sell from its own buffer stock. Thus P_c would be a good proxy for a price index of non-traded goods.

2 A. Suehuro and O. Yasuda, *Industrialization of Asia Series no. 3*, Institute of Developing Economies, Tokyo, 1987 (in Japanese). Quoted in World Bank (1989, p. 82).

3 There are many categories under the socio-economic category: farm operators with or without land, fishing and forestry, entrepreneurs in trade and industry, professionals, labourers, and other workers. Each of these broad groups has a varying number of subgroups. The education category has ten subgroups. By contrast, gender and urban/rural have just two subgroups each. Clearly the groupings have some influence on the proportion of inequality change attributed to "between-group" and "within-group" factors.

4 Sussangkarn (1987) and Mazumdar (1997). Mazumdar estimated that, in the urban labour market, the mean earnings in the formal sector were 81 per cent higher than in the informal sector in 1988, decreasing to 65 per cent higher in 1996. At the same time, the proportion of workers in the formal sector remained more or less unchanged at 61 per cent of the total. The formal sector in this analysis was defined as the sum of public sector employees, all employers in the sector, employees in private enterprises with more than six workers, and those self-employed who had more than 14 years of education (to include the professional own-account workers).

5 The details of the formula for the calculation of changes in Gini and the results can be obtained from the author upon request.

6 The dependent variable of the earnings function was the log of labour earnings. The explanatory variables were: education (measured by years of schooling); potential experience and its squared value (in years); and sets of dummies for gender, occupation, industry, region, and size of enterprise. The adjusted R^2 was 0.49 in 1988, increasing to 0.59 in 2002 for the public sector, and 0.56 and 0.57 respectively for the private sector.

7 In Sussangkarn's study, secondary school leavers earned about 50 per cent more than those with primary schooling, while those with university education reached a peak of three times the level of the latter in 1980, with the differential falling gently to 2.75 in 1984.

8 Real wages declined by 0.7 per cent in 1997 and 2.9 per cent in 1998 in the aftermath of the Asian crisis.

9 See Warr (1999, pp. 635–636) and also Warr and Nidhiprabha (1996), reporting the details that went into the construction of the earlier version of this index.

13 The case of Vietnam

1 We are grateful to Dipak Mazumdar and Albert Berry for extremely helpful comments on earlier drafts. Remaining errors are our own.

2 The only published work uncovered, which analyses the overall size distribution, is JDR (2006, pp. 15–17).

3 The categories used in the sectoral breakdown are a modified version of Singelmann (1978).

4 See, for example, Vijverberg and Haughton (2004).

5 Results of the second and third surveys were published in Ronnås and Ramamurthy (2001) and Kokko and Sjöholm (2006), respectively.

6 The capital–labour ratio is also highest for mid-sized firms in the 100–199 size groups. The index of K/l is 83 for the smallest two size groups and increases to 132 for the 100–199 slab, before declining for the next two groups (index for 500+ is 100) (own calculations from the Enterprise Survey data).

7 It should be noted that official usage of the term "small-scale" referred to the non-state sector

8 The one major exception concerns significant urban wage premiums, which may reflect urban residency registration for formal sector jobs (JDR 2006, 89).

9 See, for example, Tenev *et al.* (2003, pp. 62, 75) and Nguyen and Ramachandran (2006, pp. 205–207).

10 These findings are complementary to those in the broader literature, which has found significant barriers to entry in the export market due to fixed costs in Latin America (Roberts and Tybout, 1997) and sub-Saharan Africa (van Biesebroeck, 2005).

11 Similarly, Levy (1991) argued that the presence of small-scale export traders in Taiwan, and their relative absence in Korea, is one important variable explaining the much heavier reliance on SMEs in the export sector in the former. Such traders allowed Taiwanese SMEs to overcome economies of scale in marketing associated with high fixed costs of search and negotiation.

12 Domestic non-state firms include those with public shares up to 49 per cent.

13 It should be noted that only the 2000, 2003, and 2004 rounds of the census contain identifiers of export status.

14 The one major caveat about the VHLSS data concerns the under-reporting of internal migrants. Comparison of data from the VHLSS 2004 and the population census of Ho Chi Minh City suggest that the former captured less than 4 per cent of the 20 per cent of residents with temporary registration status found in the latter (JDR 2008, p. 24). If temporary migrants are disproportionately in the lower consumption brackets, the data will understate levels and changes in inequality (and, likely, poverty).

15 If the focus is on absolute inequality, a different picture emerges. The absolute gap between the consumption expenditure of the top and bottom quintiles more than doubled in real terms between 1993 and 2004, from around 2000 VND to over 5000 VND. The size of the gap places Vietnam at the mid to high end of the Asian average when measured in US$ PPP (ADB, 2007, p. 7).

16 The stata code used, and exposition of parts of the technique, draws on Lopez-Feldman (2006).

17 The VLSS questionnaires in the 1990s did not include a question which would allow one to apportion income from non-farm, non-silviculture, and non-aquaculture businesses into secondary and tertiary income categories.

Conclusions

1 Khan reports that there was an underestimate of incomes in 2005 in those components of income which are particularly unequalizing and hence the Gini indices for this year are probably underestimated.

2 The Gini measure was of course lower for household consumption (Khan 2009, Table 7).

3 This is not surprising since modern manufacturing had quite a limited development in 1990.

4 A significant difference is made to the measure of inequality if earning migrants are included with the family members left behind in rural areas who are non-earning.

References

Part I, Part II, and Conclusions

Ace, Z.J. and Audrestch, D.B. (eds) (1993) *Small Firms and Entrepreneurship: An East–West Perspective*, Cambridge: Cambridge University Press.

Admiraal, P.H. (ed.) (1996) *Small Firms in the Modern Economy*, Oxford: Blackwell Publishers.

Ahsan, A. and Pages, C. (2007) "Are All Labour Regulations Equal? Assessing the Effects of Job Security, Labour Dispute and Contract Labour Laws in India", *Policy Research Working Paper*, WPS 4259, Washington DC: World Bank.

Asian Development Bank (ADB) (2008) "Accounting for Inequality in India: Evidence from Household Expenditures", *Working Paper Series No. 117*, Manila: Economics and Research Department.

Asian Development Bank (2009) *Key Economic Indicators 2009. Special Chapter on Enterprise Size*, Manila: ADB.

Asian Development Bank (2010a) *Key Economic Indicators 2010. The Growth of the Middle Class*, Manila: ADB.

Asian Development Bank (2010b) *Poverty, Inequality and Inclusive Growth in Asia: Measurement, Policy Issues and Country Studies*, Manila: ADB.

Athukorala, P. (2008) "Export Performance in the Reform Era: Has India Regained the Lost Ground?", draft February 2008, Division of Economics, Australian National University.

Audretsch, D.B. (2002) "The Dynamic Role of Small Firms: Evidence from the US", *Small Business Economics*, 18, pp. 13–40.

Aziz, J. and Cui, L. (2007) "China`s Low Consumption: The Neglected Role Of Household Consumption", *IMF Working Paper*, WP/07/81, July.

Banerjee, A. and Picketty, T. (2005) "Top Indian Incomes 1922–2000", *World Bank Economic Review*, 19, 1, pp. 1–19.

Bardhan, P. (2010) *Awaking Giants: Feet of Clay*, Princeton, New Jersey: Princeton University Press.

Bauer, P.T. and Yamey, B.S. "Economic Progress and Occupational Distribution", *Economic Journal*, 61, 244, pp. 741–755.

Beng, C.S. (1988) *Small Firms in Singapore*, Singapore: Oxford University Press.

Benjamin, D. and Brandt, L. (2003) "Agriculture and Income Distribution in Rural Vietnam during Reform: a Tale of Two Regions", in D. Dollar and P. Glewee (eds), *Economic Growth, Poverty and Human Welfare: Policy Lessons from Vietnam*, Washington DC: World Bank.

Benjamin, D., Brandt, L., Giles, J., and Wang, S. (2008) "Income Inequality During China's Economic Transition", Chapter 18 in L. Brandt and T.G. Rawski (eds), *China's Great Economic Transformation*, New York: Cambridge University Press.

Besley, T. and Burgess, R. (2004) "Can Labor Regulation Hinder Employment Performance? Evidence from India", *Quarterly Journal of Economics*, 17, 3, pp. 91–134.

Bhalla, S. (2010) "Growth Patterns", in S. Acharya (ed.) *Essays in Honour of Montek Ahluwalia,* Delhi: Oxford University Press.

Bhagwati, J. (1993) *India in Transit: Freeing the Economy,* Oxford: Clarendon Press.

Bhattacharjea, A. (2006) "Labour Market Regulation and Industrial Performance in India: A Critical Review of the Empirical Evidence", *Indian Journal of Labour Economics*, 49, 2, pp. 211–232.

Bosworth, B and Collins, S.M. (2007) "Accounting for Growth: Comparing China and India", *Journal of Economic Perspectives*, 22, 1, pp. 45–66.

Brandt, L. and Rawski, T.G. (eds) (2008) *China's Great Economic Transformation*, Cambridge: Cambridge University Press.

Cai, F., Park, A., and Zhao, Y. (2008) "The Chinese Labor Marker in the Reform Era", Chapter 6 in L. Brandt and T.G. Rawski (eds), *China's Great Economic Transformation*, Cambridge: Cambridge University Press.

Carlsson, B. (1984) "The Development and Use of Machine Tools in Historical Perspective", *Journal of Economic Behavior and Organization*, 5, pp. 91–114.

Carlsson, B. (1993) "Book Review of *The Competitiveness of Small Firms* by Cliff Pratten", *Journal of Economic Literature*, 31, pp. 920–921.

Carlsson, B. (2006) "Small Business, Flexible Technology and Industrial Dynamics", in P.H. Admiraal (ed.), *Small Firms in the Modern Economy*, Oxford: Blackwell Publishers.

Cawthorne, P. (1995) "Of Networks and Markets: the Example of Tirupur's Cotton Knitwear Industry", *World Development*, 23, 1, pp. 43–57.

Chakravarty, D. (2010) "Trade Unions and Business Firms: Unorganized Manufacturing in West Bengal", *Economic and Political Weekly*, 65, 6, pp. 45–52.

Chari, S. (2004) *Fraternal Capital: Peasant Workers, Self-Made Men, and Globalization in Provincial India*, Stanford: Stanford University Press.

Deaton, A. (1997) *The Analysis of Household Surveys: A Microeconometric Approach to Development Policy*, World Bank, Washington: Johns Hopkins Press.

Debroy, B. and Kaushik, P.D. (eds) (2005) *Reforming the Labour Markets*, New Delhi: Academic Foundations.

Dougherty, S.M. (2008) "Labour Regulations and Employment Dynamics at the State Levels in India", *Economics Department Working Paper No. 624*, Paris: OECD.

D'Souza, E. (2009) "Labour Market Flexibility: Insurance versus Efficiency and the Indian Experience", in R. Kanbur and J. Svener (eds), *Labor Markets and Economic Development*, London and New York: Routledge.

Fields, G. (2003) "Accounting for Income Inequality and its Changes: A New Method and Applications to the Distribution of Earnings in the United States", *Research in Labour Economics*, 22, 1, pp. 1–38.

Government of India (2011) *Economic Survey 2011*, Delhi: Ministry of Finance, Government of India.

Hashim, S.R. and Sarkar, S. (2011) "Poverty Line: Does it Require Upward Adjustment?", Paper presented at International Seminar on "Revisiting the Poverty Issue: Measurement, Identification and Eradication Strategy", Patna (India), 20–22 July, 2007.

Huang, Y. (2003) *Selling China: Foreign Direct Investment During the Reform Era*, New York: Cambridge University Press.

Huang, Y. (2008) *Capitalism with Chinese Characteristics: Entrepreneurship and the State*, New York: Cambridge University Press.

Jeong, H. (2005) "Assessment of Relationship between Growth and Inequality: Micro-evidence from Thailand", *IEPR Working Paper*, 5, 20, Institute of Policy Research, University of Southern California.

Karan, A. and Sarkar, S. (2000) "Labor Flexibility and Industrial Relations: A Study of Organized Manufacturing Sector in India", *Indian Journal of Labour Economics*, 42, 4, pp. 1156–1168.

Kathuria, V., Rajesh Raj, S.M., and Sen, K. (2011) "The Effects of Economic Reforms on Manufacturing Dualism", *Working Paper No. 30/2011*, Institute of Development Policy and Management, University of Manchester.

Khan, A.R. (2009) "Measuring Inequality and Poverty in Bangladesh", *Bangladesh Development Studies*, XXXI, nos 3–4, pp. 1–34.

Kundu, A. and Mohanan, P.C. (2009) "Employment and Inequality Outcomes in India", Paper presented at OECD Seminar on Employment and Inequality in Brazil, China and India, April OECD Publishing House, Paris.

Kuznets, S. (1966) *Modern Economic Growth: Rate, Structure, and Spread*, New Haven: Yale University Press.

Lin, C.-H.A. and Orazem, P. (2004) "A Re-examination of the Time Path of Wage Differentials in Taiwan", *Review of Development Economics*, 8, 2, pp. 295–308.

Little, I.M.D., Mazumdar, D., and Page, J. (1987) *Small Manufacturing Enterprises: A Comparative Analysis of India and Other Economies*, New York: Oxford University Press for the World Bank.

Mazumdar, D. (1973) "Labour Supply in Early Industrialization: The Case of the Bombay Textile Industry", *Economic History Review*, XXVI, 3, pp. 477–496.

Mazumdar, D. (1983) "Segmented Labor Markets", *American Economic Review*, 73, 2, pp. 254–259.

Mazumdar, D. (1984) "The Rural–Urban Wage-gap, Migration and the Working of Urban Labor Markets: An Interpretation Based on a Study of the Workers of Bombay City", *Indian Economic Review*, 18, 2, pp. 169–198 (reprinted in the *World Bank Reprint Series*, Number 300).

Mazumdar, D. (1991) "Import-Substituting Industrialization and Protection of the Small-Scale", *World Development*, 19, 9, pp. 1197–1213.

Mazumdar, D. (2003) "Small and Medium Enterprise Development in Equitable Growth and Poverty Alleviation", in C.M. Edmonds (ed.) *Reducing Poverty in Asia; Emerging Issues in Growth, Targeting and Measurement*, Asian Development Bank, Cheltenham: Edward Elgar.

Mazumdar, D. (2010) "Decreasing Poverty and Increasing Inequality in India", Chapter 4 in OECD, *Tackling Inequalities in Brazil, China, India and South Africa: The role of Labour Markets and Social Policies*, Paris: OECD Publishing.

Mazumdar, D. and Basu, P. (1997) "Macroeconomic Policies, Growth and Employment: the East and South-East Asian Experience", in A.R. Khan and M. Muqtada (eds) *Employment Expansion and Macroeconomic Stability under Increasing Globalization*, London: Macmillan.

Mazumdar, D. and Mazaheri, A. (2003) *The African Manufacturing Firm*, London and New York: Routledge.

Mazumdar, D and Sarkar, S. (2008) *Globalization, Labor Markets and Inequality in India*, London: Routledge.

McKinsey Global Institute (2007) *The Bird of Gold: The Rise of India's Middle Class*, San Francisco: McKinsey Institute.

Mookherjee, D. and Shorrocks, S. (1982) "A Decomposition Analysis of Trends in Income Inequality", *Economic Journal*, 92, pp. 886–902.

Naughton, B. (2007) *The Chinese Economy: Transitions and Growth*, Cambridge, Mass.: MIT Press.

Organization for European Co-operation and Development (OECD) (2010) *Tackling Inequalities in Brazil, China, India and South Africa*, Paris: OECD Publications.

Papola, T.S. (2005) "Emerging Structure of the Indian Economy—Implications of Intersectoral Imbalances", Presidential Address of the 88th Annual Conference of the Indian Economic Association, 27–29 December, Vishakhapattam.

Psacharopoulos, G. and Patrinos, H.A. (2002) "Returns to Investment in Education: A Further Update", *Policy Research Working Paper*, no. 2881, September, Washington DC: World Bank.

Ramaswamy, K.V. (2006) "Employment in Indian Manufacturing and New Services: Impact of Trade and Outsourcing", paper presented in the conference on Labour and Employment Issues in India, 27–29 July, Institute for Human Development, Delhi.

Ravallion, M. (2009) "The Developing Worlds' Bulging (but Vulnerable) 'Middle Class'", *Policy Research Working Paper*, No. 4816, Washington DC: World Bank.

Rodrik, D. and Subramanian, A. (2004) "From 'Hindu Growth' to Productivity Surge: The Mystery of the Indian Growth Transition", *IMF Staff Papers*, 52, 2, pp. 193–228.

Roy, S. (2010) "Garments Industry in India: Perspectives and Future Challenges", *Draft Report*, Delhi: Institute of Human Development.

Sarkar, S. (2009) "Income and Earnings Inequality", Chapter 4 in *Employment Report for India*, Draft, Institute of Human Development, Delhi.

Sarkar, S. (2011) "Footwear Industry in India, Case Study of the Unorganized Industry", unpublished draft, Delhi: Institute of Human Development.

Sarkar, S. and Mehta, B.S. (2010) "Income Inequality in India: Pre- and Post-Reform Periods", *Economic and Political Weekly*, XLV, 37, pp. 45–55.

Singh, A. and Dasgupta, S. (2005) "Will services be the new engine of economic growth in India?", *ESRC Centre for Business Research, Working Paper 310*, ESRC Centre for Business Research.

Shukla, R.K., Drivedi, R.K., and Sharma A. (2004) *The Great Indian Middle Class*, Delhi: National Council of Applied Economic Research.

Streefkerk, H. (2001) "Thirty Years of Industrial Labour in South Gujarat: Trends and Significance", *Economic and Political Weekly*, 36, June 30, pp. 2398–2411.

Tewari, M. (1998) "Intersectoral Linkages and the Role of the State in Shaping the Conditions of Industrial Accumulation: A Study of Ludhiana's Manufacturing Industry", *World Development*, 26, 8, pp. 1387–1411.

Tewari, M. (2006) "Adjustments in India's Textile and Apparel Industry: Reworking Historical Legacies in a Post-MFA World", *Environment and Planning A*, 38, pp. 2325–2344.

Topalova, P. (2008) "India: Is the Rising Tide Lifting All Boats?", *Working Paper No. 08/54*, Washington DC: International Monetary Fund.

UNCTAD (annual) *Trade and Development Report*, Vienna: UNCTAD.

Ushikawa, S. (2011) "Knowledge Spillover in Indian Automobile Industry", *IDE Discussion Paper*, no. 303, Institute of Developing Economies, Tokyo.

Vasudeva-Dutta, P. (2005) "Accounting for Wage Inequality in India", *Indian Journal of Labour Economics*, 48, 2, pp. 273–295.

World Bank (1993) *The East Asian Miracle*, New York: Oxford University Press.

World Bank (2010) *India's Employment Challenge: Creating Jobs, Helping Workers*, Delhi: OUP.

World Bank (various years) *Doing Business Surveys*, Washington DC: World Bank.

World Bank (various years) *Investment Climate Assessment Surveys*, Washington DC: World Bank.

Xu, X. (2009) "Size Structure of Manufacturing Enterprises in China", *Unpublished Draft Consultant Report,* Economics Department, Asian Development Bank, Manila.

Japan

Allen, G.C (1940) "Japanese Industry: Its Organization and Development to 1937", in E.B. Schumpeter (ed.) *Industrialization of Japan and Manchukuo 1930–1940*, New York: MacMillan Company.

Broadbridge, S. (1966) *Industrial Dualism in Japan.* London: Frank, Cass & Co.

Chenery, H.B., Sishido, S., and Watanabe, T. (1962) "The Pattern of Japanese Growth 1914–1954", *Econometrica*, 30, 1, pp. 98–139.

Fields, G. (1980) *Poverty, Inequality and Development,* Cambridge: Cambridge University Press.

Friedman, D. (1988) *The Misunderstood Miracle: Industrial Development and Political Change*, Ithaca: Cornell University Press.

Hayashi, M. (2005) *SMEs, Subcontracting and Economic Development in Indonesia: With Reference to Japan's Experience*, Tokyo: Japan International Cooperation Publishing.

Ishikawa, S. (1962) "A Comparison of the Size Structures in Indian and Japanese Manufacturing Industries", *Hitotsubashi Journal of Economics*, 2, 2, pp. 50–79.

Kaneda, H. (1980) "Development of Small and Medium Enterprises and Policy Responses", *Studies in Employment and Rural Development No. 32*, Washington DC: World Bank Economics Department.

Klein, L. and Ohkawa, K. (eds) (1968) *Economic Growth: the Japanese Experience since the Meiji Era*, Yale Growth Center, Homewood: Richard D. Irwin Inc.

Kuznets, S. (1938) *Commodity Flow and Capital Formation*, New York: National Bureau of Economic Research.

Mazumdar, D. and Sarkar, S. (2008) *Globalization, Labor Markets and Inequality in India*, London: Routledge.

Minami, R. (1976) "The Introduction of Electric Power and its Impact on the Manufacturing Industries", in H. Patrick (ed.) *Japanese Industrialization and its Social Consequences*, Berkeley and Los Angeles: University of California Press, pp. 299–326.

Minami, R. (1978) "The Turning Point in the Japanese Economy", *Quarterly Journal of Economics*, 82, 3, pp. 380–402.

Minami, R. (1986) *The Economic Development of Japan*, London: MacMillan Press.

Nishiguchi, T. (1994) *Strategic Industrial Sourcing: The Japanese Advantage*, New York: Oxford University Press.

Odaka, K. (1967) "Employment and Wage Differential Structure in Japan: A Survey", *Hitotsubashi Journal of Economics*, 8, 1, pp. 41–64.

Paukert, F. (1973) "Income Distribution at Different Levels of Development", *International Labor Review*, 108, pp. 97–108.

Patrick, H. (ed.) (1976) *Japanese Industrialization and its Social Consequences*, Berkeley: University of California Press.

Rapp, W.V. (1976) "Firm Size and Japan's Export Structure: A Microview of Japan's Export Competitiveness since Meiji", in H. Patrick (ed.) *Japanese Industrialization and its Social Consequences*, Berkeley: University of California Press, pp. 201–248.

Shaw, W.H. (1947) *Value of Commodity Output since 1869*, New York: National Bureau of Economic Research.

Shinohara, M. (1970) *Structural Changes in Japan's Economic Development*, Tokyo: Kinokuniya.

Shinoya, Y. (1968) "Patterns of Industrial Development", in L. Klein and K. Ohkawa (eds) *Economic Growth: the Japanese Experience since the Meiji Era*, Yale Growth Center, Homewood: Richard D. Irwin Inc.

Uyeda, T. (1938) *The Small Industries of Japan: their Growth and Development*, London and New York: Oxford University Press.

World Bank (1993) *The East Asian Miracle: Economic Growth and Public Policy*, New York: OUP.

Yosuba, Y. (2006) "The Evolution of Dualistic Wage Structure", in H. Patrick (ed.) *Japanese Industrialization and its Social Consequences*, Berkeley: University of California Press, pp. 249–298.

Taiwan

Abe, M. and Kawakami, M. (1997) "A Distributive Comparison of Enterprise Size in Korea and Taiwan", *The Developing Economies*, vol. XXXV, 4, pp. 382–400.

Amsden, A. (1991) "Big Business and Urban Congestion in Taiwan: The Origin of Small Enterprise and Regionally Decentralized Industry (Respectively)", *World Development*, 19, 9, pp. 1124–1135.

Bourguignon, F., Fournier, M., and Gurgand, M. (2001) "Fast Development with a Stable Income Distribution", *Review of Income and Wealth,* 72, 2, pp. 139–163.

Chou, T.C. (1995) *Industrial Organization in a Dichotomous Economy: the Case of Taiwan.* Aldershot: Avebury.

Chu, W. (1997) "Causes of Growth: A Study of Taiwan's Bicycle Industry", *Cambridge Journal of Economics*, 21, pp. 55–72.

Fei, J., Ranis, G., and Kuo, S. (1978) "Growth and Family Income Distribution by Factor Components", *Quarterly Journal of Economics,* XCII, 1, pp. 1–68.

Galenson, W. (ed.) (1979) *Economic Growth and Structural Change in Taiwan*, Ithaca and London: Cornell University Press.

Ho, S.P.S. (1980) "Small-Scale Enterprises in Korea and Taiwan", *World Bank Staff Working Papers*, no. 384, Washington DC.

Ho, S.P.S. (1982) "Economic Development and Rural Industries in South Korea and Taiwan", *World Development*, 10, 11, pp. 973–990.

Kuo, S.W.Y. (1983) *The Taiwan Economy in Transition*, Boulder, Colorado: Westview Press.

Kuznets, S. (1955) "Economic Growth and Income Inequality", *American Economic Review*, 45, 1, pp. 1–28.

Kuznets, S. (1979) "Growth and Structural Shifts", Chapter 1 in W. Galenson (ed.). *Economic Growth and Structural Change in Taiwan*, Ithaca and London: Cornell University Press.

Levy, B. (1991) "Transaction Costs, the Size of Firms and Industrial Policy", *Journal of Development Economics*, 34, pp. 151–178.

Lin, C.-H.A. and Orazem, P. (2004) "A Re-examination of the Time Path of Wage Differentials in Taiwan", *Review of Development Economics*, 8, 2, pp. 295–308.

Lunjow, P. and Stern, N. (eds) (1988) *Economic Development in Palanpur over Five Decades,* Delhi: Oxford University Press.

Ranis, G. (1979) "Industrial Development", Chapter 3 in W. Galenson (ed.), *Economic Growth and Structural Change in Taiwan*, Ithaca and London: Cornell University Press.

Smith, H. (2000) *Industrial Policy in Taiwan and Korea in the 1980s*, Cheltenham, UK: Edward Elgar.

Sylia, R.M. (1974) *The Industrialization of Taiwan: Some Geographical Considerations*, Jerusalem: Jerusalem Academic Press.

Thorbecke, E. (1979) "Agricultural Development", Chapter 2 in W. Galenson (ed.), *Economic Growth and Structural Change in Taiwan*, Ithaca and London: Cornell University Press.

Thorbecke, E. and Wan, H. (eds) (1993) *Taiwan's Development Experience,* Norwell, Mass: Kluwer Academic Publishers.

Tzannatos, Z. and De Silva, M. (1998) "SME Experience in East Asia: Case of Japan, Republic of Korea and Taiwan", unpublished draft, Washington DC: Economic Development Institute (EDI), World Bank.

Vere, J.P. (2005) "Education, Development, and Wage Inequality: The Case of Taiwan", *Economic Development and Cultural Change*, 53, 3, pp. 712–735.

Korea

Amsden, A.H. (1989) *Asia's Next Giant*, New York and Oxford: Oxford University Press.

Bai, M.-K. (1982) "The Turning Point in the Korean Economy", *The Developing Economies*, 20, pp. 117–140.

Chenery, H., Robinson, S., and Syrquin, M. (1986) *Industrialization and Growth*, New York: Oxford University Press for the World Bank.

Choo, H. (1978) "Growth and Income Distribution in Korea", *Korean Development Institute Working Paper*, no. 7810.

Corbo, V. and Suh, S. (eds) (1992) *Structural Adjustment in a Newly Industrializing Country: The Korean Experience*, World Bank, Baltimore and London: Johns Hopkins University Press.

Fields, G. and Yoo, G. (1998) "Falling Labour Income Inequality in Korea's Economic Growth: Patterns and Underlying Causes", unpublished, Korean Labour Institute, Seoul, May.

Hong, W. (2000) "Labor Surplus in Korea: A Reassessment", *International Economic Journal*, 14, 4, pp. 125–141.

Hout, M. and Dohan, D.P. (1996) "Two Paths to Education Selection in Sweden and the United States", in R. Erikson and O. Jonsson (eds), *Can Education be Equalized?*, Boulder, Co: Westview Press, pp. 207–302.

Kim, K. and Leipziger, D.M. (1993) *Korea: A Case of Government-led Development,* Washington DC: World Bank.

Kim, L. and Nugent, J. (1994) "The Republic of Korea's Small and Medium-Size Enterprises and their Support Systems", *World Bank Policy Research Working Paper*, No. 1404, Washington DC.

Leipziger, D.M., Dollar, D., Shorrocks, A.F., and Song, S.Y. (1992) *The Distribution of Income and Wealth in Korea*, EDI Development Studies, Washington DC: World Bank.

Mazumdar, D. (1990) "Korea's Labour Markets under Structural Adjustment", *World Bank Working Paper*, No. WPS 554, Washington DC.

Mazumdar, D. (1993) "Labour Markets and Adjustment in Open Asian Economies", *World Bank Economic Review* 7, 1, pp. 349–380.

Moon, S.H. (2001) "The Skill Wage Differential of Korea After the 1980s: The Effect of Supply, Demand and International Trade", unpublished, Korean Development Institute, November.

Nugent, J. (1996) "What Explains the Trend Reversal in the Size Distribution of Korean Manufacturing Establishments", *Journal of Development Economics*, 48, 2, pp. 225–251.

Nugent, J. and Yhee, S.J. (2002) "Small and Medium Enterprises in Korea: Achievements, Constraints and Policy Issues", *Small Business Economics*, 18, pp. 85–119.

Richardson, R. and Kim, B.W. (1986) "The Structure of Labor Markets in LDCs: Overview for South Korea", *Development Research Department Discussion Paper*, No. DRD162, World Bank, Washington DC, March.

Rodgers, G. (ed.) (1994) *Workers, Institutions and Economic Growth in Asia*, International Institute of Labour Studies, Geneva: ILO.

Seong, S. (1993) *Economic Development and Policy for Small and Medium-Sized Enterprises in Korea*, Korean Development Institute, Policy Monograph 93–06, Seoul.

Suh, S. (1985) "Economic Growth and Income Distribution: the Korean Case", *Korean Development Institute Working Paper*, No. 8508, Seoul.

United Nations Industrial Development Organization (1986) "SMEs in the Evolution of Italian and Indian Industrialization Systems", Vienna: UNIDO.

World Bank (1993) *The East Asian Miracle: Economic Growth and Public Policy*, New York: OUP.

Yoo, J. (1990) "The Industrial Policy of the 1970s and the Evolution of the Manufacturing Sector in Korea", *Korean Development Institute Working Paper*, No. 9017, Seoul.

Thailand

Ahuja, V., Bidani, B., Ferreira, F., and Walton, M. (1997) *Everyone's Miracle? Revisiting Poverty and Inequality in East Asia*, Washington DC: World Bank.

Christensen, S., Dollar, D., Siamwala, A., and Vichyanand, P. (1993) *Thailand: The Political and Institutional Underpinnings of Growth*, Washington DC: World Bank.

Coxhead, I. and Plangpraphan, J. (1999) "Economic Boom, Financial Bust and the Decline of Thai Agriculture", *Chulalongkorn Journal of Economics,* 11, 1, pp. 76–96.

Feder, G., Onchan, T., Chalamwong, Y., and Hongladarom, C. (1988) *Land Policies and Farm Productivity in Thailand*, Baltimore: The Johns Hopkins University Press.

Institute of Population Research (1995) *Report on Internal Migration in Thailand,* Bangkok.

Jeong, H. (2005) "Assessment of Relationship between Growth and Inequality: Macro-evidence from Thailand", *IEPR Working Paper 05:20,* Institute of Economic Policy Research, University of Southern California.

Mazumdar, D. (1993) "Labour Markets and Adjustment in Open Asian Economies", *World Bank Economic Review* 7, 1, pp. 349–380.

Mazumdar, D. (1997) "Growth and Inequality in Thailand: A Study of Labor Market Issues", unpublished draft, World Bank, November.

Mazumdar, D. and Tzannatos, Z. (1997) *Labor Markets and Employment in Thailand*, unpublished draft, Washington DC: World Bank.

Pholphirul, P. (2005) "Competitiveness, Income Distribution, and Growth in Thailand: What Does the Long-Term Evidence Show?", *International Economic Relations Program*, Bangkok: Thai Development Research Institute.

Pholphirul, P. (2007) "Labour Market Issues under Trade Liberalization: Implications for the Workers", *Asia-Pacific Development Journal*, 14, 1, pp. 41–71.

Susssangkarn, C. (1987) "The Thai Labor Market; A Study of Seasonality and Segmentation", paper presented at the International Conference on Thai Studies, Australian National University, Canberra.

Sussangkarn, C. (1988) "Production Structures, Labor Markets, and Human Capital Investment: Issues of Balance for Thailand", *NUPRI Research Paper Series*, No. 46, Nihon University, Population Research Institute, Tokyo.

Sussangkarn, C. (1994) "Thailand", in S. Horton, R. Kanbur, and D. Mazumdar (eds) *Labor Markets in an Era of Structural Adjustment*, Washington DC: World Bank EDI Development Studies.

Warr, P. (1993) *The Thai Economy in Transition*, Cambridge: Cambridge University Press.

Warr, P. (1999) "What Happened in Thailand?", *The World Economy*, 22, pp. 631–650.

Warr, P. and Nidhiprabha, B. (1996) *Thailand's Macroeconomic Miracle*, World Bank, Kuala Lumpur: Oxford University Press.

World Bank (1983) *Country Economic Report on Thailand*, Washington DC: World Bank.

World Bank (1989) "Thailand: Country Economic Memorandum Building on the Recent Success", *Report No. 7445-TH*, Washington DC.

Bangladesh

Ahmed, N. and Bakht, Z. (2010) "A Review of Macro and Fiscal Incentives in the Manufacturing Sector: Implications for Future Policies", *Background Studies for the Sixth Five Year Plan*, BIDS and the Planning Commission, GOB.

Ahmed, N. and Yunus, M. (2010) "Trade Liberalization, Changes in Industrial Structure, and Job Creation in Bangladesh", BIDS (mimeo).

Bakht, Z. (1993) "Economic Reforms, Industrial Strategy and Employment Growth", *Social Dimensions of Economic Reforms in Bangladesh*, ILO-ARTEP.

Bakht, Z. (2001) "Trade Liberalization, Exports and Growth of Manufacturing Industries in Bangladesh", in M. Huq and J. Love (eds) *Strategies for Industrialization: The Case of Bangladesh*, Dhaka: UPL.

Government of Bangladesh (GOB) (2009) *Economic Review*, Dhaka: Ministry of Finance.

Islam, R. (2006) "The Nexus of Economic Growth, Employment and Poverty Reduction: An Empirical Analysis", in R. Islam (ed.) *Fighting Poverty: The Development Employment Link*, Boulder and London: Lynne-Rienner Publishers.

Mazumdar, D. (2003) "Small and Medium Enterprise Development in Equitable Growth and Poverty Alleviation", in C.M. Edmonds (ed.) *Reducing Poverty in Asia; Emerging Issues in Growth, Targeting and Measurement*, Asian Development Bank, Cheltenham: Edward Elgar.

Rahman, M. and Bakht, Z. (1997) "Constraints to Industrial Development: Recent Reforms and Future Direction", in M.G. Quibria (ed.) *The Bangladesh Economy in Transition*, Asian Development Bank, Oxford: Oxford University Press.

Further references

Ahmed, N. (2009) "Promoting Employment Intensive Growth in Bangladesh: Policy Analysis of the Manufacturing and Service Sectors", *Employment Working Paper*, No. 38, ILO, Geneva.

Bakht, Z. (2008) "Development of SME Sector in Bangladesh", *Emerging Issues in Bangladesh Economy, Independent Review of Bangladesh's Development 2005–06*, Dhaka: Centre for Policy Dialogue and University Press Ltd.

Chowdhury, N. (2006) "Employment Generation Through Growth in Manufacturing in Bangladesh: Some Analysis and a Broad Brush Prognosis', paper presented at the Roundtable on Bangladesh's Economy, Bangladesh Institute of Development Studies, 23 May.

Islam, R. (2007) "What Kind of Economic Growth is Bangladesh Attaining?", paper presented at the International Conference on Development Prospects of Bangladesh: Emerging Challenges, Bangladesh Institute of Development Studies, 2–3 December.

Khan, A.R. (2006) "Employment Policies for Poverty Reduction", in R. Islam (ed.) *Fighting Poverty: The Development-Employment Link*, Boulder and London: Lynne-Rienner Publishers.

Osmani, S.R. (2005) "The Role of Employment in Promoting the Millennium Development Goals", *Discussion Paper No. 18*, ILO-UNDP Joint Program on Promoting Employment for Poverty Reduction.

Rahman, R.I. and Islam, K.M.N. (2003) "Employment Poverty Linkages: Bangladesh", in *Issues in Employment and Poverty*, Discussion Paper 10, Recovery and Reconstruction Department, International Labour Office, Geneva.

Rahman, R.I. and Islam, K.M.N. (2006) "Bangladesh: Linkages among Economic Growth, Employment, and Poverty", in R. Islam (ed.) *Fighting Poverty: The Development-Employment Link*, Boulder and London: Lynne-Rienner Publishers.

World Bank (2007) "Bangladesh: Strategy for Sustained Growth", *Bangladesh Development Series Paper*, No. 18.

Vietnam

Akram-Lodhi, H. (2005) "Vietnam's Agriculture: Processes of Rich Peasant Accumulation and Mechanisms of Social Differentiation", *Journal of Agrarian Change*, 5, 1, pp. 73–116.

Asian Development Bank (ADB) (2007) *Inequality in Asia*, Manila: Asian Development Bank.

Bales, S. and Rama M. (2001) "Are Public Sector Workers Underpaid?", *World Bank Policy Research Working Paper*, No. 2747, Washington DC: World Bank.

Belser, P. and Rama, M. (2001) "State Ownership and Labour Redundancies: Estimates Based on Enterprise-Level Data from Vietnam", *World Bank Policy Research Working Paper*, No. 2599, Washington DC: World Bank.

Berry, A. (2010) "Improving Measurement of Latin American Inequality and Poverty with an Eye to Equitable Growth Policy", in S. Anand, P. Segal, and J. Stiglitz (eds) *Debates on the Measurement of Global Poverty*, Oxford: Oxford University Press.

Dapice, D. (2006) "Fear of Flying: Why is Sustaining Reform so Hard in Vietnam?", paper prepared for the Review of 20 Years of *Doi Moi*, in Vietnam Roundtable Meeting, 15–16 June, Hanoi.

Fforde, A. (2007) *Vietnamese State Industry and the Political Economy of Commercial Renaissance: Dragon's Tooth or Curate's Egg*, Oxford: Chandos Publishing.

Fforde, A. and de Vylder, S. (1996) *From Plan to Market: The Economic Transition in Vietnam*, Boulder: Westview Press.

General Statistics Office (2008) *The Situation of Enterprises through the Results of Surveys Conducted in 2005, 2006, 2007*, Hanoi: Statistics Publishing House.

Hakkala, K. and Kokko, A. (2007) "The State and the Private Sector in Vietnam", *Stockholm School of Economics Working Paper*, No. 236, Stockholm, June.

Harvie, C. (2008) "SME Development Strategy in Vietnam", in C. Harvie and B. Lee (eds) *Small and Medium Sized Enterprises in East Asia*, Cheltenham: Edward Elgar.

Hill, H. (2000) "Export Success Against the Odds", *World Development*, 28, 2, pp. 283–300.

International Monetary Fund (1999) "Vietnam: Statistical Appendix", *IMF Staff Country Report No. 99/56*, Washington DC, July.

International Monetary Fund (2003) "Vietnam: Statistical Appendix", *IMF Country Report No. 03/382*, Washington DC, December.

International Monetary Fund (2007) "Vietnam: Statistical Appendix", *IMF Country Report No. 07/386*, Washington DC, December.

Jenkins, R. (2004) "Why Has Employment Not Grown More Quickly in Vietnam?", *Journal of the Asia Pacific Economy*, 9, 2, pp. 191–208.

Joint Donor Report (JDR) (2006) *Vietnam Development Report 2006 – Business*, Hanoi.

Joint Donor Report (JDR) (2008) *Vietnam Development Report 2008 – Social Protection*, Hanoi.

Kokko, A. and Sjöholm, F. (2006) "The Internationalization of Vietnamese Small and Medium Enterprises", *Asian Economic Papers*, 4, 1, pp. 152–177.

Lall, S. (2003) "Technology and Industrial Development in an Era of Globalisation", in H.J. Chang (ed.) *Rethinking Development Economics*, London: Anthem Press.

Lerman, R. and Yitzhaki, S. (1985) "Income Inequality Effects by Income Source: A New Approach and Applications to the United States", *Review of Economics and Statistics*, 67, pp. 151–156.

Levy, B. (1991) "Transaction Costs, the Size of Firms and Industrial Policy", *Journal of Development Economics*, 34, pp. 151–178.

Lopez-Feldman, A. (2006) "Decomposing Inequality and Obtaining Marginal Effects", *The Stata Journal*, 6, 1, pp. 106–111.

Malesky, E. and Taussig, M. (2008) "Where is Credit Due? Legal Institutions, Connections, and the Efficiency of Bank Lending in Vietnam", *Journal of Law, Economics and Organization*, 25(2), pp. 535–578.

Mazumdar, D. (2003) "Small and Medium Enterprise Development in Equitable Growth and Poverty Alleviation", in C.M. Edmonds (ed.) *Reducing Poverty in Asia; Emerging Issues in Growth, Targeting and Measurement*, Asian Development Bank, Cheltenham: Edward Elgar.

Mekong Economics (2002) "SOE Reform in Vietnam", *Vietnam SOE Sector Paper*, Hanoi.

Ministry of Planning and Investment (2006) *Small and Medium Enterprise Development: 5 Year Plan 2006–2010*, Hanoi, January.

Nadvi, K. and Thoburn, J. (2004a) "Vietnam in the Global Garment and Textile Value Chain: Impacts on Firms and Workers", *Journal of International Development*, 16, pp. 111–123.

Nadvi, K. and Thoburn, J. (2004b) "Challenges to Vietnamese Firms in the World Garment and Textile Value Chain, and the Implications for Alleviating Poverty", *Journal of the Asia Pacific Economy*, 9, 2, pp. 249–267.

Nguyen, T. and Ramachandran, N. (2006) "Capital Structure in Small and Medium-Sized Enterprises", *ASEAN Economic Bulletin*, 23, 2, pp. 192–211.

Ocampo, J. and Vos, R. (2008) *Uneven Economic Development*, New York: Zed Books.

Prasad, E. (2009) "Rebalancing Growth in Asia", *National Bureau of Economic Research Working Paper*, No. 15169, Cambridge, Mass., July.

Riedel, J. (1997) "The Emerging Private Sector and the Industrialisation of Vietnam", *Private Sector Discussion Paper*, No. 1, Mekong Project Development Facility, Hanoi.

Roberts, M. and Tybout, J. (1997) "The Decision to Export in Colombia: An Empirical Model of Entry with Sunk Costs", *American Economic Review*, 87, 4, pp. 545–564.

Ronnås, P. (1998) "The Transformation of the Non-State Manufacturing Sector in the 1990s", *Stockholm School of Economics Working Paper in Economic and Finance*, No. 241, Stockholm, May.

Ronnås, P. (2001) "The Transformation of the Non-State Manufacturing Sector in the 1990s", in P. Ronnås and B. Ramamurthy (eds) *Entrepreneurship in Vietnam: Transformation and Dynamics*, Copenhagen: Nordic Institute of Asian Studies Publishing.

Ronnås, P. and Ramamurthy, B. (eds) (2001) *Entrepreneurship in Vietnam: Transformation and Dynamics*, Copenhagen: Nordic Institute of Asian Studies Publishing.

Singelmann, J. (1978) *From Agriculture to Services, The Transformation of Industrial Employment*, Beverley Hills: Sage Publications.

Social Watch (2008) *Country Report: Vietnam*, Montevideo: Social Watch.

Stark, O., Taylor, J., and Yitzhaki, S. (1986) "Remittances and Inequality", *Economic Journal*, 96, pp. 722–740.

Steer, L. and Taussig, M. (2002) "A Little Engine that Could…: Domestic Private Companies and Vietnam's Pressing Need for Wage Employment", *World Bank Policy Research Working Paper*, No. 2873, August.

Tenev, S., Carlier, A., Chaudry, O., and Nguyen, Q.-T. (2003) *Informality and the Playing Field in Vietnam's Business Sector*, Washington DC: World Bank and International Finance Corporation.

Thoburn, J. (2004) "Globalisation and Poverty in Vietnam: Introduction and Overview", *Journal of the Asia Pacific Economy*, 9, 2, pp. 127–144.

Van Arkadie, B. and Mallon, R. (2004) *Vietnam: A Transition Tiger?* Canberra: Asia Pacific Press at the Australian National University.

Van Biesebroeck, J. (2005) "Exporting Raises Productivity in Sub-Saharan African Manufacturing Firms", *Journal of International Economics*, 67, 2, pp. 373–391.

Vietnam Academy of Social Sciences (VASS) (2006) *Vietnam Poverty Update Report 2006: Poverty and Poverty Reduction in Vietnam 1993–2004*, Hanoi, December.

Vijverberg, P.M. and Haughton, J. (2004) "Household Enterprises in Vietnam: Survival, Growth and Living Standards", in P. Glewwe, N. Agrawal, and D. Dollar (eds) *Economic Growth, Poverty and Household Welfare in Vietnam*, Washington DC: World Bank.

Webster, L. and Taussig, M. (1999) "Vietnam's Undersized Engine: a Survey of 95 Larger Private Manufacturers", *Private Sector Discussion Paper*, No. 8, Mekong Project Development Facility, Hanoi.

Index

Page numbers in *italics* denote tables, those in **bold** denote figures. Notes are denoted by the letter 'n'. A letter will follow the note where there are the same references on the page.